Reaching New Horizons

Gifted and Talented Education for Culturally and Linguistically Diverse Students

Editors
Jaime A. Castellano

Eva I. Díaz

Allyn and Bacon

Boston ▪ London ▪ Toronto ▪ Sydney ▪ Tokyo ▪ Singapore

Series Editor: *Aurora Martínez Ramos*
Editorial Assistant: *Elizabeth Slater*
Editorial-Production Administrator: *Joe Sweeney*
Editorial-Production Service: *Colophon*
Composition Buyer: *Linda Cox*
Electronic Art and Composition: *Omegatype Typography, Inc.*
Manufacturing Buyer: *Julie McNeill*
Cover Administrator: *Kristina Mose-Libon*

Library of Congress Cataloging-in-Publication Data

Reaching new horizons : gifted and talented education for culturally and linguistically diverse students / editors, Jaime A. Castellano & Eva Diaz.
    p. cm.
   Includes bibliographical references and index.
   ISBN 0-205-31413-9 (alk. paper)
    1. Gifted children—Education—United States.   2. Linguistic minorities—Education—United States.   3. Education, Bilingual—United States.   I. Title: Gifted and talented education for culturally and linguistically diverse students.
II. Castellano, Jaime A.   III. Diaz, Eva.

LC3993.2 .R43 2001
371.95—dc21

                                    2001034097

Printed in the United States of America

10 9 8 7 6 5 4 3 2 1   06 05 04 03 02

To my wife, Lillian Castellano, for her love, patience, and support, and for keeping me grounded in spite of myself; to my children, Jaime, Alejandro, Gabriel, and Gisell, for being such a wonderful part of my life and of whom I am so very proud; to my brother and sisters, their spouses (Frank and Yolanda Corona, Sergio and Cynthia Barrera, Olympia Castellano, and Michael and Kelly Castellano) and their children and/or grandchildren, who are an inspiration and joy; to the memory of my parents, Tony and Lilia Castellano, whom I miss very much; and to my father- and mother-in-law, Ismael and Delia Torres, for their encouragement and support.

Jaime A. Castellano

I dedicate this book to my son, Anastassios-Emmanuel, whose perspicacity as a young bicultural and bilingual child inspires me to continue my work on ethnicity, bilingualism, and talent development.

Eva I. Díaz

CONTENTS

FOREWORD

When I began teaching in a school for the gifted forty years ago, at the height of post-Sputnik endeavors to educate the gifted (and at the zenith of average SAT scores), there was only a handful of minority students enrolled. These students were mostly the sons and daughters of physicians and lawyers, while the White students in attendance represented broader socioeconomic backgrounds. Over the years, the proportion of children from nondominant ethnic groups who have been selected for gifted and talented (GT) programs has increased slightly, but so has the proportion of White children.

As the demographics of our society have been changing inexorably toward greater proportions of minority students in our schools, many educators have realized that if the United States is to consolidate its position of leadership in the world, minority gifted youth will have to be found and educated to the fullest extent possible. One of the greatest challenges faced by GT programs in this regard is posed by gifted children who are not only culturally diverse, but also limited-English-proficient.

The culturally different are difficult enough to accommodate by traditional GT educators, who would prefer to change nothing about their programs, but only make special efforts to "identify" more minority GT students who meet traditional criteria. By implication, these traditionalists would try to change or reconfigure minority GT students to resemble White GT students. Furthermore, the accommodation of the *linguistically* different in GT programs has been, until recently, a topic altogether threatening—or at least too organizationally disquieting—to discuss in professional or community circles. When dialogue does occur, it should include individuals from bilingual education, English as a Second Language classes, and gifted education. These administrators, teachers, and other primary stakeholders who represent the demographics of the school community should come together to develop a framework for successfully facilitating the inclusion of culturally and linguistically diverse students in gifted education programs.

The truly gifted adults in our society—not the clawing, upwardly mobile members of the "Volvo Vigilantes," mind you, but the secure, accomplished contributors to the professions, arts, and sciences—are starting to articulate their concern that the best and brightest youngsters from all groups in our society must be cultivated in ways that build on their strengths, not necessarily their similarities to middle class White Americans. In doing so, the diversity of these students will place new elements into the commixture from which we draw our collective creativity. The concerns of these adults for our society and its inadequate response to the education of gifted children are at last bringing out their leadership in this area.

Reaching New Horizons: Gifted and Talented Education for Culturally and Linguistically Diverse Students presents state-of-the-art solutions to educational questions that, in some cases, have not yet been asked by GT educators as a group. If these educators share the concern for reaching all gifted children, however, they will read this book. Theoretical issues and practical steps are emphasized in every topic, because all of the authors realize that both of these elements are needed if defensible opportunities for all GT children are to evolve into effective praxis. Propositional knowledge is provided to the reader wherever possible, and as for the rest, the authors share the best of what is known.

Moving into the area of educating the culturally and linguistically gifted student still requires a certain level of courageous experimentation and badly needed documentation and evaluation. As of now, there is no magic wand. The idea is to eschew deracination, draw the best from the notion of integration, promote mutual understanding through a multicultural curriculum, and build the linguistically different gifted children's capacities for high levels of bilingual proficiency.

Ernesto M. Bernal

PREFACE

This edited collection was compiled as part of a shared vision of professionals enticed by the promise of bilingual gifted education. The editors of and contributors to this book are familiar with the ethnic and linguistic diversity of the United States and well aware of the upward, accelerated growth in diversity, especially among children and youth. We also believe in the interdependent nature of educational excellence and equity, and the imperative of providing equitable, high-end learning experiences to culturally and linguistically diverse children.

Origins

Systemic reform efforts aiming at academic excellence and equity have galvanized the movement to address the needs and strengths of culturally and linguistically diverse students. Within this context and in a ground-breaking move, the U.S. Department of Education's Office of Educational Research and Improvement (OERI) and the Office of Bilingual Education and Minority Language Affairs (OBEMLA) sponsored a national meeting in January of 1997 to discuss the issues faced by students with outstanding talents and limited English proficiency. At last, acknowledged leaders in the fields of bilingual and gifted education were brought together to initiate a national dialogue, which began to break down the stoicism, cynicism, and disconnection of the fields. Although, prior to this meeting, the editors and contributors were all involved in the education and advocacy of culturally and linguistically diverse students, including children with limited English proficiency, and gifted potential and talents, it was at this meeting that the possibility of collaboration emerged, thus enabling the editors to actuate their dream of publishing a book of this nature.

Goals and Purpose

Originally, this book was intended to bring together the fragmented and somewhat scarce knowledge available on the issues. In fact, up to the moment of sending this book for publication, the editors were not aware of any other single book dealing primarily with issues of *linguistic diversity*, gifted education, and talent development. A sizable body of literature exists regarding identification and programming issues for gifted and talented students who are from different cultural backgrounds. Nonetheless, most of this literature neglects the linguistic component, thus leaving only a few significant yet scattered pieces of literature available in professional journals, books, and electronic sources. Consequently, this book was conceived bearing in mind our interest and commitment to these issues, the scarcity of foundational resources in this area, and the esoteric visibility of this student population.

This book is intended to provide, for the first time, a synopsis and accessible discussion of foundational, interdependent topics, including relevant research findings and educational practices, on linguistic diversity, giftedness, and talent development, thus bridging a gap in the literature and bringing the discussion of these issues to the forefront. We have also attempted to develop a guiding resource for educators, counselors, administrators, preservice teachers, and other practitioners, based on thorough reviews of the literature, theory-driven works, and applications to practice. In addition, we hope that educational researchers and policy makers will view this book as a basic reference to pertinent issues. In the end, we hope this book will enable readers to develop a basic theoretical understanding of the issues and to advance more responsive programs and experiences for these students.

Themes and Topics

The theme of the insoluble and reciprocal dependency of excellence and equity in education permeates this book. We understand that educational excellence cannot be brought to fruition without educational equity, and as long as educational discussions focus on excellence overriding equity, all children will be missing the promise of developing to their maximal potential. This is particularly relevant in light of the unrelenting debate of excellence versus equity in the field of gifted education, with recurrent arguments sustaining the need to forgo equity in the name of academic excellence. Similarly, as long as the education of culturally and linguistically diverse students focuses on their perceived deficiencies (e.g., limited English proficiency), these students will be prevented from enjoying their right to excellence and equity in education. We are convinced that bilingual gifted education offers the opportunity for culturally and linguistically diverse students with outstanding gifts and talents to obtain both excellence and equity in their education.

As the reader will discover, this book includes a diversity of topics, content, and perspectives (e.g., historical, empirical, and practical), allowing all of the contributors to use their own voices. In spite of the differences in opinion at times, there is a sense of consensus among the contributors. We see this as a strength of this book, yet we also acknowledge that some people may perceive this as a hindrance to achieving a sense of unity throughout the book. Broadly speaking, topics included in this book are history, legislation, policy, and theory of bilingual education and gifted education, advanced cognitive development and bilingualism, creativity, identification of and programs for children with gifted potential or performance, curriculum and pedagogy, teacher preparation and recruitment, parent and family involvement, and research.

Organization of This Book

For purposes of organization, sections and chapters have been arranged in the way they seem to fit best or that helps ideas to flow. This book is divided into five sections, each containing a preamble and a set of chapters. The fifteen chapters are written by contributors from throughout the United States who we considered visionary people devoted to helping culturally and linguistically diverse students reach their potential. We all share a common interest in the education of these students; we share a vision.

Following the Introduction is the first section, Contextualizing the Intersect of Cultural and Linguistic Diversity Giftedness, and Talent Development. Chapter 1 provides an overview of relevant historical events in education, particularly bilingual and gifted education, from the late 1800s to the 1980s. The purposes, policies, practices, and criticisms of each field are examined, and visible historical trends are rendered. Critical connections are also framed to help researchers and practitioners reflect on the evolving field of bilingual gifted education. Chapter 2 places the field of bilingual gifted education within a contemporary context. For this purpose, the most recent reform movement in U.S. education and its relevance to the field of bilingual gifted education are examined.

The second section, Conceptualizing Advanced Cognitive Development, Creativity, and Bilingualism, includes Chapters 3 and 4. Chapter 3 reviews the literature on the relationship between advanced first- and second-language learning and cognitive development in children and discusses the historical evolution of the methodological designs used in research studies on bilingualism and cognition since the 1960s. Suggestions to improve the methodological design and measurement of variables when studying cognition and bilingualism are also offered. Chapter 4 provides evidence in support of a symbiotic relationship between bilingualism and creativity. For this purpose, different levels of bilingualism and characteristics of creativity are discussed, and examples of lessons that enhance bilingual students' creativity are provided.

The third section, Identifying and Nurturing Gifted Potential and Bilingualism contains Chapters 5 through 11. The purpose of Chapter 5 is to expound on (1) the barriers that culturally and linguistically diverse students faced when trying to gain admission into gifted and talented programs; and (2) inclusionary approaches and strategies for identification and placement. Chapter 6 outlines current gifted program and service delivery models in the United States. Sociocultural and political factors influencing the extension of these models to culturally and linguistically diverse students are also addressed. Chapter 7 discusses four major issues to consider when designing new curriculum paradigms, including bilingual children, teachers, teaching, and learning strategies. This chapter concludes with sample units, guides, and recommendations for future directions. Chapter 8 raises awareness about the similarities among the methodologies of teaching English to Speakers of Other Languages (ESOL) and gifted education. Issues of identification are also considered. Chapter 9 describes the Schoolwide Enrichment Model (SEM), developed by Joseph S. Renzulli, a well-known leader in the field of gifted education. This chapter also proposes an educational project connecting the SEM and a two-way bilingual program model for providing excellence and equity to culturally and linguistically diverse students. Chapter 10 presents success stories of programs serving talented culturally and linguistically diverse students in the United States, including Project GOTCHA in Florida, the gifted bilingual program in the Milwaukee Public School System, and Project EXCEL in the San Diego, California, public schools. Chapter 11 describes the key elements of an early advocacy, service delivery model to address the needs of gifted, English language learners (in preschool to second grade). An integrated approach of student readiness, teacher training, and parental involvement is emphasized.

The fourth section, Strengthening Teacher Preparation and Parental Involvement, includes Chapters 12 and 13. Chapter 12 delineates a field-tested model for the recruitment and preparation of teachers for bilingual gifted and talented programs. Chapter 13 presents a comprehensive parent-involvement model implemented as a summer orientation program in gifted magnet centers for Hispanic populations in a large urban school district.

The last section, Living Visions: Learning from and Informing Educational Research and Policy, includes the last two chapters of this book and an afterword. Chapter 14 examines formal and informal policymaking issues at the classroom, school, school district, community, state, and federal levels regarding English as a second language and talent development. Chapter 15 briefly reviews research done in bilingual gifted education and identifies promising research directions. The Afterword engenders a shared vision of the pressing issues discussed throughout this book. In the end, we hope that each chapter contributes to a better understanding of the evolving field of bilingual gifted education.

Eva I. Díaz

Acknowledgments

I acknowledge certain individuals and groups who have helped this book become a reality. First, I thank Lucy Bravo for her technological expertise and patience throughout the early formatting of this project. Second, I am grateful to the Gifted Education Special Interest Group (SIG) of the National Association for Bilingual Education (NABE) and the Special Populations Division of the National Association for Gifted Children (NAGC), which have tirelessly advocated for the historically underrepresented student. Next, I express my most sincere thanks to those contributing authors with whom I share a common vision, and who took the time from their busy personal and professional lives to contribute to this book. I especially thank Eva I. Díaz, co-editor of this book, for having the "ganas" to see this project through. Finally, I acknowledge all those educators who make a positive difference in the lives of gifted and talented culturally and linguistically diverse students.

Jaime A. Castellano

I wish to extend my gratitude to Jaime A. Castellano, co-editor of this book, for his hard work, determination, and renewing energy at times when completing this project seemed almost impossible. I am grateful to the contributing authors, who also helped realize the dream of completing a book of this nature. I am also deeply thankful to my husband and our families, whose unconditional love and support were a constant source of strength. Lastly, I gratefully acknowledge the unseen, yet powerful inspiration of two very talented women in academia: Dr. Sally M. Reis, role model, colleague, and friend; and Dr. Lourdes Díaz Soto, university professor, who unexpectedly opened a window in 1989, exposing me to a new world. I thank both of you so very much.

Eva I. Díaz

INTRODUCTION

During the last four decades, a gradually increasing amount of attention has been devoted to the education of culturally and linguistically diverse students in U.S. schools. This attention is due partly to an acknowledgment of the growing numbers and participation rates of these students in schools, which in turn challenges the educational system to provide them with equitable, high-quality education—an enriched education that is sensitive to their cultures and languages while also being challenging and exciting.

This book begins to address issues of cultural and linguistic diversity within the framework of bilingual gifted and talented education in the United States. The intention is to provide a multifaceted discussion of fundamental and interdependent issues in the education of gifted and talented students from culturally and linguistically diverse backgrounds in a manner unlike any other book. However, given (1) the inter- and intradiversity of students from culturally and linguistically diverse backgrounds, (2) the limited research base and body of knowledge concerning issues of gifted and talented education in relation to specific ethnic groups, and (3) the predominance of bilingual programs for Spanish speakers, this book focuses primarily on students from Latino backgrounds.[1]

This introduction serves the following purposes:

1. It clarifies conceptualizations and definitions of key terms. The reader must be aware, however, that these definitions are not final, because terms evolve in nature as knowledge germinates.
2. It provides an overview of demographics and educational information on culturally and linguistically diverse students in the United States.
3. It describes the overall conditions of gifted and talented students from culturally and linguistically diverse backgrounds.
4. It introduces the critical issues that will be discussed throughout the book, including the emergence of bilingual gifted and talented education seeking equity and excellence in the education of culturally and linguistically diverse students.

Nomenclature

A challenge that is frequently faced when talking about people or things is that of labeling. Throughout the years, terms or labels have experienced transformations, and the field of education is not immune to this process. As happens with change in general, this periodic change of the terms used causes controversy in regard to which terms are acceptable (Tiedt & Tiedt, 1998). To some, these transformations are trendy changes resulting from the fad of an era, but in reality, the concepts remain fairly similar. For others, these transformations are healthy changes based on contemporary knowledge, which in turn carry a significant conceptual shift. In any case, choices in labeling need to be made, especially because, most often, choice of terminology represents someone's assumptions and beliefs. However, defining and making choices in labeling people and their attributes is a difficult process due to the complexity of understanding the interconnections among the terms—a phenomenon in the fields of bilingual education and gifted and talented education.

For the purposes of this book, and in order to facilitate understanding, the following guiding definitions have been chosen from a multitude of alternatives. We have decided to use the term *culturally and linguistically diverse students* to refer to students from early childhood to grade 12 who represent inter- and intradiversity[2] in cultural or ethnic minority groups (definition follows), including language backgrounds other than English. Thus, for the most part, their first language (the language that is learned first and which may also be the one with which the individual identifies) is other than English, and they learn English as their second language. A term often used interchangeably with that of culturally and linguistically diverse is *language minority*. However, it is our understanding that this term, within the U.S. context, not only ascribes a tacit lesser value to languages other than English and their native speakers, but also circumscribes significant cultural elements.

Cultural and Linguistic Diversity:
Linguistic Complexities

A significant issue in a discussion of who may be identified as a culturally and linguistically diverse person is the presence of substantial variation due to the complexities of second-language learning and linguistic contact. For instance, culturally and linguistically diverse students may develop simultaneously their ethnic minority language and English. However, it could also happen that, given a variety of generational and schooling factors, students become dominant in English while their first language stagnates developmentally. This could occasionally happen to the extent of their becoming monolingual in English while growing up in an ethnically or culturally diverse household (identifies with English rather than with the ethnic minority group's characteristic language; see Skutnabb-Kangas & Cummins, 1988). As a result, the term *culturally and linguistically diverse student* includes the group of students commonly identified as limited English proficient, as well as bilingual.

On one hand, the term *limited English proficient* makes reference to culturally and linguistically diverse students "whose English proficiency is not yet developed to the point where they can profit fully from English-only instruction" (August & Hakuta, 1997, p. 15). Nevertheless, although this term is well established both in the educational field and in legislation,[3] it is often perceived as a negative label due to its focus on the student's perceived linguistic weakness or problem. For this reason, the term *English language learner (ELL)* has emerged as a more positive label for students identified as having LEP (Rivera, 1994). However, this term has also been used in the literature as a synonym for the term *culturally and linguistically diverse* in general, not only for students identified as having (LEP), in which case, we understand that this label is misused. Moreover, the term could be misleading, as it overlooks the cultural dimension of students—a dimension we believe is intimately connected to language but too often disregarded. Besides, a monolingual native English speaker could be labeled in this way, too, thus causing confusion and neglecting the complexity of bilingualism.

On the other hand, culturally and linguistically diverse students who are *bilingual* have developed proficiency in their first languages "and enough proficiency in English not to be disadvantaged in an English-only school environment" (August & Hakuta, 1997, p. 16). *Bilingualism*, then refers, very broadly speaking, to attainment of proficiency in two languages. Defining this concept proves to be a challenge, as there is no consensus, and multitudinous definitions and typologies exist, which in turn depend on multifarious factors such as conditions for language development, language use, and students' social status.[4] For instance, bilingualism could be differentiated as additive or subtractive, considering the conditions for development (e.g., impact of instructional program). *Additive bilingualism* denotes the preservation of the first language while acquiring a second language, thus resulting in an enrichment experience. To the contrary, *subtractive bilingualism* implies the partial or total stifling of first-language development while developing the second language. This is usually the case with most culturally and linguistically diverse students in the United States (August & Hakuta, 1997). Meanwhile, if considering language use then, *balanced bilingualism* could be distinguished from *dominant bilingualism*. The former suggests well-developed competencies in two languages at approximately equal levels of proficiency. The latter involves a higher level of proficiency in one of the two languages (Baker, 1996). In any case, it is important to recognize that a student's two languages are always evolving.

Cultural and Linguistic Diversity: Culture

When referring to culturally and linguistically diverse students, there is a deliberate recognition of the pivotal role of students' cultures in all aspects of their lives. According to the Council on Anthropology and Education of the American Anthropological Association (Saravia-Shore & Arvizu, 1992), *culture* refers to a "dynamic, creative, and continuous process that includes behaviors, values, and substance shared by people that guides them in their struggle for survival and gives meaning to their lives" (p. xviii). In other words, culture is a shared organization or set of complex ideas (cultural knowledge) mediated by changes that influences the way people perceive, relate, and interpret things (worldview) and in turn makes the results of these processes by-products of their culture.

Culturally and linguistically diverse students belong to *cultural* or *ethnic groups*, that is, groups of people that share a sense of group identification or identity (distinctiveness); racial and physical attributes; national origin; and religious, linguistic, or cultural heritages that differ from those of other groups within a society. For example, Bennett (1999) explained that the ethnic group of people in the United States who identify with an Anglo-Western European culture, otherwise called White Anglo-Saxon Protestants (WASPs), comprises the predominant society. African Americans, Native Americans, Asian Americans, and Latinos also constitute ethnic groups. An individual's subjective and chosen affiliation with or sense of belonging to a cultural (reference) group is commonly referred as an individual's *ethnicity*. According to Tiedt and Tiedt (1998), "ethnicity is an umbrella term that includes varied groupings based on national or linguistic background" (p. 13).

An ethnic group also may be considered an *ethnic minority group*. Sometimes, the term *minority* implies a numerical minority, yet oftentimes it signifies a subordinate status in a society (even if the group represents a numerical majority), or both. Therefore, often, so-called ethnic minority groups are singled out and relegated to an inferior position within a society and are thus discriminated against on the basis of their group characteristics (e.g., race, culture, language, and religion), even if they represent a numerical majority in a specific area. For these reasons, African Americans, Native Americans, Asian Americans, and Hispanics or Latinos have been identified as ethnic minority groups in the United States. Still, the concept of minority has become increasingly confusing, misleading, and unavailing in the United States as societal changes take place and the general population becomes more diverse (Banks, 1997). Similarly, the term *ethnolinguistic minority group* implies an ethnic minority group, as described, but one whose most salient and indispensable characteristic is its language (e.g., Latinos). Common in the literature are the terms *minorities* and its synonym *people of color*, denoting members of ethnic minority groups. However, these labels are confusing—the former, as explained, and the latter, because all human beings are people of color.

A last set of terms to be considered in relation to ethnic groups is that of *Latinos* or *Hispanics*. These terms refer to Mexicans, Puerto Ricans, Cubans, Central and South Americans, and people with origins in other Spanish-speaking countries (e.g., those whose origins are in Spain) (Jones-Correa & Leal, 1996; Kanellos, 1993). Currently, Mexican Americans comprise the largest Hispanic group (64.3%), followed by Puerto Ricans (10.6%) and Cubans (4.7%). Although Hispanics share a common origin and linguistic base, the groups that make up the Hispanic population are not monolithic, because they differ in many important ways. According to Bean and Tienda (1987), Hispanics living in the United States come from twenty-three different countries. Therefore, major demographic, historical, cultural, political, and experiential differences exist among these groups. Their unique experiences have influenced them in different ways, both before and after immigration to the United States.

Demographics

The number of culturally and linguistically diverse individuals living in the United States increased steadily throughout the twentieth century, especially after 1970.[5] This trend of increasing racial, cultural, and linguistic diversity is expected to continue in the future. For instance, Hollmann, Mulder, and Kallan (2000) predict an increase in legal immigration to the United States between 1999 and 2020 as an aftermath of the implementation of the Immigration Reform and Control Act of 1986. This act allowed millions of people not only to legalize their status and become citizens, but also to sponsor the legal immigration of their immediate relatives. Immigration projections for the period between 2021 and 2100 also augur growth.

Foreign-Born Population

According to the U.S. Census Bureau (2000), the foreign-born population of the United States totaled 25.8 million as of 1997, representing the largest number in U.S. history.[6] This figure represents a 30 percent increase since the 1990 census and a 168 percent increase since 1970, when the United States had the lowest foreign-born population in the century. Moreover, the Census Bureau estimated that one in ten people in the United States was foreign born in 1997—the highest proportion since 1930 and equivalent only to proportional figures in 1850. In this regard, the Census Bureau indicated that

> the 1997 figure is midway between the highest figures during a period of large-scale migration from Europe (14 percent in 1870 and 15 percent in 1890 and 1910) and the lowest figure during the culmination of a long period of limited migration (5 percent in 1970). (p. 1)

Among the foreign-born population, 51 percent were from Latin America (i.e., Central America, the Caribbean, and South America), 27 percent were from Asia, 17 percent were from Europe, and the remaining 5 percent were born in other regions of the world.

Culturally and Linguistically Diverse Populations: Foreign and Native Born

As foreign-born populations increase, native-born[7] culturally and linguistically diverse populations also increase, resulting in striking growth rates, particularly for the Hispanic and Asian and Pacific Islander populations in the past two decades (Smith, Ahmed, & Sink, 2000). For example, although the total U.S. population grew by 9.6 percent, the Hispanic population had a 39.7 percent increase, and the Asian and Pacific Islander population had a gain of 44 percent between 1990 and 1999. As a result, the Hispanic population comprised 11.5 percent of the population (from 9% in 1990) of the U.S. total population in 1999. Similarly, the Asian and Pacific Islander population constituted 4 percent of the population (from 3% in 1990).

As expected, these changes in U.S. population also meant changes in language usage. In 1980, Census data indicated that 23 million people (11%) in the United States (both foreign born and native) spoke a language other than English at home. By 1990, this figure had increased to nearly 32 million (13.8%)—a 38.1 percent increase since 1980 (U.S. Census Bureau, 1990). Likewise, between 1979 and 1989, the number of Spanish speakers five years of age and older increased by 65 percent, and the number of speakers of Asian and Pacific Island languages increased by 98 percent (McArthur, 1993).

Culturally and Linguistically Diverse Students

In 1996, McLeod reported that ten million children live in homes in which languages other than English are spoken (i.e., a 22.4% increase since 1980), Spanish (73%) being the most widely spoken language, followed by several Asian languages (10% to 15%)—a mirror reflection of the trends just discussed. Currently, of the over 329 languages spoken in the United States, approximately one hundred are represented among students with LEP, a subset of the culturally and linguistically diverse population.[8] Public K–12 school enrollment figures for the 1996–1997 academic year indicated that approximately 3.4 million of these children were identified as students with LEP (Macías, 1998a; National Clearinghouse for Bilingual Education [NCBE], 1998; Waggoner, 1999). This figure represented an 8 percent increase over the figure reported for the 1995–1996 schoolyear and a 57 percent increase from that reported for the 1990–1991 period.[9] More recent figures are not available, but Garcia (1995) estimated that by 2000, there would be approximately six million students with LEP. In addition, Garcia also predicted that this number would be fifteen million, or 25 percent, of school-aged children by 2026.

These students account for one-fifth of school-age children, or approximately 5 percent of all public school students and 31 percent of all Native American/Alaska Natives, Asian/Pacific Islander, and Hispanic students enrolled in U.S. public schools. In this regard, Anstrom and Kindler (1996) and the NCBE (1998) cautioned that substantial variance exists among estimates of the population of students with LEP by virtue of the broad range of definitions of LEP used across State Educational Agencies (SEAs). Macías (1998b) further stated that these figures might underestimate the number of students with LEP. A 1997 U.S. Department of Education report stated that "no matter which estimate is most accurate, U.S. Census figures indicate that linguistic diversity among students will persist and increase" (p. 13).

According to Fleischman & Hopstock, (1993, cited in August & Hakuta, 1997), 6 percent of school districts in the nation are serving a student population that comprises at least 40 percent students with LEP. The National Center for Education Statistics [NCES] (1997) reported that these students (1) are concentrated in the West, (2) live in urban areas, and (3) attend large schools (750 or more students) with a high minority student enrollment. This report also indicated that (1) 82 percent of students with LEP live in five states: California, Texas, Florida, New York, and Illinois[10]; and (2) 40 percent of all these students live in California, also accounting for one-fourth of all public school students in that state.

Fifty-three percent of students with LEP are enrolled in grades K–4 and are being served in the public school system through a continuum of approaches and programs—for example, (1) "sink or swim" approaches, in which no accommodations are made for students[11]; (2) programs that provide supplemental English teaching, using a minimal amount, or none at all, of the student's first language, such as English as a Second Language (ESL), Structured English Immersion (SEI), Teaching English to Speakers of Other Languages (TESOL), and English for Speakers of Other Languages (ESOL) programs[12]; and (3) multiple types of bilingual education programs, including but not limited to, transitional, maintenance, and two-way bilingual education.[13] Bilingual education programs differ in many ways due to school and community characteristics, the extent of native language and English language use, length of student placement, teaching methodology, goals, and outcomes, especially in relation to levels of bilingual development. As a result, an extensive assortment of programs and designs exists. Within these programs, in addition to the use of both first-language and English instruction in academic subjects, the majority of students receive ESL instruction or a combination of ESL and compensatory education services (e.g., Title I). Notwithstanding, students with LEP in urban, high-minority schools are more likely to participate in bilingual programs using their native language for content instruction.

In this regard, the NCBE (1998) reported that 76.8 percent of students identified as having LEP (in public and nonpublic schools) in 1996–1997 were being served in a variety of federal, state, and local programs, at times concurrently. Of those, 32.2 percent were served in local or state bilingual education programs, 19.9 percent were enrolled in local or state ESL-only programs, and 30.7 percent were in other special programs offered by local or state agencies. For federal programs, Title I served about 53.7 percent of students identified as having LEP, the Emergency Immigrant Education program served 21.6 percent, and approximately 14 percent were served in federally funded bilingual programs.

In comparison to the 1992–1993 figures, Title I is currently serving a higher number of students identified as having LEP, and local or state bilingual programs decreased their enrollment from almost 50 percent to 32 percent in the 1996–1997 period (Anstrom & Kindler, 1996). This change in services could reflect not only changes in federal policies under the Improving America's School Act of 1994 (P.L. 103-382), but also the difficulty of serving children from many different cultural and linguistic backgrounds in bilingual education programs. In other words, students identified as having LEP are served more often by Title I (i.e., the Helping Disadvantaged Children Meet High Standards Act of IASA) than by Title VII programs (i.e., Bilingual Education, Language Enhancement, and Language Acquisition programs).

About 50 percent of students identified as having LEP are recent immigrants (foreign born), while the other 50 percent are born in the United States (native). The former students comprise a heterogeneous group that usually differs greatly in age, native language development and/or literacy, English proficiency, academic preparation, and familiarity with U.S. culture (U.S. Department of Education, 1997). Culturally and linguistically diverse students, including those with LEP, are also likely to come from low-income families (McLeod, 1996). For example, 1990 U.S. Census data suggested that approximately 37 percent of culturally and linguistically diverse students (referred to as *language minority*) are poor, compared with about 17 percent of all other students (U.S. General Accounting Office, 1994). As a result, 77 percent of the former students are eligible for reduced-price lunches and attend schools with high poverty rates. The U.S. Department of Education report entitled, *School Reform and Student Diversity* (1997), asserted the following:

> Nearly all LEP students and other language minority students are members of ethnic and racial minority groups and nearly all are poor. Their neighborhoods are likely to be segregated and beset with multiple problems—inadequate health, social, and cultural services; insufficient employment opportunities; crime, drugs, and gang activity. Their families are likely to suffer the stress of poverty, to worry about their children's safety in dangerous environments, and to fear for their future, given their few positive prospects. LEP and other language minority students also swim against the tide of discrimination. (p. 14)

U.S. Secretary of Education, Richard W. Riley, said,

> Let me highlight just one shortcoming in the teaching force: 54 percent of all teachers have limited English proficient (LEP) students in their classroom, yet only one-fifth of teachers feel very prepared to serve them. . . . We need teachers who not only know more than one language but also have the background and training to maximize the learning potential of students with diverse backgrounds. (Riley, 2000a, p. 4)

Accordingly, a highly debated issue concerning the education of these students is the absence of knowledge about, or misunderstanding of, their cultural, linguistic, and cognitive skills, which in turn fosters prejudicial and discriminatory action against them. For instance, this misunderstanding has resulted in limited educational policies, school programs, or educational services that address their unique needs, interests, and strengths. A precise portrayal of the academic achievement of students with LEP nationwide is difficult to attain, because until recently, these students were exempted from statewide testing due to their limited proficiency in English (NCES, 2000). Yet, evidence exists concerning culturally and linguistically diverse students in general.

The evidence regarding the academic outcomes or educational attainments, at the national level, of culturally and linguistically diverse students or language-minority students illustrates the consequences of inappropriate decisions. According to Moss and Puma (1995), culturally and linguistically diverse students, particularly those with LEP, (1) are usually perceived by teachers as having lower academic abilities or being "underachievers," (2) receive lower grades, and (3) obtain lower scores in math and reading standardized tests. The NCBE (1998) confirmed that, in general, these students scored lower in math and reading tests. These students are also prone to (1) take fewer academic courses; (2) lag behind in writing, science, and mathematics; and (3) have higher dropout rates (Moss & Puma, 1995). According to Fleischman and Hopstock (1993, cited in August & Hakuta, 1997), a large percentage of culturally and linguistically diverse students, especially those with LEP, are classified as educationally disadvantaged, particularly in the upper grade levels. For instance, 20 percent of these students in the average high school and 12 percent of those in the average middle school have missed more than two years of schooling. In addition, up to 1993, limited federal support had forced districts to rely mostly on state and local sources to educate the majority of culturally and linguistically diverse students. As a result, the schooling experience of these students has often been marked by issues of access, such as inequities in funding, teacher quality, curriculum, technology, class size, and the prevailing view that if students do not achieve, it is their own fault. Moreover, culturally and linguistically diverse students with gifted potential and talents, especially those with LEP, have also been ignored.

Unrealized Promises: Gifted Potential and Outstanding Talent among Culturally and Linguistically Diverse Students

Currently, it is widely recognized in the literature that giftedness and talents are found in all cultural and socioeconomic groups and that culturally and linguistically diverse children with gifted potential and talents, especially those with LEP, have historically been neglected.[14] Yet, although the panorama for culturally and linguistically diverse children with gifted potential and talents in the U.S. educational system seems to have improved in past decades, this improvement has been gradual; as a result, these students are still dramatically underidentified and underserved in gifted and talented programs (Bermudez & Rakow, 1993; Clasen, Middleton, & Connell, 1994; Maker, 1996; Mitchell, 1988; Richert, 1987). A growing body of research-based knowledge, greater awareness among practitioners, somewhat more flexible state policies, and increased efforts at identification, placement, and programming have yielded only limited success, because these students' underrepresentation in gifted and talented programs is widespread—a phenomenon referred to as the "time bomb" of gifted education (Renzulli, 1999).

The educational system often overlooks these students because they are learning English as their second languages and are being raised with values and attitudes different from those found in U.S. mainstream society (Udall, 1988). Consequently, many of these students are denied the learning experiences and educational services necessary to develop their potential, thus possibly resulting in undeveloped gifted potential and talents and underachievement. Other factors contributing to the lack of student identification and provision of gifted and talented services relate to (1) educators' low expectations, erroneous preconceptions, and negative attitudes (Clark, 1993; High & Udall, 1983); (2) nonresponsive curriculum and instructional strategies (Diaz, 1994); (3) differing manifestations of high potential and inappropriate identification methods (de Bernard, 1985; Frasier, 1997; Johnson et al., 1985; Ortiz & Volloff, 1987); and (4) discrimination, misunderstanding, and disinterest from the educational system and the society at large (institutional racism).

A recurring issue in the identification and service of gifted and talented students from culturally and linguistically diverse backgrounds is that of the inappropriateness and misuse of standardized tests. It has been proved that standardized tests often underestimate the abilities of these students, especially those who are in the process of developing English as their second language and experiencing acculturation (Gonzalez, 1996; Zappia, 1988). Hartley (1987) claimed that most of the standardized tests used for the identification of gifted and talented students are primarily dependent on English oral and written language. Moreover, minimal consideration, if any, is given to the procedural complexities of acquiring a second language and adapting to new contexts, as well as important psychosocial and cultural elements. Some experts in the field consider standardized testing to be a tool that denies equal educational opportunity to these students by using test scores to demonstrate "that the students obtain lower scores compared with majority children due to internal factors, such as race" (González & Yawkey, 1993, p. 43).

Among the numerous barriers to the participation and success of culturally and linguistically diverse students in gifted and talented programs are lack of identification; the scarcity of funding to develop, implement, improve, and maintain effective programs; the dearth of qualified personnel to work with these students; and inappropriate placement and services. Those who "make it" are usually placed in programs that focus on developing abilities that are valued by the mainstream culture, resulting in students having to work twice as hard to succeed, overcoming obstacles of differing value systems, behavioral patterns, inadequate academic preparation, and differing language (Leung, 1981). In fact, many of the few culturally and linguistically diverse students actually placed in gifted and talented programs drop out. For example, Machado (1987) found that one-fifth of Hispanic students designated as gifted drop out of school, while the number of Hispanic students in gifted classes is less than half of what would be expected from their numbers in the general population.

The Promise of Bilingualism

In several addresses, former U.S. Secretary of Education, Richard W. Riley, proclaimed the promise of bilingualism and declared that narrow, long-standing beliefs, such as a child's native language, if other than English, being a weakness, or that immigrants and their children should speak nothing but English, represent the dismissing of "one of the greatest opportunities of this new century" (Riley, 2000a, p. 3). Thus, Riley pledged to support solid bilingual programs, especially dual-language or two-way programs, which he described as "the wave of the future" (p. 3). He further stated,

It is high time we begin to treat language skills as the asset they are, particularly in this global economy. Anything that encourages a person to know more than one language is positive—and should be treated as such. Perhaps we should begin to call the learning of a second language what it truly is—"biliteracy.". . . Proficiency in English and one other language is something that we need to encourage among all young people. . . . Our nation can only grow stronger if all our children grow up learning two languages.

He also highlighted this message at the Seventh Annual State of American Education Address (Riley, 2000b) and acknowledged the need for avoiding the "old tyranny of low expectations" (p. 4). At the National Hispanic Education Meeting (Riley, 2000c), former Secretary Riley affirmed that knowledge is power and that the knowledge of a second language is power; thus, *bilingualism brings power*. He encouraged schools to adopt an "English plus one" approach—challenging young people to meet high standards in two languages.

This unusual position of the U.S. Department of Education regarding bilingualism was actually observed in the Improving America's Schools Act (IASA) of 1994. For instance, Title VII of the IASA included the Bilingual Education Act and the Foreign Language Assistance Act. Both of these Acts endorsed the essential role that proficiency in languages other than English has on the U.S. capacity for economic competition, national security, and global understanding. However, this position has been politically and publicly attacked because of its educational implications.

In the past, and even currently, mixed messages persist in regard to the development of bilingualism. For example, the study of foreign languages, since its revival in the 1980s, has been validated by opponents of bilingual education as a bona fide intellectual endeavor, but only for a few. In this regard, Casanova (1992) asserted,

So many, including former Secretary Bennett, have endorsed foreign language competence as an advantage in the world of business and social interaction, but the same people consistently oppose native language instruction for SOLs [Speakers of Other Languages]. This suggests that languages spoken by native speakers are not "foreign," or that children from language minority populations are not expected to fill positions where bilingual competence may be not only useful but also required. The first explanation is illogical, the second smacks of racism. Whether due to faulty logic or to racism, these beliefs encourage policies that lead to subtractive bilingualism and contribute to the creation of our own disadvantaged populations. (pp. 338–339)

More recently, Padilla (1998) exposed the same enduring and puzzling paradox:

Following this line of reasoning, the schools should wipe out skills in the non-English mother tongue that students might bring with them to the first grade, only to insist later on foreign language study in high school as a college entrance requirement and for graduation from college. So, the people who turn out to be bilingual in the end of the educational pipeline are not those who seemingly would start school with the advantage of a non-English language. Rather, the bilinguals are those students who have the opportunity to study abroad and who are encouraged to learn a "foreign" language. Those for whom a foreign language is not foreign are forbidden from mastering it. In short, what is a great education for the well to do is forbidden learning for the poor and the immigrants. (p. 1)

This manner of thinking debases culturally and linguistically diverse students' abilities (e.g., linguistic assets) and their dignity. Therefore, the persistence of this mentality and course of action is no longer justifiable (not that it ever was). Culturally and linguistically diverse students in the United States constitute a national strength with unique funds of talent. Their linguistic diversity opens the door to linguistic (e.g., bilingual), social (e.g., cross-cultural understanding), and academic (e.g., the bilingualism connection to high achievement) enrichment, not only for themselves, but for all students. Research evidence demonstrates that bilingualism is not a disability but an opportunity for cognitive growth and support of students' creativity (Kessler & Quinn, 1987; Gonzalez, Bauerle, & Felix-Holt, 1996). The funds of talent are waiting to be nurtured and manifested. In order to do so, it is indispensable to look at these students and interpret their behaviors in light of their uniqueness. For example, Arroyo and Sternberg (1993) stated,

> Among disadvantaged children, giftedness is reflected in qualities, in addition to, and sometimes other than, measurable intellectual capacity. It includes behaviors that allow disadvantaged students to cope with social and economic deprivation. Because these adaptive behaviors are themselves governed by cognitive abilities that constitute intelligent behavior, it is reasonable to assume that the behavioral characteristics displayed by some disadvantaged children are reflective of giftedness.

As part of their human rights and as the national resource they represent, these students need to be nurtured and encouraged to achieve optimal developmental levels, just like any other student in the U.S. educational system. For this purpose, educational alternatives founded on the principles of equity and excellence are imperative.

Fulfilling the Promise: Equity and Excellence in Educational Opportunities

As mentioned in the Preface, the insoluble interdependency of excellence and equity in education underlies our work in gifted education.[15] It is understood that educational excellence cannot be brought to fruition without educational equity, and as long as educational discussions focus on excellence overriding equity, all children will be missing the promise of developing to their maximal potential. This is particularly relevant, bearing in mind the deeply entrenched dilemma of excellence versus equity in the field of education, but notably in gifted education.[16]

In 1997, Gallagher alleged that society was giving emphasis once again to equity and that, for this reason, gifted services were being reduced. Similarly, Colangelo and Davis (1997) stated,

> Society swings back and forth between the goals of equity versus excellence. . . . When equity is the primary concern, as in the 1960s, the early 1970s, and resurfacing in the 1990s, planning suitable educational programs for gifted students is put on the back burner or in the closet. *Equity* typically is translated as helping slow learning, disadvantaged, and other at-risk students become more equal. Unfortunately, treating issues of equity and excellence as antagonistic and mutually exclusive is destructive to the development of sound educational practices that meet the educational needs of every individual student. (p. 3)

Therefore, if equity has been the educational ideal at times and *we* (researchers, educators, practitioners, etc.) have interpreted it as "helping slow-learning, disadvantaged, and other at-risk students become more equal" (by way of classical, diminishing descriptions often attached to racially, culturally and linguistically diverse students), how is it possible that culturally and linguistically diverse students still experience such critical educational conditions in general? Moreover, how is it possible that culturally and linguistically diverse students are still on the back burner or in the closet of gifted education? Could it be that the long-standing view of equity as the "dumbing down" of educational experiences is still evident in the field? As long as the field of gifted education fails to realize how complex it is to reconcile these two educational ideals, we must embrace these ideals and commit ourselves to a genuine search for ways of achieving them. Otherwise, gifted education is going to be under attack. Thus, in agreement with Colangelo and Davis' position, placing these ideals against each other is counterproductive and, in the end, detrimental to students.

Renzulli (1999) presented a more recent example of how the debate over excellence versus equity in gifted education is fueled by prejudice. While addressing issues of eroded financial support to gifted education, Renzulli explained that low-cost programming alternatives, such as regular classroom differentiation, are increasingly being adopted by school districts. He suggested further that a contributing factor to school districts' accepting the move toward "meeting the needs of gifted students in the regular classroom" is the school districts' tacit notion that "it will minimize the appearance of minority underrepresentation" (p. 131). Thus, are changes in school districts' support for and advocacy for gifted and talented programs and services based on what the districts believe is best for gifted and talented children, or are the changes based on their lack of initiative in tackling, thoughtfully, the issue of minority underrepresentation? These types of justifications are ill conceived and fruitless and only engender resentment.

It is essential to understand high-quality education as a fundamental prerequisite to quality and have an appreciation of the diversity that makes up the United States. By the same token, as long as the education of culturally and linguistically diverse students focuses on their perceived deficiencies (e.g., LEP), these students will be prevented from developing their high potential and enjoying their right to excellence and equity in education.

Bilingual Gifted and Talented Education: Pursuing the Ideals of Excellence and Equity

As detailed carefully throughout this book, bilingual gifted and talented education has the potential to facilitate excellence and equity of educational opportunities not only to culturally and linguistically diverse students, but also to other students with high potential. By focusing on inclusion rather than selectivity, the base of student participation is broadened. Moreover, this type of education is concerned with both the provision of access to services and the provision of quality education (opportunity). In this manner, bilingual gifted and talented education nurtures students' high potential in enriched learning contexts that are sensitive to their diverse needs and strengths, and nurtures it in an atmosphere of acceptance and encouragement. Furthermore, bilingual gifted and talented education not only promotes individual development, but also contributes to the well being of the society. Thus, bilingual gifted and talented education aims at the following goals:

1. Providing students with accepting learning environments that value and respect their personal, cultural, and linguistic diversity while they are engaged in high-end, creative learning
2. Providing students with stimulating and challenging learning environments that (1) tap their diverse human resources, (2) respect their peculiar ways of expressing their gifted potential and talents, and (3) support their motivation, self-concept and self-image, which in turn bolsters their manifestation of gifted potential and talents
3. Promoting students' bilingual, biliterate, academic, and cross-cultural development
4. Empowering students politically, socially, and economically

Summary

The United States is a country in transition, because considerable demographic changes are taking place. Its racial, cultural, and linguistic diversity is unparalleled. Although this diversity vitalizes the United States, it also poses serious challenges to deeply rooted habits of the mind, to assumptions, and to conduct. An example of this is the educational challenge posed by increasing numbers of culturally and linguistically diverse students in U.S. schools. Data on their educational status indicate that a primarily disabling approach has been used to face this challenge, and, as a result, these students have been averted from tapping into their cultural, linguistic, and cognitive resources. Nevertheless, a better understanding of these students, through an expanded body of knowledge and increased awareness, calls for a type of education that capitalizes on the growing linguistic diversity of students in the United States by assisting these students to tap their potential and unmanifested sources of talent. In this manner, the students' cultural and linguistic diversity is conceptualized as a unique opportunity for educational enrichment. As is well known, culturally and linguistically diverse students most often arrive at school with the gift of a language other than English. However, the interplay of complex factors could mask the expression of their gifted potential and talents. Nevertheless, provided access and the right conditions, culturally and linguistically diverse students would have lesser possibilities of belonging to the category of the underrepresented and the underserved in programs for the gifted and talented. At least, this is what is hoped. It is better to be hopeful than not.

REFERENCES

Anstrom, K., & Kindler, A. (1996). *Federal policy, legislation, and educational reform: The promise and challenge for language minority students.* Washington, DC: National Clearinghouse for Bilingual Education.

Arroyo, C. G., & Sternberg, R. J. (1993). Against all odds: A view of the gifted disadvantaged. In B. Wallace & H. B. Adams (Eds.), *Worldwide perspectives in the gifted disadvantaged* (pp. 29–43). Oxon, England: AB Academic.

August, D., & Hakuta, K. (1997). *Improving school for language-minority children: A research agenda.* Washington, DC: National Academy Press.

Baker, C. (1996). *Foundations of bilingual education and bilingualism* (2nd ed.). Clevedon, England: Multilingual Matters.

Banks, J. A. (1997). *Teaching strategies for ethnic studies* (6th ed.). Boston: Allyn and Bacon.

Bean, F. D., & Tienda, M. (1987). *The Hispanic population of the United States.* New York: Russell Sage Foundation.

Bennet, C. I. (1999). *Comprehensive multicultural education: Theory and practice* (4th ed.). Boston: Allyn and Bacon.

Bermudez, A. B., & Rakow, S. J. (1993). *Examining identification and instruction practices for gifted and talented limited English proficient students.* (ERIC Document Reproduction Service ED 360 871.)

Bilingual Education Act, 20 U.S.C. § 7401–7405 (1994).

Casanova, U. (1992). Shifts in bilingual education policy and the knowledge base. In R. V. Padilla & A. H. Benavides (Eds.), *Critical perspectives on bilingual education research.* Tempe, AZ: Bilingual Press.

Clark, B. (1993). *Growing up gifted* (4th ed.). Columbus, OH: Charles E. Merrill.

Clasen, D. R., Middleton, J. A., & Connell, T. J. (1994). Assessing artistic and problem solving performance in minority and nonminority students using a non-traditional multidimensional approach. *Gifted Child Quarterly, 38* (1), 27–32.

Colangelo, N., & Davis, G. A. (1997). *Handbook of Gifted Education.* Boston: Allyn & Bacon.

Davis, G. A., & Rimm, S. B. (1998). *Education of the gifted and talented* (4th ed.). Boston: Allyn and Bacon.

de Bernard, A. E. (1985). Why José can't get in the gifted class: The bilingual child and standardized reading tests. *Roeper Review, 8* (2), 80–82.

Díaz, E. I. (1994). *Underachievement among high ability Puerto Rican high school students: Perceptions of their life experiences.* Unpublished doctoral dissertation, Pennsylvania State University at University Park.

Feldman, D. H. (1999). A developmental, evolutionary perspective on gifts and talents. *Journal for the Education of the Gifted, 22* (2), 159–167.

Foreign Language Assistance Act, 20 U.S.C. § 7511–7516 (1994).

Frasier, M. M. (1997). Gifted minority students: Reframing approaches to their identification and education. In N. Colangelo & G. A. Davis (Eds.), *Handbook of gifted education* (2nd ed., pp. 498–515). Boston: Allyn and Bacon.

Gallagher, J. J. (1997). Issues in the education of gifted students. In N. Colangelo & G. A. Davis (Eds.), *Handbook of gifted education* (2nd ed., pp. 10–23). Boston: Allyn and Bacon.

García, E. E. (1995). The impact of linguistic and cultural diversity on America's schools: A need for new policy. In M. C. Wang & M. C. Reynolds (Eds.), *Making a difference for students are risk: Trends and alternatives* (pp. 156–185). Thousand Oaks, CA: Corwin Press.

Gonzalez, V. (1996). Do you believe in intelligence? Sociocultural dimensions of intelligence assessment in majority and minority students. *Educational Horizons, 75* (1), 45-52.

Gonzalez, V., Bauerle, P., & Felix-Holt, M. (1996). Theoretical and practical implications of assessing cognitive language development in bilingual children with qualitative methods. *Bilingual Research Journal, 20* (1), 93–131.

Gonzales, V., & Yawkey, T. (1993). The assessment of culturally and linguistically different students: Celebrating change. *Educational Horizons,* (1), 41–49.

Gordon, E. W. (1996). The promise of accountability and standards in the achievement of equal educational opportunity. In E. C. Lagemann & L. P. Miller (Eds.), *Brown v. Board of Education: The challenge for today's schools* (pp. 151–156). New York: Teachers College Press.

Hartley, E. A. (1987). *How can we meet all their needs? Incorporating education for the gifted and talented into the multicultural classroom.* (ERIC Document Reproduction Service No. ED 336 968.)

High, M. H., & Udall, A. J. (1983). Teacher ratings of students in relation to ethnicity of students and school ethnic balance. *Journal for the Education of the Gifted, 6* (3), 154–166.

Hollmann, F. W., Mulder, T. J., & Kallan, J. E. (2000). *Methodology and assumptions for the population projections of the United States: 1999 to 2100.* U.S. Census Bureau, Population Division Working Paper No. 38 [On-line]. Available: www.census.gov/population/www/documentation/twps0038.pdf

Improving America's Schools Act, 20 U.S.C. § 5801 (1994).

Johnson, S. T., Starnes, W. T., Gregory, D., & Blaylock, A. (1985). Program of assessment, diagnosis, and instruction (PADI): Identifying and nurturing potentially gifted and talented minority students. *The Journal of Negro Education, 54* (3), 416–430.

Jones-Correa, M., & Leal, D. L. (1996). Becoming "Hispanic": Secondary panethnic identification among Latin American-origin populations in the United States. *Hispanic Journal of Behavioral Sciences, 18* (2), 214–254.

Kanellos, N. (1993). *The Hispanic-American almanac: A reference work on Hispanics in the United States.* Detroit, MI: Gale Research.

Kessler, C., & Quinn, M. E. (1987). Language minority children's linguistic and cognitive creativity. *Journal of Multilingual and Multicultural Development, 8* (1 & 2), 173–186.

Leung, E. (1981). *The identification and social problems of gifted bilingual-bicultural children.* (ERIC Document Reproduction Services ED 203 653.)

Machado, M. (1987). Gifted Hispanic underidentified in classrooms. *Hispanic Link Weekly Report, 5* (7), 1–2.

Macías, R. F. (1998a). *How many school-aged limited English proficient students are there in the U.S.? How many in each state?* [On-line]. Available: www.ncbe.gwu.edu/askncbe/faqs/01leps.htm

Macías, R. F. (1998b). *How has the limited English proficient student population changed in recent years?* [On-line]. Available: ncbe.gwu.edu/askncbe/faqs/08leps.htm

Maker, C. J. (1996). Identification of gifted minority students: A national problem, needed changes and a promising solution. *Gifted Child Quarterly, 40* (1), 41–50.

McArthur, E. K. (1993). *Language characteristics and schooling in the United States, a changing picture: 1979 and 1989* (National Center for Education Statistics, NCES 93-699). Washington, DC: U.S. Government Printing Office.

McLeod, B. (1996). *School reform and student diversity: Exemplary schooling for language minority students.* Washington, DC: National Clearinghouse for Bilingual Education.

Miller, L. R., & Tanners, L. A. (1996). Diversity and new immigrants. In E. C. Lagemann & L. P. Miller (Eds.), *Brown v. Board of Education: The challenge for today's schools* (pp. 71–80). New York: Teachers College Press.

Mitchell, B. M. (1988). A strategy for the identification of the culturally different gifted/talented child. *Roeper Review, 10* (3), 163–165.

Moss, M., & Puma, M. (1995). *Prospects: The congressionally mandated study of educational growth and opportunity: First year report on language minority and limited English proficient students.* Washington, DC: U.S. Department of Education.

National Center for Education Statistics. (1997). *A profile of policies and practices for limited English proficient students: Methods, program support, and teacher training* (SASS 1993–94). Washington, DC: U.S. Government Printing Office.

National Center for Education Statistics. (2000). *Increasing the participation of special needs students in NAEP: A report on 1996 NAEP research activities* [On-line]. Available: www.nces.ed.gov/pubsearch/pubsinfo.asp?pubid=2000473

National Clearinghouse for Bilingual Education. (1998). *Summary report of the survey of the States limited English proficient students and available educational programs and services 1996-1997* [On-line]. Available: www.ncbe.gwu.edu/ncbepubs/seareports/96-97/part1.htm#academic

Ortiz, V., & Volloff, w. (1987). Identification of gifted and accelerated Hispanic students. *Journal for the Education of the Gifted, 11* (1), 45–55.

Padilla, R. V. (1998). Title VII ESEA: The ambivalence of language policy in the United States. *Bilingual Research Journal* [On-line], *22* (1). Available: brj.asu.edu/v221/intro.html

Renzulli, J. S. (1999). Reflections, perceptions, and future directions. *Journal for the Education of the Gifted, 23* (1), 125–146.

Richert, S. (1987). Rampant problems and promising practices in the identification of disadvantaged gifted students. *Gifted Child Quarterly, 31* (4), 149–154.

Riley, R. W. (2000a). *Excelencia para todos—Excellence for all: The progress of Hispanic education and the challenges of a new century* [On-line]. Available: www.ed.gov/speeches/03-2000/000315.html

Riley, R. W. (2000b). *Remarks at the National Hispanic education meeting* [On-line]. Available: www.ed.gov/speeches/06-2000/hispaniceduc.html

Riley, R. W. (2000c). *Seventh annual state of American education address: Setting new expectations* [On-line]. Available: www.ed.gov/speeches/02-2000/000222.html

Rivera, C. (1994). Is it real for all Kids? *Harvard Educational Review, 64* (1), 55–75.

Saravia-Shore, M., & Arvizu, S. F. (1992). Introduction to cross-cultural literacy: An anthropological approach to dealing with diversity. In M. Saravia-Shore & S. F. Arvizu (Eds.), *Cross-cultural literacy: Ethnographies of communication in multiethnic classrooms* (pp. xv–xxxviii). New York: Garland Publishing.

Skutnabb-Kangas, T., & Cummins, J. (1988). *Minority education.* Clevedon, England: Multilingual Matters.

Smith, A. S., Ahmed, B., & Sink, L. (2000). *An analysis of state and county population changes by characteristics: 1990–1999.* U.S. Census Bureau, Working Paper Series No. 45 [On-line]. Available: www.census.gov/population/www/documentation/twps0045/twps0045.html#secl

Tiedt, P. L., & Tiedt, I. M. (1998). *Multicultural teaching: A handbook of activities, information, and resources* (5th ed.). Boston: Allyn and Bacon.

Udall, A. (1988). Curriculum for gifted Hispanic students. In J. C. Maker & S. W. Schiever (Eds.) *Critical issues in gifted education: Defensible programs for cultural and ethnic minorities* (Vol. II) (pp. 41–56). Austin, TX: PRO-ED.

U.S. Census Bureau. (2000, August). *Census Brief—Coming to America: A profile of the Nation's foreign born* [On-line] (CENBR/00-2). Available: www.census.gov/prod/2000pubs/cenbr002.pdf

U.S. Census Bureau. (1990). *Language use and English ability, persons 5 years and over, by state: 1990 census* [On-line] (CPHL-96). Available: www.census.gov/population/socdemo/language/table1.txt

U.S. Department of Education. (1997). *School reform and student diversity*. Washington, DC: U.S. Government Printing Office.

U.S. General Accounting Office. (1994). *Limited English proficiency: A growing and costly educational challenge facing many school districts*. Washington, DC: U.S. Government Printing Office.

Waggoner, D. (1999, May) *Numbers and needs: Ethnic and linguistic minorities in the United States*, [On-line] *9* (3), 1–6. Available: www.asu.edu.educ/cber

Zappia, I. (1988). Identification of gifted Hispanic students: A multidimensional view. In J. C. Maker & S. Schiever (Eds.), *Critical issues in gifted education: Defensible programs for cultural and ethnic minorities*, (Vol. II) (pp. 19–26). Austin, TX: PRO-ED.

NOTES

1. For additional information on Hispanics and issues of gifted and talented education, see: Díaz, E. I. 1999). Hispanic Americans: USA. In A. Y. Baldwin & W. Vialle (Eds.), *The many faces of giftedness: Lifting the masks* (pp. 23–44). Albany, NY: Wadsworth.

2. The term *diversity* is a broadly inclusive term recognizing significant variation among people in our society in relation, especially, to people's cultural heritages, racial and ethnic identities, gender, and class experiences (Miller & Tanners, 1996; Sarvia-Shore & Arvizu, 1992).

3. Title VII: Bilingual Education, Language Enhancement, and Language Acquisition programs of the Improving America's Education Act of 1994 (P.L. 103–382), Part E, Sec. 7501(8) established that

The terms 'limited English proficiency' and 'limited English proficient,' when used with reference to an individual, mean an individual

(A) who
  (i) was not born in the United States or whose native language is a language other than English and comes from an environment where a language other than English is dominant; or
  (ii) is a Native American or Alaska Native or who is a native resident of outlying areas and comes from an environment where a language other than English has had a significant impact on such individual's level of English proficiency; or
  (iii) is migratory and whose native language is other than English and comes from an environment where a language other than English is dominant; and
(B) who has sufficient difficulty speaking, reading, writing, or understanding the English language and whose difficulties may deny such individual the opportunity to learn successfully in classrooms where the language of instruction is English or to participate fully in our society.

4. For comprehensive discussions of definitions and typologies of bilingualism, see Beardsmore, H. B. (1986). *Bilingualism: Basic principles* (2nd ed.). Clevedon, England: Multilingual Matters; Baker, C. (1996). *Foundations of bilingual education and bilingualism*. Clevedon, England: Multilingual Matters.

5. The U.S. Census 2000 information release schedule is available at: www.factfinder.census.gov.home/resease schedule.html

6. *Foreign born* is defined as not U.S. citizens at birth, including people from Latin America, Europe, Asia, and other regions. See also U.S. Census Bureau (1993). *We the American . . . Foreign born* [On-line]. Available at: www.census.gov/apsd/wepeople/we-7.pdf

7. *Native* is defined as born in the United States or a U.S. island area such as Puerto Rico, or born abroad of a U.S. citizen parent.

8. Among the 329 languages spoken in the United States are Vietnamese, Hmong, Cantonese, Cambodian, Korean, Laotian, Navajo, Tagalog, Serbian, Russian, French Creole, Arabic, Portuguese, Japanese, Armenian, Chinese, Mandarin, Farsi, Hindi, and Polish

9. K–12 public enrollment figures for the 1994–1995 schoolyear indicated that there were 3,184,696 LEP students (from 2.3 million in 1990–1991). In 1996–1997, this figure was 3,405,915. Moreover, Anstrom and Kindler (1996) stated that from 1985 to 1994, the reported number of LEP students increased an average 9.6 percent per year in contrast to 1 percent for the total student population.

10. K–12 public LEP enrollment figures for the 1996–1997 schoolyear: California, 1,381,393; Texas, 513,634; Florida, 288,603; New York, 220,840; and Illinois, 118,246. Waggoner, D. (1999, May) *Numbers and needs; Ethnic and linguistic minorities in the United States*, *9* (3), 1–6. Available at: www.asu.edu.educ/cber

11. *Submersion* or U.S. immersion, is a "sink or swim" approach, in which students with limited English proficiency are taught in English-only classrooms without any language assistance. This model also promotes assimilation to U.S. society and subtractive bilingualism. This type

of approach is a violation to these students' civil rights under the Supreme Court's *Lau v. Nichols* (1974) decision (see Chapter 1). This model is different from the *Canadian Immersion Model*, in which majority language speakers (i.e., English) learning a second language (French) aim at biliterate development through second-language–oriented pedagogy.

12. *ESL* programs usually involve removing students from submersion classrooms for a short period of time, either daily or several times a week, to provide instruction about English, either grammar-based or communicative-based (pull-out within the student classroom, in a resource room, or in a resource center that brings together students from a number of schools). These programs may also provide content-based English instruction, also known as *Sheltered English*. *Structured English Immersion* (SEI) refers to intensive instruction in and about English with between 10 percent and 30 percent of instructional time in the students' first language. For recent discussions of SEI, see Baker, K. (1998). Structured english immersion: Breakthrough in teaching limited-English-proficient students. *Phi Delta Kappan, 80* (3), 199–204; Baker, K. (1999). How can we best serve LEP students: A reply to Nicholas Meier and Stephen Krashen. *Phi Delta Kappan, 80* (9), 707–710; Krashen, S. (1999). What the research really says about Structured English Immersion: A response to Keith Baker. *Phi Delta Kappan, 80* (9), 705–204; Krashen, S. (2000). *Another response to Keith Baker* [On-line]. Available at: ourworld.compuserve.com/homepages/jwcrawford/krashen6.htm

13. *Bilingual education* could be generically defined as educational programs designed to allow students to learn academic concepts in their home language while learning a second language. *Transitional bilingual education* (TBE) or early-exit bilingual education is a type of compensatory bilingual program in which content area support in first-language instruction is provided while gradually teaching the student English. As students are phased into English instruction, it is expected that students' mainstreaming to English-only classrooms would take place as soon as possible (usually between one and three years). This type of program fosters generally subtractive bilingualism and assimilation. *Maintenance* or late-exit bilingual programs involve students from a single linguistic background receiving instruction in their first and second languages. This program model promotes biliteracy, additive bilingualism, and academic excellence. *Two-way* bilingual education, dual-language instruction, or bilingual immersion represents an enrichment model in which culturally and linguistically diverse students from a single linguistic background and native English speakers are grouped together, aiming at additive bilingualism, biliteracy, and high academic achievement.

14. As used herein, the term *gifted potential* refers to an unmanifested high capacity for outstanding performance or achievement. Meanwhile, *giftedness* alludes to manifested outstanding behaviors or performance. As with the term *bilingualism*, there is no consensus about a single definition of giftedness, and a broad range of definitions are available in the literature. The term *talent* is related to the term *giftedness* in that they both denote individuals' capacities or abilities for outstanding performance, but the term *talent* usually alludes to more specific, within-domain capacities (Feldman, 1999). What is generally accepted is that (1) these terms imply multidimensionality and evolving abilities, and (2) the interpretation of their meaning is mediated by sociocultural factors. In spite of the ongoing debate over labels in the field of gifted education, these terms were chosen in order to bring clarity to the terminology used throughout this book. For discussions about these terms, see Davis, G. A., & Rimm, S. B. (1998). *Education of the gifted and talented* (4th ed.). Englewood Cliffs, NJ: Prentice-Hall; Feldhusen, J. F. (1996). Talent as an alternative conception of giftedness. *Gifted Education International, 11* (3), 124–127; Gagné, F. (1997). Critique of Morelock's (1996) definitions of giftedness and talent. *Roeper Review, 20* (2), 76–85. (see also related articles in this same volume and issue); Morelock, M. J. (1999). On the nature of giftedness and talent: Imposing order on chaos. *Roeper Review, 19* (1), 4–12; and the entire edition of the *Journal for the Education of the Gifted* (1999) 22 (2).

15. According to Gordon (1996), the term *equity* connotes fairness and social justice, and the term *equality* alludes to sameness and the absence of discrimination.

16. For an example of the rhetoric surrounding the dilemma of equity versus excellence in gifted education, see Tannenbaum, A. J. (1998). Programs for the gifted: To be or not to be? *Journal for the Education of the Gifted, 22* (1), 3–36.

1

Framing An Historical Context for the Education of Culturally and Linguistically Diverse Students with Gifted Potential: 1850s to 1980s

EVA I. DÍAZ

1850s to 1900: A New-Sprung America

Socioeconomic and Political Context

Prior to the 1850s, a population with mostly rural living and farming as the primary occupation characterized U.S. society. The United States was divided between North and South, with slavery predominating in the latter. Up to that point, most immigrants had come from Northern Europe and industrialized, literate countries (e.g., Germany). However, from the mid to late 1800s to the 1920s, U.S. society experienced several profound changes, including mass immigration, industrialization, urbanization, and an increased complexity of capitalism (e.g., investment banking in the 1870s). The second half of the nineteenth century was also marked by (1) the Civil War (1861–1865) and its reconstruction period; (2) the Spanish-American War in 1898; (3) significant inventions, such as telephones, electric power plants, and airplanes; and (4) the proliferation of business "tycoons," or industrial entrepreneurs who created financial empires (e.g., John D. Rockefeller and Andrew Carnegie) and had a powerful influence over the government.

Immigration and Being an "American" The massive inflow of immigrants during the period between 1850 and 1900 was overwhelmingly from southern and eastern Europe (e.g., the Irish, Italians, Jews, Greeks, Rumanians, Poles, etc.), with only a small number of Asian background (e.g., Chinese, Japanese). During this time, Mexicans and other Hispanics were also present, especially in today's California and the Southwest, yet they remained "invisible." In general, a significant number of these immigrants were

1

poor, illiterate, and of diverse religions. For the most part, these immigrants had an urban destination in the Northeast, in order to fill the labor needs of an expanding industrial society (e.g., textiles, railroads, machinery, and manufacturing), and in the Midwest for mining and agriculture. Asian immigrants, though, were mostly brought to the United States as cheap labor for agriculture in California, but their immigration quickly became restricted through unprecedented, racially discriminatory legislation.

Along with these changes, class- and culture-related issues emerged. For example, members of higher social classes perceived an increase in poverty and crime among people in lower social classes living in urban areas. This perception translated into the belief that crime and poverty were connected and that they originated in individual, moral failure. Thus, increased cultural heterogeneity was linked to "immorality" and "deviance," based on a belief in immigrant inferiority and White supremacy (Katz, 1976). A reactive, fearful response called for homogenization and the creation of a common moral and political culture (Kastle, 1982). As a result, the assimilation and deculturalization of immigrants was at the core of the movement to form a national identity, and the English language became the unifying force (Anglo-Saxonism). An outcome of these events was a new definition of being "American": giving up the "old life" and becoming a monolingual literate in English. In other words, bilingualism, or the use of native languages other than English, was perceived as unAmerican. This mentality extended beyond the continental United States to its territories abroad. During this time, Blacks also were victims of blatant racism and segregation. For instance, in 1896, the U.S. Supreme Court, in *Plessy v. Ferguson*, legitimized racial segregation in public places, thus giving way to the "separate but equal" tenet.

Educational Context

Throughout the 1800s, cultural diversity and bilingualism were common (Crawford, 1999; Rothstein, 1998), yet the use of the English language was expanding steadily. During the nineteenth century, linguistic heterogeneity underlined the nationwide occurrence, although not without controversy, of native language instruction, bilingual education, and bilingualism (Crawford, 1999; Rothstein, 1998).

Native Language Instruction   Because local communities had control of the schools, schools responded mostly to the needs of their communities, including religion and native languages. For example, German schools were established in Pennsylvania, Illinois, and Colorado, among other states. Likewise, native language instruction was offered in Italian, French, and Chinese. In addition, Spanish-English bilingual education existed in New Mexico. However, circumstances and practices changed with the advent of the common school.

According to Rothstein (1998), on one hand, several immigrant groups were successful in obtaining native language instruction and English as a Second Language (ESL) classes in public and parochial schools throughout the second half of the nineteenth century and early in the twentieth century. On the other hand, submersion in English gradually became "the approach" to educate immigrants (either native-born or foreign-born), as antinative language instruction and antibilingual education legislation flourished, although these were not always enacted. Rothstein also stated that these measures, sponsored primarily by Republican politicians and school boards, were often a reaction to the intense immigration experienced during this era. Furthermore, Rothstein argued that not only was the immersion of immigrants in U.S. public schools far from successful, but the majority of all students was not succeeding in school either. High dropout rates and sporadic attendance, or no attendance at all, were pervasive among all students, but worse among immigrant students. For example, Cockcroft (1995) claimed that in the early 1900s, less than one of five Mexican children attended school. Moreover, the children of Mexican seasonal workers were, for the most part, deprived of schooling.

The Common School   During the mid- to late 1800s and at the turn of the century, the common school or public school movement prevailed in the United States. This movement responded to the conditions of the era (e.g., mass immigration, industrialization, and urban growth) with a capitalist, Protestant, White Anglo-Saxon, and Republican orientation (Cockcroft, 1995; Katz, 1976). That is, not only were schools perceived as places for children to develop moral character and work ethics, but also as agencies to lessen crime and poverty and facilitate assimilation and cultural standardization, especially among immigrants. Schools, which were booming in urban areas, were intended to "unify" Americans, enabling people to become "true Americans" and "good members of society." Therefore, schools aimed primarily at (1) shaping behaviors and attitudes, (2) alleviating perceived social problems, and (3) reinforcing standing social structures rather than cultivating cognitive skills and intellectual abilities. These industrialist aims (i.e., unity, social order, and obedience) were further supported by the capitalistic emphasis on "citizenship training" for culturally and linguistically diverse, immigrant people. As a result, the provision of native language instruction or bilingual education declined, and language restrictionism promoted the establishment of English-only instruction laws in a few states at the beginning of the twentieth century. Furthermore, English proficiency became a measure of assimilation and loyalty to the host country (Crawford, 1999). Thus, Americanization through public schooling suppressed immigrants' languages and cultures.

Given the socioeconomic changes and conditions of U.S. society at the time, compulsory attendance was imposed, special classes were created to serve "retarded" students, a differentiated curriculum was introduced, and increased attention was given to socialization. According to Tropea (1987), special classes permitted the legitimate segregation of students, especially in urban systems. During this time, de jure segregation of Blacks and de facto segregation of Latinos were the rule. However, segregation along racial lines had not gone unnoticed by Black and Latino parents, who strove to counteract it (Cockcroft, 1995).

Hereditary Intelligence   Concurrently, school leaders during this time promoted a talent model, in which the ideal of achievement was available, supposedly, on the basis of ability and in which the "able should rise simply by virtue of their own talents" (Katz, 1976, p. 401). Katz argued that this line of thinking on meritocracy, free of unfairness, implied that failure once again was a reflection of weak individual responsibility and lack of ability. In reality, the prevailing model was one of social status transmission, which in turn advanced status as an inherited blessing from father to son.

During this time, the concepts of intelligence and giftedness emerged as a significant area of research. For instance, in the late 1800s, Galton [in Davis & Rimm, 1998] carried out research on the components of genius, intelligence, and intelligence testing, underscoring the keenness of senses as a measure of intelligence and the hereditary nature of intelligence. Nevertheless, the study of "intelligence" can be traced back to the late 1700s. Between 1870 and 1900, "pupils of more than average capability," "highly capable," "brilliant children," "exceptionally bright [children]," "genius," and "pupils of supernormal mentality" were identified as those who demonstrated high scholastic attainments or achieved high intelligence quotients (IQs). Additionally, Davis and Rimm (1998) suggested that scattered, mostly local efforts to provide gifted education were underway.

Recapitulation

In sum, the period between 1850 to 1900 in the United States was characterized by the startling growth of cities, diverse immigrant populations, and industries. These societal changes engendered concerns about poverty and crime, which were often perceived to be caused by the cultural inferiority of recent immigrants. As a result, the assimilation of immigrants gained momentum. In the educational environment, the common school movement responded to the social conditions of the time and aimed at developing morality, a sense of citizenship, and social order. Typifying events in the educational arena were (1) the imposition of compulsory attendance, (2) the decline of bilingual and native language instruction, (3) the establishment of special classes, (4) the introduction of a "differentiated curriculum," and (5) the emergence of research interest in the concept of intelligence.

1900 to 1950s: National Identity and Historic War Conflicts

Socioeconomic and Political Context

The first half of the twentieth century is distinguished by its progressive reforms. Starting with Republican President Theodore Roosevelt (1901–1909), these modern, liberal attempts sought the development of collective thought and a controlled economy in a rapidly changing society (Karier, 1972). During these years, while business interests were having a strong impact on the government, the United States became involved in world politics and engaged in extensive military campaigns.

During prewar years, the United States enjoyed a magnificent economic boom. For instance, the industrial expansion of the period prompted a love affair with automobiles and airplanes. However, it also strengthened (1) hierarchical social class divisions, which sustained U.S. capitalist society; and (2) an economy dependent on a racial division of labor. On one hand, the notion of the masses as often irrational and prone to conflict and violence still predominated. "The uncontrolled immigrant masses of our urban ghettoes" were perceived as a problem with potential chaotic consequences, in need of "nonviolent but coercive means of social control" (Karier, 1972, p. 60). On the other hand, a common perception about the existing distribution of wealth, power, and status being "rooted in nature itself" existed; this meant that White, Anglo-Saxon, native-born individuals were inherently superior, and anybody else was inferior and had to accommodate the dominant group.

One of the responses to industrialism and the social transformations of the era was the emergence of the ideal of social efficiency; that is, "experts" were sought to provide rational knowledge on facilitating social order. In this regard, Stevens (1972) wrote the following:

> The concept of social efficiency as it emerged in the Progressive Era was used to denote a method whereby maximum predictability and probability might be achieved in any socially oriented process. In the early twentieth century, advocates of social efficiency usually adopted what they called scientific methods for achieving these ends. Some, however, continued to rely upon moral suasion. Collectively, social efficiency was a method for achieving social stability *in* and control *of* the environment. In general, then, the term denoted a method for effecting social control. (p. 18)

On April 2, 1917, Democratic President Woodrow Wilson declared war against Germany in the name of democracy. This war ended on November 11, 1918, resulting in postwar times marked by a depressed economy and joblessness. Nevertheless, immigrants, not war, were blamed and used as a scapegoat for the economic and social troubles of the time. It was not until 1923 that the U.S. economy experienced some prosperity.

Antiimmigrant Attitudes and "Americanization"   Early in the 1900s and continuing into the early 1920s, antiimmigrant, particularly anti-German, feelings permeated the national atmosphere. This antiimmigrant attitude was also observed as a "Brown Scare," targeting Mexicans and provoking their deportation on the basis of their being undesirable and troublemakers. Paradoxically, Mexicans were being brought to the United States during this same time as sources of cheap labor for farming, in order to sustain the nation's commercialized agriculture industry (Cockcroft, 1995). Moreover, this antiimmigrant position reached a crucial point when the harshest immigration restrictions ever (i.e., the 1921 Emergency Quota Act) were instituted under Republican President Warren G. Harding's administration (1921–1923).

During the first quarter of the twentieth century, the protection of the "American way" required the socialization of the masses and a need to "Americanize" immigrants. According to Hansot and Tyack (1982), a strategy to achieve such goals was the creation of centers for community organization. Hansot and Tyack explained that, under this cover, these social centers were really aimed at transmitting proper values, molding moral citizens, and enabling individuals to use their leisure time in commendable ways. It was believed that free time would interfere with building a socially efficient, orderly, and stable society. Moreover, Crawford (1999) explained that "as Americanization took a coercive turn, proficiency in English was increasingly equated with political loyalty; for the first time, an ideological link was forged between speaking good English and being a 'good American' " (p. 26). In this regard, Lewis (1980) stated that "the thirty years from 1890 onward have been referred to as 'the heyday of xenophobic legislation,' and that the U.S. Supreme Court in 1967 referred to the era as the 'period of extreme nativism' " (p. 367). By 1923, though, the furor over Americanization and the attempts to legislate loyalty to the English language were on the decline.

The Great Depression and Catastrophic Times of War   Starting in 1929, with a peak in 1933 (lasting until 1940), the Great Depression sank the economic health of the United States. In response to this situation, Democratic President Franklin D. Roosevelt (1933–1945) proposed his New Deal program, which took aim at a controlled economic recovery through federal regulation, especially in the areas of banking, agriculture, and public welfare. Simultaneously, large-scale industries, banking, insurance companies, and labor unions were growing. By 1937, the U.S. economy had recovered somewhat, but was still in recession and in the midst of World War II. It was precisely through government intervention in the economy during World War II that military priorities were met (e.g., automakers building tanks) and that the defense industry emerged.

In the military arena, Japanese military forces attacked Pearl Harbor in 1941 and the United States declared war. Individuals of Japanese background were moved to isolated camps (1942), and during the next few years, U.S. forces were involved in many military interventions. In 1944, World War II was waning, and it ended in 1945. Democratic President Harry S. Truman authorized U.S. military forces to drop atomic bombs on Hiroshima and Nagasaki, Japan. From 1946 to 1947, the Cold War against the former Soviet Union began to take shape. In 1950, the United States was at war with Korea, with that conflict ending in 1953, after which, Republican President Dwight D. Eisenhower (1953–1961) focused on maintaining world peace. In addition to the threat of nuclear war, the 1950s also marked an era of space exploration, suburban expansion, Hula Hoops, and rock and roll.

During these war times, the United States continued the importing of Mexican labor (i.e., the Bracero Program, 1940–1964) to counterbalance the abrupt insufficiency of workers in the railroad and agricultural industries. Puerto Ricans were hired as postal workers and Native Americans as "code talkers," primarily because the bilingualism of each group enabled the U.S. Department of Defense to scrutinize and monitor significant sources of information and communicate in unidentifiable ways or codes unknown to its adversaries.

In spite of this general scenario, increased concern (albeit embryonic) about social issues, such as racism, the melting-pot idea, and forced assimilation, had begun in the late 1930s. Intellectuals of the time called for tolerance, understanding, communication, and cultural pluralism, and they warned society about the dangers of racial conflict and forced melting-pot assimilation. They also pinpointed the attitudinal roots of intolerance and the curative power of arts and creativity in eliminating fear, prejudice, and stereotyping. In accord, intercultural and human relations programs were developed, stressing the commonality of all people. Goodenow (1975), a critic of this movement, charged these scholars with treating issues of race and ethnicity only superficially, thus failing to address the real issues. He argued that they not only took little action, but also neglected the structural, institutional nature of racism and the role of race relations. Furthermore, Goodenow asserted that progressive theory and rhetoric were really used to rationalize segregation and assimilation.

The Unexpected Social Aftermath of World War II   Meanwhile, the United States was actively engaged in war conflicts, and social issues such as racial violence, prejudice, and discrimination kept swelling. Surprisingly, World War II—a war against Nazi racism—influenced the understanding of racism within the United States and animated the blooming of a civil rights movement that empowered ethnic minorities. For instance, in 1948, President Truman ordered the desegregation of the Armed Forces. Simultaneously, as Black and Latino veterans were coming back from war, they infused their renewed vitality in the search for rights into the burgeoning civil rights movement. Most of these emerging Black and Latino civil right groups initially responded to the challenge of school segregation. Moreover, the rationale for the Cold War had an impact on U.S. racial matters in education, as will be explained later in this chapter.

After World War II, the U.S. economy experienced a magnificent boom, accompanied by the "Baby Boom" and the increase of the middle class. New industries emerged (e.g., aviation and electronics) and well-established businesses consolidated. The U.S. work force gained in productivity, but the small-scale farming or agricultural businesses could no longer compete with big agribusiness ventures. Increased demands for housing and other middle class demands fostered the development of suburbs and shopping centers. In fact, President Truman's Fair Deal program supported most of these social and economic changes. In 1957, the first Soviet satellite reached outer space, and soon after, in 1958, the first U.S. satellite, "Explorer I," was successfully launched. With this achievement, an era of space exploration began.

Educational Context

Progressivism in the First Quarter of the Twentieth Century   From 1890 to 1920, and within a framework of Americanization through schooling, "administrative progressives" emerged, creating more centralized, impersonal, and bureaucratic school systems (Gelb, 1989). The purpose of this movement was to introduce the corporate model of administration into public schools. These progressive school reformers transferred the overall power of school decisions to experts, who established templates for practice using a behaviorist, top-down model. This time was also an era of "educational professionalism" (e.g., creation of teacher organizations) and psychological testing. Public schools were viewed as the "master agency for adjustment" (Stevens, 1972, p. 19) for the common good, which often represented the interests of the dominant group and the necessities of an industrial society but disempowered others. Karier (1972) indicated the following:

> In the process, education of the individual was sacrificed for the greater need for social control and security. As a consequence, large numbers of people were not educated to be critical individual citizens, but trained to seek security and comfort in the symbols and mythologies manipulated by Madison Avenue social science experts. (p. 76)

Karier added, "In this way, neither science nor technology was effectively employed to enhance democracy (rule by the people) but rather became an effective tool of the powerful in controlling the social system" (p. 76). An example is the creation of the junior high school in the early 1900s. Kliebard (1995) wrote, "the creation of a new educational institution, the junior high school, was given special impetus by the perceived need to 'explore' children's needs and capacities before entering upon the high school period" (p. 94). However, a more significant expression of social control took place during the Depression era, when high numbers of teenagers with no work entered public schools, especially at the secondary level. According to Kliebard (1995), this challenge encouraged the idea of "education according to need" or "education according to predicted social and vocational roles" (p. 85). Curriculum differentiation and specialized courses, primarily at the high school level, were introduced. For example, vocational, industrial, and cooperative education programs flourished in industrial centers and cities around the United States. In these programs, schools and local factories collaborated to train students to become "efficient workers with love for their country" (McBride, 1974). These strategies were not primarily about individual well-being but about reducing inefficiency in education and sustaining a social order attuned with the new industrial society. Franklin (1989) argued that curriculum differentiation emerged as an instrument of social control to preserve the political and economic power of the upper classes at the expense of the working classes, particularly the urban poor and ethnic and racial minorities. He explained that concerns about a more diverse student population in class, ethnicity, and ability brought about more "functional" school programs or specialized courses of study. These programs channeled students into roles based on their backgrounds and abilities, thus sustaining racism and the concept of social utility.

Standardized testing, differentiated curriculum, and tracking were components of an instant and vital solution to the quest for order and stability on the basis of science, merit (fairness), and progress. These methods served the purpose of matching individuals with what was perceived as their ineluctable roles, given their inborn abilities. In other words, prognostication of the roles of these students was determined based on what the dominant group perceived as their predestination. For example, in 1917, special classes or learning centers were introduced for slower learners, newly arrived students, and limited English speakers who had IQ scores in the low 70s, but whose actual learning abilities were far above their test scores and could, with some special help, be brought to an "efficient school level" (Raftery, 1988, p. 79). As mentioned, curriculum differentiation or different forms of education for different kinds of children had also emerged by 1918. Thus, tracking involved providing academic subjects to college-bound students or to those deemed able to deal with ideas, and providing manual training to those students who were believed to be able to benefit from a more utilitarian school experience. Clearly, the school system aimed at preparing students for their "expected" adult lives. Furthermore, mental testing had become the source of modern, scientific rationalization for all of these educational practices.

A Movement on Mental and Psychological Testing   According to Davis and Rimm (1994), a movement toward developing measures of mental ability had been underway since the early 1900s, and was represented by Binet, Cattell, and Terman. Goodard,

Yerkes, and Thorndike also were popular figures in this movement. However, it was Binet's preponderant scale that was used most frequently. By the 1920s and 1930s, IQ testing was widely adopted by school systems, leading to tracking based on elitist, racist, and hereditarian beliefs of testing, as well as legitimizing the underrepresentation of immigrants, Blacks, and the poor in the upper tracks (Ackerman, 1995; Cohen & Rosenberg, 1977). Although there were contradictory evidence, complaints, and an increased recognition that mental capacity could not be measured or represented by a single entity called *general intelligence* (accumulated from the 1930s to the 1950s), this knowledge remained largely overlooked. Cultural biases and the inadequacy of translations were also identified as limitations of mental tests. For example, Raftery (1988) pointed out that a few administrators were searching for more "suitable tests for non-English speaking children, particularly Mexicans" (p. 79), because there were data suggesting that translated tests were unreliable, due to cultural and linguistic biases. Unfortunately, lack of English proficiency was still perceived as a manifestation of low mental ability instead of as a lack of experience with a new language and culture, in which case, total submersion in English classes and assimilation were considered the answer.

Research on Language and Intelligence in Immigrants   During this same period of time, studies (e.g., as cited in Hakuta, 1986: Brigham, 1923; Goddard, 1917; and Young, 1922) on the relationship of language, intelligence, and cognitive development were published, supporting the belief that immigrants were genetically inferior (e.g., a racially based lack of intelligence). These publications portrayed an hereditarian view and claimed that immigrants' lack of English learning was due to their lower levels of intelligence. As a result, it was understood that not even schooling could do much for them—schools could certainly not make immigrants intelligent. In any case, this line of thinking suggested that trying to educate immigrants was not worth the effort, because immigrants could not help advance the country anyway. Other studies (as cited in Hakuta, 1986: Smith, 1931, 1939; Yoshioka, 1929) pointed to the immigrants' bilingualism as the cause of their lower intelligence and academic achievement levels. This "language handicap" or "experiential" position further argued that bilingualism promoted linguistic confusion and led to emotional and educational maladjustment. Therefore, this view sustained the belief that the use of native languages (other than English) at home interfered negatively with cognitive development to the extreme of causing mental retardation. These understandings were subsequently fueled by the results of biased intelligence tests. (The evidence gathered on these studies, though, has been found to lack validity due to significant methodological flaws in the design and implementation of the studies as well as in the interpretation of results.) Still, these findings were used as scientific evidence to legitimize the restrictions on immigration and the linguistic assimilation promulgated by politicians.

This "new body of knowledge," along with an antiimmigrant attitude and the emphasis on social control, contributed to the decline of instruction in languages other than English. After 1920, not only did native language instruction and bilingual education fade, but foreign language education for native-born students was outlawed. Moreover, by the early 1920s, thirty-four states had English-only requirements in the schools. However, the outlaw of foreign language study was soon declared unconstitutional. In this regard, Crawford (1999) states that although the hostility had started to decline by 1923, "public attitudes had changed fundamentally: learning in languages other than English now seemed less than patriotic" (p. 29). Moreover, "minority tongues were devalued in the eyes of the younger generation" (p. 29). Public schooling through English-only instruction remained focused on assimilating immigrant students.

The Unexpected Aftermath of World War II and the Cold War in Education   As explained, the World War II era of the 1940s marked the onset of the civil rights movement that empowered culturally and linguistically diverse individuals to restore their cultures and obtain equal educational opportunity. For instance, in 1946 and 1947, Latino parents in California brought a class action suit, known as *Mendez v. Westminster School District*, to the Ninth Circuit Court, which in turn declared that the Plessy doctrine of "separate but equal" was unconstitutional (cited in Cockcroft, 1995).With this antecedent, the 1954 Supreme Court decision *Brown v. Board of Education of Topeka, Kansas* dismissed the "separate but equal" doctrine, or de jure segregation, and supported the desegregation of U.S. schools.

According to Cockcroft (1995), a significant factor in this court decision was the so called "Cold War Imperative," or "the need to eliminate apartheid at home in order to justify charging the Soviet Union with human rights violations" (p. 46). Correspondingly, the *Brown* decision sustained that school segregation based on race is unconstitutional and that equitable, high-quality education is a right of all children. Although this decision did not contemplate nor have a bearing directly upon members of other minority groups, it has served as a precedent in the search for equality for culturally and linguistically diverse students. For instance, in the *Reyes v. School District #1, Denver, Colorado, 1973*, the Supreme Court ruled that Latinos were covered by *Brown*. Fischer (1982) claimed that "the Supreme Court decision in Brown has generated more litigation, more court involvement in education, and more reexamination of educational policy than any other single decision in history" (p. 63). He further wrote,

> Historically, our courts have relied on voluntary compliance to their orders and decrees. . . . In desegregation cases, however, courts had to resort to unusual practices to mobilize public support for their orders, and even then the results were at best a mixture of partial success and continued hostility, resentment, and resistance. (p. 66)

After World War II, college education increased in value, and educational opportunity became a political issue. Violations of equal opportunity were viewed as the result of social prejudice, cultural expectations, and economic inequality. Contemporaneously, by the late 1950s, controversy reemerged about the wide use of mental testing in schools, especially the charge of discriminating against minorities and the poor. Actually, it was perceived that testing would not only infringe on educational opportunities, but also deny them. The 1950s also saw the revitalization of foreign language teaching, primarily for national defense purposes (i.e., the National Defense Education Act of 1958).

Intelligence, Giftedness, and Gifted Education   During the first half of the twentieth century, the field of gifted education also experienced several crucial happenings. For instance, in 1920, Guy Whipple coined the term *gifted* to designate those students that were "highly intelligent" or high academic achievers (Passow, 1981). During that time, researchers focused on identifying the traits and characteristics (physical, medical, and character) of gifted individuals in order to determine the nature of giftedness. After all, it was believed that high intelligence, and therefore giftedness, was inherited (passed through the genes). In the early 1920s, Terman's research findings reinforced the concept of giftedness as a particular cut-off IQ score. Yet, this concept of giftedness disregarded artistic or creative talents. His model was attuned with the social efficiency philosophy of the era. His work has also been criticized for overlooking racial minorities (Colangelo & Davis, 1997; Witty, 1981).

In 1926, Cox highlighted the potential influence of factors such as persistence, self-confidence, and willpower on giftedness. During this time, Leta Hollingworth (1926) also pinpointed the emotional dimension of giftedness, the importance of early identification, and the role of enrichment learning. Still, minor interest was devoted to the education of gifted children or the development of special abilities. According to DeHaan and Havighurst (1961), gifted programs in the United States have been in place since the nineteenth century, with mostly acceleration and homogeneous grouping models up to the 1930s. Acceleration, with increasing attention to enrichment for gifted children within regular classrooms, started in the 1930s to 1940s. Regarding the identification of gifted children, researchers had grown somewhat aware of the limitations of intelligence tests in defining and identifying gifted children. However, in practice, practitioners were still encouraged to use ability and aptitude tests as a fair means for identifying talented youth with the potential to attend college (Ackerman, 1995).

During the 1940s and 1950s, there was a growing recognition of untapped human resources. The concepts of creativity and special abilities gained more acceptance in the field, especially in the 1950s. Also, in 1951, Witty's report, *The Gifted Child*, sparked renewed interest in the topic, including an expanded definition of this group to include "10 or 15 percent of the age group instead of only 1 or 2 percent, which had been the tendency before 1940" (DeHaan & Havighurst, 1961, p. 13). By the early 1950s, some state laws on gifted education, such as in Louisiana (McHardy, 1985), were in place. Experimental programs for gifted students flourished by the mid-1950s. Then, a particular historical event, the successful launching of the Soviet satellite Sputnik in 1957, introduced a frenzy of national panic in order to compete, accompanied by a perceived need for the sustained progress of gifted education (Tannenbaum, 1979, 1981).

By the late 1950s and early 1960s, a short-lived call to discover and nurture the talents of the brightest resulted from the Congress' approval of the National Defense Education Act of 1958. According to DeLeon and VandenBos (1985), this Act not only reinforced the connection between federal involvement in education and national defense, but also provided funds to strengthen instruction in modern foreign languages, mathematics, and science. It also granted funds to assist in establishing gifted services, including testing programs for identifying those with special ability and guidance counseling for others. Zettel (1982) argued that gifted services all of a sudden increased in number during the 1959 to 1963 period, due primarily to state and private foundations' efforts to advance gifted education. Tannenbaum (1979) described this period of time as the "Great Talent Hunt" or "a period of great talent mobilization, requiring the most able-minded to fulfill their potentials and submit their developed abilities for service to the nation" (p. 12). He also stated that research and professional interest related to giftedness and gifted children increased at the time.

Recapitulation

In short, the U.S. society of the first half of the twentieth century was distinguished not only by its progressive, liberal orientation, but also by its disturbing war involvements and economic vacillations. Industrialism and social change called for the ideals of social efficiency or social control, especially through Americanization in schools, yet this process was radically influenced by the unexpected impact of World War II on social attitudes and education. Before World War II, schools had become the preferred medium for molding students in accordance with the established order. However, after this war and the Cold War, social issues such as racism gained attention and gains were made in addressing issues of educational equity (e.g., desegregation). In relation to gifted education, not only did the concepts of creativity and special abilities expand long-standing views of giftedness, but gifted programs also flourished. Still, the primary interest remained on the intellectually gifted or on students with very high IQ scores.

1960s to 1990: Love Me . . . Love Me Not and Social Justice

Socioeconomic and Political Context

Politics in the 1960s and 1970s   In 1961, with the youngest man ever elected President, John F. Kennedy, an era of neoprogressive unrest began. Although Kennedy's economic plans brought prosperity to the United States, it was his activism and efforts on behalf of equal rights (e.g., affirmative action) that distinguished his administration. For example, Kennedy signed Executive Order 10925 in 1961, establishing the need for affirmative action in the hiring of Blacks by defense contractors. Kennedy's efforts on behalf of equal rights were in response to the social uprising among members of minority groups, mostly Blacks and Hispanics, involved in the civil rights movement (e.g., mass marches led by Martin Luther King, Jr., the Chicano revolt in the Southwest, and the Puerto Rican rising in the Northeast). However, Kennedy became the youngest president to die in office when he was assassinated in 1963. As a result, it was his successor, Lyndon B. Johnson (1963–1969) who continued Kennedy's measures, including a milestone civil rights bill in 1964.

The landmark Title VI of the Civil Rights Act prohibited discrimination on the basis of race, color, or national origin in all programs receiving federal assistance; violation of this legislation would result in the termination of that federal assistance. The Act was directed at counteracting racial segregation and seeking equality. The Office for Civil Rights (OCR) of the Department of Health, Education, and Welfare (HEW) became responsible for enforcing Title VI. Later, in 1965, Johnson also signed Executive Order 11246, requiring federal contractors to take affirmative action to provide equal opportunity without regard to a person's race, religion, or national origin, thus extending protection to all racial and ethnic minorities (Curry, 1996). Women were included as a protected group in 1968, and people with disabilities in 1973. In addition, Johnson proposed an extensive "Great Society" program, which focused on social welfare and, in turn, made significant contributions to the poor (antipoverty programs) and the elderly. All of these domestic events were taking place while the United States was engaged in the Vietnam War (1964–1973).

In 1969, Republican Richard M. Nixon became president, and the first walk on the moon was accomplished. While in office, Nixon concentrated primarily on world politics, reducing tensions with China and the Soviet Union. However, the economic panorama in the United States was deteriorating quickly as a new global economy, with cheap labor markets abroad and automation, bolstered inflation and unemployment, which in turn led to increasing federal budget deficits throughout the 1970s. Similarly, in the social sphere, affirmative action and civil rights acquired a Republican interpretation. For example, Marable (1996) stated that Nixon utilized a "liberal reform for conservative objectives: the expansion of the African-American middle class, which might benefit the Republican Party" (p. 7). After Nixon's resignation in 1974, Republican Gerald R. Ford became president. Facing a depressed economy, many of Ford's measures were aimed at stimulating the economy. In 1977, Democrat Jimmy Carter won the presidential election. He continued to battle economic problems, and, although there was some improvement, the economic instability continued. However, in the international arena, Carter was known as a champion of human rights and the president who established the Department of Education.

Immigration   In 1959, the Cuban Revolution provoked a significant influx of Cuban refugees into the United States. In 1960, legislation was enacted whereby the United States opened its doors to world refugees. Not long after, by the end of the 1970s and into the 1980s, the United States faced the second largest immigration wave, due to a variety of reasons, including the relaxation of provisions in the 1965 Immigration Act and a booming economy. This wave of immigrants differed in many ways from previous waves, in that these immigrants, many without legal status, were predominantly non-White, were from Third World countries (especially Asia and Latin America), and were highly diverse in comparison to earlier European immigrants. For instance, immigrants (1) came from diverse countries and socioeconomic levels, (2) tended to be more educated and skilled than were previous waves of immigrants, and (3) had diverse reasons for immigrating (Porter & Rumbaut, 1990). In this regard, Garcia and Gonzalez (1995) indicated that from 1981 to 1990 over seven million people immigrated to the United States, representing a 63 percent increase in comparison to that of the previous decade.

Not surprisingly, this increase in the number of immigrants, at a time when the U.S. economy was experiencing a serious recession, generated another swell of anti-immigrant feeling in the 1980s and 1990s. For instance, the Immigration Reform and Control Act (IRCA) of 1986 was enacted, imposing fines on employers who hired undocumented workers and granting amnesty to illegal immigrants that met certain requirements in order to create a stable labor force for growers. Nevertheless, this law backfired as it (1) unexpectedly drove legal immigration to high levels, (2) established the networks necessary for continued immigration, (3) made more visible the lack of resources to enforce the law, (4) did not result in the intended stable labor force for agriculture, and (5) provoked a new wave of illegal immigration. In fact, Freedberg and McLeod (1998) described the Act as "perhaps the most important immigration legislation of the century and now widely viewed as one of the government's biggest failures" (p. A1). Another example is the emergence of the movement in the early 1980s that sought to make English the official language of the United States. Since then, this movement has also attempted to pass legislation that amends the Voting Rights Act (e.g., to repeal bilingual voting requirements) and the Immigration and Nationality Act (e.g., to require that naturalization ceremonies be conducted entirely in English) and repeals the Bilingual Education Act. As a counteracting force, the English Plus movement emerged in 1987. According to Lewelling (1992), this movement "is based on the belief that all U.S. residents should have the opportunity to become proficient in English *plus* one or more other languages [emphasis in original]" and that the cultural diversity of the United States is "a national strength" (p. 1). Lewelling also states that, through its advocacy role, the English Plus movement has facilitated the adoption of state and local resolutions supporting linguistic pluralism.

Reagan and Bush in the 1980s   General discontent with the economic and social conditions grew during the 1970s. Thus, in 1980, the newly elected Republican President, Ronald Reagan (1981–1989), promised to reverse the economic downfall of the 1970s. Reagan's administration was characterized by a sober economic plan aimed at stimulating the economy. In contrast to the 1960s and 1970s, government expenditures were drastically reduced and many social programs were eliminated during Reagan's two terms in office. Still, the country withstood an intense recession in 1982. For example, business bankruptcies rose 50 percent over the previous year, with farmers hit hard. By 1983, the economy seemed to be recovering, although federal deficits kept rising (largely due to Reagan's increased defense spending), and a stock market crash in 1987 called the public's attention to the instability of the economy. Regarding military campaigns, the Iran–Contra affair in the early and mid-1980s was one of the most notable.

During the Reagan administration, U.S. society experienced an increase in White supremacy activism, and thus an increase of violence along racial lines. Moreover, a so-called White backlash (i.e., the belief in reverse discrimination against White men) turned against affirmative action, civil rights, social programs, and immigration. The latter, immigration, was perceived to be the cause of the economic and social problems experienced during the 1980s. According to Williams (1996), Reagan and the subsequent Bush administration particularly supported this perception. In 1989, Republican George Bush became president, and soon afterward the United States invaded Panama and the Gulf War against Iraq (1990) began. Using immigrants as scapegoats, "working and middle-class Americans were encouraged to divert their attention away from the global economy and technological roots of their problems" (p. 249). Likewise, their attention was drawn away from the economic aftermath of the U.S. involvement in the Vietnam War and many other detrimental military decisions and economic policies made during these and previous administrations.

Educational Context

During the 1960s, many different groups (e.g., women, ethnically diverse people, individuals with disabilities, and others) had grown more outraged that the schools were consciously being used to perpetuate inequalities based on class, gender, race, and ethnicity. Thus, these groups demanded attention and used the law as an instrument of change. For example, Blacks and Latinos achieved major school victories in the 1960s and 1970s, respectively. These victories compelled school systems, administrators, educators, and practitioners to be more responsive to long-excluded groups.

The late 1960s and early 1970s composed an era when the ideals of equity and excellence were polarized as two conflicting goals of education. By the mid-1970s, the pendulum was shifting, as public schooling was being characterized as a declining industry. Accordingly, the excellence movement reemerged in the late 1970s, with concerns of "quality" over equity.

In 1983, the report, *A Nation at Risk: The Imperative for Educational Reform* (National Commission on Excellence in Education, 1983) was published, declaring that public education in the United States was a failure. This, according to Cizek (1999), marked the beginning of the "manufactured crisis" in American education. As a result, public education achieved top priority on the national agenda. Moreover, Pipho (1999) argued that as soon as the first set of international comparisons appeared after the NCEE report, it was believed that the United States would, because of its failing schools, languish in the global economy. From that point on, the purpose of general education was to make the United States competitive in the global economy. For this purpose, educational efforts were directed away from equity and toward the pursuit of academic excellence, defined and assessed in English (McGroarty, 1992). This concern over improving the U.S. quality of education led to the growth of a minimum competency movement at the state level, which in turn created an emphasis on testing. In 1986, the report, *A Nation Prepared*, called for replacing the factory-like education with an education more attuned to the new Information Age. Among the report's initiatives were the creation of charter schools and support for the higher order thinking movement (Resnick, 1987). Not too long afterward, many Republican politicians invoked the restoration of educational authority (i.e., standards and testing) and reinvention, with no real systemic reform of the school system. This political sector proclaimed itself against multicultural or bilingual education and affirmative action, thus supporting the assimilation or Americanization of culturally and linguistically diverse people. Moreover, these Republican politicians accused the movement for equality of educational opportunities of creating a decline in academic standards in U.S. schools.

Paradoxically, the warning of an educational crisis led to the framing of the importance of languages other than English as a component of new, rigorous academic standards, thus counteracting U.S. students' lack of competence in foreign languages. Being able to speak other languages was deemed critical to being effective in the global market. As a result, a revived interest in foreign languages took place in the 1980s. However, the repercussion of this perspective was really observed in the 1994 reauthorization of Title VII.

Aside from these events, the Middle School Movement emerged in the 1960s as a result of the dissatisfaction with the concept of the junior high school as a miniature version of high schools, and as a result of new findings in the fields of human growth, development, and cognition (George & Lawrence, 1982). The number of middle schools grew quickly in the early 1970s, serving as a bridge between elementary and high schools and seeking to meet the particular educational needs of adolescents (primarily ten- to fourteen-year-olds) as they go through physical, psychological, and social-transition challenges. Similarly, multicultural education appeared in the 1970s, with an emphasis on human relations (Tiedt & Tiedt, 1998).

Federal Policy and Legal Background for Bilingual Education   In the federal policy arena, a highly significant period began in the 1960s. The establishment of the Civil Rights Act of 1964 and its emphasis on equality, as discussed previously, served as a key reactant in the design of the first federal law to aid elementary and secondary education, that is, the Elementary and Secondary Education Act (ESEA) of 1965 (P.L. 89-10) (Casanova, 1992). This legislation provided Title I funds for the education of children with low socioeconomic status (SES) and facilitated the enactment of Title VII of ESEA, best known as the Bilingual Education Act (BEA) of 1968.

The Bilingual Education Act of 1968   The Bilingual Education Act (BEA) was signed into law (i.e., P.L. 90-247) and provided federal funds (i.e., competitive grants totalling $7.5 million) for the development of programs targeting students with *limited English-speaking ability* from low-income families, preservice and in-service teacher training, the acquisition of teaching materials, and parental involvement (20 U.S.C. 880b, Sec. 704, 81 Stat. 816). The BEA encouraged the creation of "innovative" programs but did not provide significant instructional guidance nor did it mandate bilingual education.

Originally, the BEA was a response to poverty and to the failure of sink-or-swim approaches for educating culturally and linguistically diverse children. Most of these programs were remedial or compensatory in nature, thus focusing on students' perceived weaknesses. Nevertheless, the BEA's early success was, in part due to the reliance on the success of the Coral Way two-way bilingual program to serve Cuban refugees in Dade County, Florida, Public Schools and other experimental bilingual programs. Crawford (1999) lamentably noted that after the success of the Coral Way program,

> Federal and state bilingual education laws soon followed. *Government intervention changed the focus of the Coral Way experiment, however, from an enrichment model aimed at developing fluency in two languages, to a remedial effort designed to help "disadvantaged" children overcome the "handicap of not speaking English"* [italics added]. From the outset, federal aid to bilingual education was regarded as a "poverty program," rather than an innovative approach to language instruction. This decision would shape the development of bilingual programs, and the heated ideological battles surrounding them, over the next three decades. (pp. 36–37)

During the same year, the Department of Health, Education, and Welfare (HEW) issued the first interpretations and guidelines of the Civil Rights Act of 1964 and its own regulations applicable to school districts and other programs under its tutelage. According to these guidelines, those school systems receiving federal assistance "are responsible for assuring that students of a particular race, color, or national origin are not denied the opportunity to obtain the education generally obtained by other students in the system" (33 *Federal Register* 4956).

The Office for Civil Rights and Lau *v.* Nichols   In spite of the efforts initiated by the BEA, many school districts failed to take action in providing equality of educational opportunity to students with limited English-speaking ability. Complaints to the Office for Civil Rights (OCR) prompted an investigation, which determined that many school systems were discriminating against these students on the basis of their national origin. As a result, in 1970, the OCR sent a memorandum to school districts, warning them about the existence of discrimination on the basis of national origin and delineating the responsibilities of school districts in providing equal educational opportunity to these students.

Although, on one hand, this memorandum underscored the remedial, transitional nature of bilingual education (as established by the BEA) and the "language deficit, educationally disadvantaged" view concerning the language-minority students; on the other hand, this memo proved to be of significance in the legal realm. For instance, *Lau v. Nichols* (1974) was a class action suit brought on behalf of limited English proficient (LEP) students of Chinese ancestry enrolled in the San Francisco public school system. The plaintiffs alleged that the school district's conduct violated both the Fourteenth Amendment to the Constitution and Title VI of the Civil Rights Act of 1964. However, both the District Court and the Ninth Circuit Court of Appeals found no violations, but the U.S. Supreme Court unanimously overturned the lower courts' decisions, finding that the school district had indeed discriminated against these students and had violated Title VI of the 1968 regulations. The Supreme Court ruling, however, did not consider the constitutional charge. Justice Douglas cited the OCR 1970 memorandum and argued that "there is no equality of treatment merely by providing students with the same facilities, textbooks, teachers, and curriculum; for students who do not understand English are effectively foreclosed from any meaningful education" (*Lau v. Nichols*, 94 S. Ct. 786). In other words, the *Lau v. Nichols* case (1) upheld the guidelines delineated in the 1970 memorandum and (2) ascertained the rights of language-minority students by establishing the inequality of treatment in submersion programs (mainstream, English-only instruction). Yet, it did not mandate any remedy, just that alternative ways of educating these students be sought.

The Equal Educational Opportunity Act of 1974   Just a few weeks after the *Lau v. Nichols* decision, Congress passed the Equal Educational Opportunity Act (EEOA) as Title II of the Elementary and Secondary Education Act Amendments of 1974 (P.L. 93-380). The EEOA called for the most effective education possible to facilitate the development of student potential to the highest achievable levels. According to Faltis and Hudelson (1998), the EEOA extended the *Lau* decision to all public schools, not just those receiving federal assistance. It also established new responsibilities placed on school districts serving language-minority students, including the provision of special programs for these students. The EEOA stated,

> No State shall deny equal educational opportunity to an individual on account of his or her race, color, sex, or national origin, by the failure of an educational agency to take appropriate action to overcome language barriers that impede equal participation by its students in its instructional programs. (20 U.S.C. §1703[f])

In addition, the EEOA suggested that a discriminatory effect without a discriminatory intent could be considered a violation of Title VI.

The Bilingual Education Act of 1974   To clarify the ambiguity of "appropriate action," other 1974 Education Amendments were consulted, including the amendment reauthorizing the Bilingual Education Act (P.L. 93-380). This BEA (1) dropped the poverty criterion, thus expanding the eligibility for participation in Title VII programs to all students with limited English-speaking ability, particularly Native American children; (2) required schools to provide instruction in the children's native languages and cultures; (3) provided for English-speaking students to enroll in bilingual programs; and (4) included new categories of programs for teaching training, technical assistance, and instructional materials. As a result, it was inferred that bilingual education could be considered an appropriate action to overcome the so-called language barriers. Nevertheless, the focus remained on a compensatory and transitional model, rather than an enrichment model. In 1974, Congress also mandated the creation of a national clearinghouse for bilingual education and established the Office of Bilingual Education and Minority Language Affairs (OBEMLA) within the U.S. Department of Education to administer the BEA.

The Lau Remedies   In 1975, the Department of Housing, Education, and Welfare circulated the Lau Remedies (OCR, 1975), which are policy guidelines for school district compliance with the Title VI requirements upheld in the *Lau* decision. These guidelines specified some approaches, methods, and procedures for the identification, instruction, and mainstreaming of students with LEP. The Lau Remedies also determined professional standards for teachers of these students. More importantly, Lyons (n.d.) claimed that the Lau Remedies specified that "schools should instruct elementary students through their strongest language until they could participate effectively in English-only classrooms" (p. 11), hence implying the provision of bilingual education. These guidelines also established that an ESL program standing alone was not necessarily considered an appropriate action.

During the latter half of the 1970s, the OCR's compliance reviews were based on the Lau Remedies. Curiously, these guidelines lacked formality; for this reason, a process to formalize an expanded version of the guidelines was undertaken between 1978 and 1980. However, when the newly formed Department of Education announced these proposed regulations, they received a highly negative public response, mostly because they were perceived as a tremendous federal intervention in local school control. According to Crawford (1999), President Carter announced these new regulations as part of a political move to win Hispanic votes. However, the proposed regulations were withdrawn in 1981 due to the negative public response, the election of Ronald Reagan as president, and Reagan's declared aim of reducing government intervention.

The Bilingual Education Act of 1978   Meanwhile, the BEA was reauthorized as part of the enactment of the Elementary and Secondary Education Act (ESEA) of 1978 (P.L. 95-561). Thus far, the increase of bilingual programs throughout the United States had been due primarily to the BEA of 1974 and the enforcement of the Lau Remedies. However, this increase in bilingual programs was occurring simultaneously with budget cutting in other educational programs, due to the economic recession then occurring in the country. The 1978 reauthorization (1) clarified that federal funds would be used for transitional native language instruction, (2) expanded student eligibility for assistance to include all students with LEP (i.e., reading and writing), and (3) provided funds to investigate teaching and learning methods for these students. According to Stewner-Manzanares (1988), the economic climate of the time called for better accountability of federal expenses, and, for this reason, the BEA of 1978 allocated research funds for the evaluation of program effectiveness. It was within this context that bilingual education rebounded and received most of its legal and social support in the 1970s.

In the 1980s, the OCR developed a new set of Title VI compliance procedures and standards. These new criteria were based on the requirements established in the 1970 memorandum, the *Lau* decision, the analytical framework for evaluating whether a program complies with the EEOA requirement of "appropriate action" developed by the court of appeals in the *Castaneda v. Pickard* case (1981) and other court cases (e.g., *Idaho Migrant Council v. Board of Education*, 9th Circuit 1981; and *Keyes v. School District #1*, 1983). Since then, these revised guidelines have been enforced on a case-by-case basis, thus allowing greater flexibility and local control in servicing students with LEP.

The Bilingual Education Act of 1984   The increase in federal funding for bilingual education during a time of recession, the increased flexibility in the enforcement of the Lau Remedies, and President Reagan's frank personal opposition to bilingual education served to counter the increased numbers of language-minority students and, hence, students in need of bilingual education services. This increase was due primarily to the second largest migration wave, mostly from Asia and Latin America, in U.S. history. These changes were reflected in the BEA of 1984 (P.L. 98-511). This reauthorization reflected a shift in perspective, as "special alternative instructional programs or SAIPs" (English-only) were included along with transitional bilingual education programs. The BEA of 1984 also embodied a variety of new programs in family English literacy, developmental bilingual education, academic excellence, and special populations (i.e, preschool, gifted and talented, and special education). For example, this was the first time that Title VII allocated funds to serve the needs of students with LEP who were identified as gifted. (This aspect is discussed in Chapter 2, in the section, The Intersect of Bilingual and Gifted Education.)

On a curious note, transitional programs under this reauthorization were required to use structured English language instruction combined with native language, reflecting the use of research findings that these were more effective, advocated by opponents of bilingual education. However, developmental or two-way bilingual education programs that were known to promote academic achievement, bilingualism (English and the native language), and cross-cultural understanding (participation of LEP and native English speakers) did not receive any specific funding allocations. Moreover, grantees were required to inform parents about their rights to decline enrollment in any of the Title VII programs and accept enrollment of their children in mainstream classes.

The four years following the Title VII BEA reauthorization of 1984 exemplified a period of quarreling about the positions and policies of the U.S. Department of Education and those of advocates of bilingual education. A prominent figure during these years was William J. Bennett, Secretary of Education under the Reagan administration. Bennett fought to impose his views on bilingual education and recruited a clique of followers to carry out his wish of dismantling bilingual education and promoting English-only programs. It was thanks to his efforts that the debate surrounding bilingual education became highly political and symbolic, rather than pedagogical and pragmatic. His allusions to turn-of-the-century views on the relationship between language and American citizenship, including loyalty, coupled with an increasing antiimmigrant feeling in U.S. society and the rise of the movement to declare English the official language, fueled the controversy. Furthermore, it is the belief of some that Bennett and his followers used disinformation as a strategy to maintain the attack against bilingual education.

The Bilingual Education Act of 1988   Under these circumstances, the BEA was reauthorized as part of the Hawkins-Stafford Elementary and Secondary School Improvement Act of 1988 (P.L. 100-297). This process proved to be challenging for advocates of bilingual education, and a legislative compromise among the Department of Education, the National Association for Bilingual Education, and the Senate, among others, was reached (Crawford, 1999). The main amendments included in this reauthorization were (1) a three-year maximum enrollment rule for students in bilingual programs, (2) an emphasis on professional training (due to a severe shortage of qualified professionals), and (3) changes in funding formulas so that increased funds would be allocated for SAIPs (i.e., from 10% in 1984 to 25% in 1988).

Overall, the 1980s represented the declivity of the government's advocacy role in civil rights, the debilitation of Title VI (Casanova, 1992), and the abatement of bilingual education. The debate on bilingual education centered on the use of native language instruction. Meanwhile, not only did federal policy leadership deteriorate, but funding also went into remission. In spite of declining federal support, McGroarty (1992) asserted that "bilingual education has become rapidly institutionalized since the early 1970s" (p. 9). For example, more and more states have certification requirements in bilingual and ESL education, and several mainstream professional organizations, such as the National Education Association, have official positions supporting bilingual education.

To entangle the picture further, the heat of the official language debate had come upon bilingual education in the 1980s. In this regard, Crawford (1999) quoted President Reagan as saying,

> But it is absolutely wrong and against American concepts to have a bilingual program that is now openly, admittedly dedicated to preserving their native language and never getting them adequate in English so they can go out into the job market and participate. (p. 53)

Research on Bilingualism and Cognitive Development   The 1960s witnessed a great interest in cognitive development, thus increasing research in this field. Correspondingly, since then, research examining bilingualism and intellectual or cognitive development has pointed to possible positive relationships (Bialystok & Hakuta, 1994; Hakuta & Garcia, 1989). For instance, in 1962, Pearl and Lambert published their influential research findings, which suggested that balanced or full bilingualism had a positive impact on children's cognition. Pearl and Lambert found that bilingual subjects demonstrated advantages in concept formation and in tasks requiring mental or symbolic flexibility, in comparison to monolingual subjects (see also Ben-Zeev, 1977; Ianco-Worrall, 1972; Liedtke & Nelson, 1968).

Curiously, the 1980s were also characterized by a growth in the research evidence supporting the advantages of bilingualism and bilingual instruction (Diaz, 1983; Kessler & Quinn, 1987; Willig, 1985) and the developmental nature of second-language acquisition (Cummins, 1984; McLaughlin, 1987; Zentella, 1981). Nevertheless, the Baker and de Kanter report (1981) on the effectiveness of bilingual education quickly became a preferred counteracting resource by opponents of bilingual education. This highly criticized and discredited report declared bilingual education ineffective and even harmful (Crawford, 1999).

Federal Policy for Gifted Education As mentioned, the late 1950s and early 1960s are considered times of splendor for gifted education, primarily due to the belief that gifted individuals were the ones capable of redeeming the United States in light of Soviet technological advances. Simultaneously, the emphasis on cognitive development of the 1960s encouraged middle-class parents to stimulate their young children's learning, especially the gifted children (Wrigley, 1989). Concurrently, there was an increased concern for social justice, especially as a result of the court decision, *Brown v. Board of Education*, to desegregate schools. The evolving movement for equal rights gained momentum in the 1960s, especially when the Civil Rights Act was signed into law in 1964. According to Tannenbaum (1979), this emphasis on social justice not only diverted attention away from gifted education, but also disputed its (1) reliance on biased intelligence tests as for the identification and placement of gifted children and (2) its denial of access to culturally diverse students (called "socially disadvantaged" at the time). Tannenbaum further argued that no reconciliation between the interest in gifted children and the concern for culturally diverse children was achieved.

By the early 1970s, and given the economic climate and perceived state of education in the United States, a call to discover the brightest children was promulgated and gifted education gained impetus once again. In 1970, a congressional mandate, entitled "Provisions Related to Gifted and Talented Children," was added to the ESEA amendments of 1969 (P.L. 91-230, sec. 806), resulting in federal support for nationwide initiatives in gifted education. According to Jackson (1979), this action also led the U.S. Commissioner of Education, Sidney P. Marland, to launch a comprehensive study of the extent of educational provisions to meet the needs of gifted students in the United States. As a result, the report, *Education of the Gifted and Talented* (best known as the Marland Report), was submitted to Congress at the end of 1971.

The Marland Report The Marland report suggested that gifted services reach not only a minimum number of students, but also significantly underserved certain subpopulations (e.g., racially, culturally, and linguistically diverse learners). It also argued that, thus far, gifted education had been a low governmental priority with no federal leadership and that a flagrant talent loss existed in the country. This report had far-reaching implications, especially as evidenced by the Office of Education's implementation of its recommendations. Consequently, the Marland Report is considered the embryo of developments that occurred in gifted education in the 1970s.

Among the most notable achievements of the Marland Report was the proposed Marland, or Office of Education, definition of *gifted and talented children*, which was adopted by many school districts throughout the United States:

> Gifted and talented children are those identified by professionally qualified persons who, by virtue of outstanding abilities, are capable of high performance. These are children who require differentiated educational programs and/or services beyond those normally provided by the regular school program in order to realize their contribution to self and society. Children capable of high performance include those with demonstrated achievement and/or potential ability in any of the following areas, singly or in combination: general intellectual ability, specific academic aptitude, creative or productive thinking, leadership ability, visual and performing arts, and/or psychomotor ability. (p. 2)

Another example of the impact of the Marland Report was the provision, for the first time ever, of categorical funds for gifted education, including programs in training and research, and for demonstration projects, among others. In 1974, through the ESEA amendments (P.L. 93-380), Title IV, and the Consolidation of Certain Education Programs—Special Projects Act, appropriations were authorized for gifted and talented programs and other education programs. Nonetheless, the emergence of federal funding for gifted education in this context of "special programs" implied that federal support could be withdrawn as soon as the temporary need for these programs decreased. In the same year, the Office of Gifted and Talented in the U.S. Department of Education was officially established.

In addition, during this time, special classes and a search for talent reappeared, using standardized ability and achievement testing as reasonable, appropriate actions in spite of challenges to it in the 1960s. Gifted programs and psychometric testing seemed to favor children from the upper and middle classes, perpetuating the existing social order. As a result, gifted programs and the field of gifted education were charged with elitism, that is, believing that members of White middle and upper social classes deserve favored treatment by virtue of their perceived superiority in intellect, ethnic, and racial background and socioeconomic status, and thus acting in ways that excluded those individuals that did not conform to this model. In other words, the same concerns that shook the field in the mid-1960s were once again evident.

The Gifted and Talented Children's Education Act of 1978   In 1978, Congress approved the Gifted and Talented Children's Education Act, through the newly added Title IX—Additional Programs, Part A of the Education Amendments (P.L. 95-561), which continued funding for training, research, and demonstration projects. Congress also amended the definition of *gifted and talented children* by eliminating the component of psychomotor ability. This definition intended to expand the popular view of *giftedness* as a high IQ score, but it fell short of achieving this purpose. The new definition presented several difficulties, including the exclusion of nonintellectual (motivational) and cultural factors, the inconsistency of categories, and the propensity for misunderstanding.

However, in the 1980s, the Reagan administration reshaped the federal role in education by consolidating programs, proposing the elimination of the Department of Education and diminishing funds for educational initiatives (DeLeon & VandenBos, 1985). For instance, by 1982, the Reagan administration had repealed the Gifted and Talented Children's Education Act of 1978 and eliminated the Office of Gifted and Talented in the Department of Education. Interestingly, a year later, the 1983 publication of the report, *A Nation at Risk*, not only again brought to public attention the debate over educational excellence versus equity, but also pronounced gifted and talented students as an at-risk school population. DeLeon and VandenBos contended that although other reports reinforced the latter, gifted and talented education issues did not get much public attention. In this regard, Ross (1991) also argued that although there was a temporary increase in funding and gifted programs, these efforts had almost disappeared by 1990 due to state budget crises and "competing educational interests" (p. 173).

The Jacob K. Javits Gifted and Talented Students Education Act of 1988   In 1988, the Hawkins–Stafford Elementary and Secondary School Improvement Amendments (P.L. 100-297) established the Jacob K. Javits Gifted and Talented Students Education Act as part of the new ESEA Title IV—Special Programs, Part B—Provisions for Gifted and Talented, and reinstated federal presence in the field. The Javits Act aimed at providing national leadership in identifying and serving gifted and talented students, especially those that were economically disadvantaged, had LEP, or had disabilities (a program priority). Thus, it also supported the expansion and improvement of educational opportunities for these children. Funds (i.e., $10 million) were allocated for professional training, development and expansion of programs, and research. In addition, the Javits Act directed the Secretary of Education to establish a national research center and an administrative unit within the Department of Education. As a result, the National Research Center on Gifted and Talented (NRC G/T) was created to provide leadership in research and practice in gifted education.

Research and Views on Giftedness   Until the 1940s, the term *gifted children* was primarily defined as those children comprising the top 1 percent or 2 percent of their age group, as measured by standardized tests of intelligence. In the early 1950s, this definition was expanded to include the top 10 percent or 15 percent. Moreover, between the 1950s and the late 1970s, dissatisfied researchers in the field proposed broader views of giftedness, including the concepts of creativity (Torrance, 1962, 1969, 1974), multiple talents (Taylor, 1978), and special gifts in academic and social areas (Cohn, 1981). In other words, definitions and conceptions of giftedness were becoming more inclusive or liberal (Renzulli, 1986). The quest for a broader understanding of giftedness continued throughout the 1970s and 1980s. For example, Renzulli (1978) proposed a three-ring conception of giftedness. According to Renzulli, "persons who have achieved recognition because of their unique accomplishments and creative contributions possess a relatively well-defined set of three interlocking clusters of traits. These clusters consist of above average ability, task commitment, and creativity" (p. 3). Giftedness, then, was viewed as the display of gifted behaviors with a dynamic and interactive nature, as "a condition that can be developed in some people if an appropriate interaction takes place between a person, his/her environment, and a particular area of human endeavor" (Renzulli, 1986, p. 60). Other definitions, conceptions, and theories of giftedness were provided by Gagne (1985) and Sternberg (1993), among others. New views on intelligence also emerged in the 1980s, including Gardner's seven intelligences (1983) and Sternberg's triarchic theory (1985).

Coincidentally, dissonant experiences with intelligence testing also increased as (1) the charges of elitism and the quest for a broader understanding of giftedness grew and (2) the racial, cultural, and linguistic diversity present in the school system was highlighted by desegregation efforts, civil rights enforcement, and the focus on equity during the 1960s and 1970s. As a result, authorities in the field began promulgating that IQ tests were effective neither in assessing originality or creativity, nor in identifying gifted students from diverse racial and cultural backgrounds (Witty 1981).

Recapitulation

A significant increase in the number of immigrants arriving in the United States occurred between the 1960s and the early 1980s. During the 1960s and 1970s, political, judicial, and social gains in the civil rights, affirmative action, and bilingual education arenas coincided with times of economic prosperity. In the educational realm, the intervention of judicial powers was critical for culturally and linguistically diverse individuals seeking equity in education. For example, a favorable climate of federal policy and the enforcement of civil right laws supported the revival of bilingual education in the 1960s and 1970s, but these efforts were often interpreted as a need to embrace a focus either on equity or on academic excellence, thus inciting a distorted view of equity and excellence as separate, even mutually exclusive, ideals in education. In the mid-1970s, gifted education gained a renewed interest, which in turn was accompanied by efforts to expand the concept of giftedness and an awareness of the exclusion of certain groups of students based on their socioeconomic, racial, cultural, and linguistic backgrounds. However, efforts to be more inclusive or attuned with the goal of equity in education were not only resisted, but also perceived as an intrusion on academic excellence.

Once unrelenting economic times arrived in the late 1970s and the 1980s, support for civil rights, affirmative action, and bilingual education declined and an antiimmigrant climate reappeared. Several forces contributed to this decline, including political debates, reductions in federal funding, and general public unrest. In fact, during the Republican administrations in the 1980s, the enforcement of civil rights protections was deliberately forsaken, affirmative action and other antidiscriminatory programs were downplayed, and bilingual education was beleaguered. Interestingly, during the same time, two other contrasting trends were observed: (1) a building of research evidence pointing to the cognitive advantages and other benefits of bilingualism and bilingual education and (2) an increase in the numbers of culturally and linguistically diverse students in need of bilingual services. The field of gifted education was also hard hit in the early 1980s when President Reagan repealed the Gifted and Talented Children's Education Act, thus leaving the field without federal leadership and support. A few years later, the field regained impetus and reestablished federal involvement.

Summary

From the 1850s to the 1980s, the evolution of the social, economic, and political realms in the United States was accompanied by a search for a national identity, economic stability, and world supremacy. In this quest, the country's rich and continuous racial, cultural, and linguistic diversity was often both embraced and rebuffed. As a result, campaigns for assimilation endured alongside campaigns for ethnic revival. Meanwhile, catastrophic times of war and economic fluctuations prevailed from the 1910s to the 1960s. Although U.S. involvement in war has decreased since the 1960s, its economic impact was felt up to the 1980s.

All of the material presented in this chapter imprinted the educational sphere. At all times, the educational system reflected the social conditions of the time. For example, up to the 1940s, schools had been agencies for molding children. However, significant gains in the struggle for educational equity (e.g., desegregation, affirmative action, and bilingual education) after World War II and the Cold War charted a different course. Similarly, because gifted individuals were perceived as being necessary to sustain U.S. world supremacy, attention to their strengths and needs increased. However, the imbalance concerning educational equity versus excellence prevailed, which in turn was exacerbated by the politization of education.

REFERENCES

Ackerman, M. (1995). Mental testing and expansion of educational opportunity. *History of Education Quarterly, 35* (3), 279–300.

Baker, K., & de Kanter, A. (1981). *Effectiveness of bilingual education: A review of the literature.* Washington, DC: Office of Planning, Budget and Evaluation, U.S. Department of Education.

Ben-Zeev, S. (1977). The influence of bilingualism on cognitive strategy and cognitive development. *Child Development, 48,* 1009–1018.

Bialystok, E., & Hakuta, K. (1994). *In other words: The science and psychology of second-language acquisition.* New York: Basic Books.

Bilingual Education Act of 1978, Pub. L. No. 95-561, 92 Stat. 2268.

Bilingual Education Act of 1984, Pub. L. No. 98-511, 98 Stat. 2370.

Bilingual Education Act, 20 U.S.C. § 880-b1 (1968).

Bilingual Education Act, 20 U.S.C. § 1703 (1974).

Bilingual Education Act, 20 U.S.C. § 3281–3283 (1988).

Brown v. Board of Education of Topeka, Kansas, 347 U.S. 483 (1954).

Casanova, U. (1992). Shifts in bilingual education policy and the knowledge base. In R. V. Padilla & A. H. Benavides (Eds.), *Critical perspectives on bilingual education research.* Tempe, AZ: Bilingual Press.

Castaneda v. Pickard, 648 F.2d 989 (5th Cir. 1981).

Civil Rights Act, 42 U.S.C. § 2000d (1964).

Cizek, G. J. (1999). Give us this day our daily dread: Manufacturing crises in education. *Phi Delta Kappa, 8* (10), 737–743.

Cockcroft, J. D. (1995). *Latinos in the struggle for equal education.* New York: Franklin Watts.

Cohen, D. K., & Rosenberg, B. H. (1977). Functions and fantasies: Understanding schools in capitalist America. *History of Education Quarterly, 17* (2), 113–137.

Cohn, S. J. (1981). What is giftedness? A multidimensional approach. In A. H. Kramer (Ed.), *Gifted children: Challenging their potential.* Unionville, NY: Trillium Press.

Colangelo, N., & Davis, G. A. (1997). *Handbook of gifted education* (2nd ed.). Boston: Allyn & Bacon.

Cox, C. C. (1926). The early mental traits of three hundred geniuses. In L. M. Terman (Ed.), *Genetic studies of genius* (Vol. 2). Stanford, CA: Stanford University Press.

Crawford, J. (1999). *Bilingual education: History, politics, theory, and practice* (3rd ed.). Los Angeles, CA: Bilingual Educational Services.

Cummins, J. (1984). *Bilingualism and special education.* San Diego: College Hill Press.

Curry, G. E. (Ed.). (1996). *The affirmative action debate.* Reading, MA: Addison-Wesley.

Davis, G. A., & Rimm, S. B. (1994). *Education of the gifted and talented* (3rd ed.). Boston: Allyn & Bacon.

Davis, G. A., & Rimm, S. B. (1998). *Education of the gifted and talented* (4th ed.). Boston: Allyn & Bacon.

DeHaan, R. F., & Havighurst, R. J. (1961). *Educating gifted children.* Chicago: University of Chicago Press.

DeLeon, P. H., & VandenBos, G. R. (1985). Public policy and advocacy on behalf of the gifted and talented. In F. D. Horowitz & M. O'Brien (Eds.), *The gifted and talented: Developmental perspectives* (pp. 409–435). Washington, DC: American Psychological Association.

Diaz, R. (1983). Thought and two languages: The impact of bilingualism on cognitive development. *Review of Research in Education, 10,* 23–54.

Elementary and Secondary Education Act, 20 U.S.C. § 863 *et seq.* (1969).

Elementary and Secondary Education Act, 20 U.S.C. § 2701 *et seq.* (1965).

Elementary and Secondary Education Amendments, 20 U.S.C. § 1863 (1974).

Equal Educational Opportunity Act, 20 U.S.C. § 1703 (1974).

Equal Educational Opportunity Act, Pub. L. No. 93-380, 88 Stat. 514 (1974).

Faltis, C. J., & Hudelson, S. J. (1998). *Bilingual education in elementary and secondary school communities: Toward understanding and caring.* Boston: Allyn and Bacon.

Fischer, L. (1982). The courts and educational policy. In A. Lieberman & M. W. McLaughlin (Eds.), *Policy making in education: Eighty-first yearbook of the National Society for the Study of Education.* Chicago: University of Chicago Press.

Franklin, B. M. (1989). Progressivism & curriculum differentiation: Special classes in the Atlanta public schools, 1898–1923. *History of Education Quarterly, 29* (4), 571–593.

Freedberg, L., & McLeod, R. G. (1998, Tuesday, October 13). The other side of the law: Despite all U.S. efforts to curb it, immigration is rising. *San Francisco Chronicle,* p. A1.

Gagne, F. (1985). Giftedness and talent: Reexamining a reexamination of definitions. *Gifted Child Quarterly, 29,* 103–112.

Garcia, E. E., & Gonzalez, R. (1995). Issues in systemic reform for culturally and linguistically diverse students. *Teachers College Record, 96* (3), 418–431.

Gardner, H. (1983). *Frames of mind: The theory of multiple intelligences.* New York: Basic Books.

Gelb, S. A. (1989). "Not simply bad and incorrigible": Science, morality, and intellectual deficiency. *History of Education Quarterly, 29* (3), 359–379.

George, P., & Lawrence, G. (1982). *Handbook for middle school teaching.* Glenview, IL: Scott, Foresman.

Gifted and Talented Children Act, 20 U.S.C. § 3311 (1978).

Goodenow, R. (1975). The progressive educator, race and ethnicity in the Depression years: An overview. *History of Education Quarterly, 15* (4), 365–394.

Hakuta, K. (1986). *Mirror of language: The debate on bilingualism.* New York: Basic Books.

Hakuta, K., & Garcia, E. E. (1989). Bilingualism and education. *American Psychologist, 44* (2), 374–379.

Hansot, E., & Tyack, D. (1982). A usable past: Using history in educational policy. In A. Lieberman & M. W. McLaughlin (Eds.), *Policy making in education: Eighty-first yearbook of the National Society for the Study of Education* (pp. 1–22). Chicago: University of Chicago Press.

Hollingworth, L. S. (1926). *Gifted children: Their nature and nurture.* New York: Macmillan.

Ianco-Worrall, A. (1972). Bilingualism and cognitive development. *Child Development, 43,* 1390–1400.

Idaho Migrant Council v. Board of Education, 647 F.2d 69 (9th Cir. 1981).

Immigration Reform and Control Act, 8 U.S.C. § 1101 *et seq.* (1986).

Jackson, D. M. (1979). The emerging national and state concern. In A. H. Passow (Ed.), *The gifted and the talented: Their education and development* (pp. 45–62). Chicago: University of Chicago Press.

Jacob K. Javits Gifted and Talented Students Education Act, 20 U.S.C. § 3061–3068 (1988).

Kastle, C. F. (1982). Presidential address: Ideology and American educational history. *History of Education Quarterly, 22* (2), 123–137.

Karier, C. J. (1972). Liberalism and the quest for orderly change. *History of Education Quarterly, 12* (1), 57–80.

Katz, M. B. (1976). The origins of public education: A reassessment. *History of Education Quarterly, 16* (4), 381–407.

Kessler, C., & Quinn, M. E. (1987). Language minority children's linguistic and cognitive creativity. *Journal of Multilingual and Multicultural Development, 8* (1&2), 173–186.

Keyes v. School District #1, Denver, Colorado 576 F. Supp. 1503 (D. Colo. 1983).

Kliebard, H. M. (1995). *The struggle for the American curriculum: 1893–1958* (2nd ed.). New York: Routledge.

Lau v. Nichols, 94 S. Ct. 786 (1974).

Lau v. Nichols, 414 U.S. 563 (1974).

Lewelling, V. (1992, December). *Linguistic diversity in the United States: English Plus and Official English:* National Clearinghouse on Literacy Education, Center for Applied Linguistics.

Lewis, E. G. (1980). *Bilingualism and bilingual education: A comparative study.* Albuquerque: University of New Mexico Press.

Liedtke, W. W., & Nelson, L. D. (1968). Concept formation and bilingualism. *Alberta Journal of Educational Research, 14,* 225–232.

Lyons, J. J. (n.d.). *Legal responsibilities of education agencies serving national origin language minority students.* The Mid-Atlantic Equity Center, the American University.

Marable, M. (1996). Staying on the path to racial equality. In G. E. Curry (Ed.), *The affirmative action debate* (pp. 3–15). Reading, MA: Addison-Wesley.

Marland, S. P., Jr. (1972). *Education of the gifted and talented: Vol. 1 Report to the Congress of the United States by the U.S. Commissioner of Education.* Washington, DC: U.S. Government Printing Office.

McBride, P. W. (1974). The Co-op industrial education movement. *History of Education Quarterly, 14* (2), 209–221.

McGroarty, M. (1992). The social context of bilingual education. *Educational Researcher, 21* (2), 7–9.

McHardy, R. (1985). *Providing programs for preschool gifted children on a statewide basis.* Paper presented at the The Fifth World Conference on Gifted and Talented Children, Manila, Philippines.

McLaughlin, B. (1987). *Theories of second-language learning.* London: Arnold.

National Defense Education Act of 1958, Pub. L. No. 85–864, § 72 Stat. 1580.

National Commission on Excellence in Education. (1983). *A nation at risk: The imperative for educational reform.* Washington, DC: U.S. Government Printing Office.

Office of Civil Rights. (1975). *Task force findings specifying remedies available for eliminating past educational practices ruled unlawful under* Lau v. Nichols. Washington, DC: Department of Health, Education, and Welfare.

Passow, A. H. (1981). The nature of giftedness and talent. *Gifted Child Quarterly, 25* (1), 5–10.

Pearl, E., & Lambert, W. (1962). The relationship of bilingualism to intelligence. *Psychological Monographs, 76* (27), 1–23.

Pipho, C. (1999). Public opinion and public education. *Phi Delta Kappa, 80* (8), 565–566.

Plessy v. Ferguson, U.S. 537 (1896).

Porters, A., & Rumbaut, R. G. (1990). *Immigrant America: A portrait.* Berkeley: University of California Press.

Raftery, J. R. (1988). Missing the mark: Intelligence testing in Los Angeles public schools, 1922–32. *History of Education Quarterly, 28* (1), 73–93.

Renzulli, J. S. (1978). What makes giftedness?: Reexamining a definition. *Phi Delta Kappa, 60* (3), 180–184, 261.

Renzulli, J. S. (1986). The three-ring conception of giftedness: A development model for creative productivity. In R. J. Sternberg & J. E. Davidson (Eds.), *Conceptions of giftedness* (pp. 53–92). New York: Cambridge University Press.

Resnick, L. (1987). *Education and learning to think.* Washington, DC: National Research Council.

Ross, P. (1991). Advocacy for gifted programs in the new educational climate. *Gifted Child Quarterly, 35* (4), 173–176.

Rothstein, R. (1998). Bilingual education: The controversy. *Phi Delta Kappa, 79* (9), 672–678.

Sternberg, R. J. (1985). *Beyond IQ: A triarchic theory of human intelligence.* New York: Cambridge University Press.

Sternberg, R. J. (1993). The concept of giftedness: A pentagonal implicit theory. In G. R. Bock & K. Ackrill (Eds.), *The origins and development of high ability* (pp. 5–16): Ciba Foundation Symposium 178.

Stevens, E. W. (1972). Social centers, politics, and social efficiency in the progressive era. *History of Education Quarterly, 12* (1), 16–33.

Stewner-Manzanares, G. (1988, Fall). *The Bilingual Education Act: Twenty years later.* The National Clearinghouse for Bilingual Education [Online]. Available: <www.ncbe.gwu.edu/ncbepubs/classics/focus/06bea.htm>.

Tannenbaum, A. J. (1979). Pre-Sputnik to post-Watergate concern about the gifted. In A. H. Passow (Ed.), *The gifted and the talented: Their education and development* (Vol. I, pp. 5–27). Chicago: University of Chicago Press.

Tannenbaum, A. J. (1981). Pre-Sputnik to post-Watergate concern about the gifted. In W. B. Barbe & J. S. Renzulli (Eds.), *Psychology and education of the gifted* (pp. 20–37). New York: Irvington.

Taylor, C. W. (1978). How many types of giftedness can your program tolerate? *Journal of Creative Behavior, 12,* 39–51.

Tiedt, P. L., & Tiedt, I. M. (1998). *Multicultural teaching: A handbook of activities, information, and resources* (5th ed.). Boston: Allyn & Bacon.

Torrance, E. P. (1962). *Guiding creative talent.* Englewood Cliffs, NJ: Prentice-Hall.

Torrance, E. P. (1969). Creative positives of disadvantaged children and youth. *The Gifted Child Quarterly, 13* (2), 71–81.

Torrance, E. P. (1974). Differences are not deficits. *Teachers College Record, 75* (4), 471–487.

Tropea, J. L. (1987). Bureaucratic order and special education in urban schools: 1890s–1940s. *History of Education Quarterly, 27* (1), 31–53.

U.S. Department of Health, Education and Welfare (1975, 11 August). *Task force findings specifying remedies available for eliminating past educational practices ruled unlawful under* Lau *v.* Nichols. Washington, DC: Author.

Williams, L. F. (1996). Tracing the politics of affirmative action. In G. E. Curry (Ed.), *The affirmative action debate* (pp. 241–257). Reading, MA: Addison-Wesley.

Willig, A. C. (1985). A meta-analysis of selected studies on the effectiveness of bilingual education. *Review of Educational Research, 55,* 269–317.

Witty, P. A. (1981). The education of the gifted and the creative in the U.S.A. In W. B. Barbe & J. S. Renzulli (Eds.), *Psychology and education of the gifted* (3rd ed., pp. 38–46). New York: Irvington.

Witty, P. E. (Ed.). (1951). *The gifted child.* Boston: Heath.

Wrigley, J. (1989). Do young children need intellectual stimulation? Experts' advice to parents, 1900–1985. *History of Education Quarterly, 29* (1), 41–75.

Zentella, A. C. (1981). Language variety among Puerto Ricans. In C. A. Ferguson & S. B. Heath (Eds.), *Language in the USA* (pp. 218–238). New York: Cambridge University Press.

Zettel, J. J. (1982). The education of gifted and talented children from a federal perspective. In J. Ballard, B. A. Ramirez, & F. J. Weintraub (Eds.), *Special education in America: Its legal and governmental foundations* (pp. 51–64). Reston, VA: Council for Exceptional Children.

2 Framing A Contemporary Context for the Education of Culturally and Linguistically Diverse Students with Gifted Potential: 1990s to the Present

EVA I. DÍAZ

As with Chapter 1, this chapter intends to provide a flexible chronological overview of relevant occurrences in education, particularly in bilingual and gifted education, and social life in the United States from 1990 to the present, thus placing the field of bilingual gifted education within a contemporary context. For this purpose, the most recent reform movements in U.S. education and their relevance to the field of bilingual gifted education are examined. This chapter also includes a few connections between the field of bilingual education and that of gifted education, in the hope that this information will be useful to researchers and practitioners who are interested in defining a direction for these growing fields, thus placing them at the forefront.

1990s to the Present: Economic Recovery, Social Distress, and Educational Reform

Socioeconomic and Political Context

As in the 1980s, in 1991, the United States was once again in a recession, but in 1991 the recession hit the financial industry harder. Banks and insurance companies felt it most, as did the automotive and steel industries. A declivitous displacement of employees was further bolstered by restructuring and downsizing in corporate America. Nevertheless, in the early and mid-1990s, many people found themselves either discharged from their jobs or with declining incomes and job insecurity due to the economic restructuring and downsizing. As a result, a new middle, working but "anxious class" erupted, with members in need of reevaluating their careers and skills in order to survive economically. Bracey (1997) observed that even people with high levels of literacy often found themselves not only earning low wages, but also losing their benefits packages and job security. In this regard, Jackson (1996) stated that the 1990s endured

> . . . a new form of economic violence. Companies like ABC and Walt Disney, Westinghouse and CBS, Viacom and Paramount, Chase Manhattan and Chemical Bank, in merging their capital will purge their workers and submerge their hopes for the future. Billionaries and millionaries will be made in the process. Let us not be misled: millions more will lose their jobs, displaced by the concentration of capital and power. (p. 289)

Jackson further argued that politicians disguised public attention to these economic issues by "feeding them the bait of race in exchange for votes" (p. 289). In so doing, immigration, affirmative action, and racial issues became scapegoats once again and were fiercely attacked throughout the 1990s.

After winning the presidential election in 1992, Democratic President William J. Clinton promised to renew the United States' economy, and during his time in office (1993–2000), the economy prospered. In 2000, the United States was the most productive country in the world, with a federal budget boasting a surplus.

A Revival of the Antiimmigrant Posture   In spite of the economic recovery, an antiimmigrant posture persisted throughout the 1990s. This antiimmigrant posture had its roots in the relationship established between the increase in the number of immigrants and the U.S. economic hardships of the 1980s. An extreme example of this posture at the state level was the California voters' approval of Proposition 187 in 1994, terminating numerous services to illegal immigrants in that state. Nevertheless, Proposition 187 became entangled in court challenges and never went into effect. Another example, at the federal level, was the reform of welfare law in 1996, which eliminated many benefits to legal immigrants as well. Although many of these welfare reforms were reversed, some reforms indeed reduced immigrants' eligibility for social services. Meanwhile, the U.S. Congress also enacted laws to increase control on the border between the United States and Mexico (California, Arizona, and Texas), hoping to diminish the largest source of illegal immigration.

Despite all of these measures, legal and illegal immigration continued to increase. For instance, while the overall U.S. population rose by 8 percent in the 1990s, the foreign-born population increased by 30 percent (Freedberg & McLeod, 1998). Accordingly, Freedberg (1998) asserted that during the 1990s, the United States admitted a record number of new legal immigrants (i.e., approximately one million a year). In response to this increase in immigration, primarily of legal immigrants, antiimmigrant legislation continued to be proposed in the late 1990s, seeking to reduce it (e.g., the Mass

Immigration Reduction Act of 1999) and deny citizenship at birth to children born in the United States of parents who are not legal residents or citizens (e.g., the Citizenship Reform Act of 1999). In this regard, Collier and Freedberg (1998) reported that many of these initiatives to restrict immigration in the 1990s were blocked by interest groups in agribusiness, civil liberties advocates, and politicians eager to win immigrants' votes.

Language Restrictionism   In the 1990s, recurrent proposals for English-only legislation also continued at the federal and state levels. For example, four Official English bills were introduced to the 106th Congress. In general, three of these bills attempted to amend Title IV of the U.S. Code to declare English the official language of the U.S. government. These bills also intended to ban bilingual ballots, bilingual education, and citizenship ceremonies in languages other than English. Similarly, a constitutional amendment sought to make English the official language of the United States. At the state level, approximately twenty-four states had Official English amendments, and at least seven other states were considering such legislation (Crawford, 2000). For example, in 2000, Utah's voters approved a measure to make English the sole language of that state's government. However, a state district judge blocked the enforcement of the initiative, based on serious constitutional issues (Associated Press, 2000).

Since its inception in the early 1980s, the English-only movement has been a great source of debate. Opponents claim that Official English laws not only are unnecessary (i.e., English is the de facto official language of the United States), but also are discriminatory (e.g., violate civil rights and First Amendment rights) and divisive (e.g., foster intolerance and prejudice). Chen (1995) argued,

> Because these laws are predicated upon false and disparaging assumptions about today's immigrants, they can only fan the flames of prejudice, mistrust and divisiveness. And because the disparaging arguments are directed against today's immigrants who are largely Hispanic and Asian, the racial undercurrents that lay beneath the surface of English-only efforts make these laws doubly dangerous and divisive. Rather than inspiring cohesion and unity, such legislation will, in the end, exacerbate societal discord and ethnic tension. (pp. 6–7).

Affirmative Action or Race and Gender Preferences?   As mentioned, affirmative action also came under attack in the 1990s. For example, in 1996, the passage of Proposition 209 in California eliminated equal opportunity programs (e.g., affirmation action, outreach, recruitment, mentoring, and tutoring) that were designed to remedy race and gender discrimination in public employment, education, and contracting. In Washington, voters passed a similar measure in 1998, called Proposition 200, banning the use of affirmative action strategies in public college admissions and government employment. In 2000, Florida's governor signed an executive order banning so-called racial preferences or quotas in higher education and in the hiring of state employees and contractors. These measures endanger the United States' commitment to equity by restricting affirmative action and, frequently, calling for race-blind criteria while overlooking the historic and current institutionalized forms of discrimination.

Educational Context

According to Spring (1997b), "the 1990s might be considered the most politically explosive period for school politics in U.S. history" (p. 118). In 1989, Republican President Bush and the nation's governors, with the leadership of then-governor Bill Clinton, established six national educational goals aimed at "transforming" the educational system in the United States in order to maintain a vigorous, internationally competitive economy and responsible democracy (U.S. Department of Education, 1991). The next year, Bush released *America 2000: An Education Strategy* as his plan for implementing these goals through national academic standards, national testing, and corporate involvement.

Goals 2000 and the Improving America's Schools Act of 1994   Interestingly, when Democrat William J. Clinton defeated Republican George H. Bush in the 1992 presidential election, the six national goals remained at the core of Clinton's plan for educational reform. With two other goals added, President Clinton signed into law the *Goals 2000: Educate America Act* (P.L. 103-227) and the *Improving America's Schools Act* (IASA) (P.L. 103-382) in 1994. The eight national education goals and the IASA were based on the premise that every child can learn, or can learn more, if challenged by high standards, which are believed to improve learning through a consistent system of curricula in alignment with assessments. That same year, Secretary of Education, Richard W. Riley, affirmed that Goals 2000 and the IASA focused on simultaneously providing excellence and equity in education and improving the education of all children (U.S. Department of Education, 1994a).

The IASA reauthorized the Elementary and Secondary Education Act (ESEA) of 1965 for five years. According to Anstrom and Kindler (1996), "the IASA is designed to tie existing federal programs to the objectives of Goals 2000 and in so doing act as a catalyst for school reform" (p. 10). Since the establishment of Goals 2000 this systemic, standards-based reform prompted multifarious initiatives nationwide to develop and implement (1) content and performance standards in academic areas (e.g., math, science, English, history) and (2) assessments aligned with these standards. These laws also supported parental and community involvement, charter schools, after-school programs, professional development, and technology, among many other initiatives (U.S. Department of Education, 2000a). In general, these two laws supplemented and advanced reforms already underway in some states and school districts, while in other places, these laws promoted the establishment of new reforms. As a result, Secretary of Education Richard W. Riley affirmed, in his Second Annual State of American Education Address in 1995, that the United States was

> . . . no longer a nation at risk toward mediocrity, but a "nation on the move" toward high standards . . . a nation turning the corner, yes, raising its standards and reaching for excellence for the 21st century. . . . This is a critical time for American Education . . . a turning point. . . . I believe we are, at long last, turning the corner . . . moving from being a nation at risk to a nation with a hopeful future. We are starting to win the battle for excellence and good citizenship in American education. . . . Why am I becoming optimistic? Student performance in reading, science and math is on the rise, and we have made up much of the ground that we lost in the 1970s. (pp. 1–2)

As of 2000, forty-nine states had standards in core subjects and forty-eight had assessments to measure student progress. A U.S. Department of Education report entitled, *Educational Progress 1992–2000* (U.S. Department of Education, 2000a), summarized findings in relation to the impact of these reforms, indicating that, since 1992, student reading and math scores on the National Assessment of Educational Progress [NAEP] had increased in the fourth, eighth, and twelfth grades, including the scores of those students in schools with the highest poverty-level enrollments. Similarly, SAT math and verbal scores had also increased. This report also pointed to the creation of one thousand new charter schools and an increased number of (1) high school graduates going directly to college, especially low-income and African American students, and (2) students taking advanced placement exams. Increased funding for advanced placement, college awareness and preparation, and tuition and loan assistance facilitated the above. In addition, this report concluded that increased federal support for initiatives such as class-size reduction, technology literacy and access, comprehensive school reform, and after-school and other extended-learning opportunities (e.g., twenty-first-century community learning centers and community technology centers) facilitated the process of meeting high standards.

Notwithstanding, both pieces of legislation were widely criticized. For example, these educational bills have been perceived as (1) an indisputable example of business-people making decisions about higher academic standards under the leitmotif of "better education for a better economy;" (2) neglecting serious structural issues, such as school funding, capacity, and other inequalities in resources (Duke, 1998); (3) overrelying on testing and standardization (Ramirez, 1999); (4) trying to meet high academic standards in a vacuum, that is, overlooking children's lives outside of the classroom; and (5) overemphasizing high standards and improved assessment without a comparable commitment to equity (Gordon, 1996). In other words, this standards- and assessment-driven reform was paradoxically perceived as jeopardizing the very goals of equity and excellence for all students that it was supposed to invoke.

In general, concurrent educational considerations during the 1990s were those related to school choice or to the concept of giving students and families options for participation in school and educational programs without regard for the neighborhoods in which they lived (Metcalf & Tait, 1999). School choice (i.e., magnet schools, alternative schools, charter schools, home schooling, and school vouchers, among others) and its consequences for demographics and equity became a serious source of debate (Goldhaber, 1999). However, the most conflictive issue was that of school vouchers (i.e., provision of public funds for use by families to pay for the public or private school of their choice) and their constitutional, social, educational, financial, and administrative complications (Doerr, 1999; Hewley, 1996; Metcalf & Tait, 1999).

The Bilingual Education Act of 1994   As mentioned, the IASA of 1994 reauthorized the ESEA, including Title VII—Bilingual Education, Language Enhancement, and Language Acquisition Programs. As part of this reauthorization, Title VII included three parts: (1) the Bilingual Education Act (BEA), (2) the Foreign Language Assistance Act, and (3) the Emergency Immigrant Education Program. Through the BEA (Title VII, Part A, P.L. 103-382), $215 million was authorized for competitive, capacity-building, collaborative (i.e., collaboration with other programs under IASA and other Acts) programs and grants to states and local school districts, including development and implementation of bilingual programs, enhancement or expansion of existing bilingual programs, and the implementation of schoolwide or districtwide bilingual programs. The purpose of the BEA was to educate limited English proficiency (LEP) students to master English and meet high content and academic performance standards. *It recognized the need to protect and develop the national linguistic resource represented by LEP students. As a result, priority was given to programs designed to ensure proficiency in English and another language for all students.* The BEA also established that 25 percent of grants in any category could be awarded by using Special Alternative Instructional Programs (SAIPs). In addition, funds were available to assist school districts (and institutions of higher education as necessary) in (1) carrying out research and program evaluation activities, (2) collecting data on LEP populations and their educational opportunities, and (3) providing professional development. Support for the National Clearinghouse for Bilingual Education also was provided.

The Foreign Language Assistance Act (Title VII, Part B, P.L. 103-382) assigned $35 million for grants to states and districts for innovative model programs to establish, improve, or expand foreign language education, especially at the elementary school level. Lastly, the Emergency Immigrant Education Program (Title VII, Part C, P.L. 103-382) authorized $100 million for grants to states and local school districts that had experienced immigrant influxes, to provide enhanced instructional opportunities and help (e.g., with transition) immigrant students.

Although the BEA of 1994 demonstrated a higher level of congruity with the latest research on bilingualism and bilingual education than did previous reauthorizations, it was berated in the political sphere and in the media. For example, at the federal level, Congress reduced BEA appropriations by 38 percent between 1994 and 1996 (Crawford, 1997). At the state level, California's voters approved Proposition 227, or "English for the Children" initiative, in 1998, resulting in the dismantling of bilingual education programs in the public schools. Proposition 227 replaced bilingual programs with a "sheltered or structured English immersion" program for students with LEP for a period of no longer than a year, thus imperiling children's academic, linguistic, and social development. In an unusual step, both President Clinton and Secretary of Education Richard W. Riley declared their opposition to this initiative (Portner, 1998). In 2000, Arizona followed California in adopting an even more restrictive English-only school initiative, Proposition 203. A similar measure also was considered in Colorado, but it did not succeed.

Arguments against bilingual education became highly visible in the 1990s in spite of the sizable body of research and literature supporting bilingualism and bilingual education (Crawford, 1997; Cummins, 1998; Krashen, 1996, 1999a, 1999b). Some of that new visibility was achieved through much media coverage, which McQuillan and Tse (1996), Crawford (1997), and Cummins (1999) described as antagonistic and misleading. This aggression against bilingual education occurred simultaneously with the enactment of English-only legislation in states throughout the country.

Within this general context, Goals 2000, the IASA, and the reauthorization of the BEA in 1994 were the cause of both skepticism and encouragement among advocates of bilingual education. As indicated, a systemic standards-based reform was intended for all students, including LEP students. However, on one hand, educational reforms in the United States had been oblivious to these students' needs, circumstances, and strengths, and warnings regarding the lack of explicitness on how these reforms would incorporate LEP students had been issued from the beginning of this new surge (Rivera & LaCelle-Peterson, 1993; U.S. Department of Education, 1994b). On the other hand, the Office of Bilingual Education and Minority Language Affairs (OBEMLA) (1995) declared that this BEA reauthorization, as a component of a major systemic reform effort, marked a "revitalization in a new direction" away from the deficiency model, which was characteristic of previous reauthorizations. Besides mentioning the inclusion of LEP or language-minority students, this standards- and assessment-based reform, as expressed in the legislative language, required that these students be included in ways that are valid, reliable, and fair. As a result, a panel of experts in the field was formed throughout the 1990s to advise on the defensible inclusion of children with LEP in the new reforms (e.g., inclusion of LEP students in the National Assessment of Educational Progress).

The Jacob K. Javits Gifted and Talented Students Education Act of 1994
In 1994, the Jacob K. Javits Gifted and Talented Students Education Act, Title X, Part B of the IASA (P.L. 103-382) was also reauthorized. Among Congress' findings, this Act declared that gifted and talented students constitute a national resource and that if their special abilities are not recognized and developed, their potential to the national interest would likely be lost. It also affirmed that *gifted and talented students from economically disadvantaged backgrounds and with limited English proficiency are at greatest risk of being unrecognized and not being provided appropriate educational services* (§ 10202 [a] 1–5). Accordingly, priority was given to model programs that identified and provided services to these populations, as well as to students with disabilities, and that offered technical assistance and dissemination of information (§ 10205, 1–2).Within a systemic reform framework of high standards for all children, this Act provided funds (i.e., $10 million) for demonstration projects, personnel training, and research. It also continued support for a national research center. In 1995, a five-year grant was awarded to the National Research Center on the Gifted and Talented (NRC G/T).

In general, issues related to gifted education and the reauthorization of the Jacob Javits Gifted and Talented Students Education Act received minimal media attention in the 1990s (Lewis & Karnes, 1995, 1997). Likewise, a search of ERIC Digests on "topics of prime current interest in education" revealed that not a single digest dealt with issues related to gifted and talented education.

The Clinton Administration Proposal for the Reauthorization of the Elementary and Secondary Education Act
President Clinton's administration proposal—the Educational Excellence for All Children Act of 1999, to reauthorize the Elementary and Secondary Education Act of 1965—presumably represented the "federal government's single largest investment in elementary and secondary education" (U.S. Department of Education, 2000b, p. 1). A fact sheet from the U.S. Department of Education (2000c) indicated that this legislation built on the ESEA reauthorization of 1994 (IASA) and ratified the crucial role of the federal government in providing high quality and equitable

education to all children. The proposed law was supposedly committed to academic equity and excellence through (1) high standards in every classroom, (2) improved teacher and principal quality, (3) strengthened accountability for student performance, and (4) support for safe, healthy, disciplined, and drug-free school environments. For these purposes, flexibility through local innovations attending to the conditions of the local context was encouraged in the bill.

This proposal represents the largest federal investment in education in over 30 years. It built on Goals 2000 and the IASA of 1994 and paid special attention to two urgent needs: (1) school modernization and construction and (2) the recruitment, preparation and training of high-quality teachers. In this regard, the U.S. Department of Education (2000a) estimated that $127 billion is needed to bring existing schools into acceptable conditions, and that 2.2 million teachers would need to be hired during the next decade.

The Bilingual Education Act of 1999   If Title VII, as designed by the Clinton administration, is reauthorized by Congress, it would include the BEA and the Emergency Immigrant Program. The proposed BEA continues the emphasis on high academic standards for LEP students and the funding priority for programs that develop proficiency in more than one language. It also proposes several changes to the reauthorization of 1994, including giving competitive priority to (1) school districts that have had little prior experience servicing LEP students, but are experiencing a rapid growth in this student population, and (2) grant applicants that demonstrate they have an effective program for helping LEP students learn English and achieve high standards. Other changes include (1) the consolidation of grant activities (i.e., the program-development and -implementation grants and enhancement grants are collapsed into a single grant program); (2) a new requirement for baseline data on the performance of LEP students and annual project evaluations, including students' English language proficiency; (3) focused professional development and teacher education programs; and (4) a provision that if projects cannot demonstrate progress in a three-year period, an action plan for improvement be submitted, and if after implementing the plan, no progress is evident, the Secretary must terminate the grant.

In 1999, the National Association for Bilingual Education communicated three concerns regarding the Educational Excellence for All Children Act of 1999: (1) the wording of the bill is prone to be misinterpreted as emphasizing learning English as quickly as possible over achieving academically while learning English, (2) the wording of the bill does not promote two-way bilingual programs that foster bilingualism and biliteracy for all students, and (3) the bill stresses aligning accountability measures over effective instruction for culturally and linguistically diverse students. Accordingly, Wiese and Garcia (1998) expressed their concern about the impact of mandated assessments for LEP students and the expectation that children would achieve English fluency in three years in order to be transferred to English-only classrooms. These authors explained that as part of the proposed accountability system, the Department of Education recommends a series of assessments for LEP students participating in Title I and Title VII programs that would result in the overtesting of this particular student population. Moreover, the proposed assessments are not clear as to how to accommodate these students' linguistic needs. Another concern was that the expectation of children achieving English fluency in three years, in order to be transferred to English-only classrooms, has no basis in sound educational theory or practice. Wiese and Garcia (1998) argued the following:

> A three-year goal for English proficiency can drive curriculum in a way that refocuses resources, staff material, and accountability on English language acquisition. This will come at the expense of other content areas such as math, science, social studies, etc. (p. 12)

In other words, the bill's content is not only contrary to the goal of developing students' linguistic strengths, but it also compromises maximum academic achievement.

The Gifted and Talented Children Act of 1999   For Title X, Part B, Gifted and Talented Children, the Educational Excellence for All Children Act of 1999 preserves most of the essence of the Jacob K. Javits Gifted and Talented Students Education Act of 1994, and proposes only minor revisions to it. For instance, it requires that the National Research Center's dissemination efforts focus on the results of its activities in schools with high percentages of economically disadvantaged students. It also authorizes, rather than mandates, program evaluation.

House and Senate ESEA Reauthorization Proposals

Bilingual Education   In 1999, the House passed H.R. 2—the Dollars to the Classroom Act—reauthorizing Title I and Title VII of the ESEA. Originally, this bill intended to deal with Title I, but ended up folding in Title VII. As a result, H.R. 2 amends Title VII and renames Part A—Bilingual Education, or the Bilingual Education Act—as the English Language Education, or the English Language Proficiency and Academic Achievement Act. Some House members indicated that although they opposed the Title VII provisions included in this bill, they still felt compelled to support the bill because it reauthorized Title I.

According to Zehr (1999), Delia Pompa, executive director of the National Association for Bilingual Education, believes that H.R. 2 discourages schools from using languages other than English and makes more difficult the provision of high-quality bilingual programs. For example, in comparison to the Clinton Administration bill, H.R. 2 (1) replaces the current discretionary grant program with a state formula grant program when appropriations for bilingual education exceed $220 million (the FY 2000 appropriation was $248 million); (2) requires states, under the formula grant program, to discontinue funding if the majority of students are not attaining English language fluency and reaching state standards after three years; (3) eliminates the 25 percent maximum limit on funds that may be used for SAIPs; (4) requires school districts to obtain informed parental consent prior to student placement; (5) eliminates the Foreign Language Assistance Program; (6) deletes authorizations for Academic Excellence grants and for the National Clearinghouse for Bilingual Education; and (7) renames the OBEMLA as the Office of Educational Services for Limited English Proficient Children, among other provisions. The Senate's proposal (i.e., S. 2) is similar to the Clinton Administration proposal, yet it repeals two grant programs and the provisions for intensified instruction, among others.

Gifted and Talented Education   The House and Senate also have proposals for gifted education that are similar to each other and are generally perceived as "friendly." The House proposal—Title V, Jacob K. Javits Gifted and Talented Students Act of 1999— amends the ESEA Title X (Programs of National Significance) to revise requirements for Part B—Jacob K. Javits Gifted and Talented Students Act of 1994. The House proposal (1) provides that a portion of any increase over the FY 2000 level be used to increase the size of awards to state educational agencies; (2) establishes a new formula grant program once the appropriation reaches $50 million, with funds awarded on the basis of the number of children aged five to seventeen, whereupon state educational agencies are expected to award 95 percent of the funds to local educational agencies on a competitive basis; and (3) eliminates the current law requirement that half of the grants be used to serve students who are not otherwise served through traditional methods. Similar to the Clinton administration plan, the House proposal continues the current discretionary grant program and authorizes the National Center. As part of the House plan for the reauthorization of the ESEA, Title IV—Indian, Native Hawaiian, and Alaska Native Education—revises Title IX of the ESEA of 1994. Part of the proposed revisions is the repeal of grants for gifted and talented programs targeting these particular student populations.

The Senate proposal resembles the House plan, but it (1) does not stipulate any increase in the size of awards if FY 2000 level increases, (2) requires that state educational agencies award 88 percent of funds to local educational agencies, and (3) adds model development to the list of activities to be carried out by the National Center. According to Peter D. Rosenstein (Sack, 2000), executive director of the National Association for Gifted Children, "This is the first time Congress is really recognizing the needs of these children and saying to states 'You have to do something' " (p. 32).

Recapitulation

In sum, the 1990s experienced a revitalized economy accompanied by a persistently negative attitude toward immigrants, affirmative action, and language diversity. In the educational sphere, the 1990s was a period of significant activity at all levels of the spectrum. The passage of Goals 2000 and the IASA of 1994 represented a new surge of educational reforms sweeping the country. As a result, academic standards, aligned assessments, and accountability gained momentum. In the process, equity concerns were either disregarded or not addressed with the same commitment devoted to high standards.

As part of the IASA of 1994, the BEA and the Jacob K. Javits Gifted and Talented Students Education Act were reauthorized. On one hand, the BEA of 1994 was significant in that, for the first time, it established a priority for programs that promoted bilingualism and was congruent with the growing body of research supporting bilingualism and bilingual education. However, bilingual education came under fire from its opponents. On the other hand, the Jacob K. Javits Gifted and Talented Students Education Act closely resembled its previous reauthorization and reaffirmed that children with LEP are usually overlooked.

Current proposals for the reauthorization of the ESEA of 1965 continue an emphasis on standards, assessments, and accountability, but add a new focus on teacher quality and school modernization. In 1999, the Clinton Administration, the House of Representatives, and the Senate submitted proposals for the reauthorization of both the BEA and the Jacob K. Javits Gifted and Talented Students Education Act. Interestingly, all of the proposals to reauthorize the BEA included significant changes in their wording, thus reflecting the antibilingual sentiment characteristic of the mid- to late 1990s. Meanwhile, the House and Senate proposals for the reauthorization of the Javits Act appear more appealing to the field of gifted education than the Clinton Administration plan.

The Intersect of Bilingual and Gifted Education

In 1968 and following the calls of the time, Gowan pointed out that U.S. schools "have been the prime agency for enculturing and Americanizing many minority groups," and it was the practitioners' responsibility to ensure equality of opportunity for the "disadvantaged gifted" (p. 118). Gowan further claimed that "the disadvantaged gifted student deserves the full attention of American Education." Since the late 1980s, increasing concern has emerged in regard to the needs of diverse racial, ethnic, and cultural groups of gifted children (Maker & Schiever, 1989). For example, for the first time at the federal level, bilingual education funds were devoted to the high potential of culturally and linguistically diverse children. The BEA of 1984 was the first law to provide federal funds for the establishment and implementation of gifted and talented programs for students with LEP. More recently, the Jacob K. Javits Gifted and Talented Students Education Act of 1988 also provided federal funds for research on the identification of culturally and linguistically diverse students and the implementation of programs. This Act also established that "outstanding talents are present in children and youth from all cultural groups, across all economic strata, and in all areas of human endeavor" (U.S. Department of Education, 1993, p. 26).

In 1991, the OCR specified its policy on LEP students and gifted and talented programs in a memorandum entitled, "Policy Update on Schools' Obligations toward National Origin Minority Students with Limited English Proficiency (LEP Students)":

> The exclusion of LEP students from specialized programs such as gifted/talented programs may have the effect of excluding students from a recipient's programs on the basis of national origin, in violation of 34 C.F.R. § 100.3(b) (2), unless the exclusion is educationally justified by the needs of the particular student or by the nature of the specialized program. LEP students cannot be categorically excluded from gifted/talented and other specialized programs. If a recipient has a process for locating and identifying gifted/talented students, it must also locate and identify gifted/talented LEP students who could benefit from the program. (p. 8)

Results from a study of the OCR's involvement in gifted education during the period from 1992 to 1995 indicated that most complaints dealt with minority students' access to gifted education (mostly African American and Hispanic/Latino students). Specifically, about 17 percent of these complaints involved students with LEP (Karnes, Troxclair, & Marquardt, 1997).

During the 1990s, the field of gifted education tried to embrace equity by promoting the incorporation of talent development for all children (Passow & Rudnitski, 1994; Renzulli, 1991, 1994) and formally recognizing the presence of talents in children and youth from all cultural groups and socioeconomic levels. The 1972 Marland definition was superseded by the definition of outstanding talent offered by the Office of Educational Research and Improvement (OERI), U.S. Department of Education, in a report entitled, *National Excellence: A Case for Developing America's Talent* (1993). According to the U.S. Department of Education (1993), the following definition of *children with outstanding talent* "is based on the definition used in the federal Javits Gifted and Talented Education Act," and it "reflects today's knowledge and thinking" (p. 26):

> [These children] perform or show the potential for performing at remarkably high levels of accomplishment when compared with others of their age, experience, or environment. These children and youth exhibit high performance capability in intellectual, creative, and/or artistic areas, possess an unusual leadership capacity, or excel in specific academic fields. They require services or activities not ordinarily provided by the schools. Outstanding talents are present in children and youth from all cultural groups, across all economic strata, and in all areas of human endeavor. (p. 26)

This same report also characterized the education of gifted students as a "quiet crisis" that might receive national attention only when it reaches a catastrophic level. Additionally, Ross (1994) argued that this report has considerably augmented efforts to deal with issues related to culturally diverse students with gifted potential. For example, this report stated clearly that "special efforts are required to overcome the barriers to achievement that many economically disadvantaged and minority students face" (p. 28), and, shortly after, the Jacob K. Javits Gifted and Talented Students Education Act of 1994 indicated a priority for the development and implementation of model programs for culturally and linguistically diverse, talented students. Still, in defiance of the advances, the preeminence of defining *giftedness* as a narrow, static reflection of the individual's intelligence (psychometric terms) is evident, because most school districts still use IQ measures or cut-off scores (most often above the 95th percentile) for the identification of gifted students. These are precisely the districts that are more prone to neglect culturally and linguistically diverse, gifted students.

In a discussion of gifted identification as a constitutional issue, Brown (1997) argued that "states who require a certain test score or percentile are not only permitting discrimination, they are requiring it" (p. 159). Reports in the early 1990s (Coleman & Gallagher, 1992; Patton, Prillaman, & VanTassel-Baska, 1990) showed that the vast majority of states (over 90%) still used norm-referenced tests and that some suggested the use of nontraditional measures (e.g., out-of-school activities, work samples, multiple sources of referral) to identify gifted students. In relation to diverse populations, a few states had alternative criteria, child-study teams, preprogram trials, and retesting strategies in place. Actually, Coleman and Gallagher (1992) argued that a majority of states seemed to have inclusive policies for the identification and service of gifted students to such an extent that these written policies did not appear to be preventing services to diverse populations. Ironically, these authors also acknowledged that actual diverse student participation in gifted programs within the same states demonstrated the opposite.

In 1998, Landrum, Katsiyannis, and DeWaard reported that approximately 12 percent of states (five of forty-two) participating in their survey indicated that they had specific provisions for underrepresented groups. These authors also stated that nearly 36 percent of the participating states reported increasing efforts to provide opportunities for minority and "disadvantaged" gifted students in response to the initiatives stated in the National Excellence Report. In other words, it seems that although several efforts have been made in the past decade to overcome these limitations, school districts and individuals still find themselves either lacking support and guidance in designing, implementing, and evaluating their efforts or just ignoring the available body of knowledge.

The pervasive disparity in the proportion of culturally and linguistically diverse students, particularly among students of Native American and Latino backgrounds (with the exception of students of Asian backgrounds, who are overrepresented), identified and served in programs for the gifted is a major concern in both fields, and has become an important item on the agenda. In this regard, Landrum, Katsiyannis, and DeWaard (1998) pointed out that minority student participation in gifted programs ranged from less than 1 percent to more than 5 percent across states in 1996. The primary reason cited in the literature for the underrepresentation of these students is the absence of adequate assessment procedures and programming efforts (Bernal, 1989; Castellano, 1995; Cohen, 1988; Frasier, García, & Passow, 1995; Frasier & Passow, 1994; Kitano & Espinosa, 1995; Leung, 1981; Masten, 1985; Mills & Tissot, 1995; Smith, LeRose, & Clasen, 1991). In fact, Frasier (1997) claimed that issues of identification and programming for minority students have been pervasive for the past 40 years and have consistently focused on "(1) differences in test performance among racial, cultural, and ethnic groups; and (2) the effects of cultural, economic, and language differences or deprivations on the ability of minority students to achieve at levels associated with giftedness" (p. 498). She further contended that proposed solutions to such issues have not only done little in reversing the underrepresentation of minorities in gifted programs, but also have emphasized perceived student deficiencies, weaknesses, and cultural differences as the primary causes of their underrepresentation in gifted programs.

The literature also suggests that few educational models or programs have been designed specifically to identify and develop talents in culturally and linguistically diverse students. In some ways, these programs promote primary and second language development as well as cultural expression through the different academic areas. "Model Rocketry and the Space Sciences for the Gifted" (Cary, 1990), Project EXCEL (Hermanson & Perez, 1993; Perez, 1998), and Project FIRST STEP (Perez, 1998), developed in the San Diego Unified School District, are examples of such programs. Another program that addresses this goal is the Tucson Unified School District program, GATE, which integrates bilingual education and gifted education, focusing the attention on students with LEP and on other minority students (Barkan & Bernal, 1991, Perez, 1998). Notwithstanding, Bermudez and Rakow (1993) stated that there is an absence of specialized programs or instructional models that focus on gifted LEP students.

Currently, new alliances and initiatives are shaping the path. For instance, the National Association for Bilingual Education (NABE) and the National Association for Gifted Children (NAGC) have established special-interest groups of culturally and linguistically diverse students with high potential. Since 1995, the NABE has offered national symposia on issues related to the education of culturally and linguistically diverse, gifted students. The NAGC has also supported several presentations on this topic. Additional efforts have come from other individual institutions or agencies, such as Confratute, a summer institute on enrichment teaching and learning at the University of Connecticut. Since 1994, Confratute has offered weeklong strands on developing talents among culturally and linguistically diverse student populations. The NRC/GT has also sponsored several research studies on culturally and linguistically diverse, talented students since 1992 (see Diaz, 1994, 1998; Kloosterman, 1997; Reis, Hebert, Diaz, Maxfield, & Ratley, 1995). In addition, in the early 1990s, the OERI sponsored two investigations on gifted students among the Pueblo peoples. In January 1997, the OERI and the OBEMLA sponsored the first collaborative initiative on the education of students with LEP and outstanding talents. During this invitational meeting, experts and well-known representatives of each field discussed the current state of affairs in educational research and practice (see U.S. Department of Education, 1998).

Recapitulation

In short, although efforts to include racially, ethnically, culturally and linguistically diverse students, including students with LEP, into gifted and talented programs began in the 1980s, programs and funding really developed during the 1990s. During this period, some federal leadership backed up field initiatives and the OCR facilitated its help to school districts in order to counteract the underrepresentation of racially, ethnically, culturally, and linguistically diverse students in gifted and talented programs. The challenge of inclusion proved to be distressing for many school systems, and concerns over equity and excellence emerged constantly. Indeed, advances were made in this regard, but much work stands ahead of educators, administrators, and researchers, among others.

Common Ground

At first glance, the fields of bilingual education and gifted education appear far from each other. In fact, they have followed clearly different historical directions. In spite of this polarity, however, these two fields appear to share a few broad commonalities:

1. *No federal mandate.* A federal mandate that would provide much-needed federal leadership and support does not currently exist for gifted and bilingual education. Therefore, these fields are vulnerable to U.S. social and political mood swings (e.g., changes in legislation, given social events and governmental leadership), especially because both fields have been perceived as offering "special" programs or "catering" to limited populations.

2. *Demand but not enough supply.* Although both fields are designed to sensibly address the needs of particular student populations, neither has been able to provide educational

programming for all qualifying children, due to misunderstanding, underfunding, and understaffing (see Cohen, 1996; Crawford, 1997; Sternberg, 1995). Thus far, bilingual and gifted programs have aimed at maximizing students' strengths and academic potential, although with different foci—bilingualism and special talents, respectively. However, federal as well as state and local support has been scarce and prone to cutbacks.

3. *Lack of collaboration across programs.* Researchers and practitioners in both fields recognize that their own programs lack collaboration with other stakeholders. As a result, these programs often remain in peripheral positions within schools.

4. *Persistence of unfavorable social views of these fields.* According to Sternberg (1995), society holds a negative view of gifted individuals, thus ignoring and devaluing them. Similarly, Hornblower (1995) wrote that bilingual education "is exploding into one of the nation's most divisive political issues, fueled, on one hand, by a backlash against immigration and affirmative action and, on the other, by the failures and ideological strictures of some existing bilingual programs" (p. 38). Krashen (1996) contended that bilingual education was facing the strongest opposition ever. In other words, neither of the two fields have been "in grace," at least during the past decade.

5. *Misinformation as a common malady.* Unfortunately, research findings in both fields have not always found their way into policy and practice or into the knowledge of the general public. As a result, information about bilingual and gifted education is manipulated inappropriately, and serious misconceptions are sustained (see Cummins, 1989; Cohen, 1996; Samway & McKeon, 1999).

Recapitulation

The fields of bilingual education and gifted education have followed different historical courses. However, some commonalities, such as cuts in funding and support, changes in paradigms (i.e., views on bilingualism and giftedness), and the call for reconciliation of the equity versus excellence dispute have given way to collaboration between these fields.

Summary

The 1990s represent an era of significant economic, social, and educational change in the United States. After a dramatic economic downfall in the 1980s and early 1990s, a recovery, starting in the mid- to late 1990s, took the United States back to the top of world economic supremacy. Nevertheless, significant social issues, such as discrimination on the basis of race, ethnicity, or language, escalated to disconcerting levels. In the educational arena, the 1990s was a time of extensive yet "wholesale-like" reforms, determined primarily by Goals 2000 and the IASA of 1994.

During the 1990s, the fields of bilingual education and gifted education experienced changes in legislation and practice that enabled them to increase collaboration, thus taking the initial steps to overcome past alienation and extend the promise of better educational practice to more children. The issues addressed by the bilingual/gifted education fields have actually been around for a while, but they have been rediscovered and placed in the forefront, due to increasing numbers of students and awareness. In this way, the fields of bilingual education and gifted education intersected and emerged with promising ways of achieving the goal of equal educational opportunities, not only for culturally and linguistically diverse students, but for *all* students.

REFERENCES

Anstrom, K., & Kindler, A. (1996). *Federal policy, legislation, and educational reform: The promise and the challenge for language minority students.* Washington, DC: National Clearinghouse for Bilingual Education.

Associated Press (2000). *Utah Official-English rule blocked* [On-line]. Available: <news.findlaw.com/apstories/other/1110/12-2000/20001201185133930.html>.

Barkan, J. H., & Bernal, E. M. (1991). Gifted education for bilingual and limited English proficient students. *Gifted Child Quarterly, 35* (3), 144–147.

Bermudez, A. B., & Rakow, S. J. (1993). *Examining identification and instruction practices for gifted and talented limited English proficient students.* (ERIC Reproduction Services ED 360 871).

Bernal, E. (1989). "Pluralism and power"—Dare we reform education of gifted along these lines. In C. J. Maker & S. W. Schiever (Eds.), *Critical issues in gifted education: Defensible programs for cultural and ethnic minorities* (pp. 34–36). Austin, TX: Pro-Ed.

Bilingual Education Act, 20 U.S.C. § 7401-7405 (1994).

Bracey, G. W. (1997). The seventh Bracey report on the condition of public education. *Phi Delta Kappan, 79* (2), 120–136.

Brown, C. (1997). Gifted identification as a constitutional issue. *Roeper Review, 19* (3), 157–160.

Cary, A. (1990). Model rocketry and the space sciences for the Hispanic bilingual/gifted child. *Gifted International, 6* (1), 46–53.

Castellano, J. (1995). Revisiting gifted education opportunities for linguistically and culturally diverse students. *National Association for Bilingual Education News, 18* (6), 27–28.

Chen, E. M. (1995). *Implications of "Official English" legislation* [On-line]. Available: <www.aclu.org/congress/chen.html>.

Cohen, L. M. (1988). *Meeting the needs of gifted and talented minority language students: Issues and practices.* (ERIC Reproduction Services ED 309 592).

Cohen, L. M. (1996). Mapping the domains of ignorance and knowledge in gifted education. *Roeper Review, 18* (3), 183–189.

Coleman, M. R., & Gallagher, J. J. (1992). *Updated report on state policies related to the identification of gifted students.* Chapel Hill: Gifted Education Policy Studies, University of North Carolina at Chapel Hill.

Collier, R., & Freedberg, L. (1998, October 16). Frustrating search for solutions: Workplace called key to immigration control. *San Francisco Chronicle*, p. A1.

Crawford, J. (1997). *Best evidence: Research foundations of the Bilingual Education Act* [On-line]. Available: <www.ncbe.gwu.edu/ncbepubs.reports>

Crawford, J. (2000). *Language legislation in the U.S.A.* [On-line]. Available: <ourworld.compuserve.com/homepages/jwcrawford/langleg.htm>.

Cummins, J. (1989). *Empowering minority students.* Sacramento: California Association for Bilingual Education.

Cummins, J. (1998). *Beyond adversarial discourse: Searching for common ground in the education of bilingual students* [On-line]. Available: <ourworld.compuserve.com/homepages/jwcrawford.cummins.htm>.

Cummins, J. (1999). *Research, ethics, and public discourse: The debate on bilingual education* [On-line]. Available: <ourworld.compuserve.com/homepages/jwcrawford/ cummins2.htm>.

Diaz, E. I. (1994). *Underachievement among high ability Puerto Rican high school students: Perceptions of their life experiences.* Unpublished doctoral dissertation, Pennsylvania State University, University Park.

Diaz, E. I. (1998). Perceived factors influencing the underachievement of talented Puerto Rican descent students. *Gifted Child Quarterly, 42* (2), 105–122.

Doerr, E. (1999). Give us your money. . . . *Phi Delta Kappa, 80* (10), 778–779.

Duke, D. L. (1998). Challenges of designing the next generation of America's schools. *Phi Delta Kappa, 79* (9), 688–693.

Emergency Immigrant Education Act, 20 U.S.C. § 75-41-7549 (1994).

English Plus Resolution, H. Con. Res. 4, 105th Cong., 1st Sess. (1997) [On-line]. Available: <thomas.loc.gov/cgi-bin/query>.

English Plus Resolution, H. Con. Res. 4, 106th Cong., 1st Sess. (2000) [On-line]. Available: <thomas.loc.gov/cgi-bin/query>.

Foreign Language Assistance Act, 20 U.S.C. § 7511-7516 (1994).

Frasier, M., & Passow, A. H. (1994). *Toward a new paradigm for identifying talent potential* (RM94112). Storrs: University of Connecticut, National Research Center on the Gifted and Talented.

Frasier, M. M. (1997). Gifted minority students: Reframing approaches to their identification and education. In N. Colangelo & G. A. Davis (Eds.), *Handbook of gifted education* (2nd ed., pp. 498–515). Boston: Allyn & Bacon.

Frasier, M. M., García, J. H., & Passow, A. H. (1995). *A review of assessment issues in gifted education and their implications for identifying gifted minority students* (RM 94112). Athens: NRC G/T—University of Georgia.

Freedberg, L. (1998, October 16). Fierce debate on flow of legal migrants: Congress has squelched moves to cut numbers. *San Francisco Chronicle*, p. A7.

Freedberg, L., & McLeod, R. G. (1998, October 13). The other side of the law: Despite all U.S. efforts to curb it, immigration is rising. *San Francisco Chronicle*, p. A1.

Goals 2000: Educate America Act, 20 U.S.C. § 5811-5812 (1994).

Goldhaber, D. D. (1999). School choice: An examination of the empirical evidence on achievement, parental decision making, and equity. *Educational Researcher, 28* (9), 16–25.

Gordon, J. D. (1996, December). Teachers from different shores. *Equity and Excellence in Education. 29* (3), 28–36.

Gowan, J. C. (1968). Issues in the education of disadvantaged gifted students. *Gifted Child Quarterly, 12,* 115–119.

Hewley, W. D. (1996). The false premises and false promises of the movement to privatize public education. In E. C. Lagemann & L. P. Miller (Eds.) Brown *v.* Board of Education: *The challenge for today's schools* (pp. 135–142), New York: Teachers College Press.

Hermanson, D., & Perez, R. I. (1993). *Project EXCEL.* San Diego: San Diego City Schools, School Services Division, Exceptional Programs Development.

Hornblower, M. (1995, October 9). Putting tongues in check. *Time*, pp. 40–42, 49–50.

Improving America's Schools Act, 20 U.S.C. § 5801 (1994).

Jackson, J. L. (1996). Race-baiting and the 1996 presidential campaign. In G. E. Curry (Ed.), *The affirmative action debate* (pp. 288–296). New York: Addison-Wesley.

Jacob K. Javits Gifted and Talented Students Education Act, 20 U.S.C. § 8031-8037 (1994).

Karnes, F. A., Troxclair, D. A., & Marquardt, R. G. (1997). The Office of Civil Rights and the gifted: An update. *Roeper Review, 19* (3), 162–165.

Kitano, M. K., & Espinosa, R. (1995). Language diversity and giftedness: Working with gifted English language learners. *Journal for the Education of the Gifted, 18* (3), 234–254.

Kloosterman, V. I. (1997). *Talent identification and development in high ability, Hispanic, bilingual students in an urban elementary school.* Unpublished doctoral dissertation, University of Connecticut, Storrs.

Krashen, S. (1999a). *Bilingual education: Arguments for and (bogus) arguments against* [On-line]. Available: <ourworld.compuserve.com/homepages/jwcrawford/krashen3.htm>.

Krashen, S. (1999b). *Condemned without a trial: Bogus arguments against bilingual education.* Portsmouth, NH: Heinemann.

Krashen, S. D. (1996). *Under attack: The case against bilingual education.* Culver City, CA: Language Education Associates.

Landrum, M. S., Katsiyannis, A., & DeWaard, J. (1998). A national survey of current legislative and policy trends in gifted education: Life after the National Excellence report. *Journal for the Education of the Gifted, 21* (3), 352–371.

Leung, E. (1981). *The identification and social problems of gifted bilingual-bicultural children.* (ERIC Document Reproduction Services ED 203 653).

Lewis, J. D., & Karnes, F. A. (1995). Examining the media coverage of gifted issues. *Gifted Child Today, 18* (6), 28–30.

Lewis, J. D., & Karnes, F. A. (1997). A portrayal of the gifted in magazines. (ERIC Reproduction Services EC 305 430).

Maker, C. J., & Schiever, S. (Eds.). (1989). *Critical issues in gifted education: Defensible programs for cultural and ethnic minorities* (Vol. 2). Austin, TX: Pro-Ed.

Masten, W. (1985). Identification of gifted minority students: Past research, future directions. *Roeper Review, 8* (2), 83–85.

McQuillan, J., & Tse, L. (1996). Does research matter? An analysis of media opinion on bilingual education 1984–1994. *Bilingual Research Journal, 20* (1), 1–27.

Metcalf, K. K., & Tait, P. A. (1999). Free market policies and public education: What is the cost of choice? *Phi Delta Kappa, 81* (1), 65–75.

Mills, C. J., & Tissot, S. L. (1995). Identifying academic potential in students from under-represented populations: Is using the Raven's Progressive Matrices a good idea? *Gifted Child Quarterly, 39* (4), 209–217.

Office of Civil Rights (1991, September 27). *Memorandum—Policy update on schools' obligations toward* national origin minority students with limited English proficiency (LEP students). Washington, DC: Author.

Passow, A. H., & Rudnitski, R. A. (1994). Transforming policy to enhance educational services for the gifted. *Roeper Review, 16*, 271–275.

Patton, J. M., Prillaman, D., & VanTassel-Baska, J. (1990). The nature and extent of programs for the disadvantaged gifted in the United States and territories. *Gifted Child Quarterly, 34* (3), 94–96.

Perez, R. (1998). Inclusive and authentic gifted education for English language learners: The San Diego experience. In U.S. Department of Education, *Talent and diversity: The emerging world of limited English proficient students in gifted education* (pp. 25–36). Washington, DC: Author.

Portner, J. (1998, May 6). Administration, Congress weigh in on bilingual education. *Education Week* [On-line] *17* (34). Available: <www.edweek.org/ew/vol17/34delay.h17>.

Ramirez, A. (1999). Assessment-driven reform: The emperor still has no clothes. *Phi Delta Kappan, 81* (3), 204–208.

Reis, S., Hebert, T., Diaz, E., Maxfield, L. R., & Ratley, M. E. (1995). *Case studies of talented students who achieve and underachieve in an urban high school* (RM95120). Storrs, CT: National Research Center on the Gifted and Talented.

Renzulli, J. S. (1991). The NRC G/T: The dream, the design, and the destination. *Gifted Child Quarterly, 35* (2), 73–80.

Renzulli, J. S. (1994). *Schools for talent development: A practical plan for total school improvement.* Mansfield Center, CT: Creative Learning Press.

Riley, R. W. (1995, February 1). *Turning the corner: From a nation at risk to a nation with a future.* Second Annual State of American Education Address. Thomas Jefferson Middle School, Arlington, VA. Washington, DC: U.S. Department of Education.

Rivera, C., & LaCelle-Peterson, M. (1993). *Will the national educational goals improve the progress of English language learners?* Washington, DC: Center for Applied Linguistics.

Ross, P. (1994). Introduction to descriptions of Javits grant projects. *Gifted Child Quarterly, 38*, 64.

Sack, J. L. (2000). *Support building for renewed focus on gifted education* [On-line]. Available: <www.edweek. com/ew/ew printstory/cfm?slug=29gifted.h19>.

Samway, K. D., & McKeon, D. (1999). *Myths and realities: Best practices for language minority students.* Portmouth, NH: Heinemann.

Smith, J., LeRose, B., & Clasen, R. E. (1991). Underrepresentation of minority students in gifted programs: Yes! It matters! *Gifted Child Quarterly, 35* (2), 81–83.

Spring, J. (1997). *Political agendas for education: From the Christian Coalition to the Green Party.* Mahwah, NJ: Lawrence Erlbaum Associates.

Sternberg, R. J. (1995). The sounds of silence: A nation responds to its gifted. *Roeper Review, 18* (3), 168–172.

U.S. Department of Education (1991). *America 2000: An education strategy.* Washington, DC: U.S. Government Printing Office.

U.S. Department of Education (1993). *National Excellence: A case for developing America's talent.* Washington, DC: U.S. Government Printing Office.

U.S. Department of Education (1994a). *Changing education: Resources for systemic reform.* Washington, DC: U.S. Government Printing Office.

U.S. Department of Education (1994b). *For all students: Limited-English-proficient students and Goals 2000.* Washington, DC: U.S. Government Printing Office.

U.S. Department of Education (1998). *Talent and diversity: The emerging world of limited English proficient students in gifted education.* Washington, DC: U.S. Government Printing Office.

U.S. Department of Education, (2000c). *Educational Excellence for All Children Act of 1999—Prospectus* [On-line]. Available: <www.ed.gov/offices/OESE/ESEA/prospectus/overview. html>.

U.S. Department of Education, (2000b). *Educational Excellence for All Children Act of 1999—Fact sheet* [On-line]. Available: <www.ed.gov.offices/OESE/ESEA/factsheet.html>.

U.S. Department of Education (2000a). *Brief on educational progress 1992–2000* [On-line]. Available: <www.ed.gov>.

U.S. House of Representatives (1999). H.R. 2—Dollars to the Classrooms Act [On-line]. Available: <thomas.loc.gov/cgi-bin/bdquery/z?106:HR0002:@@@L&summ2=m&>.

Wiese, A., & Garcia, E. E. (1998, Winter). The Bilingual Education Act: Language minority students and equal educational opportunity. *Bilingual Research Journal* [On-line], *22* (1). Available: <brj.asu.edu/v221/>.

Zehr, M. A. (1999, November 3). Bilingual ed. advocates decry changes to Title VII. *Education Week* [On-line] *19* (10), p. 22. Available: <www.edweek. org/ew/ewstory.cfm?slug= 10ling.h19>.

3

Advanced Cognitive Development and Bilingualism

Methodological Flaws and Suggestions for Measuring First- and Second-Language Proficiency, Language Dominance, and Intelligence in Minority Children

VIRGINIA GONZÁLEZ

This chapter has the objective of reviewing literature on the relationship between advanced first- and second-language learning and cognitive development in children. Emphasis is given to the critical discussion of the historical evolution of methodological designs used in research studies on bilingualism and cognition conducted since the 1960s to the present. Throughout this critical literature review, the discussion of methodological flaws of research studies conducted during these four decades receives special attention, with derived suggestions to improve the methodological design and measurement of variables when studying cognition and bilingualism. In light of this critical literature review of research findings and its derived suggestions, an effort is made to include explicit discussions of educational implications for the assessment and instruction of gifted, culturally and linguistically diverse students.

As an overview of the sections in this chapter, a brief discussion of the three major methodological designs used by studies conducted since the 1960s until the 1990s is presented first, with a focus on (1) first- and second-language proficiency, language dominance, and advanced cognitive development in minority children; and (2) socioeconomic status (SES) factors. Next is a critical discussion, with support of literature reviewed and in a more specific manner, of the methodological problems still present in research studies on advanced cognition and bilingualism that attempt to measure advanced cognitive development, first- and second-language development, and language dominance in bilingual children. The second section is a discussion of between-subjects design studies comparing bilinguals and monolinguals. In the third section is a discussion of within-subjects design studies comparing low versus high second-language proficiency, divided into studies that have used standardized tests and studies using experimental tasks. The fourth section covers a discussion of the complexity of measuring SES factors due to the multidimensionality of this omnibus variable.

Overview of Major Methodological Designs

Research Studies Focusing on First- and Second-Language Proficiency, Language Dominance, and Advanced Cognitive Development in Minority Children

During the early 1960s, the first studies controlling for confounding factors affecting the positive influence of bilingualism on cognitive development in children were conducted. Actually, a landmark study was conducted in Canada by Peal and Lambert in 1962, which compared monolingual and advanced bilingual children, and controlled for the first time for SES factors. Only balanced bilinguals (i.e., children who were proficient in their first and second languages) were included in this pioneer study, which also matched monolinguals and bilinguals in their socioeconomic characteristics. It was not until the middle 1980s that researchers started to conduct and endorse studies with between-subjects designs, which compared low versus high first-language proficiency in bilingual children from low SES backgrounds. This methodological design was abandoned in the late 1980s for regression models, which could control statistically for individual differences in first- and second-language proficiency, language dominance, and SES factors in bilingual children.

Even though there have been improvements in the methodological designs of research studies conducted since the 1960s until the present, there are still methodological problems with the actual instruments used to measure the level of first- and second-language proficiency, language dominance, and advanced cognitive development in minority children. At present, most studies conducted on bilingualism and cognition control for confounding factors and aim to demonstrate the advantages of early advanced bilingualism on cognition. However, very few of the studies conducted since the 1960s until the present have used valid alternative assessments of cognition and language for minority low SES children.

As this extensive and meticulous literature search revealed, since the early 1960s until the present most research studies on bilingualism and cognitive development continue to use discrete-point standardized tests that assess the following:

1. Limited language skills (e.g., only vocabulary at the receptive level), instead of the multidimensionality of expressive and receptive language skills (i.e., writing, reading, speaking, listening) in different linguistic areas (pronunciation, vocabulary, syntax, grammar, semantics [understanding symbolic and sociocultural meaning] and pragmatics [social use of language for communicating within a culture])

2. Unidimensional aspects of cognitive development, focusing primarily on logical-mathematical skills, and not representing other cultural dimensions of contemporary models of intelligence

These standardized tests were originally developed during the early and middle decades of the twentieth century under the influence of the traditional medical assessment model. These traditional tests have been demonstrated by numerous research studies conducted during the 1970s and 1980s to be invalid and unreliable for bilingual children from minority and low SES backgrounds. (For an extended discussion, see Gonzalez & Yawkey, 1993; Gonzalez, Brusca-Vega, & Yawkey, 1997.) However, these standardized tests continue to plague with methodological flaws most contemporary research studies on bilingualism and cognition, resulting in the invalid measurement of these variables in low SES, language-minority children. Even contemporary studies, conducted during the middle and late 1980s and 1990s, that recognized the need for the change of theoretical and methodological paradigms for the study of bilingualism and cognition, still used standardized tests for the measurement of these variables. Thus, even though the weight of research evidence is overwhelming for the methodological flaws of standardized tests when used with language-minority children, there seems to be a need to develop new ways of implementing experimentally an alternative way of measuring advanced cognition in bilinguals.

In terms of educational implications of the state-of-the-art of measurement of language proficiency, dominance, and cognitive development in gifted children, the same situation in research is also true for practice in the U.S. public school system. Still the use of discrete, unidimensional, traditional, standardized tests of language and intelligence represents the most common, widespread practice in educational settings for both mainstream and language-minority students who are evaluated for potential giftedness. As stated, these traditional standardized tests were developed about fifty years ago and do not follow the basic standards of test development, published in 1985, proposed by the American Educational Research Association (AERA), the American Psychological Association (APA), and the National Council on Measurement in Education (NCME).

Research Studies Focusing on the Effect of Socioeconomic Status Factors

Most contemporary studies on cognition and bilingualism recognize the overwhelming effect of SES factors, but they do not control for confounding variables such as paternal/maternal occupations and educational levels and sociocultural environmental factors present in the home and school settings that affect development (e.g., whether the mother works outside of the home, number of siblings, language use at home by parents and siblings).

Methodological Problems in Measuring Advanced Cognitive Development, First- and Second-Language Proficiency, and Language Dominance in Bilinguals

Between-Subjects Designs Comparing Bilinguals with Monolinguals

For more than thirty-five years, studies on the relationship between bilingualism and cognition that have used between-subjects designs have shown that bilingual children's cognitive processes develop at higher levels in comparison to their monolingual counterparts (e.g., Lambert & Tucker, 1972; Peal & Lambert, 1962). The weight of research evidence has demonstrated that advanced bilingualism positively influences performance of cognitive tasks involving concept formation processes such as classification, meta-linguistic awareness, creativity, analytical reasoning, and problem-solving abilities (e.g., Bialystock, 1991; Cummins, 1978; Hakuta, 1991; Torrance, Gowan, & Aliohi, 1970).

The first attempt to explain the positive influence of bilingualism on cognition was made by Peal and Lambert (1962) in their code-switching hypothesis. They explained their findings that balanced bilinguals outperformed their monolingual counterparts, when controlling for SES factors, with the code-switching hypothesis. They proposed that the advantage of cognitive flexibility is provided by the bilingual children's ability to think in two languages. Later, Lambert and Tucker (1972) explained that bilingual children engaged in "incipient contrastive linguistics" (p. 207), as they stated, "We think that the process may start as a type of translation game . . . then the comparison and contrast of codes starts to become more systematic as the children notice salient differences in word order. . . , of gender" (p. 207); there was also "an early development of a linguistic 'detective' capacity, that is, an attentive, patient, inductive concern with words, meanings, and linguistic regularities" (p. 208). However, Diaz and Klingler (1991) questioned the validity of the code-switching hypothesis, because, they argued, "there is no empirical evidence (beyond anecdotal accounts of questionable validity) that bilinguals indeed switch language while performing cognitive tasks" (p. 168).

Another methodological study present in Peal and Lambert's study (1962) is the measurement of nonverbal cognitive abilities. They use the Raven Progressive Matrices, which only measure a reduced domain of cognitive abilities: spatiotemporal relationships. However, bilinguals still outperformed monolinguals when SES and intelligence quotient (IQ) of children in the Raven test were controlled by using analysis of covariance. Peal and Lambert adjusted the mean scores in which the two groups differed before comparing them, using analysis of variance. However, one wonders whether cognitive abilities were comparable in monolingual and bilingual children, or whether the balanced bilinguals selected for the study were more intelligent than other nonbalanced bilingual children. That is, balanced bilingualism may not be the result of learning two languages (as was explained by Peal & Lambert), but the result of individual differences present in children prior to their bilingualism. As commented on by

McLaughlin (1990), "Lacking fully random selection, it is impossible to say whether bilingual experiences lead to positive cognitive consequences or whether differences in initial aptitude lead to bilingual experiences" (p. 162).

Lambert and Tucker (1972) conducted another important study, the St. Lambert Experimental Bilingual Program, which was offered to French- and English-speaking children. They attributed their findings, which showed advantages of bilingualism, to the transfer of skills across languages. They argued that content learned through the use of one language also developed and showed in the other language. In their discussion of their findings, they raised an important issue—knowledge representation in bilinguals: "We wonder whether in these cases [of learning and development spreading across languages] there actually was a transfer of any sort or whether some more abstract form of learning took place that was quite independent of the language of training" (p. 209). They recognized that research on bilingual children could open a window to the relationship between language and thought, such as transfer of learning.

In a related vein, Vygotsky (1962) acknowledged the important influence of learning two languages, representing two different cultural views, on transfer of cognitive skills and knowledge. He stated, "The child can transfer to a new language the system of meanings he already possesses on his own" (p. 109). Vygotsky also recognized the importance to the child of learning a second language for development of explicit knowledge of one's own native language's structures and rules. Vygotsky (1962) explained this process based on the child's exposure to multiple representations of concepts: "The child learns to see his language as one particular system among many, to view its phenomena under more general categories, and this leads to awareness of his linguistic operations" (p. 110).

More recently, Diaz and Klingler (1991) argued that the positive influence of bilingualism on cognitive development shown by studies conducted during the 1970s and 1980s can be explained by the cognitive executive functions of self-regulation that language processing offers. They asserted that the use of private speech allows bilingual children to systematically separate form and meaning, and when provided with high-level cognitive tasks, they can access implicit knowledge, resulting in metalinguistic awareness.

Other researchers (e.g., Bialystock & Cummins, 1991; Diaz, 1985; Diaz & Klingler, 1991; Kessler & Quinn, 1987) have also asserted the positive influence of bilingualism on higher level cognitive processes, such as creativity, and divergent and convergent thinking. Kessler and Quinn (1987) compared sixth-grade, Spanish–English bilingual, Mexican American children with monolingual English children from "an upper socioeconomic suburban area in the eastern part of the United States" (p. 176). Both groups of children were exposed to an experimental treatment: an inquiry-based science program, which trained them to formulate scientific hypotheses within a problem-solving setting. When they evaluated the quality of the hypotheses, based on syntactic and semantic variables, the bilingual children outperformed the monolinguals in convergent thinking skills, because the bilinguals used the English language in a metaphorical and creative manner. Kessler and Quinn defined a *metaphor* as the development of a "similarity between apparently unlike things in the process of creating and transferring meaning from one universe of knowledge to another" (p. 181). Actually, these researchers considered that a metaphor provides a semantic context for the child to relate linguistic and cognitive processes, and to make meaningful connections between the two cultural worlds in which they live (the mainstream school culture and the minority family culture). As they stated, "Metaphor formation interacts with experience of the physical world and cultural dimensions of the environment in which language and cognitive creativity function" (p. 181).

Kessler and Quinn also asserted that

> the metaphors generated by bilingual children in formulating scientific hypotheses reflect a creativity which also takes into account their universe . . . it draws on the culture of which they are a part and which they bring to the schooling process. (p. 182)

In addition, the bilingual children who participated in Kessler and Quinn's study, showed higher levels of divergent thinking than did the monolingual children. That is, bilingual children used the English language with more fluency than did monolingual children. Bilinguals also provided more unique, creative, complex, and multiple solutions to science problems than did monolinguals. These researchers used Torrance's definition of creativity, which he developed in 1965: "the process of searching for solutions, formulating guesses or hypotheses, testing and retesting them, and finally communicating the results" (cited in Kessler & Quinn, 1987, p. 181). Kessler and Quinn interpreted the presence of higher level convergent and divergent thinking abilities in bilinguals, in comparison to that of monolinguals, as "aspects of a common underlying creativity and the interaction between both left and right hemispheres" (p. 182). They considered convergent thinking as the expression of synthesis, and divergent thinking as the expression of analysis; both thinking processes related to creativity, which is stimulated by the high degree of first- and second-language proficiency of balanced bilingual children.

Even though Kessler and Quinn's study provides very interesting results and uses experimental ways of measuring higher level cognitive processes, such as metaphor formation, there is no indication of the validity of the measures used. In addition, their study also has major methodological flaws, because there is no control of confounding variables, such as the measurement of first- and second-language proficiency in bilingual children and the SES levels of both groups of subjects. These authors simply asserted that the language-minority children were "additive bilinguals from whom the second language, English, developed without loss to the first language, Spanish" (p. 176), because (1) the bilingual children lived in "the lowest socioeconomic barrio of San Antonio" (p. 175), in which it was "possible to function in daily life using Spanish almost exclusively" (p. 176); and (2) "all had participated in a bilingual education program from the beginning of their schooling in the primary grades" (p. 176). However, no valid measure was administered to the language-minority children to prove the degree of their first- and second-language proficiency. Another related methodological flaw is that both groups of children were exposed to very different mainstream cultures, and hence dialects of the English language: The monolingual children lived in the eastern region of the United States, and the bilingual children lived in the southwest region of the country. Another methodological flaw of the measurement, or lack thereof, of the

SES levels of both groups of subjects was that the authors only inferred the value of this variable from the neighborhoods in which the children lived.

Diaz and Klingler (1991) recognized that there is a need for a test of "the validity of an explanatory model of how and why bilingualism has much positive effects" (p. 167). They proposed that this explanatory "model should be formulated, developed, and tested within a solid theoretical framework regarding the relation between language and thought in development . . . and should explain the reliable findings to date on bilingual cognitive development" (p. 169). However, it is this author's argument that due to methodological problems still present in the measurement of cognition and language development in bilinguals, and of SES mediating factors, findings of research studies are contradictory and thus not reliable. Moreover, this author wishes to clarify that this explanatory model should be different than models explaining first-language learning in monolingual children. It is this author's belief that one monolingual child plus one monolingual child does not equal a bilingual child. Thus, researchers who study bilingualism and cognition should also take into account how socioeconomic and sociocultural variables affect the development of culturally and linguistically diverse children.

Furthermore, in relation to advanced cognitive development in bilinguals, Diaz and Klingler (1991) argued that it is not explained yet "how bilinguals' metalinguistic skills are related to advantages in cognitive abilities *not* [italics added] directly related to language, such as classification." Thus, they considered classification as a nonlinguistic cognitive skill and developed "an explanatory model of the relationship between bilingualism and cognitive abilities that specifies the role of language awareness [or metalinguistic awareness] in the development of non-linguistic cognitive skills [such as classification]" (p. 167). Actually, this author argues that classification is indeed a concept formation process directly related to language. In fact, verbal and nonverbal classification tasks, administered in both first- and second-language study, were demonstrated by Gonzalez (1991, 1994, 1995) to lead bilingual children to the formation of semantic representations in which symbolic sociocultural connotations underlie linguistic structures and markers. These verbal and nonverbal classification tasks have demonstrated a measurement of the interaction among cognitive, linguistic, and cultural concept formation processes in bilingual children.

In conclusion, as observed in this discussion of between-subjects design studies, and following Diaz's and Klingler's (1991) arguments, the cause-and-effect direction of the relationship between bilingualism and advanced cognition has not been demonstrated as yet by an explanatory model. This author believes that the use of more sophisticated research designs can be fruitful avenues for studying the cause–effect relationship between bilingualism and advanced cognition. This author also thinks that it is possible to demonstrate the positive influence of bilingualism on cognition, if methodological flaws still present in the measurement of first- and second-language proficiency, language dominance, and cognitive development, and of SES factors, are resolved. For instance, regression models that use within-subjects designs and that control statistically for individual differences (i.e., first- and second-language proficiency, language dominance, and SES factors) can be more productive. In addition, as discussed by Bialystock and Cummins (1991) and Diaz (1985), a longitudinal research strategy can be ideal for the control of individual differences that occur in cross-sectional research studies.

From a more educationally applied point of view, the cause-and-effect relationship between bilingualism and cognition also offers important implications. First of all, educators and administrators in the U.S. public school system need to emphasize individual differences in learning in order to accommodate all of the idiosyncratic characteristics present in the developmental and learning needs of the culturally and linguistically diverse children. It is only when educators understand the idiosyncratic ways in which young children deal with cultural and linguistic differences that they can identify at-risk students who are potentially gifted. These resilient students typically show some form of verbal and/or nonverbal giftedness that is also tinted by their minority cultural backgrounds. This cultural and/or linguistic giftedness present in language-minority, low SES, young students can only be evaluated by committed evaluators using alternative measures. (For a further discussion of this topic and presentation of case studies, see Clark & Gonzalez, 1998; Gonzalez and Clark, 1999.) That is, these students have some internal psychological characteristics (e.g., temperament, personality traits, potential) and/or enjoy the scaffolding presence of mentors and role models in their communities (i.e., parents, siblings, grandparents, extended family members, and/or teachers). The interaction of these internal and external factors make these children resilient to the potential negative effect of poverty, to the point of showing the benefits of additive bilingualism on their cognitive development.

Continuing with the discussion of the relationship between advanced cognition and bilingualism, the following section presents within-subjects design studies conducted with standardized tests and experimental tasks.

Within-Subject Designs Comparing Low versus High Second-Language Proficiency Levels in Bilinguals

Studies Using Standardized Tests

Use of the within-subjects design began during the 1980s and was proposed and endorsed by researchers such as Kenji Hakuta and Rafael Diaz (1985), who categorized degrees of bilingualism into three groups: proficient, partial, and limited. A methodological flaw in some of the within-subjects design studies is the use of standardized measures assessing discrete cognitive and language abilities. Even though a positive influence of bilingualism on cognition is shown by these studies, the use of standardized discrete measures narrows the scope of cognitive and linguistic abilities assessed. When alternative, experimentally based measures are used by researchers, different and broader dimensions of children's cognitive and linguistic abilities may be assessed.

Serious methodological flaws are found in studies conducted during the 1980s that used the within-subjects designs, due to the invalid psychometric characteristics of standardized tests of language proficiency and cognitive development. For instance, Hakuta and Diaz (1985) compared language-minority, Puerto Rican children attending kindergarten and first-grade bilingual maintenance educational programs, who showed different degrees of bilingualism (with variation in their English-language proficiency and controlling for their Spanish-language proficiency). Hakuta and Diaz used the

Spanish Peabody Picture Vocabulary Test (PPVT) for controlling for individual differences in first-language proficiency and the Raven Progressive Matrices for measuring the dependent variable of nonverbal cognitive development.

In Hakuta and Diaz's study, multiple regression analyses supported a causal model in which children's degree of bilingualism influenced their nonverbal cognitive ability, even when these subjects were immigrant children of low SES background. However, both standardized tests used by Hakuta and Diaz were discrete measures of abilities. The PPVT measures only oral productive language skills, and the Ravens device measures only spatiotemporal relationships. Subsequently, Diaz (1985) conducted a study using the same sample but divided it into low and high English-proficiency levels, and also controlled for Spanish-language proficiency. Diaz used a modified version of the subtest of opposite analogies of the Stanford-Binet Intelligence Scale for measuring cognitive development. One of the limitations of this adapted standardized measure is that only one specific "correct" answer per item was accepted in Diaz's study.

Multiple regression analyses showed that

> in both kindergarten and first grade, degree of bilingualism predicted significant portions of the cognitive variance for children of low second language (English) proficiency level, while the effects attenuated or virtually disappeared for children of high second language proficiency of the same age. (Diaz & Klingler, 1991, p. 178)

Diaz and Klingler explained the results obtained by Diaz (1985), using Cummins (1976) threshold hypothesis and the pseudobilingualism hypothesis proposed by Peal and Lambert (1962). These two hypotheses attempted to explain the contradictory results obtained by studies of the relationship between bilingualism and cognition. The underlying ideas common to these hypotheses are that there are both

1. Positive effects of developing two languages simultaneously to a high degree (or having a strong first language) on cognition, resulting in additive bilingualism
2. Negative effects of low first- and second-language proficiency levels on cognition, resulting in substractive bilingualism or pseudobilingualism

Similarly, Skutnabb-Kangas and Toukomaa (1976) explained the academic problems and cognitive disadvantages that occur in some immigrant language-minority children as the result of semilingualism, or the lack of proficiency in both first- and second-languages. Moreover, Diaz and Klingler (1991) also used as an explanation the timing of positive effects of bilingualism on cognition, which "seem to occur more strongly for children at early stages of bilingual development and attenuate as children become more proficient bilinguals" (p. 177). Diaz and Klingler also concluded that "the effects of bilingualism on cognitive development are most likely mediated through the processes and experiences associated with early phases of second-language learning in an additive context" (p. 179).

An alternative explanation for the age hypothesis proposed by Diaz and Klingler, in relation to contradictory results of previous studies using standardized measures, can be the presence of methodological flaws in the measures of variables used. This author thinks that studies using the Raven Progressive Matrices as a measure of nonverbal cognitive abilities in bilinguals, and the PPVT as a measure of language proficiency (e.g., Diaz, 1985; Hakuta, 1987; Hakuta & Diaz, 1985), have major validity problems, especially when these traditional measures are used with Spanish-dominant children who show low levels of English proficiency. It seems that results of studies using the Raven Progressive Matrices with bilingual children do not show an attenuation of cognitive advantages due to bilingualism. Actually, this author would explain differently the findings obtained by these studies: For older children with higher degrees of English as a second language proficiency, the Raven test may be a more valid measure of their nonverbal, spatiotemporal, cognitive abilities. Therefore, the children's higher degree of bilingualism explains a lower percentage of the variance of the Raven scores within a regression model—and vice versa for younger children with lower degrees of English as a second language proficiency.

Furthermore, it is this author's position that for all bilingual children (even mainstream young children), regardless of their levels of first- and second-language proficiency, discrete-point standardized tests (e.g., the Raven and the PPVT) are unidimensional measures of complex and multidimensional constructs, such as cognitive and language development. As explained by Harley, Cummins, Swain, and Allen (1990), "The problem is directly related to the way in which language proficiency has been conceptualized—specifically the extrapolation from conversational fluency in English to overall proficiency in the language" (p. 8). Harley et al. supported the use of different methodologies for studying language proficiency, due to the difficulty of operationalizing this construct and also due to the presence of differences in learning experiences.

Thus, this author proposes that both hypotheses (i.e., age and level of bilingualism) are based on standardized measures of cognitive and language abilities. Therefore, these studies are influenced by interfering variables such as the following:

1. Schooling and learning effects
2. Lack of validity, due to bilingual children's linguistic and cultural unfamiliarity with test items and to standardization problems
3. The lack of construct validity of theoretical frameworks underlying standardized tests when used with language-minority children, especially when these children come from low-SES backgrounds

In sum, there are two major methodological problems in studies that obtain different findings for the effect of older and younger children's degree of bilingualism on cognition:

1. The narrow or discrete domain of cognitive abilities measured by standardized tests (Gonzalez et al., 1997; Oller, 1991; Oller & Damico, 1991), such as the Raven Progressive Matrices, which measures only spatiotemporal relationships representing perceptual and nonverbal concept-formation processes
2. The lack of validity and reliability of the Raven test for minority children, due to the influence of schooling, learning, standardization, cultural, and linguistic factors on their test performance (Rogoff & Chavajay, 1995)

Thus, from these methodological flaws that occur in research studies conducted with bilingual children from low-SES backgrounds, some educational, practical implications can be derived. Given the state of the art of standardized tests, it is still a challenge for school districts to screen and assess language dominance and language proficiency levels in minority children in a valid and reliable manner. As contemporary research has demonstrated, it is problematic to categorize degrees of bilingualism when using measures from the traditional psychometric paradigm. That is why training educators in alternative assessment models and methodologies is key for the appropriate use of more valid and reliable alternative batteries, representing the effect of bilingualism and biculturalism on young children's bicognitivism. This contemporary training needs to focus primarily on the change of attitudinal, belief, and knowledge systems in preservice and in-service educators, administrators, and supporting school personnel (i.e., school psychologists, educational diagnosticians, social workers) who participate in the assessment and instructional process of at-risk students.

Secondly, when evaluating at-risk, language-minority children who come from culturally and linguistically diverse backgrounds, there is a need to analyze the interaction of the internal and external social factors impacting their development. This interaction between psychological and ecological factors may be positive or negative, resulting in fewer children in additive bilingualism and resilient characteristics or potential giftedness. Most language-minority children suffer from low achievement levels, due primarily to substractive bilingualism reflecting the negative impact of their low socioeconomic environment. In addition to income and tangible resources in the community and home, levels of education, social status of occupation, degree of acculturation, and English language proficiency levels tend to be much lower in poor families than in middle and upper class families. Reciprocally, levels of stress and distress, number of children, and presence of mental and health problems tend to be much higher in poor families than in their middle and upper class counterparts.

Poverty is associated with many complex social status and family-structure factors, which may place language-minority children at risk of presenting as low achievers. Thus, the resilient children who are potentially gifted are also protected by some mediational factors, such as a positive family environment (for a further discussion of this topic, see Gonzalez & Oviedo, 2000). These resilient children also develop social and/or academic proficiency in both first and second languages at a younger age, and in a faster manner; as research demonstrates, however, their progress is not shown consistently by standardized tests. That is why, if these potentially gifted, language-minority, poor, young children are assessed with standardized tests only, they will not be identified.

It is not a matter of whether giftedness exists among bilingual, poor children, but a matter of sensitivity of evaluators and the instruments they select to use for a specific purpose and in a specific manner. As demonstrated by Gonzalez, Bauerle, Black, and Felix-Holt (1999), the same gathered data, when used by evaluators from different cultural and linguistic backgrounds, prior knowledge levels, and attitudinal and belief systems, can be used to demonstrate that a child belongs to opposite categories in special education (i.e., gifted and talented, learning disabled, mentally retarded, or speech and language disordered). In addition, the sensitivity of instruments is also a key factor for identifying potentially gifted children from minority and poor backgrounds (as discussed in Gonzalez, Clark, & Bauerle, 2000). As discussed in the next section, the contradictory results found in studies using standardized tests are absent in studies using alternative methodologies, such as experimental tasks of cognitive and language development.

Studies Using Experimental Tasks

Findings of studies using experimental tasks of verbal and nonverbal abilities have also shown a positive relationship between bilingualism and cognitive development. For instance, Diaz and Padilla (1985) studied the performance of Mexican American bilingual preschoolers on three experimental tasks the authors had designed: block designs, classification, and story sequencing. Multiple regression equations showed that "children's degree of bilingualism . . . predicted significant portions of performance variance in both classification and story sequencing tasks" (Diaz & Klingler, 1991, p. 172). Degree of bilingualism was operationalized by Diaz and Padilla (1985) as the control for Spanish-language proficiency, allowing for individual variations in English-language proficiency levels.

In addition, Gonzalez, Bauerle, and Felix-Holt (1996) found that the performance of bilingual, low-SES kindergarten and first-grade children on verbal and nonverbal classification tasks was influenced by five factors:

1. First- and second-language administration
2. Verbal and nonverbal assessment procedures
3. Multiple measurements and informants
4. The individualizing of assessment
5. Evaluator characteristics, such as prior knowledge of cultural and linguistic minority factors, hypothesis and theories endorsed, knowledge level of constructs measured, and, especially, attitudes and cultural value systems

These classification tasks, called QUEST (Qualitative Use of English and Spanish Tasks), were developed by Gonzalez (1991, 1994, 1995). In a series of validation studies, QUEST has proved to be a valid assessment of cognitive and language development in bilingual children (e.g., see Clark & Gonzalez, 1998; Felix-Holt & Gonzalez, 1999; Gonzalez et al., 1994, 1996, 1997; Gonzalez & Clark, 1999; Oviedo & Gonzalez, 1999).

Diaz and Klingler (1991) recognized that "a major problem in understanding and explaining the relationship between bilingualism and cognitive development is that research has focused mostly on outcome rather than [on] process variables" (p. 180). In addition, Bialystock (1991) asserted that it is only recently that the study of the relationship between bilingualism and cognition has shifted "from product description to process models" (p. 5). She stated that "the relevant questions are whether or not bilingualism affects the way in which children process language, and the insights which they subsequently derive about the structure of language" (p. 7). Moreover, Bialystock explained that the focus of contemporary research conducted with bilingual children is on "the contextual factors that define the bilingual situation" (p. 7).

The current research focus on outcome, in this author's belief, is due to the widespread use of standardized tests of cognition and language, which have a discrete and narrow scope, reducing the multidimensional complexity of these variables to unidimensional views. Further, the use of experimental higher level cognitive tasks, such as the verbal and nonverbal classification tasks included in QUEST, can offer a window to cognitive and semantic processes in bilinguals, such as thinking styles and strategies, and to metacognitive and metalinguistic processes. In addition, it is also important to analyze these experimental tasks measuring higher level cognitive processes not only statistically, but also qualitatively, such as proposed in the scoring system used with QUEST in this study. The qualitative analysis allows researchers to understand and explain why bilingual children's thinking processes are different from those of their monolingual counterparts. As stated by Diaz and Klingler (1991), "Although we have an abundance of data on the outcome of bilingual children's performance on psychometric and experimental tasks, it is not clear whether bilingual children simply do better (more of the same) than monolinguals or whether they perform differently on the tasks" (p. 180).

Actually, the verbal and nonverbal classification tasks included in QUEST measure conceptual formation from perceptual to metalinguistic levels. Bilingual children are asked probing questions and are provided with counterexamples that contrast form and meaning and stimulate children to think about language. In the several validation studies conducted with QUEST (e.g., Clark & Gonzalez, 1998; Felix-Holt & Gonzalez, 1999; Gonzalez et al., 1994, 1996, 1997; Gonzalez & Clark, 1999; Gonzalez, Oviedo, & O'Brien de Ramirez, 2000; Oviedo & Gonzalez, 1999), it has been found that a high proportion of bilingual children tend to think at metalinguistic levels in both nonverbal and verbal tasks, showing a positive influence of bilingualism on cognition.

Even when children showed low levels of first- and second-language proficiency, Gonzalez and collaborators (e.g., Gonzalez et al., 1996) found that nonbalanced bilinguals performed at high developmental levels, even showing metalinguistic abilities, in nonverbal classification tasks of QUEST. Young, nonbalanced bilingual children from low-SES backgrounds were able to use metaphors, to think about the meaning of words, to understand that the label was independent from the attributes of the real-world object, to understand that labels are the result of cultural and linguistic conventions, and to think creatively with language.

Relatedly, Diaz and Klingler (1991) stated that "bilingual children show consistent advantages in tasks of both verbal and non-verbal abilities" (p. 183), because "the cognitive effects of bilingualism appear relatively early in the process of becoming bilingual and do not require high levels of bilingual proficiency nor the achievement of balanced bilingualism" (p. 184). Thus, nonbalanced bilingual children *do* have the potential to show the advantages of bilingualism in their testing performance. However, very few culturally and linguistically sensitive instruments exist that can provide higher level tasks for nonbalanced bilinguals to show their high cognitive potential. QUEST provides language-minority, low-SES children an opportunity to demonstrate their learning and cognitive potential, which has not yet actualized in the form of knowledge, skills, or abilities.

In addition, Gonzalez and collaborators (e.g., Gonzalez et al., 1996) found that it is also important to compare nonbalanced bilingual children's performance on QUEST when administered in their first and second languages. This form of comparison was described by Bialystock and Cummins (1991) as "an evaluation of the way in which bilingual children approach a particular task in their first and second language" (p. 228). That is the reason why the qualitative analysis of higher level conceptual tasks, such as QUEST, is so important for understanding (1) the qualitative differences of how bilingual children think in their first and second languages and (2) the cultural and linguistic differences in their cognitive processes when compared with those of monolingual children. Bilingual children think qualitatively different than do monolingual children.

Thus, it is important to use valid alternative measures of cognitive processes that are sensitive to the cultural and linguistic differences in language-minority children. On the other hand, it is also important to compare bilingual children with monolingual children in order to understand "those aspects that are unique to speakers of two languages and those that appear not to be influenced by linguistic competence (Bialystock & Cummins, 1991, p. 228). According to Bialystock and Cummins, by comparing linguistic and cognitive development in bilingual and monolingual children (with between- and within-groups designs), general principles of cognitive development can be derived. They suggested that new research problems can be enlightened by comparing bilingual and monolingual children; for example, "issues such as interdependencies between language and thought, as well as interrelations among various aspects of language proficiency are essentially inaccessible to study if one considers only the progress of monolingual children' " (p. 228).

In doing these comparisons, it is also important not to lose sight of individual differences, which prevail over the issue of how bilingualism or monolingualism influences, similarly or differently, children's cognitive development. As Bialystock and Cummins (1991) stated, "There is no reason to expect a uniform pattern of development across all operations for bilingual children, or across all bilingual children" (p. 231). In fact, there is even solid research evidence for the existence of differences within the same bilingual child in relation to concept processing and representation, attesting, as stated by Hakuta (1991), for the flexibility of the human mind. For instance, Gonzalez (1991) found that cultural and linguistic factors influenced whether bilingual children would form one or two semantic representations, and that the same bilingual child would present both forms of representations, unique and common for both languages. Actually, these within-subject differences were related to the cultural and linguistic characteristics of stimuli and classification tasks used.

As Hakuta (1991) suggested, "The kind of procedure involved influences whether the subject behaves as though the two languages are interdependent or independent and whether there are coordinate or compound systems" (p. 103). Then, assessments of bilingualism and cognition should present alternatives for children to display their mental flexibility in cognitive processing. Actually, according to Hakuta, "Malleability of results is directly related to the problem of individual differences" (p. 103). That is, multiple ways of cognitive processing may be present in bilinguals, which may be influenced by multiple variables such as cultural and linguistic content, social context of second-language acquisition, first-language background, first- and second-language strategies, level of task difficulty, personality factors, individual differences, and so on. Therefore, researchers must keep a multidimensional, innovative view when conducting studies with bilinguals, such as providing them with complex tasks.

Thus, when attempting to study the relationship between cognition and language,

> [I]t will most likely be the study of the diversity, that exists among bilingual children in their social, cognitive, and linguistic proficiency that will lead to the most universal understanding of the ways in which language and cognitive processing is carried out by bilingual children. (Bialystok & Cummins, 1991, p. 231)

However, the challenge for researchers is that "differences between bilinguals and monolinguals in cognitive ability could ultimately be attributed to differences in confounding social variables" (Diaz, 1985, p. 1377). One way of controlling for these confounding individual differences is by using statistical designs, such as multiple regression models and analysis of covariance for partialing out the effects of social and first- and second-language proficiency factors.

Furthermore, the cognitive potential of nonbalanced bilingual children, who in some instances are not proficient in English or in Spanish, is expressed in their metalinguistic awareness of linguistic form and meaning, resulting from the influence of early exposure to two languages and two cultures on their cognition. In relation to this issue, Diaz and Klingler (1991) concluded, in their discussion of the literature on the advantages of bilingualism, that "at an early age, the exposure to two languages in a systematic fashion leads to an objective awareness of language. Bilinguals' metalinguistic awareness includes . . . non-communicative [cognitive] uses and functions of language" (p. 187), leading "to an increased use of language as a tool of thought . . . [and of] self-regulatory control over different language functions . . . [and] an advantage in cognitive performance across verbal and non-verbal tasks . . . that demand non-automatic processing" (p. 188).

In conclusion, there is a need for research studies that provide empirical evidence of the cognitive advantages of bilingualism, even of nonbalanced bilingual children from low-SES backgrounds, by evaluating validly their higher level cognitive processes through the use of alternative assessments. As discussed by Hakuta (1986), research has focused historically on "good" and "bad" bilingualism and intelligence. However, as discussed in this chapter, contemporary researchers have realized that cognitive development in bilingual children is a multifaceted, complex variable influenced by numerous factors, such as SES. The cognitive development of monolingual and bilingual children cannot solely be researched as an issue of language acquisition, but must take into account external social, economic, and cultural factors, as will be discussed in the next section.

These same recommendations are also applicable to educational practitioners in the U.S. public school system when serving bilingual children. As demonstrated by alternative research paradigms and methodologies, nonbalanced bilinguals can be potentially gifted. Therefore, it is important to use alternative assessments that are administered in both first- and second-languages and to use batteries of measures that take into consideration the interactional effect of psychological and ecological factors (such as SES) on cognitive and language development and achievement levels.

Methodological Problems in Measuring Socioeconomic Status Factors in Minority Children

Current studies of bilingualism and cognitive development have found that the SES of a child can be a powerful predictor of cognitive development. For instance, Diaz (1985) found that when comparing bilingual kindergartners and first-grade Puerto Rican children, "findings indicate that observed cognitive differences between second-language-proficiency groups can be attributed to group differences in socioeconomic variables" (p. 1376). However, researchers have been plagued by the difficulties of accurately measuring the SES of the child and his or her parents. Some researchers have focused on school children receiving reduced or free school lunches, while others have looked at the occupations of the children's parents. Controversy has arisen over the methods because they do not reliably provide complete information about the everyday living conditions of the children. For instance, Diaz (1985) used the occupation of the head of the household, the family's length of residence in the United States, and the number of bedrooms in the household divided by the number of persons in the household as measures of the SES of bilingual children. Hakuta (1991) considered that "the number of years in residence in the United States is obviously related to the knowledge of English and the level of acculturation to American society" (p. 21).

Compounding the problem discussed in the preceding section, regarding how to measure first- and second-language proficiency levels in bilinguals, there are also variations in SES levels within groups of bilingual children. Many of the studies focusing on developmental outcomes of at-risk, minority, low-SES children have a more complex methodology for measuring the complex SES variable, but they show the same methodological problems in the measurement of cognitive and language developmental areas in minority children. Even though some of these studies focusing on SES effects on minority children's development also focus on some language-minority groups, such as Hispanics and Asian Americans, they do not recognize the compounding effect of the possible presence of two languages on other developmental outcome variables measured with invalid standardized tests. In the descriptions of their samples, they merely recognize the presence of different ethnic groups as a factor within the complex SES variable but do not explore the presence of a minority-language effect on other developmental areas, such as cognition.

The fact that some of the participating children were bilingual is never explored in studies with an emphasis on developmental outcomes of at-risk conditions, such as studies of resiliency in minority children. This author proposes that within the complex definition of SES factors, researchers also include within family-structure factors, such as the language used for communication at home by parents and children. We cannot ignore a major expression of culture such as language, which influences the quality and quantity of interactions between caretakers and children. Whether the mainstream or the minority language is used at home will be a reflection of the level of acculturation of parents, their cultural values and beliefs, and, overall, their teaching practices for socializing their children as monocultural or bicultural. Thus, parents and children may display monolingualism in the minority language, different degrees of bilingualism in the minority and mainstream languages, and, at the same time, monoculturalism in the minority culture, or different degrees of biculturalism in the minority and mainstream cultures. Many SES factors, such as the social class and educational levels of parents, are going to influence the parents', children's, and, in general, the family's degree of acculturation. Affective or emotional developmental areas in minority children also reflect the influence of cultural factors present in the SES complex variable; such as identity, self-efficacy, self-esteem, and self-concept domains.

Thus, compounding the scarcity of studies with bilingual children, we have the presence of major methodological flaws in the SES variables taken into account for selecting subject samples, as well as for measuring developmental complex variables such as cognitive and first- and second-language proficiency. As stated by Diaz (1985), there is still a major methodological flaw in most contemporary studies conducted with bilingual children, and with minority children in general; that is, "in certain bilingual populations in the United States, degree of bilingualism is somewhat confounded with socioeconomic variables" (p. 1384). Diaz found that when using LISREL models, which take into account the simultaneous effect of variables, bilingualism seem to be the cause of cognitive advantages in young children, even when SES factors were controlled for. That is, he found that "significant initial group differences [based on extreme high and low second-language proficiency] in cognitive variables disappeared when SES and parental employment were used as covariates" (p. 1385). Based on the results of his study, Diaz suggested the use of within-subjects designs, with the control of ability in the dominant language and SES factors.

There is need to study a possible threshold acculturation level in minority parents and their children, which would make possible their successful adaptation to the mainstream school culture. Actually, making a parallel with first- and second-language learning principles and hypotheses discussed in the preceding section, there must also be a degree of first-culture identification, internalization, socialization, and adaptation that is necessary for minority children to successfully acculturate to the mainstream social environment. That is, minority children need a strong first language and a strong first-culture identity in order to develop a healthy bicultural identity that would permit them to function and adapt to life between two cultural worlds. Minority children need to adapt to the family and the school environment, and later the larger society, and to become productive citizens of the United States. The microculture of the family environment may have similarities and differences with the macroculture represented in the school and society at large.

Individuals within a cultural group

1. Hold cultural ideologies, sociocultural meanings, values, and beliefs about the education and development of children
2. Practice specific teaching behaviors, social interactional patterns, and caregiving strategies

Both later processes, the first a psychological aspect of culture and the second a behavioral one, are transmitted and modeled by parents to their children in their mediational, mentorship roles within the cultural system. In sum, when studying developmental outcomes in language-minority children, researchers have to pay careful attention to external factors such as SES levels and family structure, which in turn reflect cultural and linguistic differences.

In terms of practical educational applications, research findings suggest that it is poverty, not limited English proficiency or degree of bilingualism, that primarily affects cognitive and language development and academic achievement levels. The negative impact of poverty on developmental and achievement levels is independent of bilingualism and can be mediated by family factors, such as degree of acculturation. Thus, when assessing and teaching language-minority children, educators need to understand the significant role of low SES on the particular forms of potential cognitive giftedness that these children may present. Giftedness in mainstream, middle and upper class children will manifest also in higher achievement levels. In contrast, language-minority, poor children could be limited English proficient and present lower achievement levels, but still be potentially culturally and linguistically gifted (for further discussion of this point, see Clark & Gonzalez, 1998; Gonzalez & Clark, 1999).

Recommendations for Researchers for Validly Measuring Socioeconomic Status

Entwisle and Astone (1994) were commissioned by the Society for Research in Child Development to generate some guidelines for measuring social constructs such as race/ethnicity and SES in young children. They highlighted that only general guidelines can be formulated, resulting in the need for adapting measures to the nature of a particular study, and also to the purpose for which measures of these social constructs are collected by a researcher. In preparing this paper, they took "into account current practice at the Bureau of the Census, research traditions developed by sociologists who have mainly been concerned with adults, and challenges posed by the changing character of the U.S. populations and its family forms" (p. 1521). They recommended that researchers collect information about race/ethnicity and SES directly for the parents' children by the time permission for the children's participation in the study is sought.

Based on the U.S. Bureau of the Census practices, people should identify themselves in categories of race/ethnicity; however, these categories

1. Confound race and ethnicity (e.g., Non-Hispanic White and Hispanic categories leave out many overlapping race and ethnic categories: Are all Hispanics homogeneous in their race? Are there some Hispanics who are White or of other races?

2. Subsume diverse ethnic groups within larger cultural groups (e.g., Tohono O'Dahams and Navajos within the Native Americans category)

For the measurement of SES level, Entwisle and Astone (1994) recommended avoiding the direct measure of annual income, due to its rapid fluctuation within short periods of time. Instead, they advised researchers to collect information on the children's fathers' (or male figures') educational levels, occupations, and labor force status. In the absence of a male figure, they recommended that researchers be careful with data about the mothers' (or female figures') occupations, due to the tendency for women to earn less than men when doing the same kind of work, or to the higher concentration of women in positions with social prestige but low payment (e.g., school teachers, social workers). They also advised researchers to be sensitive to nontraditional family structures, more common in the United States during the 1990s (e.g., stepfamilies, single-parent households, teen-age mothers, grandparents caring for children, etc.).

In addition, Sameroff, Seifer, Barocas, Zax, and Green (1987, cited in Garcia Coll, 1990) generated a multiple-risk index representing ten environmental variables correlated with SES, including: "mental health status, anxiety, parental education, occupation, minority status, family support, family size, and life events" (p. 279). Actually, as suggested by Garcia Coll (1990), growing up as a minority child in the United States is not only reflected in the cultural family environment, but also in the social class culture (SES level) and the ethnic group culture. For example, teaching strategies used by mothers and the general didactic aspects of the child-rearing environment have been found to be related to the mothers' educational levels by Laosa (1978, 1980, cited in Garcia Coll, 1990), which are also associated with their social class. Other studies (e.g., Gutierrez, Sameroff, & Karrer, 1988, cited in Garcia Coll, 1990) have shown that the parental acculturation level is related to the complexity level of parental explanations of their children's development, as well as to other SES factors, such as educational level, and the degree and contact with poverty that their children experienced. Thus, Garcia Coll (1990) recommended that researchers "elucidate the processes by which these different yet overlapping sources of influence affect the development of minority infants" (p. 280) and study SES as a "marker variable that needs to be dissected into its components" (p. 281).

Financial, Human, and Social Capital Measures of Socioeconomic Status Factors in Minority Children

Entwisle and Astone (1987) also recommended that researchers "use separate indicators of financial, human, and social capital to measure the socioeconomic background of a child" (p. 1526). These three indicators were defined by Coleman (1988, cited in Entwisle & Astone, 1987). *Financial capital* was defined as money available in the household for buying material goods that the children need for their proper development (e.g., food, clothing, housing, books, educational toys, etc.). For low-SES, minority families, it is important that researchers gather information not only about wages or yearly income, but also about money or services (e.g., welfare, public housing, disability, etc.). It is also important that researchers gather information about household size for calculating the family income, and whether or not family incomes are below the poverty line. According to Entwisle and Astone (1994), "a family of four, for example, in 1990 would be judged below the poverty line if income was $12,293 or less" (p. 1527). The official poverty line is revised annually, and is also used by schools for determining whether low-SES children qualify for free meal programs. However, as commented by Hauser (1994), the poverty line measure is a dated official measure of poverty based on "a minimum cost family diet developed by the Department of Agriculture in the middle 1950s . . . [which is] just three times the food budget updated to current dollars" (p. 1544). However, current families below the poverty level find housing to be more expensive than food and have to pay about 10 percent of their earnings in taxes which did not occur during the 1950s. Thus, Hauser recommended not using the official poverty line as a measure of SES, but instead using family income and the number of children and adults in the family.

Entwisle and Astone and Hauser recommended that subsidized meals at school should not be used as SES measures, because "very crude measurements of income and family size are used to determine eligibility for school lunch programs" (p. 1544). Entwisle and Astone explained this as follows: "Full subsidy is provided if the student's household income is 130% or less of poverty level, partial subsidy is provided for those with family income of 131% to 180% of poverty level" (p. 613). *Human capital* was defined by Entswisle and Astone as the nonmaterial resources that parents can provide for their children, which is connected with the parental educational levels, especially the mothers', which is highly correlated with the fathers' educational levels—for instance, the parents' educational values and expectations and their levels of English language proficiency, literacy skills, and academically related knowledge that can assist children with their homework.

Social capital was defined by Entwisle and Astone (1994) as the social network that the children's parents can make available, "which represents the resources embodied in social relationships; we recommend using measure of household and family structure" (p. 1527). The indicators that are recommended by Entwisle and Astone as measures of household structure are "how each household member is related to the child . . . number of birth parents in the home, [and] . . . whether there is a stepparent [or grandparent] in the home" (p. 1527). Parents can act as mentors or advocates for children, as well as cultural mediators within the larger social environment—for instance, parents' resourcefulness for finding help and support from social institutions for solving family problems (e.g., mother–child health care programs from federal or state programs for poor families).

Given the complexity of measuring the SES family background, the use of indicators of financial, human, and social capital may be a very useful, productive, and interesting way of gathering and categorizing SES data in language-minority children. This author has conducted many previous experimental studies (e.g., Felix-Holt & Gonzalez, 1999; Gonzalez, & Oviedo, 2000; Gonzalez et al., 1996) with first-, second-, and third-generation Mexican American bilingual and monolingual children from low-SES backgrounds in the southwest region of the United States (primarily Texas and Arizona). In these studies, the children that were identified as gifted by teachers, parents, and evaluators tended to come from households with only scarce financial capital but that were abundant in human and social forms of capital. These minority, low-SES children had only their basic needs met (i.e., food, clothing, and housing), but their family environments were very well structured and supportive of their educational needs.

The most important component of the human capital present in these minority gifted-children's parents is the emotionally stable and safe family environment. In a case study paper, this issue of emotionally stable family environments has been discussed (Clark & Gonzalez, 1998). Parents are able to create an atmosphere of security in the home, which helps minority, gifted children develop a strong self-concept, high self-esteem, and a minority cultural identity. Many of these minority parents may or may not be acculturated to mainstream U.S. culture, and therefore to the dominant school culture. However, they do have a strong minority cultural identity and social Spanish language proficiency, functioning as strong role models for their children's healthy identity and language development in the minority culture and language.

In relation to SES measures, these gifted minority children tend to come from two-parent households, in which the father is employed in a blue-collar position, the mother is the primary caretaker of the children (she may function as a housewife or may be a part-time blue-collar worker), they have three or fewer siblings, and parents offer emotional support for their children's development. These Hispanic parents most often are mono-lingual and have educational backgrounds limited to elementary school or uncompleted high school (usually in Mexico), but they instill in their children the value of achieving a higher educational level as a means to improve the children's adult lives and provide a bet-ter SES for their grandchildren. These parents also have an interest in communicating in the school environment; they may attend English classes or literacy programs in the com-munity or in their children's schools. Even though these minority parents do not have previous experience with the mainstream school culture, they are interested in learning academic skills, so that they can support their children's educational efforts. Thus, these minority parents do function as mentors and advocates for their children, serving as human and social forms of capital for stimulating their children's development.

Using the criteria proposed by Coleman (1988, cited in Entwisle & Astone, 1994) to interpret the conclusions reached by Garcia Coll in her critical literature review (1990), it can be shown that human and financial capital are central factors in explaining the development of minority infants and young children (from birth to three years of age). After conducting a thorough review of the literature, Garcia Coll concluded that studies have shown the existence of "5 major sources of influence on the developmental outcome of minority infants . . . cultural beliefs and caregiving practices [developmen-tal goals and interaction], health status and health care practices [of some minority groups in general], family structure and characteristics, socioeconomic factors, and bio-logical factors" (p. 270). She explained the "at-risk" health care condition of minority children as the result of social and cultural factors present in African Americans, Native Americans, and some groups of Asian Americans and Hispanics. After a thorough review of the literature, Garcia Coll recognized that the most important factor was "the under-utilization of health services, especially general preventive care, due to socioeco-nomic, linguistic, and cultural barriers" (p. 275). In relation to the health condition of minority infants, she recognized an interaction between biological and external condi-tions, with more weight on cultural and SES factors. For instance, neurodevelopmen-tal problems, for which premature minority infants are biologically at risk, are compounded, or are much more likely to surface, when children are reared in below-poverty-line households (a social at-risk condition). However, there are family-structure factors in some minority families, such as the presence of an extended family bringing meaningful interaction, with mediators or mentors for the mother and child, that may increase the resiliency of these biologically at-risk minority infants. Garcia Coll pro-posed the need for research to examine "family processes . . . as a function of different structures, functional arrangements, and compositions" (p. 278).

In sum, Entwisle and Astone (1994) recommended that researchers use multiple measures of SES factors in young children, because this social construct is multidi-mensional in nature and includes the mother's educational level, the income of the household, and the three measures of household structure explained previously. More-over, Hauser (1994) stated, based on results of previous studies of the educational attain-ment of brothers and sisters (Hauser & Featherman, 1976, cited in Hauser, 1994), "that even a complete and carefully measured set of social background characteristics will not account for more than about half the resemblance between siblings" (p. 1545). He cau-tioned researchers about the complexity of the measurement of SES family levels, as he stated, "A standard set of racial/ethnic and socioeconomic variables, however well mea-sured, cannot serve as all-purpose statistical controls for family background" (p. 1545).

Studies of Biologically At-Risk, Minority, Low-SES Children   Bradley, White-side, Casey, Kelleher, and Pope (1994) studied the effect of the quality of the caregiving environment on a large sample of biologically at-risk minority infants (premature and with low birth weight) from predominantly African American (70% of the sample), and Hispanic (29%) ethnicities. These researchers concluded that "children, who showed early signs of resiliency, differed from non-resilient children in that they were receiving more responsive, accepting, stimulating, and organized care. They were also living in safer, less crowded homes" (p. 346).

Bradley, Whiteside, and Mundfrom (1994) generated a cumulative protection index encompassing six aspects of caregiving, resulting in resilience as a multidimen-sional outcome:

1. Density of household
2. Provision of a safe play area for exploration and privacy
3. High levels of acceptance of the child's behavior by caretakers
4. Presence of learning materials
5. Variety of stimulation
6. Responsivity of caregivers

Thus, the social and physical conditions present in the home environment were related to the quality and quantity of stimulation and support available to a child. However, the child's individual psychological characteristics were also important fac-tors in how caregivers responded and in the level of acceptance they displayed when interacting with the child. That is, more resilient children "tend to have fewer habits that distress their parents during infancy . . . [and] temperamental characteristics that elicit positive attention" (Bradley et al., 1994, p. 351). In addition to individual psy-chological differences in resilient children, other cultural, linguistic, and SES factors interactively influence patterns of parenting. That is, as stated by Bradley, Whiteside, and Mundfrom (1994), "The quality of the home environment is not uniform across families living in poverty" (p. 347), "which may serve as a protective mechanism" (p. 348). According to Rutter (1987, cited in Bradley et al., 1994) these ecological fac-tors may function as protective mechanisms for biologically at-risk, minority children because of their association with "reduction of risk impact . . . [and of] negative chain reactions, . . . establishment and maintenance of [adequate and strong] self-esteem and self-efficacy [through secure attachments with caretakers], and . . . opening opportunities" (p. 357).

Findings of the study of Bradley, Whiteside, and Mundfrom (1994) showed that it was highly probable that a biologically at-risk, minority child will show signs of resiliency only when at least three protective aspects were present in his or her environment. Other individual factors in a small number of children, such as excellent perinatal health, and in very few parents, such as high maternal intelligence level, also offered some protection to biologically at-risk, minority children. The maternal intelligence level was measured using the Peabody Picture Vocabulary Test (PPVT), a very discrete point standardized test that only measures vocabulary knowledge (not the complex construct of intelligence), and is, therefore, not valid for use with minority populations—hence, another methodological flaw in the measurement of the variables of this study.

In the study of Bradley, Whiteside and Mundfrom (1994), only 10 percent of the biologically at-risk, minority children appeared to be resilient at ages twelve and thirty-six months. As these reasearchers stated, "The serious impact of the 'double jeopardy' accruing to the combination of prematurity and poverty was clear in evidence" (p. 357). Some limitations in the validity of measures used for the construct of resiliency show the presence of methodological flaws in this study, and thus bias the findings. These researchers defined *resiliency* as "cognitive competence, behavioral competence, health status, and growth status" (p. 351), and in order for a child to be considered resilient, he or she had to function "in acceptable ranges for *all* four health/developmental areas at 3 years of age" (p. 351). A score of at least 85 in the Stanford-Binet intelligence scale was required for a child to be considered resilient in the developmental area of cognitive competence. This standardized test of intelligence is highly loaded with mainstream cultural content, which primarily measures knowledge level of school content. The bias of this measure is very well represented in the following reported result: The percentage of minority children not qualifying to be considered resilient based on this measure alone was higher, than based on their performance in any other criteria (p. 355).

Moreover, Garcia Coll (1990) also suggested that cultural beliefs, values, and ideologies held by minority parents are also expressed in the following ways:

1. The developmental goals they have for their infants
2. Their perceptions and reactions to their infant's cues, behaviors, and demands
3. "The hierarchy of goals that parents follow in their interactions with their infants [such as] physical health and survival . . . behavioral capacities for economic self maintenance, . . . and behavioral capacities for maximizing other cultural values" (as proposed by Levine, 1977, cited in Garcia Coll, 1990, p. 271).

Other factors that may affect parental interactions with infants were suggested by Field and Widmayer's study (1981, cited in Garcia Coll, 1990), such as level of acculturation, social prestige of the minority group within the society at large, and the specific ethnic group or subcultural group represented in the parental values (e.g., Puerto Rican mothers were found to act differently than Cuban and South American mothers).

Garcia Coll highlighted the important role of the external cultural environment, as represented in the family context within different ethnic groups and subcultures, on how young minority children canalized their potentials and interacted with the environment. Following Sameroff and Chandler (1975, cited in Garcia Coll, 1990), Garcia

Coll emphasized "the multifactorial nature of early development and the dynamic aspects of the transactions between the child and the immediate caregiving environment" (p. 271). She recognized the presence of cultural differences in the timing, intensity, and context of developmental outcomes in young minority children that are sensitive to cultural factors, such as emotional processes. However, she also recognized the presence of universals in the occurrence of certain developmental milestones and patterns that are very resistant to the effect of environmental factors, such as motor and other physical maturational skills. Therefore, cultural and environmental factors can interact to produce both individual and group differences within minority children, which can be expressed in subtle aspects of more sensitive emotional processes and intermediately sensitive cognitive and language processes.

Garcia Coll (1990) asserted that researchers studying minority infants confounded ethnic differences with SES factors and used the majority literature as a framework for comparing developmental outcomes in minority infants, resulting in major methodological flaws. She emphasized that these studies viewed diversity as deficiencies and, therefore, recommended remedial actions without taking into account the confounding effects of not differentiating between ethnicity and social class. These studies, she asserted, also failed to account for sampling biases and cross-sectional designs and did not recognize the lack of validity of the instruments used to measure variables and the biases brought to the study by the evaluators. According to Garcia Coll, most of these studies also used single measures of variables, did not systematically study parental cultural beliefs and goals, and did not take into account the cultural context of parental behaviors when interacting with their children. Thus, she recommended that researchers conduct longitudinal studies with the use of multiple measures of developmental or internal variables, as well as of SES external variables that occur across minority and mainstream environmental contexts. That is, researchers need to acknowledge and reflect in their methodologies that minority children live between two cultural worlds.

Garcia Coll found that studies of the minority family context in Hispanics and African Americans were "characterized by younger mothers, a higher percentage of single heads of households, but also large, extended families" (p. 270). She proposed that these diverse cultural contexts in minority children's families would also result in exposure to "different patterns of social and affective interactions, . . . learning experiences . . . [resulting] in the acquisition of different modes of communication . . . , different means of exploring their environment, and the development of alternative cognitive skills" (p. 274).

In sum, when studying biologically at-risk, minority children, it is important that researchers take into account ecological or external factors stemming from the cultural and family environments that surround these children. Special attention needs to be given to low-SES backgrounds, which are related to socialization patterns used by parents, and nontraditional family structures and diverse cultural family contexts. It is also important that research methodologies differentiate among ethnicity, culture, and social class.

Studies of Socioeconomically At-Risk, Minority Children

Walker, Greenwood, Hart, and Carta (1994) reported a longitudinal study of thirty-two low-SES, minority children (Hispanics and African Americans, representing 47% of the sample) and thirty-two majority children who were administered measures of language development and academic achievement from kindergarten through the third grade. These researchers reported that "nineteen percent of the sample lived at or below the national poverty level . . . [and] almost half of the children attended schools serving low-income families" (p. 608). They also measured three variables related to SES factors: parental educational levels, annual family incomes, and types of employment. Using these indicators, they formed a composite index by ranking each child on these three variables.

As with most of the previously discussed studies, the study by Walker et al. (1994) also has some methodological flaws. These were due to the following:

1. Confounding the effect of ethnicity and SES, because subject grouping was based only on low-SES factors
2. An invalid measure of intellectual ability (the Stanford-Binet test), receptive and spoken language (the PPVT), and student ability (Ottis-Lenon School Abilities Test) for low-SES, minority children
3. Researchers merely stating that "the first language of all children was English" (p. 608) without providing any valid measure of first- and second-language proficiency for the minority children as proof of this "assumed proficiency," which resulted in the confounding effect of SES, ethnicity, and language-minority status

These researchers found two trends in their data:

1. Children's differences in SES were also reflected in their differences in the intelligence quotient (IQ) on the Stanford-Binet test and in their spoken vocabulary, as measured by the PPVT.
2. The composite index of SES variables correlated significantly with the children's IQs.

Walker et al. (1994) attributed the differences found among the children "to SES-related factors and not specifically to their minority or cultural background" (p. 618). However, they did not measure how the cultural diversity of these minority children might have been expressed in culturally different ways in their language and cognitive development and academic achievement levels. Simply showing differences in standardized, mainstream measures of developmental abilities between minority and majority children does not mean that the same developmental constructs were measured in both groups. That is, the minority children performed at lower levels in the Stanford-Binet, PPVT, and Ottis-Lenon School Abilities Test, but this does not indicate that they actually had lower developmental levels or that minority children showed diverse functions in comparison to majority children. These results showed the methodological flaws, which occurred because of a lack of alternative measures that would have represented the cultural and linguistic backgrounds of the minority children. Just because these minority children showed some level of social English proficiency does not mean that they were academically proficient in English; nor does it show that they did not have different levels of acculturation and degrees of biculturalism in comparison with the majority children.

Duncan, Brooks-Gunn, and Kato (1994) studied the longitudinal impact of poverty on African American children's cognitive development and externalization of behavior problems. These researchers found that the duration of poverty had significant effects on children's development and that the detrimental effects were highly significant during both early infancy and early childhood stages. They found that "the effects of persistent poverty were roughly twice as large as the effects of transitional poverty" (p. 312) and that "the effects of poverty are cumulative" (p. 313).

There were some mediators, shown in this study, for the effect of poverty on children's development:

1. Neighborhood-based measures of economic resources, with low-income neighbors acting as significant predictors of externalizing behavior problems
2. Parental characteristics and behaviors, especially on the mother's side, such as amount and quality of time parents spent with their children (i.e., the affective relationship between child and parent), aspects of the home learning environment (i.e., level of stimulation, physical environment), and the emotional and mental health of the parents (i.e., coping strategies and depression)

Duncan et al. (1994) concluded that the most important factor predicting children's cognitive development was family income, which is mediated by maternal characteristics and behaviors related to being able to psychologically cope with poverty. That is, poor children not only suffer from lack of educational resources in their home learning and neighborhood environments, but also indirectly suffer the detrimental psychological effects of poverty on their parents' behaviors and mental health. These researchers explained that "the apparent effects of female headship on child cognition are due mostly to the lower family incomes of female-headed families" (p. 313).

In sum, throughout the preceding sections on biologically and economically at-risk minority children, research studies have shown the tremendous importance of mediating family factors on developmental outcomes. The presence of mentors for guiding the development of at-risk, minority children is a very powerful buffer, leading to possible resilience, even when children are biologically at risk. When measuring SES factors, researchers must include family-structure characteristics (e.g., parental educational levels and occupations, parental mental health, number of siblings, etc.), which have been proved by research to influence early childhood development.

Summary

When conducting research on the relationship between advanced cognition and bilingualism, researchers need to be very critical about possible methodological flaws in their designs that are due to invalid measures of variables (i.e., first- and second-language proficiency, language dominance, cognitive development, SES). In addition, researchers need to take into account the interactional effect of internal psychological and external ecological variables that affect the development of young, minority, poor children. Thus, in research, we need to move to multidimensional designs that control for individual differences and the confounding effect of external factors in diverse children.

In terms of educationally practical implications, it can be concluded that we need to use multiple measures when assessing culturally and linguistically diverse students. These batteries of assessment need to include alternative measures that take into account the interaction of external sociocultural and internal or psychological factors. Special attention needs to be given to the fact that most language-minority students come from low-SES backgrounds. As the literature review discussed throughout this chapter attests, language-minority children suffer from a double jeopardy of poverty and not having protective mechanisms in their social and family environments.

Thus, using only traditional standardized tests confounds the effect of social class, poverty, and the negative impact of external social problems with deficiencies in language-minority, poor children. In fact, children who come from diverse SES, ethnic, cultural, and linguistic backgrounds also present diversity in their developmental and learning patterns. That is why educators and evaluators cannot compare the performance of poor, language-minority children with the performance of middle and upper class, mainstream children by using standardized tests. These traditional tests assess the effect of confounding external factors on language-minority children, not the constructs they were designed to measure in mainstream students. (For further discussion of this topic, see Gonzalez, 1998; Gonzalez and Yawkey, 1993; and Gonzalez et al., 1997.)

In addition, these batteries of assessment also need to have a longitudinal approach in order to link assessment with instruction. Classroom teachers and parents also need to be included as key players in interdisciplinary assessment teams. In this manner, the performance of language-minority, poor children should be evaluated across social and cultural contexts. Moreover, this longitudinal and interdisciplinary assessment process should be completed by different informants, because the external and internal constructs measured are very complex by nature. For example, the construct of poverty is complex because, as reviewed in this chapter, research has demonstrated that the duration and degree of poverty has a significant effect on minority children's development and learning outcomes.

Finally, the mediational effects of the presence or absence of scaffolding family and social environments may result in (1) assisting the child to cope with at-risk situations and become resilient, such as the potential giftedness examined in this chapter; or (2) a negative impact on the child's development and learning, with underachievement as an outcome. Thus, in educational practice, we need to move to alternative assessment and instructional paradigms that respect individual, social, cultural, and linguistic differences.

REFERENCES

AERA, APA, NCME (1985). *Standards for educational and psychological testing* (pp. 9–23, 73–87). Washington, DC: American Psychological Association.

Bialystock, E. (1991). Introduction. In E. Bialystock (Ed.), *Language processing in bilingual children* (pp. 1–9). Cambridge: Cambridge University Press.

Bialystock, E., & Cummins, J. (1991). Language, cognition, and education of bilingual children. In E. Bialystock (Ed.), *Language processing in bilingual children* (pp. 222–232). Cambridge: Cambridge University Press.

Bradley, R. H., Whiteside, L. Y., Mundfrom, D. J. (1994). Early indications of resilience and their relation to experiences in the home environments of low-birth-weight, premature children living in poverty. *Child Development, 65,* 346–360.

Clark, E. R., & Gonzalez, V. (1998). *Voces* and voices: Cultural and linguistic giftedness. *Educational Horizons*, 77 (1), 41–47.

Cummins, J. (1976). The influence of bilingualism on cognitive growth: A synthesis of research findings and explanatory hypotheses. *Working Papers on Bilingualism*, 9, 1–43.

Cummins, J. (1978). Bilingualism and the development of metalinguistic awareness. *Journal of Cross-Cultural Psychology*, IX (2), 131–149.

Diaz, R. M. (1985). Bilingual cognitive development: Addressing three gaps in current research. *Child Development*, 56, 1376–1388.

Diaz, R. M., & Klingler, D. (1991). Towards an exploratory model of the interaction between bilingualism and cognitive development. In E. Bialystock (Ed.), *Language processing in bilingual children* (pp. 167–192). Cambridge: Cambridge University Press.

Diaz, R. M., & Padilla, K. A. (1985). *The self-regulatory speech of bilingual preschoolers*. Paper presented at the April Meeting of the Society for Research in Child Development, Toronto, Canada.

Duncan, G. J., Brooks-Gunn, J., & Kato, P. K. (1994). Economic deprivation and early childhood development. *Child Development*, 65, 296–318.

Entwisle, D. R., & Astone, N. M. (1994). Some practical guidelines for measuring youth's race/ethnicity and socioeconomic status. *Child Development*, 65, 1521–1540.

Felix-Holt, M., & Gonzalez, V. (1999). Alternative assessment models of language-minority children: Is there a match with teachers' attitudes and instruction? In V. Gonzalez (Vol. Ed.), *Language and cognitive development in second language learning: Educational implications for children and adults* (pp. 190–226). Boston: Allyn & Bacon.

Garcia Coll, C. T. (1990). Developmental outcome of minority infants: A process-oriented look into our beginnings. *Child Development*, 61, 270–289.

Gonzalez, V. (1991). *A model of cognitive, cultural, and linguistic variables affecting bilingual Spanish/English children's development of concepts and language*. Doctoral Dissertation. Austin, Texas: The University of Texas at Austin. (ERIC Document Reproduction Service No. ED 345 562).

Gonzalez, V. (1995). *Cognition, culture, and language in bilingual children: Conceptual and semantic development*. Bethesda, MD: Austin & Winfield.

Gonzalez, V. (1994). A model of cognitive, cultural, and linguistic variables affecting bilingual Hispanic children's development of concepts and language. *Hispanic Journal of Behavioral Sciences*, 16 (4), 396–421.

Gonzalez, V., Bauerle, P., Black, W., & Felix-Holt, M. (1999). Influence of evaluators' beliefs and cultural-linguistic backgrounds on their diagnostic and placement decisions for language-minority children. In V. Gonzalez (Vol. Ed.), *Language and cognitive development in second language learning: Educational implications for children and adults* (pp. 269–297). Boston: Allyn & Bacon.

Gonzalez, V., Bauerle, P., & Felix-Holt, M. (1994). A qualitative assessment method for accurately diagnosing bilingual gifted children. *NABE Annual Conference Journal 1992–1993*, 37–52. Washington, DC: NABE.

Gonzalez, V., Bauerle, P., & Felix-Holt, M. (1996). Theoretical and practical implications of assessing cognitive and language development in bilingual children with qualitative methods. *Bilingual Research Journal*, 20 (1), 93–131.

Gonzalez, V., Brusca-Vega, R., & Yawkey, T. D. (1997). *Assessment and instruction of culturally and linguistically diverse students with or at-risk of learning problems: From research to practice*. Boston: Allyn & Bacon.

Gonzalez, V., & Clark, E. R. (1999). *Folkloric* and *historic* views of giftedness in language-minority children. In V. Gonzalez (Vol. Ed.), *Language and cognitive development in second language learning: Educational implications for children and adults* (pp. 1–18). Boston: Allyn & Bacon.

Gonzalez, V., Clark, E. R., & Bauerle, P. (February, 2000). *A validated model for the identification of gifted bilingual students*. Invited paper presented at the Research and Evaluation SIG, NABE 29th Annual International Conference, San Antonio, TX.

Gonzalez, V., & Felix-Holt, M. (1995). Influence of evaluators' prior academic knowledge on the diagnosis of cognitive and language development in bilingual Hispanic kindergartners. *New York State Association for Bilingual Education (NYSABE) Journal*, 10 (1), 34–45.

Gonzalez, V., & Oviedo. M. D. (February, 2000). *Family structure effects on the cognitive development of Hispanic children referred for giftedness evaluation*. In L. Malavé, V. Gonzalez, J. Castellano, B. Irby, & R. Lara-Alecio, *Current research policy and applications: Gifted and talented students*. Invited symposium conducted at the Gifted and Talented Special Interest Group (SIG), NABE 29th Annual International Conference, San Antonio, TX.

Gonzalez, V., Oviedo, M. D., & O'Brien de Ramirez, K. (April, 2000). Developmental, SES, and linguistic factors affecting bilingual and monolingual children's cognitive performance. In V. Gonzalez, R. Lara-Alecio, & B. Irby, *Developmental and assessment issues in bilingual Hispanic children referred for potential giftedness*. Symposium presented at the AERA Annual Meeting, Bilingual Education Research Special Interest Group (SIG), New Orleans, LA.

Gonzalez, V., & Yawkey, T. (1993). The assessment of culturally and linguistically diverse students: Celebrating change. *Educational Horizons, 72* (1), 41–49.

Hakuta, K. (1986). *Mirror of language: The debate on bilingualism*. New York: Basic Books.

Hakuta, K., & Diaz, R. M. (1985). The relationship between degree of bilingualism and cognitive ability: A critical discussion and some new longitudinal data. In K. E. Nelson (Ed.), *Children's language* (Vol. V.) Hillsdale, NY: Lawrence Erlbaum Associates.

Harley, B., Cummins, J., Swain, M., & Allen, P. (1990). The nature of language proficiency. In B. Harley, P. Allen, J. Cummins, & M. Swain (Eds.), *The development of second language proficiency* (pp. 7–25). Cambridge: Cambridge University Press.

Hauser, R. M. (1994). Measuring socioeconomic status in studies of child development. *Child Development, 65*, 1541–1545.

Lambert, W. E., & Tucker, G. R. (1972). *Bilingual education of children: The St. Lambert experiment*. Rowley, MA: Newbury House.

McLaughlin, B. (1990). The relationship between first and second languages: Language proficiency and language aptitude. In B. Harley, P. Allen, J. Cummins, & M. Swain (Eds.), *The development of second language proficiency* (pp. 158–174). Cambridge: Cambridge University Press.

Oller, J. W., Jr. (1991). Language testing research: Lessons applied to LEP students and programs. Paper conducted at the *First Research Symposium on Limited English Proficient Students' Issues: Focus on Evaluation and Measurement*. Washington DC: Office of Bilingual Education and Minority Languages Affairs, U.S. Department of Education.

Oller, J. W., Jr. & Damico, J. S. (1991). Theoretical considerations in the assessment of LEP students. In E. V. Hamayan & J. S. Damico (Eds.), *Limiting bias in the assessment of bilingual students* (pp. 77–110). Austin, TX: Pro-Ed.

Oviedo, M. D., & Gonzalez, V. (1999). Case study comparisons of standardized and alternative assessments: Diagnoses accuracy in minority children. In V. Gonzalez (Vol. Ed.), *Language and cognitive development in second language learning: Educational implications for children and adults* (pp. 227–268). Boston: Allyn & Bacon.

Peal, E., & Lambert, W. E. (1962). The relation of bilingualism to intelligence. *Psychological Monographs, 76*, 1–23.

Rogoff, B., & Chavajay, P. (1995). What's become of research on the cultural basis of cognitive development? *American Psychologist, 50* (10), 859–877.

Skutnabb-Kangas, T., & Toukomaa, P. (1976). *Teaching migrant children's mother tongue and learning the language of the host country in context of the sociocultural situation of the migrant family*. Helsinki: The Finnish National Commission for UNESCO.

Torrance, E. P., Gowan, J. W., & Aliohi, N. C. (1970). Creative functioning of monolingual and bilingual children in Singapore. *Journal of Educational Psychology, 61*, 72–75.

Vygotsky, L. S. (1962). *Thought and language*. Cambridge, MA: M.I.T. Press.

Walker, D., Greenwood, C., Hart, B., & Carta, J. (1994). Prediction of school outcomes based on early language production and socioeconomic factors. *Child Development, 65*, 606–621.

4

Voice and Validation

Creativity and Bilingualism

**JO ANN ROBISHEAUX AND
MARY M. BANBURY**

Stanley Prusiner, a maverick American scientist who for two decades endured derision from his peers as he tried to prove that bizarre infectious proteins could cause brain diseases such as "mad cow disease" in people and animals, Monday was awarded the ultimate in scientific vindication: the Nobel Prize in Physiology or Medicine. Until Prusiner came along no one knew that simple proteins could reproduce themselves as though they were alive. Indeed, the concept was so revolutionary that he was shunned as a man who had overreached the limits of sensibility.

> "It's terrific," said David Baltimore, the Massachusetts Institute of Technology immunologist and 1975 Nobel laureate, who for years counted himself among Prusiner's doubters. "These are the mythological stories of science-people who have really kept their own faith for so many years and lived through a period of opprobrium and finally are discovered to be right," Baltimore said. "Stories like these are not that common, but they provide an important lesson for young people in science: They say 'Be true to yourself.' " (Weiss, 1997, p. A–4)

This short passage from a newspaper article entitled, "Heretical Scientist Awarded Nobel," captures the essence of a creative personality. The objective of this chapter is to argue the point that the creative personality (as illustrated in the introductory quote) is very similar to the successful bilingual personality. It is our position that an individual's creativity supports his or her bilingualism and that an individual's bilingualism in turn nurtures his or her creativity. Therefore, the purpose of this chapter is twofold: first, to argue a causative relationship between creativity and balanced bilingualism, and, second, to give our fellow educators ideas about how to encourage creativity among students acquiring a second language.

This chapter begins with explanations and descriptions of how the characteristics of creativity mesh with the characteristics of bilingualism. We then move on to definitions of the levels of bilingualism as well as definitions of creativity. Following these definitions, we argue the point that there is a synergism between bilingualism and creativity. The chapter concludes with several suggestions for teaching strategies that can be used in helping second-language students access their creativity in order to reach the highest levels of bilingualism. This chapter is not intended to be a comprehensive review of the literature on creativity or bilingualism, but to explore the possibilities of an existing synergism between the two.

The Interface of Creativity and Bilingualism

According to Tardiff and Sternberg's (1988, pp. 435–436) review of the literature, the most frequently cited characteristics of creative individuals are the following:

- Risk taking
- Willingness to confront antagonism, ability to freely reject external limits and rules, and propensity for self-organization
- Perserverance, total absorption, focus, discipline, commitment
- Curiosity, inquisitiveness
- Openness to new experiences, deep emotions, and growth
- High intrinsic motivation

These characteristics are precisely those evident in successful bilingual individuals. In order to master a second language, an individual must be a risk taker. Only risk takers will venture forth into a foreign community and try out the new language. These risk takers are open to new experiences and are not primarily concerned with whether they will look foolish when they try on their new language, but whether they can communicate with members of the new language group.

Individuals desiring to become bilingual must have high intrinsic motivation in order to persevere. After the first few easily acquired language features are mastered, learners then face the challenges of precise vocabulary and grammar. Perseverance makes the difference between a person who speaks the second language like a tourist and one who speaks the second language like a native. Likewise, curiosity and inquisitiveness support fluent bilingualism. Truly bilingual people are anxious to learn idiomatic phrases and cultural references that will help them to master both languages.

Personal attributes that influence creative behavior, however, should also be viewed within context of the individual's environment and his or her social and cultural context. Csikszentmihalyi (1988) believes that creativity is a dynamic circular interaction among three systems: (1) the creative individual, (2) the cultural domain or symbol system, and (3) the social institution, the field, or social organization of the domain.

Figure 4.1 is one way to represent the dynamic interactive relationship of Csikszentmihalyi's work.

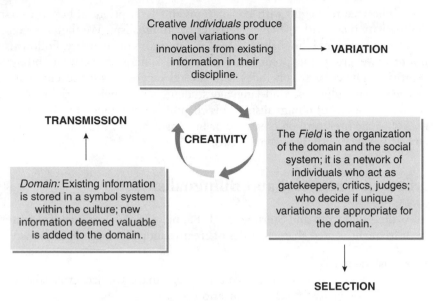

FIGURE 4.1   Csikszentmihalyi's Theory.

This dialectal process is complex, time-consuming, and generative. For example, Nobel Prize winner Stanley Prusiner inherited knowledge from the domain of science about infectious agents containing genetic material. He recognized gaps in existing knowledge, redefined problems, and discovered a novel variation—"simple infectious proteins could reproduce themselves as if they were alive." At first, other scientists in the field considered this hypothesis heretical; they rejected and derided him. Prusiner prevailed, however, and twenty years later, his research was validated by the highest authority in the field—the Nobel committee. His work, which has now been transmitted to, included in, and accepted by the scientific culture, is stimulating new research in Alzheimer's disease and other neurodegenerative syndromes. According to Csikszentmihalyi, "The model represents a cycle in the process of cultural evolution . . . " "variation, selection, and transmissions are the three main phases of the cycle" (p. 333), and creativity is the catalyst.

Likewise, in bilingual individuals, the domain is the interaction of the first and second languages, and the field is the culture of native speakers of the languages. When the bilingual speakers formulate language, they produce individually novel variations or innovations from their existing cognitive information by creating an interaction among the languages. Then, a positive reaction from the native speakers causes the bilingual speakers to store the new information as an addendum to the growing symbol system of the new language.

Csikszentmihalyi's system's view of creativity provided the framework for the lens Howard Gardner (1993a) used in *Creating Minds* to examine the lives of seven creative individuals, each of whom exemplified one of the seven intelligences detailed in his earlier theory of Multiple Intelligences. Using a rubric with the headings "Individual Level," "Domain Level," and "Field" to guide his "anatomy of creativity," Gardner explores and examines the major characteristics, forces, and influences throughout the life of a creator; in particular, he probes the relationships among the talented individual, other persons, and the creative work. He also posits his own definition of a creative individual as "a person who regularly solves problems, fashions products, or defines new questions in a domain in a way that is initially considered novel but that ultimately becomes accepted in a particular cultural setting" (p. 35).

Gardner's rubric may be used to research and analyze creative individuals within a particular culture. For example, startling glimmers of the life of Luis J. Rodriguez, poet, author, and peacemaker, are introduced in Bullard's (1993) interview " Una Vida de Esperanza." At the "Individual Level," Rodriguez was a child who did not speak English. Forsaken and belittled by the school system, he initiated a club for protection against teens with guns and was labeled a troublemaker. As a teen-ager, barred from society by racial, economic, and linguistic barriers, he joined a street gang and engaged in criminal acts. Then a crystallizing experience occurred; he met Chente, a Chicano community activist, a mentor, and Rodriguez discovered his "voice." The mature Rodriguez reflects, "After having been silent for so long and then finding a voice, once I found it, I realized how powerful language was. It practically saved my life. I needed to have my story told and my life validated. I found poetry" (p. 14).

Luis Rodriguez survived and his spirit prevailed in spite of his experiences in the school system, a deprecating environment that stifled his creativity and demeaned his culture. In his words:

> Schools should be places where kids are allowed to be expressive. I found I could not study or learn within school structure, but I was very curious. I learned a lot on my own. I did drawings, paintings, even writing. I think there are a lot of kids like myself who drop out because they can't function within the system. There have to be other ways in which they can be given some validity, be allowed to develop and grow and use their natural sense of curiosity to learn. The schools need to find ways to really connect with young people again. (Bullard, 1993, p. 14)

For Luis Rodriguez, the problem was compounded. Because school personnel did not recognize his creative behaviors or understand his cultural ones, they were not able to use his culture, language, or experiences to assist him to adjust, learn, and thrive. As Sternberg (1988b) notes, "A potentially creative individual may wither in an environment that does not foster, or that actively inhibits, a display of creative behavior" (p. 146). As Maker, Nielson, and Rogers (1994) urge, "The cultural and linguistic diversity of this country needs to be honored, valued, and represented in our special programs for gifted students, but unless significant changes occur, this will not be possible" (p. 5). For these significant changes to occur, it is imperative that educators understand both creativity and bilingualism: definitions, characteristics, and implications for the teaching/learning process.

Definitions of Bilingualism

The term *bilingual* is often used to identify a person who is able to speak two languages. In everyday conversation, this term may be sufficient, but in linguistics, the word *bilingual* gives an incomplete description of what a person's language abilities truly are. For example, language is made up of four basic areas: listening, speaking, reading, and writing. Many students who study foreign languages in secondary schools find themselves proficient in reading and writing the language but unable to understand the oral language of anyone except their teachers. Producing the language in a free-flowing verbal form is perhaps the most difficult skill of all. Conversely, people who grow up speaking a language other than English in their homes and communities find that they have great facility in listening and speaking but very few skills in writing (especially standard spelling) and reading.

It is inaccurate, then, to term both types of bilinguals equally. Can students be considered bilingual if they haven't mastered all of the language arts? Furthermore, what about Cummins' (1984) idea of cognitive competence in a language? Schooling requires students to use language to reason and to communicate that reasoning. Because this chapter deals specifically with the relationship between bilingualism and creativity, cognition is included as a fifth area of language.

Therefore, more descriptive terms are necessary to label a person who is "bilingual." Cummins (1984) uses the term *incipient bilingualism*, which refers to speakers with a minimal competence in a second language, such as beginning second-language students or tourists. Bilinguals who tend to be dominant in one of their languages are referred to as *dominant bilinguals*. These are individuals who may exhibit second-language fluency in some areas of language but who have a natural preference for their native language. Typically, dominant bilinguals use their native language most of the time, and use the second language only when the situation calls for it.

The final term, *balanced bilinguals*, refers to a category of individuals who have equally developed competencies in both languages. This is the highest level of bilingualism and implies that individuals can move easily from one language to another in order to accomplish any language purpose. Whereas a dominant bilingual may be able to use a second language for most situations, only a balanced bilingual would be able to use the second language for cognitive functions.

To confound this point even further, it must be realized that an individual's level of bilingualism does not fall neatly into one of these three categories; rather, that bilingualism runs the gamut from incipient to balanced. This point becomes extremely important in any discussion of bilingualism and creativity. If one wants to investigate the level of creativity in a bilingual person, that person's level of bilingualism becomes a factor in the investigation.

In some of the seminal work in this field, Cummins (1975, 1977) found that balanced bilingual students were superior to other nonbalanced bilingual students on the fluency and flexibility scales of verbal divergence and were marginally superior in measures of originality. He also compared the scores of monolingual students with the balanced bilingual students and the nonbalanced bilingual students. The monolingual group scored at a level similar to that of the nonbalanced bilinguals and substantially lower than that of the balanced bilinguals. As a result of this study, Cummins (1977) noted that there may be a threshold level of linguistic competence that a bilingual child must attain to avoid cognitive deficits and to allow the potentially beneficial aspects of becoming bilingual to influence his cognitive growth (p. 10).

Cummins' work gave rise to the Bilingual Threshold Theory, which posits that competence in a second language below a certain threshold level may fail to give any cognitive benefits. Therefore, incipient and dominant bilingual students may fail to do well on tests of intelligence or creativity if the tests are given in their second language. Ricciardelli (1992) states that bilingual students must "achieve high levels of linguistic proficiency in both of their languages before bilingualism can promote cognitive development."

Definitions of Creativity

According to Csikszentmihalyi, creativity depends on the existence of and interactions among the domain (symbol system), the talented individual, and the field (social system). This is similar to Gardner's view of creativity, which includes novel problems, products, and questions in a domain that are eventually accepted by the culture. Amabile (1989) concurs with both of these theorists. She believes that a child's behaviors, performances, and products are creative if experts consider the products or ideas "novel" and "appropriate." In addition, she contends that the child is most likely to be creative when the following three components of creativity intersect: domain skills, creative thinking and working skills, and intrinsic motivation (Figure 4.2).

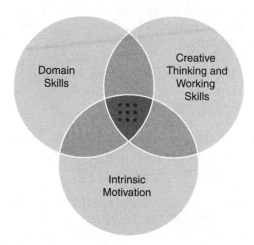

FIGURE 4.2   The Creativity Intersection.

Source: From *Growing Up Creative* (p. 63), by T. M. Amabile, 1989, Buffalo, NY: Creative Education Foundation. Reprinted with permission.

These theorists agree that creativity emerges from knowledge and experiences existing within a domain. Individuals cannot transform information unless they first possess innate or nurtured skills within a specific discipline, such as language arts, mathematics, science, social studies, art, music, sports, and so on. The literature (Sternberg, 1988a) also supports the belief that certain personality types are more predisposed to creative thinking, more willing to substitute, change, adapt, modify, put to other uses, eliminate, or rearrange existing forms and content. Finally, creativity occurs because creative people are intrinsically motivated; they "desire to do something for its own sake, because it is interesting, satisfying, or personally challenging" (Amabile, 1989, p. 50). A more in-depth examination of these characteristics of the creative personality and creative cognitive skills may assist in the identification and instruction of creative bilingual individuals.

Characteristics of the Creative Personality

Davis and Rimm (1998, pp. 36–38) synthesized the literature on personality characteristics of creative people and sorted these myriad traits into eight clusters. These clusters are used as a framework to describe and explain how these personality characteristics mesh with characteristics of bilingualism. These traits are discussed in the following sections.

Awareness of Creativity   When passing through customs, Oscar Wilde was once asked, "Do you have anything to declare?" Wilde responded, "Only my genius." Creative people, in particular adults and adolescents, are often aware of their creativity. Walberg's (1988, p. 356) biographical research with adolescents who won awards in science and art reveals that these high school students were "interested in and self confident of their own creativity and intelligence," and selected creativity more often than wealth and power as the "best characteristic to develop in life." Vygotsky (cited in Starko, 1995, pp. 40–41) suggests in his developmental theory that the linking of a child's imagination and creative play to purposeful thought and creative production begins in adolescence and reaches maturity in adulthood.

Confidence and Risk-Taking   Often described as individuals who "march to the tune of a different drummer" or as people who "push the envelope," creative people who are willing to take risks may do the following:

- Challenge assumptions, question transitions and status quo, express ideas or opinions that differ from those of their peers and authority figures
- Organize and participate in social causes, protests, or political actions
- Perform or exhibit original work
- Post novel ideas, theories, designs, or inventions to audiences or experts

For individuals who are becoming bilingual, the need for self-confidence and taking risks is tantamount to success. Fillmore (1985) described the social characteristics of successful child second-language acquirers as those who join a group and act as if they understand what's going on, even if they don't, and who give the impression that they can speak the language by using a few well-chosen words. Such social processes are the steps by which bilingual individuals create a social situation in which target language communication is possible and desired. Accomplishing such a social situation requires creativity.

High Energy and Adventurousness   Creative people tend to heed the adage, "If at first you don't succeed, try, try, again." They also adhere to Torrance's (1988, p. 68) suggestion: "Don't be afraid to 'fall in love' with something and pursue it with intensity (You will do best what you like to do the most.)" Creative individuals are

- Task oriented—if they select the task
- Internally controlled
- Intensely involved and able to persist over time in spite of obstacles, failure, lack of recognition, or reward
- Compelled to achieve or succeed

Curiosity   Even though creative people may have been told that "curiosity killed the cat," they believe that "information brought it back." Curious individuals

- Are open to new and varied ideas, experiences, feelings, actions, values, and aesthetics
- Question and inquire "Who? What? When? Where? Why? How?"
- Explore and examine subject areas more broadly and more in-depth
- Like to collect things and tend to have unique hobbies
- Are passionate about learning

Humor and Playfulness   Creative people understand Peter Pan's declaration, "I'll never grow up!" Freud (cited in Gardner, 1993a, p. 25) himself drew a parallel between creativity and the childlike nature of play. Creative individuals

- Like to play with ideas, words, and objects
- Enjoy playing with possibilities, wondering "What would happen if?"
- Possess a sense of humor, are open to zaniness; recognize absurdities and incongruities

The last characteristic is especially true of bilingual individuals. When acquiring a second language, learners are often struck by the humorous situations that could arise if words are mispronounced. For example *pescado–pecado* in Spanish (fish–sin) and *vowel–bowel* in English. Likewise, creative learners of English enjoy the use of puns and rhymes.

Idealism and Reflectiveness   Maslow (cited in Davis, 1992, p. 3) ties creativity to self-actualization. He notes that self-actualized people "have deep feelings of brotherhood with all mankind; are benevolent, altruistic, democratic, unprejudiced in the deepest possible sense." Creative people tend to be more sensitive to social issues and more open to viewing the world through someone else's eyes. They reflect on what they want to do and why they want to do it. They ponder their roles in the great scheme of things. Some believe that they can achieve the impossible: They are like the Queen in Alice in Wonderland, who said, "Why, sometimes I've believed as many as six impossible things before breakfast."

Alone Time   Creative people need some "thinking" time to themselves when they can reflect, contemplate, play with possibilities, produce, or solve problems. They immerse themselves in their inner worlds, focusing on creative production. They need to work alone.

Artistic and Aesthetic Interests   In artistic and aesthetic areas, creative individuals are the consumers as well as the producers. They are much more likely than noncreative persons to attend the ballet, opera, concert, or theater; to visit the art gallery, the museum, or the special exhibit on photography or sculpture; to turn the TV channel to Arts & Entertainment and to listen to National Public Radio. They take the scenic route through life, taking time to admire and enjoy the views, the performances, the people, the productions, and the events. Dacey (1989) identifies eight additional characteristics of the creative personality. He, however, maintains that "tolerance of ambiguity," the ability to operate within a loosely defined framework, is the trait that is most "vital to the creative process," and that the other seven contribute both to the existence of this trait and to its role in promoting creativity" (p. 18). Figure 4.3 depicts these relationships.

In a comic strip, two children are walking down a school hallway, consoling each other after an exam. One of them states, "Don't worry about it. Remember, life is not a true–false test." For the most part, life does not consist of clear convergent questions, situations, or problems with expected responses, exact rules, precise procedures, and right and wrong answers. Life presents "messy" situations that are often confusing and ambiguous; there are myriad problems, with divergent or open-ended questions, fuzzy areas, hidden agendas, and numerous possible solutions. "By its nature, creative problem solving involves considerable ambiguity . . . ideas will evolve from the original

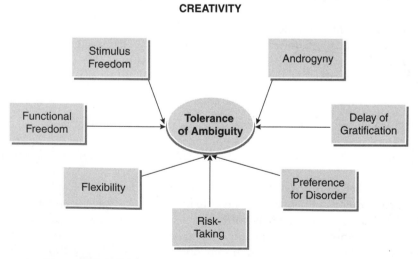

FIGURE 4.3   Personal Qualities and Creativity.

Source: From *Fundamentals of Creative Thinking* (p. 19), by J. S. Dacey, 1989, Lexington, MA: Lexington Books. Adapted by permission.

insight through a series of modifications, approximations, and improvements—which requires coping with uncertainty and ambiguity." (Davis, 1992, p. 77). The seven traits that contribute to tolerance of ambiguity are the following:

1. *Stimulus Freedom:* Realizing that there is more than one way to view a problem; the ability to break away from first impressions, response patterns, and traditional assumptions
2. *Functional Freedom:* Recognizing that objects may have multiple uses beyond their original purposes (e.g., how many uses can you think of for a hanger?)
3. *Flexibility:* Seeing all elements of the situation, points of view, or components of the problem; generates numerous categories of responses
4. *Risk Taking:* Taking chances—a trait that correlates highly with a penchant for open-ended situations
5. *Preference for Disorder:* Liking things that are more complex, chaotic, and asymmetrical, as opposed to preferring simplicity, starkness, everything in its place, and symmetry
6. *Delay of Gratification:* Willing to persevere, to remain committed to the task; able to confront failure or rejection; able to sustain intensity and action without a need for immediate success, acclamation, or reward
7. *Androgyny:* Exhibiting both male and female qualities; not bound by stereotypic gender responses

Dacey's model comes closest to replicating the personal qualities necessary for a successful balanced bilingual. To use a second language, speakers must realize that there is more than one way to view a problem. With stimulus freedom, a bilingual person can leave behind traditional assumptions about how language is used in culturally specific situations. Likewise, flexibility allows the bilingual person to see all culturally influenced points of view and to generate numerous responses to a stimulus. The qualities of risk taking and perseverance are discussed in other parts of this chapter.

Above all else, it is the bilingual individual's tolerance for ambiguity that most closely intersects with the traits of highly creative individuals. During the period in which the learner constructs an interlanguage (a language system that has a structurally intermediate status between the native language and the target language), the learner must tolerate that uneasy feeling of never being certain about the second language. Without perseverance, intrinsic motivation, and tolerance for ambiguity, the learner would never pass beyond the stage of incipient bilingualism.

The Synergism of Bilingualism and Creativity

It is our position that a person's creativity is supported by his or her bilingualism and that a person's dual language proficiency is supported by his or her creativity. This symbiotic relationship creates a type of synergism and results in a total effect that is greater than the sum of the individual effects. Whether balanced bilingualism or high creativity acts as the synergist is not able to be determined.

The findings of research conducted in this area are mixed. Kessler and Quinn (1987) conducted an empirical investigation into the effects of bilingualism on the linguistic and cognitive creativity of language-minority children who were "proficiently bilingual" in Spanish and English. The subjects for this study were sixth-grade students in two self-contained classrooms. One classroom was populated with monolingual English-speaking children and the other with Spanish-English bilingual children. The children were asked to participate in an inquiry-based science program during which they learned to formulate scientific hypotheses in a problem-solving setting. Bilingual students outperformed monolingual students on measures of syntactic and semantic linguistic variables in the creation of hypotheses. The researchers also noted that the qualitatively high scientific hypotheses expressed by the bilingual students indicated that linguistic and cognitive creativity is enhanced by bilingual language proficiency. They concluded that children with a high degree of bilingual language proficiency are capable of entering into creative processes in divergent and convergent thinking more fully than can their monolingual peers.

It is important to note that Kessler and Quinn differentiated their subjects as those with "a high degree of bilingual language proficiency." Studies on the creativity of bilingual persons may be flawed if those bilinguals have not yet reached the stage described as "balanced bilinguals." This point was supported by Ricciardelli (1992), who surveyed twenty-four studies of the relationship between creativity and bilingualism. Ricciardelli concluded that a majority of the studies suggested that bilinguals tend to be more creative than monolinguals, and that bilinguals exhibit superior linguistic performance in other areas, such as metalinguistic awareness, concept formation, and perceptual disembedding.

What about the studies in the Ricciardelli survey that did not support the symbiotic synergistic nature of bilingualism and creativity? For the most part, these can be explained by the Bilingual Threshold Theory, which implies that if bilingual subjects have not yet attained the level of a balanced bilingual, then tests of creativity that are given in the subject's second language may be negatively influenced. Therefore, research that strives to measure creativity must also ensure that the bilingual subject has equal linguistic capabilities in both languages.

Teaching Strategies

In the poem, "The Quest for Flight," Luis J. Rodriguez (1991) writes of his visit to the home of a Puerto Rican family.

> *A middle-aged man greeted us, smiling large*
> *and waving us in as if we were a kind wind*
> *on a scorched day. A gray-haired woman shuffled*
> *in the kitchen. As we entered, she began*
> *to relate the latest chisme to her daughter.*
> *The man took my arm to a table where he*
> *displayed a bottle of Mescal. He explained*
> *how he learned to drink Mescal after having*
> *gone to Korea and fought with Mexicans in the war.*

Personally, I said, give me dark rum.
Dinner came and, again, as if in my honor,
enchiladas were served. I liked Mexican food,
but I suggested that their culture didn't have
to be displaced for my sake. "Please,
I get this every day,"
I said. "Let's enjoy
what you enjoy. Let me have some black beans
and rice with pice. How about lenchon y salsa
de bacalao?"

In Rodriguez's work the crossover between cultures and languages is a vital part of the creative force that shapes his writing. The interplay of two languages supports his voice and validates his experiences of the bilingual and bicultural environment in which he lives. His talent is similar to that of many bilingual students in our nation's schools. Although Rodriguez suffered vilification by his teachers because of his lack of English proficiency and his Mexican ancestry, the recognition of language-minority students' right to native-language instruction and acknowledgement of minority students' cultures has changed the experiences of non-English-speaking students in our schools. What remains to be done by educators in today's schools is the modification of teaching methods, so that creativity and bilingualism can be nurtured. Examples of these types of teaching strategies follow the recommendations of Schall (1997), who gathered "voices of experience" from teachers of second-language learners. The following is a partial list of "winning strategies" shared by those teachers (p. 1):

1. Get to know children's culture, customs, school experiences, and background. Display artifacts from different cultures. Students use maps, family histories, and personal items to maintain and strengthen their identifies. Research the communication and behavioral patterns of culturally different students.

2. Make and share personal history books. Throughout the year, students compile, label, and describe photographs/sketches/pictures of important people, places, animals, objects, and events in their lives.

3. Use bilingual cooperative learning groups.

4. Set up mentor pairs to figure out the "hidden" curriculum—the unwritten rules, procedures, and policies of the school and the classroom.

Strategies such as these focus on affective needs; they help to build a sense of community and respect for individual differences. Moll and Diaz's (1987) qualitative research regarding instructional practices for language-minority students also reveals, however, that there is a dire need to provide students with intellectually challenging opportunities. Their research revealed that language-minority students' capacities "often are underestimated and thus they are subjected to incessant drill on skills they have already mastered" in their native languages. "They rarely are afforded opportunities to discuss ideas and complex concepts, apply principles, or experiment with implications of ideas" (p. 5). These are the very intellectual abilities that are essential for developing creativity.

These intellectual abilities can be nurtured despite the second-language learners' overt and covert cultural differences. Frasier's (1991) review of the literature identifies cognitive characteristics shared by creative students regardless of their language background. They include the ability to

- Manipulate a symbol system valued by the subculture
- Use information to think logically
- Tap into a personal storehouse of knowledge in order to solve problems
- Reason by analogy
- Apply accumulated knowledge to new situations

The questions and assignments in the following section use various educational models and strategies designed to promote and encourage creative thinking.

Creative Models and Strategies

The following instructional models for nurturing creativity among bilingual students were adapted from strategies used to teach gifted students. The original lessons were developed by teachers of gifted students in the greater New Orleans area who were enrolled in a university teaching-strategies course (i.e., Sandy Borchgrevink, Jan Weiner, Karen Bauer, Angie Wall, and Kathleen Horvil).

Model I: The Multiple Intelligences Model

The Multiple Intelligences Model, consisting of eight different intelligences, was developed by Howard Gardner (1993b), a professor at Harvard University. Gardner recommends that teachers should use the multimodal strategies to develop and enhance the creative and cognitive strengths of all students. He believes that his model counterbalances the three biases in our society: "Westist," "Testist," and "Bestist" (p. 12): Westist mostly prizes Western cultural values, such as logical rational reasoning; Testist values only those abilities that can be quantitatively measured; and Bestist reckons that there is a definitive logical approach to problem solving. Gardner, however, maintains that if we "mobilize the spectrum of human abilities, . . . people . . . will also feel more engaged and better able to join the rest of the world community" (p. 12).

Topic: Biographies of Famous People from Your Target Language Group

Verbal/Linguistic: Write a cinquain poem in your target language about a famous person from your target language group. Use the following formula to guide you:

Line 1: Write the name of the person that you want to describe.
Line 2: Write two or three words that describe or tell about (adjectives) the person.
Line 3: Write three words that show action (verbs), detailing what the person does or did.
Line 4: Write a short phrase or a few words about the person.
Line 5: Write another word that identifies the person.

The following examples are written about Maya Lin, the creator of the Vietnam Veterans' Memorial in Washington, DC, and Pablo Neruda, a well-known Chilean poet:

Maya
Dedicated, investigative, confident
Creates, sculpts, designs
Child of Chinese immigrants
Artist

Neruda
Perceptivo, Inquieto
Crea, Escribe, Suena
Poeta de la gente

Neruda
Perceptive, restless,
Creates, Writes, Dreams
Poet of the People

Logical/Mathematical: Use your target language to construct a timeline that traces the highlights of the notable person's life.

Visual/Spatial: Design a quilt square for a "Notable Peoples Quilt." The square could contain pictures, words, or symbols that portray the person's philosophy or accomplishments, or it could represent the people, places, or events that contributed to his or her success. (Quilts can be made out of cloth, felt, cardboard, etc.)

Musical/Rhythmic: Choose a song representative of the culture and time period of the person you choose to investigate. Use your target language to write or rewrite the lyrics of an event or events from his or her life.

Bodily/Kinesthetic: Prepare a dance, mime, or simulation that captures the essence of your notable person.

Interpersonal: Working in cooperative groups, design and build a model of a monument that will commemorate the notable person.

Intrapersonal: In your journal, use your target language to reflect on the criteria for becoming famous as well as your own personal goals and aspirations; what will be your claim to fame?

Model II: Bloom's Taxonomy of Educational Objectives

Bloom's Taxonomy of Educational Objectives is a model that is hierarchical, classifying learning experiences according to their levels of complexity, from "Knowledge," a less complex thinking skill, to "Evaluation," the most complex. According to Maker and Nielson (1995), this taxonomy provides "a simple, easy-to-learn structure for developing teaching–learning activities that take students through a sequential process in the development of a concept or the learning of relationships" (p. 54).

Topic: *Urban Runoff*

Knowledge: Use your target language to write a "talking-heads" documentary, describing the urban runoff problem. Give examples of household products, chemicals, and contaminants that end up being washed down our storm drains.

Comprehension: Use your target language to construct a flow chart depicting how common household products, fertilizers, detergents, animal wastes, pesticides, motor oil, and so forth, end up in our rivers.

Application: Design a mini-action plan that will help solve the urban runoff problem. Target a problem, ask questions, research, locate resources, identify obstacles, brainstorm solutions, select evaluation criteria, evaluate solutions, design a plan, and complete a job chart. Use your target language to complete a "cause-and-effect" chart, delineating natural and human causes of urban runoff.

Synthesis: Use your target language to write a play, story, or puppet show that teaches the audience the importance of recycling used motor oil.

Evaluation: Review the ideas we have discussed and debated for reducing and preventing urban runoff. Decide which idea you think is most likely to help our rivers. Prepare a defense of your position in your target language.

Model III: Divergent Questioning Model

The Divergent Questioning Model stimulates thinking and creativity because divergent questions do not have specific right or wrong answers; therefore, a wide variety of responses are acceptable. Starko (1995), however, warns that "divergent thinking alone is not creativity. Creativity entails finding a problem or issue worth addressing, generating ideas for addressing it, and evaluating the ideas generated" (p. 196).

Topic: *Ocean Life*

Quantity/Fluency: Use your target language to list all of the possible solutions that you can think of to get a whale out of the ocean. Use your target language to list all of the ways you could use an old fishing net. Think of all of the ways you could remove trash from the ocean.

Viewpoint/Flexibility: What would an oil slick look like to a swordfish? How would an iceberg look to a manatee? What would a hurricane mean from the viewpoint of a whale? Write your answers to these questions in your target language.

Involvement: You are a dolphin caught in a tuna net. Use your target language to describe how it feels. How would you feel if you were the hook in a fish's mouth?

Forced Associations/Synectics: How is an iceberg on the ocean's surface like happiness? Which is heavier: troubles or a whale? How is a humpback whale like Cinderella? Use your target language to write the answers to these questions.

Reorganization/Provocative Questions: Suppose there were no tides. What are all of the things that might happen? What would happen if marine animals could communicate with humans? Suppose whales were the size of crabs and crabs the size of whales. Use your target language to write all of the things that might happen.

Model IV: Creative Problem Solving

Creative Problem Solving (CPS) (Maker & Nielson, 1995) is a model whereby students are presented with a scenario, sometimes called a "fuzzy situation" or a "mess." Students research the issues, brainstorm problems, target a specific problem, brainstorm solutions, identify evaluation criteria, evaluate solutions, and describe a plan to put the solution into practice. According to Starko (1995), CPS "is a powerful process that can serve students well in attacking school, social, and personal problems. . . . CPS is most potent when used to interact with the real world" (p. 215).

Topic: Oral Histories/Museums

Fuzzy Situation: Develop a museum for your local county. The County Office of Economic Development has planned a museum with the following Vision Statement as its guiding purpose: "To establish a museum to house and display artifacts and documents of oral, written, audio/visual and pictorial history, which will depict the story of the county."

The County Historical Foundation Steering Committee is in the initial stages of studying the feasibility of developing such a museum to house the history of the county. Because a primary focus of such a museum will be "to provide an enriching, educational, and cultural experience for future generations in the county," the Steering Committee members are soliciting ideas and suggestions from you as they continue to research the issue of the components of an effective museum. Because the committee members want to ensure a museum that appeals to children of all ages, as well as to adults, your input will be carefully considered. Use your problem-solving skills as you ponder the steering committee's questions:
- What qualities make a good museum?
- How can we evaluate those qualities?
- What do students hope to learn about the county on a museum tour?
- What kind of hands-on activities or displays should be included for children?
- How should classroom activities or assignments be connected to changing museum displays?

Brainstorm other possible issues, problems, and solutions that must be carefully researched in the initial developmental stage of a museum plan. Select what you consider to be the most urgent or significant problem; use CPS to decide on a course of action. Write your plan of action in your target language.

Model V: Encounter Lesson

The Encounter Technique is one that is used to motivate students to think creatively, to feel psychologically safe and free to express their thoughts and explore their feelings. This type of visualization can be used to explore issues and events related to course content. "Guided imagery that is focused on content can enhance students' memory and stimulate their writing or other creative expression" (Starko, 1995, p. 232).

Topic: Birds/Title: Wood Duck

Setting: Like the other four million wood ducks that annually migrate through the southeastern United States, you spend the winters in flooded bottom-land forests and marshes. I want you to pretend to be a wood duck who has just arrived in Jean Lafitte National Park in Louisiana. Choose your native language or your target language to respond to the following questions:

Leading Questions
1. How do you feel when you see your preferred winter home habitat rapidly eroding year by year? (Ask a question about senses or experiences.)
2. How do you feel when you fly over a fine New Orleans restaurant that is serving roasted duck dishes? (Ask a question that focuses on feelings about others, one that promotes empathy.)
3. How do you feel on the first day of the duck-hunting season in this "Sportsman's Paradise"? (Ask a question about conflict or risk about a situation that evokes fear or anxiety.)
4. What would you like to say to people who think you all look alike and have no individuality or personality? (Ask an abstract question that stimulates thinking about values or beliefs.)
5. If you could be some creature other than a bird, what would you be? (Ask a question about creative transformation.)
6. If you were a speech writer for the Louisiana Tourist Commission, what would you say about your winter home in the next TV commercial or radio advertisement? (Ask a question that requires a verbal message.)

Summary

I went over to Ray's house on that hot, dull day. He was sitting in a big rusty yellow car with the roof down. The car had no wheels and was jacked up on cinder blocks. He was sitting there just tugging the steering wheel back and forth. I said, "I don't know what you're doing but you're getting nowhere fast." So he says to me, "You're thinking too small, I'm driving the planet." (Fonseca, 1995)

When it comes to aspects of creativity and bilingualism, most educators think too small. In this chapter, we have endeavored to blur the dividing walls that educators use to separate creative individuals and bilingual individuals. The symbiotic relationship between bilingualism and creativity requires a merging of these two separate categories into one. When students add a second language, they must call on their creative characteristics to master that second language. Therefore, teaching strategies that tap into creative resources of second-language students will enhance the students' cognitive function.

The findings presented in this chapter call for further research into the relationship between bilingualism and creativity. However, caution must be exercised in identifying subjects who have fully mastered two language systems. As the Bilingual Threshold Theory has shown, assessing creativity in individuals who do not have cognitive fluency in both languages may result in invalid results. For bilingualism to positively affect creativity (and vice versa), the individual must be at the point described as a "balanced bilingual."

REFERENCES

Amabile. T. M. (1989). *Growing up creative: Nurturing a lifetime of creativity.* Buffalo, NY: Creative Education Foundation.

Bullard, S. (1993, Fall). [Interview with Luis Rodriguez]. *Teaching Tolerance,* 11–15.

Cummins, J. (1975). *Cognitive factors associated with intermediate levels of bilingual skills.* Unpublished manuscript, Educational Research Centre, St. Patrick's College, Dublin.

Cummins, J. (1977). Cognitive factors associated with the attainment of intermediate levels of bilingual skills. *Modern Language Journal,* 61, 3–12.

Cummins, J. (1984). Wanted: A theoretical framework for relating language proficiency to academic achievement among bilingual students. In C. Rivera (Ed.), *Language proficiency and academic achievement.* Gevedon, England: Multilingual Matters.

Csikszentmihalyi, M. (1988). Society, culture, and person: A systems view of creativity. In R. J. Sternberg (Ed.), *The nature of creativity: Contemporary psychological perspectives* (pp. 325–339). Cambridge: Cambridge University Press.

Dacey, J. S. (1989). *Fundamentals of creative thinking.* Lexington, MA: Lexington Books.

Davis, G. A. (1992). *Creativity is forever* (3rd ed.). Dubuque, IA: Kendall/Hunt.

Davis, G. A., & Rimm, S. B. (1998). *Education of the gifted and talented* (4th ed.). Boston: Allyn & Bacon.

Fillmore, L. W. (1985). Second language learning in children: A proposed model. In: *English Language Development.* Proceedings of a Conference on Issues in English Language Development for Minority Language Education, Arlington, VA, July 24, 1985.

Fonseca, J. (1995). *Reflection.* Unpublished manuscript.

Frasier, M. (1991). Response to Kitano: The sharing of giftedness between culturally diverse and non-diverse gifted students. *Journal for the Education of the Gifted,* 15 (1), 20–30.

Gardner, H. (1993a). *Creating minds.* New York: Basic Books.

Gardner, H. (1993b). Multiple intelligences: The theory in practice. New York: Basic Books.

Kessler, C., & Quinn, M. E. (1987). Language minority children's linguistic and cognitive creativity. *Journal of Multilingual and Multicultural Development,* 8 (1 & 2), 173–186.

Maker, C. J., & Nielson, A. B. (1995). *Teaching models in education of the gifted.* Austin, TX: Pro-Ed.

Maker, C. J., Nielson, A. B., & Rogers, J. A. (1994). Giftedness, diversity, and problem-solving. *Teaching Exceptional Children,* 27 (1) 4–19.

Moll, L. C., & Diaz, S. (1987). Change as the Goal of Educational Research. *Anthropology & Education Quarterly,* 18, 300–311.

Ricciardelli, L. A. (1992). Creativity and bilingualism. *Journal of Creative Behavior,* 26 (4), 242–254.

Rodriguez, L. J. (1991) *The concrete river.* Willimantic, CT: Curbstone Press.

Schall, J. (1997). *Unbeatable ways to reach your LEP students.* [Online]. Available: <place.scholastic.com/instructor/reaching/lep.htm#quintana119971>.

Starko, A. J. (1995). *Creativity in the classroom: Schools of curious delight.* White Plains, NY: Longman.

Sternberg R. J. (Ed.). (1988a). *The nature of creativity: Contemporary psychological perspectives.* Cambridge: Cambridge University Press.

Sternberg, R. J. (1988b). A three-facet model of creativity. In R. J. Sternberg (Ed.), *The nature of creativity: Contemporary psychological perspectives* (pp. 125–147). Cambridge: Cambridge University Press.

Tardiff, T. Z., & Sternberg, R. J. (1988). What do we know about creativity? In R. J. Sternberg (Ed.), *The nature of creativity: Contemporary psychological perspectives* (pp. 429–440). Cambridge: Cambridge University Press.

Torrance, E. P. (1988). The nature of creativity as manifest in its testing. In R. J. Sternberg (Ed.), *The nature of creativity: Contemporary psychological perspectives* (pp. 125–147). Cambridge: Cambridge University Press.

Walberg H. J. (1988). Creativity and talent as learning. In R. J. Sternberg (Ed.), *The nature of creativity: Contemporary psychological perspectives* (pp. 125–147). Cambridge: Cambridge University Press.

Weiss, R. (1997, October 7). Heretical scientist awarded Nobel. *The Times Picayune,* p. A–4.

5

Renavigating the Waters

The Identification and Assessment of Culturally and Linguistically Diverse Students for Gifted and Talented Education

JAIME A. CASTELLANO

Access to a free quality education for children may not be the number one priority of families immigrating to the United States when compared with survival issues such as civil war, hunger, religious or political persecution, and economic deprivation. After arrival in this country, however, the availability of the American educational system, with its wide-encompassing array of support services that extends beyond the academics of the classroom, quickly becomes apparent. Students are matriculated, problems are addressed, difficulties are overcome, and students are swiftly placed into classrooms with an appropriate individualized curriculum. Or are they?

Whether as a recent limited-English arrival or as a member of a bilingual–bicultural minority culture established as citizens for generations, the student who is admitted to and placed into a public school program runs the risk of never being recognized as a talented or gifted individual. In spite of achievements and accomplishments in other educational areas, the U.S. public school system often shortchanges the gifted and talented culturally and linguistically diverse (CLD) student. Considering the percentages of linguistically, racially, or culturally diverse students enrolled in public schools, the numbers identified as potentially gifted and talented are alarmingly low. Less than ten years ago, 6 percent of school-aged children needed English-language proficiency support services. Projected figures indicate that within thirty years, approximately 25 percent of the student population will have limited English proficiency. In some geographic areas the numbers are already higher, and closer to 40 percent (Kitano & Espinosa, 1995).

Three percent of the school population in the United States is estimated to be gifted. If the assumption is that giftedness crosses ethnic, linguistic, and cultural boundaries, and if we keep in mind a wonderful truism, which states, "One does not need to be fluent in English to be intelligent" (Barken & Bernal, 1991), it becomes obvious that limited English proficient (LEP) students are underrepresented in the educational programs for the gifted and talented. Traditionally, gifted programs have been filled by White middle or upper middle class students whose backgrounds have afforded them the enrichment opportunities and linguistic experiences that enhance their natural abilities in ways that support scoring well on tests designed by White middle or upper middle class experts. Enriched academic backgrounds and experiences then establish a standardized criteria that will determine future-identified gifted and talented students, thus perpetuating the preestablished cycle.

The identification of gifted characteristics and criteria used to identify potential lie at the bottom of the problem of underrepresentation of LEP students in gifted programs. Linguistic and cultural diversity, proficiency, and literacy in the first language and in English, background experiences, and range of individual talent (Kitano & Espinosa, 1995) are external problems that compound the problem. In October of 1993, the Office of Educational Research and Improvement (OERI) of the United States Department of Education submitted a report to Secretary of Education Richard W. Riley, entitled: *National Excellence: A Case for Developing America's Talent.* This document outlined the "quiet crisis" that occurs in the education of top students. The report maintains that the United States is squandering one of its most precious resources—the gifts, talents, and high interests of many students. In a broad range of intellectual and artistic endeavors, these youngsters are not challenged to do their best work. The problem is severe among economically disadvantaged and minority students, who have access to fewer advanced educational opportunities and whose talents often go unnoticed (p. 1).

One in four American children who live in poverty represent an enormous pool of untapped talent, yet most programs for these children focus on solving the problems they bring to school, rather than on challenging them to develop academic talent–related strengths. It is sometimes assumed that children from unpromising backgrounds are not capable of outstanding accomplishments. (We in bilingual/ESL/ESOL education have had to endure this attitude from others for much too long.) However, stories abound of disadvantaged children who achieve at high levels when nurtured sufficiently. The opportunities for all children to reach maximum potential must be increased.

President Bush and the nation's governors recognized this need at the 1989 Education Summit held in Charlottsville, Virginia. They defined six education goals and declared that meeting them by the year 2000 "will require that the performance of our highest achievers be boosted to levels that equal or exceed the performance of the best students anywhere. . . . We must work to ensure that a significant number of students from all races, ethnic groups, and income levels are among our top performers." This challenge cannot be ignored (pp. 5, 6). Among these groups are students identified as linguistically diverse.

The purpose of this chapter is to share with readers what works and what doesn't when targeting the identification, assessment, and evaluation of CLD students for gifted education programs and services. The research clearly documents that these students have historically been shut out of public school gifted education programs because school districts across the United States simply are not aware of the cultural and linguistic considerations that need to be taken into account throughout the referral, assessment, and evaluation process. This chapter aims to shed some light in this regard. Why these students have been denied access to gifted education is presented in the hope that these exclusionary practices will not continue to be used. More importantly, however, strategies and processes that have been used successfully and that serve as more "inclusionary" methodology to help balance the playing field are also highlighted.

A Brief Look at the History of Assessment of Culturally and Linguistically Diverse Students: The Past 100 Years

Educational placements for students have been determined by standardized test scores for over one hundred years (Tyack, 1974). Educational concerns of students from CLD backgrounds appeared to be unimportant during the turn of the twentieth century. During this historically formative period of education in the United States, debates about a national language ensued. As the number of students increased and the dollars of public budgets decreased, group testing was used to place students for differential instruction. Intelligence tests were used as the measure of educational ability to classify pupils and to provide appropriate education. This procedure determined future roles in society (Cremlin, 1961).

This process is most evident in the identification and assessment of students enrolled in programs educating the gifted and talented. The majority of early gifted programs consisted of White students who attained the needed IQ score that assured their entrance and subsequent participation. IQ scores continue to serve as an exclusionary measure, shutting out CLD students. Ultimately, this practice exacerbates issues of inequity and eliminates any opportunity of gifted placement for many of these students.

Exclusionary Practices in the Identification of Culturally and Linguistically Diverse Students for Gifted Education Programs

The reasons for underrepresentation of certain student groups from gifted education are well documented, despite the fact that gifted children can be found in every racial, ethnic, economic, and linguistic group (Castellano, 1998; Stephens & Karnes, 2000). One does not need to speak English in order to be gifted or academically talented. Gifted children are found in the poor ethnic neighborhoods in Chicago and Los Angeles, in the projects of New York and Miami, and in new immigrant populations found in West Palm Beach and San Francisco. Gifted children are found in the trailer parks and homeless shelters. They are found in rural America and in migrant camps. They are in every school these students attend, and it should be noted that the increase of "students of color" has not been matched by increases in gifted education services that meet their needs. Only now are we paying greater attention to these children. Underrepresentation is attributed to myriad factors—historical, philosophical, psychological, theoretical, social, and political. Each of these factors, alone or in combination, has had an impact on the assessment and identification of gifted students in minority student populations (Working on Gifted Issues [WOGI] Project, 2000).

An unbiased analysis reveals that the problems revolve less around the student and more around "the system." There are widespread problems, in general, in the identification of all gifted students. These problems are compounded when a student's culture or primary language is different from the norm. Among others, Richert (1992) maintains that the following reasons may be why it has been historically so difficult for diverse student populations to gain admission into such programs.

Elitist and Distorted Definitions of Giftedness

Many school districts use elitist definitions of *giftedness* that include most often only those who are White, middle class, and academically adept or successful. A major purpose of the federally legislated definition was to expand the concept of giftedness beyond IQ (Marland, 1972). Seemingly, even more limited definitions are applied. The hair-splitting distinctions between talented and gifted children, the use of designating degrees of giftedness ("highly," "severely," "profoundly," or "exotically" gifted) rather than the specification of the identification procedures used (high IQ or high achievement) create implicit hierarchies, engender elitism internal to programs, and exclude many students with gifted potential. Among those excluded are students that the school districts have also labeled culturally and/or linguistically diverse.

Confusion about the Purpose of Identification

There are several kinds of confusion about the purposes of identification. Identification is not, as too many people assume, a mere categorization of gifted abilities already made manifest. If it were, educational programs would be unnecessary. Identification is actually a needs assessment for the purpose of placing students into educational programs designed to develop their latent potential.

Teachers, administrators, and often, parents feel that entry into a program for the gifted should be a reward for achievement of "good" behavior, operationally defined as conformity to school or test-maker expectations. Many educators also seem to want the identification procedure to reaffirm the values inherent in the school system to which they have committed their own abilities. Students who are CLD are often not familiar with or have conflicting beliefs reflected in values inherent in the school.

Violation of Educational Equity

Gifted minority students are easily eliminated by present screening practices. The U.S. Department of Education's Office for Civil Rights national figures disclose that minority groups such as Blacks, Hispanics, and Native Americans are underrepresented by 30 percent to 70 percent in gifted programs (1979). These figures are collected each year, but they have not been published since 1979.

While most states formally subscribe to the comprehensive federal definition of *giftedness*, in practice many school districts seek and find only White, middle class academic achievers. Measures of academic achievement that are most often used by schools, including teacher recommendations, grades, and especially standardized tests, such as IQ, have proved to be culturally biased.

In 1982, the *National Report on Identification* (Richert, Alvino, & McDonnel, 1982) revealed that measures of academic achievement, which are not very good predictors of adult gifted achievement, effectively screened out the following subpopulations:

- Underachieving, learning disabled, handicapped, and minority students who most need programs to develop their potential
- The most creative and divergent thinkers: Inevitably, these students will be excluded by IQ tests, as Torrance (1979) has pointed out.

There is always a range of economic differences within a school district, even if there is cultural homogeneity within it. A significant finding of the 1982 *National Report* is that poor populations are consistently screened out of gifted programs because their disadvantage cuts across every other subpopulation. Data collected by Richert showed that the poor, defined by the federal standard of students qualifying for free or reduced lunches, are underrepresented from 100 percent to 500 percent.

Selective Referrals

The failure to look to minority populations for referrals in the identification process has been cited as one of the reasons these students are significantly underrepresented. Research indicates that students, teachers, and school professionals continue to have low academic expectations for CLD students, low levels of awareness of cultural and linguistic behaviors of potentially gifted minority students, insensitivity to the differences within and among groups, and inability to recognize "gifted behaviors" that minority students exhibit (Cunningham, Callahan, Plucker, Roberson, & Rapkin, 1998; Frasier & Passow, 1994; Garcia, 1994). Studies suggest that teachers view minority students as homogeneous with all members sharing the same set of values, beliefs, and characteristics. The inability of educators to recognize "gifted behaviors" exhibited by minority students contributes to their low referral rates.

Differential Cultural and Environmental Influences

Problems of underrepresentation of minority and economically disadvantaged gifted students are intrinsically related to the more general problem of the schooling of these populations. These students are more likely to be in schools that have poorer facilities, fewer instructional resources, larger classes, fewer programs for the gifted, more inexperienced teachers, and other factors that contribute to unequal educational opportunities. Significant differences in educational resources as well as the climate and learning environments are evident in those schools that serve disadvantaged populations. Such schools tend to provide fewer enrichment and higher learning opportunities and fewer occasions for students to exhibit gifted behaviors. Because such schools have fewer provisions for identifying and nurturing talent potential, referrals are limited (Passow & Frasier, 1996).

Misuse of Identification Instruments

Tests are being used in ways that test-makers never intended, sometimes to measure abilities that the tests were not designed to determine. For example, achievement and IQ tests are used almost interchangeably, thereby confusing categories of specific and general academic abilities. Instruments and procedures are also being used at inappropriate stages of identification. Diagnosis is not the purpose of initial screening procedures. However, screening through diagnostic tests, such as the Stanford Achievement Test (reading and math) and the Woodcock Johnson Reading Mastery Test, is common. Such tests are only useful for determining placement in a particular course or for measuring progress once students are placed within a program option (Richert, Alvino, & McDonnel, 1982; pp. 35, 62).

Another problem occurs when data from parents are gathered only after students have been nominated by teachers or have qualified for a talent pool through a test score. Under such procedures, disadvantaged students are easily screened out. The same error occurs when teachers assess the ability of students after they have qualified for a talent pool by a standardized test score. Most of the efforts to use data beyond achievement measures are merely cosmetic and often reinforce the exclusion of the same groups of disadvantaged students.

Test Bias

Despite the changes in demographics, many educators continue to rely on instruments designed to measure giftedness as it was perceived early in the twentieth century. Reliance on instruments inappropriate to a changing population contributes to the underrepresentation of minority students in special programs for gifted students. For example, in the Tucson Unified District, minority students make up 48 percent of the population, but only 25 percent of elementary students in programs for the gifted are minority students. Similar discrepancies exist in states across the country (Maker, 1996). Intelligence and achievement tests, once thought to be tools for predicting which students would become significant contributors in society, are now seen as predictors for success in the academic setting (Grigorenko & Sternberg, 1997). Renzulli (as cited in Maker, 1996) concluded that research indicates that vast numbers of our society who are most productive have not scored at or above the 95th percentile on standardized tests.

Cosmetic and Distorting Use of Multiple Criteria

One of the few positive trends for identification is the collection and use of data from a variety of sources. The intent of collecting a variety of data may appear to make the procedure more defensible and inclusive. However, data are often misused in several ways: the data may be unreliable, used at an inappropriate stage of identification, weighted in indefensible ways, or invalidly placed in a matrix using other data.

Inappropriate Combination of Data

The unsound practice of combining data from multiple sources in various matrices or other weighted scoring procedures was strongly criticized by a panel of national experts because doing so could obscure a variety of important indicators of gifted potential (Richert, Alvino, & McDonnel, 1982). Furthermore, combining data inappropriately also tends to identify a jack of all trades, that is, the student who develops ability, creativity, and motivation concurrently. It may eliminate the "masters of some," who especially need a gifted program to develop their potential:

▪ *Students with a very high IQ.* These students may be underachieving in school because of the extreme inappropriateness of the regular curriculum and may not receive teacher or parent nomination.

▪ *Exceptionally creative students.* These students are often screened out by IQ or achievement measures.

▪ *Creative students.* Gifted students who are independent, rebellious, and nonconforming tend not to receive teacher or parent nomination.

In addition, most of the identification procedures used, such as standardized tests, teacher recommendations, and grades, are really a measure of conformity to middle class academic values and achievement. The more measures that are used and combined inappropriately, the more likely it is that disadvantaged students (poor, minority, creative, and others who tend to be underachievers in schools) will be excluded. Therefore, the use of multiple measures, which may create the appearance of inclusiveness, can actually promote elitism in the identification process.

Problems with Using IQ Scores and Other Criteria

The use of intelligence tests can be traced back to Alfred Binet, who developed the first test in 1905 (Sarouphim, 1999). Binet's purpose in designing the test was to predict success in school, rather than to measure innate intelligence. It is interesting to note that even today, many people believe that an IQ test measures giftedness and intelligence. Intelligence tests do not take into account such factors as motivation and effort and are not normed on representative samples of the country's current demographic profile, and they reveal gender, ethnic, and cultural bias in their content (Plucker, Callahan, & Tomchin, 1996; Sarouphim, 1999). Arguments continue that standardized tests discriminate against students whose linguistic and perceptual orientation, cognitive style, learning and response styles, economic status, and cultural or social backgrounds differ from the norm group—White, middle class, native-English-speaking populations (Frasier & Passow, 1995). Observers point out that tests are designed by White, middle or upper middle class experts whose academic backgrounds and experiences have influenced the criteria that favor students from the same backgrounds (Castellano, 1998). How valid are instruments and practices developed in the Euro-American tradition for students from different cultures and environmental contexts? The greater question is, do these

tests contribute to institutionalized discrimination and racism by shaping the att
of teachers (Borland & Wright, 1994)?

Too Few Students Are Identified

Because of increasingly limited resources, there have been several counterproductive
trends among theoreticians and groups vying for services. Parents whose children are
being served through present identification practices defend the status quo because they
fear children will be excluded if other groups, such as the disadvantaged, are included.
Many administrators argue that because of limited resources, only a small number can
be served. This results in the identification of the same White middle class population
year after year.

Although there appears to be common agreement that gifted education programs
cannot serve all children, there is a national movement gaining momentum to include a
more diverse group of children in these programs, particularly those representing students who are CLD. Most of the references made to excluded groups mention minority
students in regard to race and ethnicity. Very rarely is there specific reference to students
who are limited or non-English speakers, also commonly referred to as LEP students,
CLD, English language learners (ELL), or potentially English proficient (PEP).

Problems with Identifying Talent and Ability

Identification of students for gifted and talented programs continues to be a conundrum
with which educators struggle. LEP students are affected most severely. In fact, most
LEP students fall outside the purview of schools almost entirely when students are identified for gifted and talented programs. If standardized tests or IQ tests are used exclusively, students' English language aptitude will influence their scores. Even if other
measures are used, language can influence student scores because directions may be
given in English rather than in the heritage (native) language.

In addition, researchers at the National Center on the Gifted and Talented have
identified other barriers to the identification of LEP and minority students:

- Teachers' inability to recognize indicators of potential giftedness
- Lack of a stimulating early home environment, more frequent for children from
  economically disadvantaged backgrounds
- Teachers' prejudicial attitudes (Frasier et al., 1995, pp. x–xi).

Of these major or influential factors that affect the identification of LEP students for
gifted programs, perhaps the most profound is teachers' inability to recognize indicators of abilities of LEP students. Researchers argue that this ability is affected by cultural bias in teachers inexperienced in cultural differences that affect learning styles or
parental attitudes toward school. Obviously, the extent to which teachers and other
school staff can become comfortable with the home cultures and ethnicities of their
LEP students will result in greater awareness and early recognition of potential.

The same researchers (Frasier et al., 1995) concluded that although there is a popular teacher-held perception that parents of LEP students do not involve their children in educational activities at home that support their in-school studies, this belief is actually incorrect. Again, increasing teachers' knowledge base on the home cultures of LEP students should aim at more direct home–school interactions to gain accurate perceptions of LEP students' abilities.

Most progressive gifted educators now agree that just as an expanded view of intelligence and ability is necessary, broader identification of students with outstanding aptitudes must follow. They point to the need for a multipronged identification that should include achievement data, teacher recommendations, a student portfolio, and consideration of special variables, such as language, socioeconomic background, and culture. School staff need progressive, substantive staff development to supplement and expand their knowledge of other cultural and linguistic groups. This knowledge, when supported with opportunities to pilot new programs geared toward introducing LEP students to high-status knowledge, will aid both in the development of new identification procedures, which, while perhaps imperfect, will result in expanding the numbers of LEP students eligible for gifted and talented programs (United States Department of Education, 1997).

Balancing the Playing Field

Assessments of LEP students must utilize a different set of evaluative criteria than that used for monolingual English speakers (Hamayan and Damico, 1991). The evaluator must take into account such distinct obstacles as cultural and interactive differences that may make the CLD student appear to have a disability (Westby, 1985). Educators must take into account the cultural and linguistic variables during the assessment process. The more familiar and culturally appropriate the content of the stimulus materials, the more likely that children demonstrate behavior that accurately represents their real abilities (Armour-Thomas, 1992).

LaCelle-Peterson and Rivera (1994) also emphasize that assessments must be equitable. Test procedures must not penalize students who are unfamiliar with the test language, and items on the test must be scrutinized for gender, culture, or other bias. Validity is verified when the norming population of the test is similar to the students receiving the test.

Equitable accountability of assessment depends on the background knowledge of the examiner and a flexible assessment system. The Testing and Educational Standards Commission advocate that evaluators become familiar with the adaptations necessary to provide an equitable testing situation for CLD students. Neglect of these factors may result in an invalid and conceivably harmful set of valuative recommendations for CLD students (Figueroa, 1990). Time adjustments allowed for a task, varying the mode of expression (e.g., written or oral), and providing measures of the student's proficiency in the heritage language are examples of some adaptations that may be made (LaCelle-Peterson & Rivera, 1994). Also referred to as "testing the limits," these types of adjustments in the assessment process paint a more accurate picture of the cognitive and academic abilities of CLD students.

Identification Practices

Several researchers have presented convincing evidence that a major paradigm shift is needed in the field of education in light of the national problem of underrepresentation of some cultural groups in programs for the gifted (Castellano, 1998; Frasier, 1997; Frasier & Passow, 1994; Maker, 1996; Sarouphim, 1999). The demographics of the United States are quickly changing. In 1990, four out of five foreign-born people in the United States were born in European countries; now, only one in five is of European origin. The total foreign-born population increased by 40 percent between 1980 and 1990, a greater increase than in any other ten-year period in history. The greatest increase has been in Asian (104%) and Spanish (93%) language groups. Some school districts in the Southwest have a school enrollment of 60 percent to 95 percent Hispanic children. In California and Texas, the majority of students is now what was once termed *minority* (Wagonner, as cited in Maker, 1996).

In the absence of definitive recommendations, district-level experimentation is resulting in a wide variety of approaches and strategies, accompanied by a lack of confidence about their efficacy. Unfortunately, the available literature provides little guidance on effective strategies for identifying and serving these students (Kitano and Espinosa, 1995).

Harris (1991) describes a number of issues that arise in identifying and serving gifted students who are immigrants: 1) linguistic problems stemming from the native languages that differ vastly from English in pronunciation, grammatical structure, and alphabet; 2) cultural behaviors and customs that might be perceived as strange; 3) economic and health problems, with limited access to health care; 4) attitudinal differences and emotional difficulties resulting from immigration experiences (e.g., escape from danger, violent loss of family members, legal status); and 5) conflicting expectations concerning such issues as intergenerational and gender roles and school placement and practices.

Kitano and Espinosa (1995) portray gifted students who are acquiring English as a heterogeneous group. Their diversity suggests a need for a broad range of programs that provides options for different levels of primary and English-language proficiency, different subject matter interests, and talent areas. It is also the opinion of this author that this diversity, or heterogeneity, manifests itself in the establishment of multiple considerations during the identification and assessment process.

Survey on Identification and Instructional Practices

In a landmark study, Bermudez and Rakow (1993), combined a multiple-choice and open-ended survey, examining the status of identification, placement, and instructional procedures for gifted and talented LEP students. The survey was mailed to five hundred gifted and talented coordinators from public school districts in Texas, California, Arizona, Colorado, and Florida. The target sample represented a cross section of the states' public schools with regard to size, funding, and location. There were 268 respondents who provided the following responses to the questionnaire.

I. Identification Criteria

1. Are you serving any identified gifted students who have limited English proficiency?

   Only 18.7 percent of the respondents (fifty) indicated that they had developed a means to identify gifted-talented (G/T) LEPs. This finding is particularly disconcerting in light of the fact that the states targeted for this survey have a large proportion of Hispanic students who, as a result, are not receiving the required specialized services.

2. What are some characteristics of G/T LEP students that would be masked due to language and cultural differences?

   The following behaviors were reported by those participants who have developed identification means for G/T LEP students:
   - Language (verbal and nonverbal)
   - Cognition
     - Curiosity
     - Problem-solving style
     - Prior knowledge
     - Logic and thinking
     - Attending to task
     - Spatial relationships
     - Speed in learning
   - Academic and artistic skills
     - Creativity
     - Musical skills
     - Performance in academics
     - Ability to perform on timed tests

3. Gifted students whose proficiency in English is limited (G/T LEP) can be identified in the same ways as any gifted student.

   Seventy-eight percent acknowledged the need to use different means of assessment than those used for mainstream students (Witty, 1978).

4. What criteria for identification of these students are you using?

   Seventy percent of schools responding reported the use of multiple sources in identifying G/T LEP students as recommended by the research literature (Bernal, 1974; Leung, 1981; Torrance, 1977).

5. Are these methods satisfactory?

   Thirty-two percent of the respondents found their identification process successful in dealing with the identification of G/T LEPs. Responses indicating lack of success or uncertainty about the effectiveness of these methods raise serious questions about current identification practices for these students.

6. Is the community involved in establishing criteria and characteristics of G/T LEPs?

A majority (70%) of the respondents indicated that they had no community input in the process.

II. Instructional Programs and Materials

7. Our school district has a program used successfully with G/T LEP students.

Lack of specialized programs for the G/T LEP student was evident, as only 8.6 percent of the total respondents (268) had any type of program to serve these students. Of the fifty programs that indicated having identification means in place, only 46 percent had programs.

8. Do you consider instructional technology an important medium to stimulate G/T LEP students?

Although 72 percent of the sample identifying G/T LEP students agreed that technology was important in the education of these students, there were no recommendations for these students.

9. Do you use differential instructional curriculum with G/T LEP students?

Only 8.7 percent of those respondents (two) indicating an established program for this type of student reported the use of differentiated materials. Thirty-four percent use pull-out formats, and the majority (56.5%) do not adhere to any of the identified program typologies, including mainstreamed and after-school settings.

10. Is your program based on any particular model of gifted education?

Seventy-eight percent of the established programs follow a theoretically founded model of gifted education. Of these, 22.7 percent use Renzulli's TRIAD Model, and 50 percent a combination. There were six missing responses, which could indicate the schools' lack of awareness of theoretical and research foundations available for this area.

III. Parent Involvement

11. Are the parents of G/T LEP students in your school knowledgeable about the needs of these children?

Only 38 percent of those individuals who acknowledged having identification processes in place reported that their parents were cognizant about their children's needs. That there was missing data further underscores the lack of awareness reported.

12. Are these parents supportive of school practices?

Having parents interested and supportive of school practices is an important step in developing awareness of their important role in the identification and instruction of G/T LEP students. Seventy-six percent of the schools reported that parental involvement had been realized.

According to Bermudez and Rakow (1993), the survey data seem to indicate that there are very few programs identifying and/or instructing G/T LEP students in states with high Hispanic concentrations. The majority of school district coordinators responding as having developed identification procedures for this population of students are using multiple sources to nominate and screen these students. However, only one-third of the respondents indicated any success with these measures. One reason might be that a great percentage of these individuals are excluding community input in the identification process for these youngsters. This aspect needs to be examined, as cultural and linguistic characteristics are best understood by members of the same cultural enclave.

The findings of this study also indicate that the few programs focusing on G/T LEP students do not seem to systemically follow any particular model for gifted education or have a standard research-based classroom format to instruct these students. Training teachers and other support staff in these areas is a critical component for effective instruction.

Assessment and Other Strategies for Consideration: Inclusionary Practices

In an attempt to be proactive and responsive to the needs of the ever-growing population of students from culturally and, particularly, linguistically diverse backgrounds, it is necessary to consider alternative means of identification and assessment that, when coupled with more traditional conventions, serve as a more inclusionary model for admitting these students into programs for the gifted and talented. The following sections describe several of these instruments.

The Ravens Progressive Matrices

Standardized nonverbal instruments, such as the Ravens Progressive Matrices (RPM), offer alternatives to ability measures that require English language proficiency. Saccuzzo (1993) reports that replacing the Wechsler with the RPM as the major identification measure in one large urban school district resulted in a seven-fold increase in the number of Latino students, including LEP students, enrolled in programs for the gifted over a three-year period.

The Standard Progressive Matrices

The Standard Progressive Matrices (SPM) is another standardized nonverbal instrument, which has been used in the School District of Palm Beach County, Florida, with success. Ten Title I elementary schools were transformed to gifted-education pilot centers. The use of the SPM increased the number of underrepresented students eligible for services in every school in just one year.

The Naglieri Nonverbal Ability Test (NNAT)

The NNAT uses progressive matrices to allow for a fair evaluation of a student's nonverbal reasoning and general problem-solving ability, regardless of the languages they speak or their educational or cultural backgrounds. This particular instrument has also increased the number of underrepresented students eligible for gifted education services in school districts across the United States.

Hispanic Bilingual Gifted Screening Instrument (HBGSI)

The HBGSI is a seventy-eight-item checklist designed to be completed by a student's classroom teacher. Each item is rated on a five-point scale. After rating each of the items, the scores are subtotaled by cluster. This instrument, used successfully in the Southwest, is a product of an extensive review of literature on gifted Hispanics, Hispanic familial/sociological/linguistic characteristics, Hispanic elementary children, and diverse gifted populations.

A Multiple Criteria Approach to Identification and Assessment

To use Frasier and Passow's terminology of "casting a wide net" when developing an identification process, the use of multiple-criteria assessment enhances the identification of gifted minority students. Wide agreement exists that multiple criteria or alternate criteria must provide the foundation for identification and programming for all potentially gifted students, regardless of their cultural or ethnic backgrounds (Frasier & Passow 1994; Plucker, Callahan, & Tomchin, 1996; Sternberg, 1998). Kirschenbaum (1998) proposes the use of a "funnel approach" in the identification process. More students are included in the screening process, and a variety of sources of formal and informal information (e.g., checklists, rating scales, nominations) are collected. Frasier (1997) notes that current research is helping educators to understand that because intelligence is complex and takes many forms, many criteria are necessary to measure it.

Several advantages are given for the use of multiple criteria: (1) accountability, (2) access, and (3) program development. Any system of identification of abilities that is based on one criterion does not, nor will it ever, provide educators with the sufficient depth of information to make informed pedagogical decisions. Single-criterion systems are too narrow, have a tendency to emphasize labeling a student as the primary goal, do not determine the need for gifted program services, and limit educators' ability to diagnostically address individual student needs. Moreover, when one method is used to determine eligibility for gifted services, chances are increased that qualified students will be missed. Those students who are selected will mirror the abilities reflected in that one criteria (Frasier, 1997).

Multiple criteria refers to the process of obtaining comprehensive information about a student's abilities by gathering and analyzing results from such formal and informal procedures as (1) standardized measures of aptitude, achievement, and creativity in the child's native or English language; (2) nominations by teachers, parents, the students, peers, and community/cultural groups with which the student identifies; (3) ethnographic assessment procedures whereby the student is observed in multiple contexts over time; (4) evaluations of student products and performances (performance-based or nonverbal), such as portfolios, writing samples, and samples of creativity; (5) observations using rating scales and behavior checklists; (6) past school performance; and (7) parent interviews. There is wide agreement that multiple criteria or alternate criteria must provide the foundation for identification and programming of all potentially gifted students, regardless of their cultural and ethnic backgrounds, gender, languages, and environments (Castellano, 1998; and Hadaway & Marek-Schroer; Patton; Plucker, Callahan, & Tomchin, as cited in Frasier, 1997). Moreover, assessments using profiles of ability rather than one single score recognize the complex potential of a child's talents, sustained interests, and special aptitudes across cultures, languages, and gender (Dunn, Dunn, & Treffinger, as cited in Frasier, 1997).

Castellano (in press) identifies the following multiple-criteria variables that, used in any given combination, provide a "thick picture" of a student's giftedness or potential giftedness.

Qualitative Data	*Quantitative Data*
Nomination form	Achievement test scores
Characteristics checklist	Nonverbal performance-based measures
Portfolio of student work	Test of cognitive ability (non-IQ)
Criterion-referenced measures	Current school performance
Teacher anecdotes	Past school performance
Parent interview	Language-screening results
Student interview	Awards, recognitions, achievements
Dynamic assessments	
Writing samples	
Performance-based products	
Measures of creativity	

The use of multiple criteria undoubtedly serves to include more CLD students in programs targeting the gifted and talented. Inclusionary practices also include the following strategies.

Principles of Identification

Principles for assessing identification procedures emerged through the deliberation of the national panel of experts that met as part of the *National Report on Identification* in 1982 (Richert, Alvino, & McDonnel, 1982). Practitioners should consider these carefully in decision making:

1. *Defensibility:* Procedures should be used based on the best available research and recommendations, not on the preferences of a local group.

2. *Advocacy:* Identification should be designed in the best interests of the students.

3. *Equity:* Procedures should guarantee that no one is overlooked. The civil rights of students should also be protected, and the strategies should be specified for identifying the disadvantaged gifted. Also, cut-off scores should be avoided, because they are the most common way that disadvantaged students are discriminated against.

4. *Pluralism:* The broadest defensible definition of *pluralism* should be used.

5. *Comprehensiveness:* As many students with gifted potential as possible should be identified and served.

6. *Pragmatism:* Whenever possible, procedures should allow the modification and use of instruments and resources on hand.

Selection of Tests and Instruments

The misuse of tests can be avoided by considering the following precautions:

1. Select different measures and procedures to identify each diverse gifted ability.
2. Address these issues before using any test:
    - Is the test appropriate for the ability being sought?
    - Is the test being used at the appropriate stage of identification (i.e., nomination into a broad talent pool, assessment for a specific program option, evaluation within a program)?
3. Is the test appropriate for disadvantaged subpopulations within the district? Poor, minority, creative, underachieving, and other subpopulations are typically discriminated against in measures of academic achievement.

The Role of the Psychologist and/or Diagnostician

Castellano (in press) maintains that best practices suggest there are certain dynamics that must be considered when evaluating and assessing underrepresented students for gifted education programming. Hence, school districts that are serious about increasing the representation of poor and minority students in gifted programs, including those that are linguistically diverse, should consider employing full-time school psychologists or diagnosticians in targeted schools. Inclusive methodology further dictates that any process implemented to evaluate the academic and cognitive abilities of students be flexible enough to accommodate the needs of the students being tested.

In other words, what the psychologist or diagnostician brings, *or does not bring*, to the evaluation process, in terms of attitudes, expectations, and experiences, often determines the eligibility of historically underrepresented students for gifted education. Taking the time to establish rapport with a student who may be poor and/or culturally or linguistically different has the potential of paying off in big dividends later. As adults, psychologists and diagnosticians have the experience, ability, and flexibility to set the stage for optimal student performance. The following guiding principles will assist them in this endeavor.

Setting the Stage   Psychologists and diagnosticians should consider making a minimum of two visits to the classroom of the student prior to the actual testing.

1. *First Visit:* The first visit can last as long as thirty minutes and is preplanned with the classroom teacher. Usually, fifteen to twenty minutes will suffice. The purpose is to match a name with a face and to simply observe the student in the context of the classroom. Anecdotal observations are recorded in writing.

2. *Second Visit:* The second visit could last as long as sixty minutes. It is also planned with the teacher ahead of time, and it is understood that there will be deliberate contact with the student. It is suggested that the targeted student be engaged through a small cooperative group activity with at least three of his or her classmates, chosen by the teacher. The activity can be as simple as challenging the group to use their critical thinking and problem-solving skills to solve a "brain teaser" as quickly and efficiently as possible. Anecdotal observations of the targeted student are recorded in writing.

If a cognitive assessment (IQ test) is to take place, it is imperative that the tests are given under optimal conditions. Parents who have signed the consent form for testing should be informed of the exact day, time, and location the assessment will take place. They can help prepare their child for this experience.

The Testing Situation   An informal interview lasting five to ten minutes should be held with the student just prior to testing. This is an ideal opportunity to capitalize on the former visits to the classroom and increases the comfort level of the student. It is at this time that the psychologist or diagnostician has a conversation with the student about what will occur and allows the student an equal opportunity to ask questions.

The "chunking" technique should be considered when assessing students from diverse backgrounds. This strategy allows the testing to be done in segments, or chunks, with down time between subtests.

When Testing Is Completed   Once the "official" testing is over, it is recommended that the tester summarize what was done and what will happen next. It is important for underrepresented students to know that there will be closure and that their parents will be provided copies of all results. To further cement their rapport, the adult should personally escort the student back to the classroom, generating informal conversation that is genuine and direct. Validating the student by using personalizing comments leaves both parties with a "feel-good" attitude after everything is said and done.

In the assessment of linguistically diverse students, it is important that the psychologist or diagnostician be proficient in the listening, speaking, reading, and writing of the student's home language. If this is not possible, the use of translators/interpreters should be considered. However, it is critical that translators and interpreters receive intensive training in the process of evaluation as well as the technical language associated with testing and the label being considered. Finally, the evaluation instrument itself must be a "best match" with the relevant demographics of the student.

Equitable Use of Academic Achievement Data

In a procedure approved by the United States Office for Civil Rights, the scores may be disaggregated by various populations in order to factor out the inherent bias in most standardized tests. Renorming allows the selection of the same percentage of students from each subpopulation to ensure equal representation from each group. The purpose of renorming is not merely to achieve equity. Rather than relying solely on school achievement, which is skewed by social and economic environmental differences, the major objective of renorming is to identify inherent and latent gifted potential in all populations. The following are the steps for renorming test scores:

1. Determine whether the existing procedure underidentifies any of the disadvantaged subpopulations in the district by more than 5 percent to 10 percent to determine whether the following steps should be taken.

2. Determine the percentage of students that will be identified for each program option.

3. Disaggregate the scores. Determine in which of these categories students belong:
- Economic: disadvantaged (free or reduced-price lunch); advantaged (not needing free or reduced-price lunch)
- Race, culture, language group
- Gender

4. Rank order the disaggregated scores from the various subpopulations within each group.

5. The same percentage of top-scoring students from each subpopulation is selected as from among the advantaged student population. For example, assume that a district has resources for serving 10 percent of its students, grades K–8, in homogeneously grouped classes in reading. Then, based on achievement subtest scores in reading, the top 10 percent of the African American students, the top 10 percent of Hispanic students, and so on, and the top 10 percent of the boys and the top 10 percent of the girls should be selected for services.

Students will, of course, fall into several categories (economic, social, gender, language), but a balance can be worked out so that the outcome is representative of the district's school population. If data from teachers do not differ markedly from test scores, rather than offering complementary information, the data will reflect a similar bias. In that case, data from teachers may be renormed in the same way. These procedures were used successfully in at least two federally funded Javitz grants serving more than a dozen districts in Kansas and New Jersey.

Where Do We Go From Here?

In January of 1997, for the first time in the history of public education, leaders in the fields of bilingual/ESL education and gifted education were bought together in Washington, DC, by the United States Department of Education's Office of Bilingual Education and Minority Language Affairs (OBEMLA) and the Office of Educational Research and Improvement (OERI) to discuss, on a national level, a partnership between bilingual/ESL and gifted education. As immigrants continue to find their way to the United States, and given the millions of school-aged children who speak languages other than English, school districts across the United States are hard pressed to include these students in their programs for the gifted and talented. One of the purposes of the "summit" was to develop an agenda, or an awareness, with the potential to shape future national legislation and direction, resulting in a more collaborative joining between the two fields; that is, more opportunities for CLD students.

"Here We Go Again—Yet Another 'Reform' That Will Net Little"

The prospect of yet another educational initiative—making gifted education more authentically inclusive of LEP students with outstanding abilities—may leave educators in both bilingual and gifted education, at the least, exhausted and, at best, bewildered.

Being understaffed and overworked, it may seem impossible to these school staff to authentically increase the numbers of LEP students in gifted programs—and then support them so that they succeed.

Overcoming skepticism and feelings of powerlessness is key to providing inclusive gifted education for LEP students. Most school change occurs at the local level. If changes are imposed from without, school staffs are vocal in their protests. Even when progressive public policy makes it more possible to secure funds, there is something peculiarly American about putting a local stamp on a federal or state initiative. This is abundantly clear in the current case of national content and performance standards, which are tailored to fit local needs in hundreds of districts nationwide.

What, then, are gifted and bilingual educators to do? Some basic starting points are remarkably similar to starting points for any educational reform initiative. They include, but are not limited to, the following:

- Shifting to a cognitive and philosophical view of youth as multitalented, with accompanying multipronged identification procedures to identify and nurture youth with outstanding talents
- Committing to the long-term social benefits of expanding gifted education to include LEP students
- Collaborating across programs; a willingness to negotiate and entertain different points of view
- Building on strengths and program maturity
- Establishing a clear and coherent vision of inclusive gifted education
- Bringing the issue of LEP students and gifted education to a heightened level of public awareness
- Creating an action plan with realistic timelines
- Securing adequate teacher training and inservice programs

However, not all of these variables need to be in place before change begins.

Viewing Youth as Multitalented: Establishing Multipronged Identification Procedures

If gifted education is to be truly representative of all student populations—and fully harness the talent of all ethnicities, races, and linguistic groups—school staff in all programs must shift their view of intelligence as a single, limited entity to a much broader view of talent and abilities. As staff begin to make this cognitive shift, they must also make a practical commitment to the use of multipronged identification procedures so that LEP students are not neglected. As staff transition to what may appear to be imperfect identification measures, they can be helped by the recognition that narrow, traditional measures of IQ already severely limit the numbers of youth with talents who are eligible for gifted programs. Rather than become mired in an endless debate about the best identification procedures, educators in both gifted and bilingual education need to settle on a working procedure, begin to use it, and continue to refine it as their program grows and changes.

Committing to the Long-Term Social Benefits of Expanding Gifted Education to Include LEP Students

As educators expand their views of ability and intelligence, they must also make a real commitment to the inclusion of LEP students in gifted programs. If they pursue their own argument—that losing the most able youth because appropriate educational experiences are not available to them—they will find that continuing gifted education programs that do not adequately represent LEP youth is an intolerable state of affairs. Because public monies that support public education provide public benefit, this is an especially persuasive rationale for gifted educators who want to reach as many youth with outstanding talents as possible.

Authentic and Productive Collaboration

Almost any reform effort emphasizes the need for school staff to work collaboratively with each other, with parents, and with other members of the community. Unfortunately, collaboration-like restructuring has become almost meaningless as a term, because it has been used so frequently and glibly. However, as Sizer, a nationally recognized educator with an interest in assessment and evaluation of students, has pointed out, although collaboration is difficult and demanding, it is ultimately rewarding—and necessary if programmatic efforts are to avoid parochialism (Lockwood, 1997b).

Public Awareness of LEP Students and Their Talents

The power of the press—and galvanizing public opinion—is a considerable tool that gifted and bilingual educators need to wield. As gifted and bilingual educators begin their collective efforts, involving a carefully chosen community team that serves a public relations/outreach role for the media, parents and other community members can merit positive public awareness of LEP students and their talents. This core team can garner support from a variety of community agencies, seek external funds, solicit ideas, and become a powerful tool for shaping the decisions of district administrators and school boards.

Adequate Teacher Training and Professional Development

Although both bilingual education and gifted education are particularly susceptible to funding cuts, a substantial percentage of their budgets needs to be allocated to adequate teacher training and professional development, particularly as these areas relate to inclusion and support of LEP students in gifted programs. Cross-training in both bilingual education and gifted education is necessary so that teachers are not overwhelmed by new demands placed on them. Adequate and expert professional development needs to be undertaken. It is important to undertake professional development that extends beyond the "one-shot" workshop that offers scant opportunity for teachers to apply new ideas or obtain feedback when they attempt to shift their teaching in new directions.

Ongoing Evaluation from a Variety of Sources

Evaluation is not only necessary, but vital as gifted education expands its parameters to nurture LEP students. How well are programs proceeding? What timeline is realistic? Is there an action timeline, with responsibilities assigned to each person involved in the process? Are gifted and bilingual educators able to obtain additional evaluation from an external source that will inform their ongoing efforts? Finally, are school staff prepared to deal with evaluations that are less than 100 percent positive and make necessary program changes? All these questions form the nucleus of plans for evaluation of new efforts to include and nurture LEP students in gifted programs.

Clearly, the case of LEP students and their growing role in gifted programs is a knotty and complex topic, but one that is overdue for addressing by schools and school staffs. As demographics tilt to an increasingly multicultural society, the resource of LEP students in U.S. schools needs to be identified, nurtured, and encouraged so that contemporary society can benefit from its considerable promise.

Summary

A review of the literature targeting information on the identification and assessment of CLD students for gifted education reveals that it is scarce, to say the least. Action research, involving quantitative and qualitative methodology in this area, is also scarce. However, there is an abundance of research that makes references to minority students with regard to race and ethnicity, but often to the exclusion of limited-English- and non-English-speaking students. Historically, this population of students has been on the outside looking in.

Times are changing. Educators in both bilingual education and gifted education are beginning to realize that the collaboration and promotion of inclusionary identification practices results in a win–win situation. What other program is best suited to represent diversity in terms of intelligence, language, and ethnicity than gifted education? There are pockets of successful programs across the United States. These programs must serve as a catalyst to implement similar programs in the suburbs, large urban areas, and those rural areas where CLD students are found.

The road may not be an easy one, but the whys far outnumber the why nots. Programs for gifted, or potentially gifted children, among cultural and/or linguistic groups should be designed to nurture individual giftedness and provide a classroom climate that encourages students to use their talents in productive ways.

At the national level, the tone has been set by the document *A Nation at Risk* that criticizes how U.S. schools educate their brightest students. The challenge has been issued. As a result, both bilingual and gifted educators must promote a collaborative win–win agenda that is proactive and all-inclusive.

At the state and local levels, site-based and central office administrators need to reevaluate their gifted education programs to determine whether the criteria for admission consider all students or whether their programs promote exclusionary practices. The result should be a gifted program of which all factions of the school community will be proud.

In closing, in order to consider all students for gifted education programs, it is imperative that those individuals in positions of leadership take into account the cultural and linguistic needs of LEP students. As far as these students are concerned, identification criteria should consider both formal and informal assessments, qualitative and quantitative information, and other multiple criteria that balance the playing field. Schools across the United States are not raising their ceilings high enough for our students to soar to their greatest heights. Through collaboration and networking with all factions of the school community, we can begin to make a difference on behalf of gifted and talented CLD students. Posterity challenges all advocates of children to help make that difference.

REFERENCES

Armour-Thomas, E. (1992). Intellectual assessment of children from culturally diverse backgrounds. *School Psychology Review, 21* (4), 552–565.

Barkan, J. H., & Bernal, E. M. (1991). Gifted education for bilingual and limited English proficient students. *Gifted Child Quarterly, 35* (3), 144–147.

Bermudez, A. B., & Rakow, S. J. (1993). Analyzing teachers' perceptions of identification procedures for gifted and talented Hispanic limited English proficient students at risk. *The Journal of Educational Issues of Language Minority Students, 7,* 21–33.

Bernal, E. (1974). *Gifted Mexican-American children: An ethnico-scientific perspective.* Paper presented at the annual meeting of the American Educational Research Association. (Chicago, IL, April, 1974.)

Borland, J. H., & Wright, L. (1994). Identifying young, potentially gifted, economically disadvantaged students. *Gifted Child Quarterly, 38* (4), 161–174.

Castellano, J. A. (in press). *Recommended practices that psychologists and diagnosticians should consider when evaluating culturally and linguistically diverse students for gifted education.*

Castellano, J. A. (1998). Identifying and assessing gifted and talented bilingual Hispanic students. (ERIC Document Reproduction Service, No. ED 423 104).

Cremlin, L. (1961). *The transforming of the school: Progressivism in American education, 1876–1957.* New York: Vintage Books.

Cunningham, C. M., Callahan, C. M., Plucker, J. A., Roberson, S. C., & Rapkin, A. (1998). Identifying Hispanic students of outstanding talent: Psychometric integrity of a peer nomination form. *Exceptional Children, 64* (2), 197–208.

Figueroa, R. (1990). Best practices in the assessment of bilingual children. In A. Thomas & J. Grimes (Eds.), *Best practices in school psychology—II* (pp. 93–106). Washington, DC: National Association of School Psychologists.

Frasier, M. M. (1997). Multiple criteria: The mandate and the challenge. *Roeper Review, 20,* A4–A6.

Frasier, M. M., Hunsaker, S. L., Finley, V. S., Garcia, J. H., & Martin, D. (1995, September). *Educators' perceptions of barriers to the identification of gifted children from economically disadvantaged and limited English proficient backgrounds.* Stoors, CT. The National Research Center of the Gifted and Talented.

Frasier, M. M., & Passow, A. H. (1994). *Toward a paradigm for identifying talent potential* (Research Monograph 94112). The National Research Center on the Gifted and Talented. University of Connecticut, Stoors, CT. (ERIC Document Reproduction Service No. ED 388 020).

Garcia, J. H. (1994). Nonstandardized instruments for the assessment of Mexican-American children for gifted/talented programs. *Addressing Cultural and Linguistic Diversity in Special Education: Issues and Trends.* Division for Culturally and Linguistically Diverse Exceptional Learners. Reston, VA: A division of the Council for Exceptional Children.

Grigorenko, C., & Sternberg R. (1997). Styles of thinking, abilities, and academic performance. *Exceptional Children, 63* (3), 295–312.

Hamayan, E. V., & Damico, J. S. (1991). *Limiting bias in the assessment of bilingual students.* Austin, TX: Pro-Ed.

Harris, C. R. (1991). Identifying and serving the gifted new immigrant. *Teaching Exceptional Children, 23* (4), 26–30.

Kirschenbaum, R. J. (1998). Dynamic assessment and its use with underserved gifted and talented populations. *Gifted Child Quarterly, 42* (3), 140–147.

Kitano, M. K., & Espinosa, R. (1995). Language diversity and giftedness: Working with gifted English language learners. *Journal for the Education of the Gifted, 18* (3), 234–254.

LaCelle-Peterson, M. W., & Rivera, C. (1994). Is it real for all kids? A framework for equitable assessment policies for English language learners. *Harvard Educational Review, 64* (1), 55–75.

Leung, E. K. (1981). *The identification and sound process of the gifted bilingual-bicultural children*. A paper presented at the annual conference of the Council for Exceptional Children, New Orleans, LA.

Lockwood, A. T. (1997a). *Transforming education for Hispanic youth*. Paper prepared for the Office of the Under Secretary of Education, Washington, DC: United States Department of Education.

Lockwood, A. T. (1997b). *Conversations with educational leaders: Contemporary viewpoints on education in America*. Albany, NY: State University of New York Press.

Maker, C. J. (1996). Identification of gifted minority students: A national problem, needed changes, and a promising solution. *Gifted Child Quarterly, 40* (1), 41–50.

Marland, S. P., Jr. (1972). *Education of the gifted and talented: Report to the congress of the United States by the U.S. Commissioner of Education*. Washington, DC: Department of Health, Education, and Welfare.

Office of Educational Research and Improvement. (1993). *National excellence: A case for developing America's talent*. Washington, DC: United States Department of Education.

Passow, A. H., & Frasier, M. M. (1996). Toward improving identification of talent potential among minority and disadvantaged students. *Roeper Review, 18*, 198–202.

Plucker, J. A., Callahan, C. M., & Tomchin, E. M. (1996). Wherefore art thou, multiple intelligences? Alternative assessments for identifying talent in ethnically diverse and low income students. *Gifted Child Quarterly, 40* (2), 81–90.

Richert, E. S. (1992). *Equitable identification of students with gifted potential*. Report prepared for the Kansas State Board of Education. Washington, DC: United States Department of Education.

Richert, E. S., Alvino, J., & McDonnel, R. (1982). *The national report on identification: Assessment and recommendations for comprehensive identification of gifted and talented youth*. Sewell, NJ: Educational Information and Resource Center, U.S. Department of Education.

Saccuzzo, D. P. (1993). *Identifying under-represented disadvantaged gifted and talented children: A multifaceted approach*. San Diego: San Diego State University Department of Psychology. Manuscript in preparation.

Sarouphim, K. M. (1999). Discovering multiple intelligences through a performance based assessment: Consistency with independent ratings. *Exceptional Children, 65* (2), 151–161.

Stephens, K. R., & Karnes, F. A. (2000). State definitions for the gifted and talented revisited. *Exceptional Children, 66* (2), 219–238.

Sternberg, R. J. (1998). Teaching and Assessing for Successful Intelligence. *Social Administrator, 55* (1), 26–27, 30–31.

Torrence, E. P. (1977). Ways of discovering gifted black children. In A. L. Baldwin (Ed.), *Education planning for the gifted: Overcoming cultural geographic and socioeconomic barriers*. Reston, VA: Council for Exceptional Children.

Torrence, E. P. (1979). *The search for satori and creativity*. Buffalo, NY: Education Foundation.

Tyack, D. B. (1974). *The one best system: A history of American urban education*. Cambridge, MA: Harvard University Press.

United States Department of Education (1979). *Office of civil rights report*. Washington, DC: Government Printing Office.

United States Department of Education. (1997). *Talent and Diversity: The Emerging World of United English Proficient Students in Gifted Education*. Washington, DC: Offices of Educational Research and Improvement.

Westby, C. E. (1985, November). *Cultural differences in adult–child interaction proficiency testing: Some general considerations: Assessment and intervention implications*. A mini-seminar presented at the American Speech-Language Hearing Association Convention, Washington, DC.

Witty, E. P. (1978). Equal educational opportunity for gifted minority group children: Promise or possibility? *Gifted Child Quarterly, 22*, 344–352.

6 Gifted Education Program Options

Connections to English-Language Learners

JAIME A. CASTELLANO

Organizing a program that will deliver educational services to gifted learners is one of the most complex, most researched, and least clarified areas of gifted education. The administrative structure is critical to the success of the school program. It will reflect the commitment of the school to either expand or inhibit the opportunities for learning experienced by the gifted individual (Clark, 1992). However, issues of program organization become even more clouded when schools and school districts begin to recognize and acknowledge the potential gifts and talents of students identified as English-language learners. Having been historically excluded from programs for the gifted and talented (G/T), how are these students best served, if at all? The United States Congress recognized this concern when they passed the Jacob K. Javits Gifted and Talented Students Education Act (Title IV, Part B, of P.L. 100-297). This bill stated, in part, that gifted and talented students from economically disadvantaged families and areas, and students of limited English proficiency are at greatest risk of being unrecognized and of not being provided adequate or appropriate educational services.

Programs for G/T students may be designed for faster delivery of content, for delivery of more content, for examining content in greater depth, or for dealing with more complex and higher levels of subject matter. All of these approaches are essentially accelerative in nature and are based on efforts to fit instruction to the precocity of students. Other programs for the gifted and talented may also seek to provide alternatives that will enrich the learning experiences and allow students to study topics that fit their interest. Enrichment programs often seek to provide instruction in subject matter appropriate to the children's grade level but to also allow the study and investigation of supplementary content. Still other programs attempt to provide instruction that individually and explicitly fits the achievement levels, ability, interests, and learning styles of the gifted student (VanTassel-Baska, 1998).

These program options allow all students to be accommodated in one form or another. The focus is on the skills and talents of which the child has ownership. These models transcend the ethnic, racial, cultural, or linguistic makeup of the child. The fact that there are gifted and talented students whose first language is not English does not exclude them from participating in programs for the gifted and talented. The responsibility of the school and/or school district is to create a match in which the student receives the differentiated curriculum and instruction to meet his or her needs. This is done preferably within the context of a program that accommodates the student and in which he or she will experience the most success.

The purpose of this chapter is to describe those gifted education program models most often cited in the research as options schools and/or districts can consider for their students. In reference to English-language learners, adaptations to these same models are suggested. The number of students identified as eligible for services may be the determining factor in which program model is used. Essential planning considerations necessary for formulating the model of choice, in addition to Renzulli's (1975) seven key features to a successful program, are provided. The importance of this chapter is rooted in the fact that more and more school districts across the United States are just beginning to discover the importance of matching the needs of the students to the most appropriate delivery model while maintaining the integrity and respect of their ethnic, cultural, and linguistic diversity.

Instructional Models Used with Gifted, Talented English-Language Learners: One Survey's Snapshot

Bermudez and Rakow (1993) conducted a study in six states to examine and describe the status of identification, placement, and instructional procedures for gifted and talented (G/T) limited English proficient (LEP) students. The states of Texas, California, Colorado, Florida, Arizona, and New York were chosen because of their high concentration of Hispanic students.

With specific regard to instructional programs, the following information was collected:

> *Item 7: Our school district has a program used successfully with G/T LEP students.* Lack of specialized programs for the G/T LEP student was evident, as only 8.6 percent (twenty-three) of the total respondents (268) had any type of program to serve these students. Missing data could be indicative of lack of programs, thus adding to the inadequacy of educational services for these students. Of the fifty programs that indicated having identification means in place, only 46 percent had a program for these students.

> *Item 10: Is your program based on any particular model of gifted education?* Seventy-eight percent of the established programs follow a theoretically founded model of gifted education. Of these, 22.7 percent use Renzulli's TRIAD model, and 50 percent use a combination. There were six missing responses, which could indicate the school's lack of awareness of theoretical and research foundations available for this area.

The results generated by the Bermudez and Rakow study are not surprising. School districts across the United States that serve a large number of English-language learners are often hard pressed on how to best serve this population of students. And when this same population begins to have an impact on gifted education programs, the situation is compounded even more. These students may be identified as gifted and talented, but are they placed in an appropriate program? The Bermudez and Rakow study suggests that more often than not, these students are not provided services.

Programs and Services for Talented Students

In October of 1993, the U.S. Department of Education's Office of Educational Research and Improvement (OERI) published a national report entitled, *National Excellence: The Case for Developing America's Talent*. In part, this report stated that policies alone do not guarantee that children with exceptional talents will receive a meaningful education. Most gifted and talented students spend most of the school day in a regular education classroom where little is done to adapt the curriculum to their special learning needs. Exciting pedagogy and teaching strategies have been developed and refined in some special programs for G/T students. From kindergarten through high school, the education available to talented students is largely insufficient because most schools have not been committed to seriously addressing their needs (p. 19).

As a result, through Javits grants sponsored by the U.S. Department of Education, projects seek out and provide educational programs for exceptionally talented students who are economically disadvantaged, speak limited English, or have disabilities. These programs are committed to finding and nurturing the strengths in children, providing promising students with important subject matter to study and encouraging the habits of hard work (pp. 23).

The Javits and Title VII grant money available from the federal government is funding that many school districts have been awarded to develop programs for their underrepresented populations, including those students that are identified as limited or non-English speaking who exhibit outstanding gifts and talents. Mosiac 2000 in the Chicago Public School District, Project GOTCHA, an Academic Excellence Program, and Project EXCEL in the San Diego City School District are three successful programs that have targeted these students and have framed programs to meet their needs. They are portraits of success.

Gifted Education Program Options: Connections to English-Language Learners

A four-year study sponsored by the Sid W. Richardson Foundation (Cox, Daniel, & Boston, 1985) sought to respond to three issues: (1) What programs exist for able learners? (2) Which programs are most effective and offer the best chance for adaptation to many environments? (3) What recommendations would assist schools in serving able learners?

When considering English-language learners, the questions posed by the Sid W. Richardson Foundation may be reframed in the following way: (1) What program options exist for limited or non-English speakers who demonstrate outstanding gifts or talents? (2) Which programs are most effective and offer the best chance for adaptation in schools that service G/T students from a number of different language groups? (3) What recommendations would assist schools serving only a few students versus those serving a large number from the same language group?

The program options available to schools and school districts for educating their most able students are numerous. Clark (1992) maintains that among other considerations, the planning necessary to develop a gifted program should provide the best match for the needs of the students. Therefore, special consideration must be given to those students whose primary language is other than English. This author's experience as a teacher and administrator of gifted education programs, at both the building and district levels, has been both exciting and frustrating. In one school district I was directed not to include any bilingual students because of their limited English proficiency. The program could not, or would not, accommodate their language needs. As a result, those few bilingual students who demonstrated academic talent did not receive the services they deserved.

The following gifted education program models are often cited in the research as options that schools and/or school districts can consider for their students. These same programs can be adapted and/or modified to meet the needs of underrepresented populations—in this case, students who are limited or non-English speaking and who demonstrate outstanding gifts and talents.

Part-Time Temporary Programs

There are a number of part-time temporary gifted education program models that schools can consider, adapt, or modify to meet the needs of their English-language learners.

Pull-out Programs

This may be a popular model of choice for schools who have identified a small number of gifted English-language learners from various grade levels. Multiage/grade groupings allow interstudent teaching and learning to occur on a regular basis. The emphasis is on interactive learning in the language with which the student feels most comfortable. Ideally, the teacher should be able to speak the language of the students if they are all from the same language group. If the teacher is unable to speak the language of the students, he or she should be well versed in sheltered English instruction. Either teacher, however, should have experience and training in gifted education

Of course, the pull-out program should be an extension of the core curriculum, and close communication should occur between the two instructors. The pull-out teacher may also plan seminars, specialized resource rooms, special classes, field trips, or other unique learning experiences (Clark, 1992).

Mentorship

With this option, connections are made with the greater school community to allow students to pursue specific areas of interest. Identifying adults who are experts in a particular field and who speak the heritage language of the student enhances the experience and promotes the role model–student relationship. In large urban communities with an established ethnic and cultural base, the opportunity for such a mentorship is heightened.

The focus of the mentorship program is on sharing information and experiences. Mentors may include community residents, business leaders, senior citizens, and older students. VanTassel-Baska (1998) asserts that career education surely involves much academic and affective learning through school and guidance services, but, in addition, role models, mentors, and heroes are vital parts of the career education and career-development process.

Subject Skipping

With an emphasis on acceleration, subject skipping rests on the existence of higher level courses available in the heritage language of the students. This program option is more readily found in middle schools, in high schools, and on the college or university level. Perhaps a combination of both subject skipping and the use of mentors would benefit students even more.

Bilingual students should have access to advanced coursework in which they excel. This option also allows them to remain with their age mates for other curriculum areas, thus not severing the ties completely from their friends and communities.

Balzer and Siewert (1990) maintain that, in this approach, instruction is delivered so that students move through the curriculum according to assessed skill level rather than grade level. The student moves ahead whenever mastery of content and skills is demonstrated. For many English-language learners, the foreign language curriculum comes to mind.

Telescoping

English-language learners who are enrolled in a middle, junior, or senior high school that offers a comprehensive menu of content area classes in their native language can participate in this program model. Essentially, telescoping allows students to collapse four years of high school into three, for example.

Some gifted learners, including those who are identified as English-language learners, may profit from telescoping two years of education into one or bypassing a particular grade level. Provision for such advanced placement should be based on individual student demonstration of capacity, readiness, and motivation (VanTassel-Baska, 1998).

Early Admission to College/Dual and Joint Enrollment

Following the telescoping model, the opportunity for English-language learners to enter college through early admission is available. However, early admission is contingent on placement tests and other forms of assessment that may need to be available and/or administered in their heritage languages. Their high school counselors will need to play key roles throughout the early admissions process.

The proximity of a college or university, scheduling flexibility, and cooperation between the college and the public school can form the basis for dual or joint enrollment. *Dual enrollment* allows a student to be enrolled in college courses while still in high school. The student is generally responsible for the cost of the course and transportation to and from the course but receives college and high school credit for successfully completed college work.

Similar in nature, *joint enrollment* allows a student to be enrolled in college courses while still in high school. The student is generally responsible for the cost of the course and transportation to and from the course, but the high school transcript shows only high school course work; the college transcript shows successfully completed college work (North Carolina State Department of Public Instruction, 1988). Areas of study in which linguistically diverse students may take advantage of such options include mathematics and foreign language, among others.

Accelerated Classes

Much like the subject-skipping model, the opportunity for English-language learners to enroll in accelerated coursework relies on the availability of the classes in the heritage languages. For secondary schools without a bilingual program, an alternative for these students would be that the school offer a "sheltered English" accelerated model taught by a highly trained and sensitive ESL or gifted education teacher.

The advantages of accelerated classes include the opportunity for multilanguage groups to participate in the model and the flexibility allotted to the teacher to use additional teaching methodologies, such as technology, mentoring, and telecourses.

The feature film *Stand and Deliver*, the story of high school math teacher Jaime A. Escalante, is a well-documented example of limited English proficient students enrolled in a fast-paced, more advanced math curriculum, which ultimately led to his students receiving college credit for advanced coursework.

Grade Skipping

An often-used option with monolingual English gifted students, grade skipping also should be considered for academically talented English-language learners. For gifted bilingual Hispanic students, determining heritage language standards of achievement may be easier to obtain than for other language groups. However, prior to using this model, a complete evaluation of the students should take place.

According to Davis and Rimm (1998), grade skipping is the traditional method of accelerating precocious elementary school students. It requires no special materials or facilities, no G/T coordinator, not even a G/T program. In fact, it is extraordinarily cost effective in moving the gifted or talented child through and out of the school system ahead of schedule. In elementary schools with an established K–5 or K–6 bilingual program, the opportunity exists for G/T English-language learners to be considered for grade skipping.

Correspondence Courses

This program option allows G/T linguistically diverse students to obtain college credit by taking a college course by mail, independent study, or as a form of enrichment in conjunction with the standard high school course. Having available resources in the high school for these students to tap into is a certain advantage of this model. A logical starting point may be the foreign language area, whereby they sharpen and increase their listening, speaking, reading, and writing proficiency skills in their own languages, and for college credit.

A considerable amount of self-motivation and independence is needed to complete a correspondence course successfully. Students are more likely to be successful if several of them take the same course, thus permitting mutual support, stimulation, and assistance. It also is helpful if a high school faculty member can serve as an advisor for the students in case they need help in understanding or interpreting the material or solving practice problems (Davis and Rimm, 1998).

Telecourses

When a school and/or school district has identified only a few G/T linguistically diverse students or does not have the necessary staff to implement a program that meets these students' unique needs, taking advanced coursework through telecommunications may be a viable option. However, the availability of the necessary technology is a factor that dictates whether this is even a realistic option.

Most often associated with rural school districts, telecommunications is widely employed to meet the specialized needs of gifted students found in these locations. In addition, throughout the southwestern United States, rural Mexican and Native American populations are enrolled in schools in which the budgets are sparse and personnel is limited, as is access to materials and supplies. Telecommunications may be one of the few ways that these schools may meet the needs of all students.

Full-Time Homogeneous/Heterogeneous Groupings

Once the development of the gifted education program has begun, the district must choose a program design or a combination of designs to implement the curriculum modifications. Part-time temporary groupings should be considered, as well as the following full-time homogeneous designs (Illinois State Board of Education, 1993).

Magnet Schools

Magnet schools are established for students who are interested in a specialized field of study and often include those who are G/T. In this design, the school is charged with providing specialized experiences rooted in acceleration and enrichment. The commitment of magnet school programs to recruit limited-English- and/or non-English-speaking students is suspect. Recruiting efforts targeting these students are often initiated by advocacy groups or through litigation, as the result of civil rights violations, for example.

The term *magnet school* has varying definitions, which are implemented differently throughout the United States. Those magnet schools that offer specialized training in foreign languages often include students who are English-language learners. For these dual-language magnet schools, the goal is to develop students who are truly bilingual, biliterate, and bicognitive. This program design makes sense for many of our G/T students.

Special Schools

Again, the interpretation of the term *special schools* varies throughout the country. For the most part, G/T English-language learners are excluded due to traditional standardized testing, which often includes an IQ measure. However, as an option, special schools are designed for students with special abilities or talents, with a curriculum that includes both academic content and opportunities for enrichment and accelerated training. Special schools typically draw from regional or state populations.

One example of a special school is the Illinois Math and Science Academy, located in Aurora, Illinois. From across the state, students with particular skill and talent in math and sciences are eligible for participation. This residential school design most often includes a quota system to balance the student composition for race and gender.

Because enrichment options are diverse and exciting (Davis and Rimm, 1998), opportunities to accommodate limited-English- or non-English-speaking students do exist. Enrichment programs in foreign language, music, art, and drama can be available to these students, while providing them with specialized assistance in other curriculum areas.

School within a School

The school-within-a-school option may be a very appropriate model for G/T English-language learners. For part of the school day, gifted students attend core curriculum courses taught by specially trained teachers. Flexibility is afforded school administrators who have identified a number of students who excel in a specific field of study and who require academic experiences rooted in acceleration and enrichment. The rest of the day is spent integrated with other students in the "regular" curriculum.

For a school with a highly evolved bilingual and/or ESL program, this option may best meet the needs of identified students. An additional benefit includes the fact that the students remain in the neighborhood school, close to family, friends, home, and community. According to Clark (1982), such a setting allows for more community and field experiences and flexibility of grouping without interrupting the overall school schedule. Many districts find such provisions especially attractive for highly gifted students or as a solution to low-achieving, gifted students, as the cost is little more than offering another section of a regular class.

Self-Contained Classrooms

Self-contained classrooms consisting of G/T students are found throughout the United States. These classes extend and enrich the curriculum by promoting higher order and critical thinking skills. This homogeneous model is staffed by full-time teachers and/or specialists.

School districts with a large number of English-language learners who qualify for G/T education should consider this option. This model is currently in place in the San Diego, California, City School System; the Chicago Public Schools; Socorro, Texas, Schools; the Milwaukee Public Schools; and Garland, Texas, Schools, among other large urban school districts that advocate and recognize the associated benefits afforded their English-language learners. In some cases, these classes are found in a magnet school framework.

Special Classes

Special classes for G/T students may take several forms. At the elementary level, all gifted students within a particular grade level, age, or age range may be assigned to a special class. In addition to covering prescribed grade-level objectives—and usually extending beyond them—a variety of enrichment, personal-development, and skill-development experiences are planned (Davis and Rimm, 1998).

Special classes can be especially appropriate for English-language learners who speak the same heritage language or for those models that service multiple languages in the same program. The advantages of using the heritage language for instruction is that it allows for its continued development, with particular emphasis on improving reading and writing, while at the same time encouraging the student behaviors of risk taking, elaboration, and complexity, for example.

In a special class of high ability/gifted students comprising multiple languages, the "sheltered English" approach would be the instructional method of choice. Another option is the use of the SDAIE strategy (Specially Designed Academic Instruction in English), commonly used in California. Using the special class option, gifted English-language learners would attend a specially designed class that extends or enriches the curriculum in a content area or provides enrichment activities. Examples include thinking skills, telecourses, and computer programming.

Ability Tracking/Cluster Grouping

Typically found at the middle/junior high school and senior high school levels, cluster grouping (which may be the more politically correct term to use) calls for students to be grouped for the purpose of instruction in a specified content area. For English-language learners who move up to middle or senior high school, providing opportunities to accelerate or enrich their academic experiences in the different subject areas would be meeting their high-level needs.

However, an important consideration is that the instruction be provided by a content-area specialist capable of challenging the students to higher levels. Too many times teachers assigned to instruct English-language learners at the secondary level are generalists with no content-area expertise. This should be avoided at all costs. Teachers working within this framework should also have the knowledge to differentiate the curriculum by modifying content, process, and/or product.

Multiage/Multigrade Classrooms

Primarily found at the elementary level, multiage classrooms may be one of a few viable options that a school and/or school district can consider. This model would be most appropriate in those situations when only a few English-language learners at varying grade levels are identified as gifted and/or talented. The program focus is rooted in acceleration, with emphasis on interactive learning.

This classroom with students of different ages and grades can be staffed by full-time or part-time teachers or teachers designated as specialists. Younger students learn from other students who are older. In many Hispanic cultures, for example, this approach is consistent with their value system of cooperation and collaboration.

Furthermore, according to Clark (1982), cross-grading, combining several age-graded classes into one group (e.g., first through third grade) allows easier access to materials and a pace appropriate to the gifted students' levels of development. By cross-grading, we can move away from the age-in-grade lockstep that has for years been so limiting to all students. Team teaching provides additional resources, skills, and stimulation for both teachers and learners.

Curriculum Compacting

This strategy would be very appropriate in both bilingual and regular education classrooms that include English-language learners who are identified as G/T, but where no available gifted program exists in the district. Conducted within traditional classrooms by a trained teacher, this modification compresses the content to eliminate repetition of previously mastered material, to upgrade the challenge level of the standard curriculum, and to provide time for appropriate enrichment and/or acceleration activities. To successfully implement this option, ongoing training for those participating teachers is essential. Ideally, the training should have a long-term focus, with ample opportunities for teachers to share ideas with each other.

Other Program Options

The preceding program options are not an exhaustive list. Actually, the options afforded any school district depend, in part, on how creative it can be with the resources that are available. A variety of options, such as the following, are offered at the elementary level as special services for G/T children (VanTassel-Baska, 1998).

- Seminars
- Special computer classes
- Junior Great Books program
- Foreign language instruction
- Career education, mentors, and role models
- After-school, Saturday, and summer enrichment classes
- Special classes in art, music, and dance

These options, too, can be easily modified or adapted to meet the unique needs of gifted and/or talented English-language learners, as can the following list of basic needs that are not unique to G/T youth but set forth what may be regarded as the fundamental requisites for optimum development of precocious or highly able youth (Van Tassel-Baska, 1998).

Junior High or
Middle School Services

Counseling
Group
Individual
Honors classes
Future problem solving
Junior Great Books
Odyssey of the Mind
Career education
Seminars
Mentors
Advanced placement
or college courses
Acceleration
Math
Science
English
Special opportunities
Art
Music
Drama
Dance
Special projects for the
vocationally talented
Foreign language instruction
Correspondence study
Independent study

High School Services

Counseling
Group
Individual
Honor classes
Advanced placement classes
Foreign language instruction
Seminars
Mentorships
Internships
Concurrent college enrollment
College classes in high school
Special opportunities
Art
Music
Drama
Dance
Special projects for the
vocationally talented
Debate
Correspondence study
Independent study

Why Programs Are Not Being Considered

If a plethora of both full-time and part-time programs exists, the question to be asked is, "Why are these programs not being used to accommodate those English-language learners identified as gifted?" There is no clear and simple answer. One can only speculate. Perhaps part of the reason lies in the fact that gifted education is not one of the areas associated with the Individuals with Disabilities Education Act (IDEA). In other words, because gifted education is not legislatively or legally connected to IDEA, money is not available to develop programs for this population of students. The same can be said when looking at state departments of education across the United States. There are states that mandate gifted education through policy and/or law. However, the mandate or policy may not be funded. The lack of funded mandates may serve as another rationale for why programs are not being developed (Passow & Rudnitski, 1993). Other reasons may include the possibility that schools and/or districts do not have a mechanism in place to identify gifted English-language learners, do not have the personnel qualified to meet the unique instructional and curricular needs, and/or do not have the resources and materials available for development and implementation.

The Gifted Program: Planning Considerations

Clark (1982) maintains that the planning necessary to develop a gifted program that will provide the best match for the needs of students, parent expectations, the school administration's philosophy, community resources, and the resources and commitment of the school staff is like orchestrating a symphony. There is the homework to do and the skills to perfect; there are personnel and materials to collect; beliefs and abilities to assess; cooperation to solicit. When putting it all together, the timing is crucial. Renzulli (1975d) identified seven key features that experts in the field of gifted education agree are basic to a successful program:

1. The selection and training of teachers
2. A curriculum designed to evoke and develop superior behavioral potentialities in academic areas and the arts that is both systematic and comprehensive
3. Multiple appropriate screening and identification procedures
4. A statement of philosophy and objectives that support differential education for the gifted
5. Staff orientation to promote a knowledgeable and cooperative attitude
6. A plan of evaluation
7. Delineation of administrative responsibility

There is no magic wand to wave nor spell to cast that would make a gifted education program, for any group of students, successful and effective without these seven features in combination with commitment and hard work. A collaboration of primary stakeholders is an essential ingredient for success. For those programs throughout the United States that do include English-language learners in G/T education, reaching out to diverse populations promotes a sense of cooperation and inclusion, and a validation that the contributions of these populations are welcomed and respected.

The U.S. Department of Education's Office of Educational Research and Improvement (OERI) does not collect information from school districts on the program delivery model used to service gifted students who are linguistically diverse, or who are classified as limited English proficient (LEP). Despite this fact, in adapting delivery models to be used with this population of students, "inclusionary" practices should consider the following information:

1. Number of English-language learners identified as gifted
2. Teachers trained to work effectively with gifted English-language learners

3. Available resources (fiscal, curricular, instructional)
4. Level of support from the district office and state department of education
5. Support generated from primary stakeholders such as school administration, teachers, parents, and the general school community

Furthermore, based on the work of the North Carolina Association for Gifted and Talented Task Force on Appropriate Services for Gifted Students (1988), highlights of elements essential to programs include the following:

Administrative Support and Responsibility: To have a quality program for gifted students, there must be administrative support. The administration's main responsibility is providing appropriate services for gifted students.

Definition and Identification: Identification is the process of finding those students whose characteristics match the definition. It should be noted that *giftedness* can encompass a broader range of ability than is denoted by the term *academically gifted.*

Assessment of Student Needs: While identification determines whether a student is appropriate for the program, the assessment of student needs helps to determine whether the program is appropriate for the student. The assessment of both group and individual needs should be considered.

Written Plan: A written plan outlines a system's unified efforts to provide appropriate services to its gifted students. It defines a program.

Program Options: Both group and individual program options should be combined to form a program that is flexible enough to meet the varying needs of gifted students. The key here, perhaps, is to actually have options. These need not be formal options, but any program that provides services in only one way will, sooner or later, encounter a child for whom that option is not appropriate. Time is a critical factor in determining the possible effectiveness of any option.

Curriculum: Curricula for gifted students must be responsive to the characteristics that separate the gifted from the nongifted. Curricula must also assume the existence of an adequate general education program, that curriculum modifications will directly address the academic content areas in which the students' strengths are identified, and that instruction will be on a level commensurate with the students' abilities.

Teachers: The importance of teachers in the education of gifted students cannot be overstated. The teacher that assumes responsibility for the academic content area in which the student is identified as gifted is charged with the appropriate education of that student. The teacher of the gifted must be certified in education for the gifted. Classroom teachers and others who have a significant responsibility for these children should also be trained appropriately.

Support Services: Other professionals that are important in providing services for gifted students include school counselors, media specialists, psychologists, and others. Staff development is necessary to enable these individuals to understand gifted students in order to meet their needs.

Funding: A program of appropriate services for gifted students requires adequate financial support from both the local and state levels. Federal funding through the Javits grant program from the U.S. Department of Education is also available on a competitive basis.

Community Awareness and Parent Involvement: The effectiveness and success of a program for gifted students depends on a clear understanding within the total community of that program. It is the responsibility of the school to communicate what giftedness is so that the entire community understands that program, thus justifying the mandate for appropriate services. Parents can also plan and implement programs and activities for gifted students. PAGE (Parents for the Advancement of Gifted Education) chapters have proven to be beneficial in this regard.

Factors beyond Local Control: It is recognized that there are factors such as personnel preparation, program evaluation, research and development, and demonstration programs for which the local school system is limited in how much it can do to directly support these functions. The school system can, however, encourage state, federal, and private sources to do so.

If programs are to evolve into an integral part of the district's educational program, some policies and standards must be developed and reexamined at regular intervals throughout the program (Clark, 1992). Standards for such important components of the program as the goals and objectives, responsibility for decision making, monitoring, expenditures, and staff development assure quality within the program and can provide criteria against which evaluation becomes clear and far more useful (Kaplan, 1986).

Collaboration and commitment between the school board and the parents of children identified as G/T, and every other stakeholder in between, must occur to establish programming that is meaningful and reflects the expectations of the school community and the greater society in general. English-language learners and their advocates also must be part of the process to ensure that students' unique needs are being met within the context of program development.

Summary

If the needs of gifted learners are to be met, we must have a planned, coordinated, continuous program. This program must be open and responsive to the changing individual, while providing a continuous challenge and an adequate diversity of content and process. While we may draw from more traditional gifted education models, our own communities, our parents, our students, and our staffs must make the decisions regarding structure and intent (Clark, 1992).

Traditional gifted models also can work for those English-language learners identified as G/T. Like adapting and modifying curriculum—differentiation to meet the needs of diverse student levels and talents—gifted models also can be adapted and modified with little or no emphasis on cost. The content of this chapter attempted to address how this could be done.

VanTassel-Baska (1998) acknowledges that the best models provide acceleration, enrichment, and challenging learning experiences, which help gifted youth clarify their talent, strengths, and potential and give them opportunities to move ahead to higher levels of learning at a pace that fits their abilities. The fact that there are students who are non-English or limited-English speaking is irrelevant. They deserve the same opportunity to be part of a program that accentuates their skills and talents.

Developing and activating programs and services for gifted learners are important enterprises that are ongoing and dynamic. One gifted program will not meet the needs of all gifted learners in a given school district; nor will activation of all the program-development elements described herein guarantee a sufficient effort. Only as we continue to work at the individual and collective aspects of the program-development cycle are we likely to build the quality programs we envision. The building process also takes time. Years of effort are usually required to establish and fine-tune a program of quality. Gifted program developers should view the task of program development as a major undertaking, one that is full of challenges and frustrations on the way to creating a "willed future" for gifted learners (VanTassel-Baska, 1998).

Considering the fact that English-language learners or LEP students have historically been excluded from programs for G/T students, school districts across the country should keep in mind the information detailed in this chapter. If we envision equal access for this group of students, it is our responsibility to face these challenges and frustrations head on. The process necessary to generate quality programs may take years, but our students are worth the time spent in doing so. Title VII grants from the U.S. Department of Education's Office of Bilingual Education and Minority Language Affairs (OBEMLA) and Javits grants from the OERI are two funding sources that school districts can consider to speed the process along. Finally, commitment from the local and state levels is essential for the development of quality programs for *all* students.

REFERENCES

Alvino, J., McDonnel, R., & Richert, S. (1981). National survey of identification practices in gifted and talented education. *Exceptional Education, 48* (2), 124–132.

Assouline, S. G., & Lupkowski-Shoplik, A. E. (1997). Talent search: A model for the discovery and development of academic talent. In N. Colangelo & G. A. Davis (Eds.), *Handbook of gifted education* (2nd ed., pp. 170–179). Boston: Allyn & Bacon

Belcastro, F. P. (1987). Elementary pullout program for the intellectually gifted—boon or bane? *Roeper Review, 9* (4), 4–11.

Bermudez, A. B., Rakow, S. J., Marquez, J. M., Sawyer, C., & Ryan, C. (1993). Meeting the needs of the gifted and talented limited English proficient students. National Association for Bilingual Education (1990–1991). Washington, DC.

Bermudez, A. B., & Rakow, S. J. (1993). Examining identification and instruction practices for gifted and talented limited English proficient students. (ERIC Reproduction Service ED 360 871).

Bernal, E. M. *Mexican American perceptions of child giftedness in three Texas communities.* Paper presented at the First National Conference on the Disadvantaged Gifted, Ventura, CA, March 1973.

Bernal, E. M. Alternative avenues of assessment of culturally different gifted. Speech presented to the Department of Educational Psychology, University of Georgia, Athens, February 1978.

Bernal, E. M. (1979). The education of the culturally different gifted. In A. H. Passow (Ed.), *The gifted and the talented* (pp. 395–400). Chicago: National Society for the Study of Education.

Bordie, J. (1970). Language tests and linguistically different learners: The sad state of the art. *Elementary English, 47,* 814–828.

Chislett, L. M. (1994). Integrating the CPS and schoolwide enrichment models to enhance creative thinking. *Roeper Review, 17* (1), 4–7.

Clark, B. (1982). *Growing up gifted.* New York: Merrill.

Colangelo, N., & Davis, G. A. (1991). *Handbook of gifted education.* Boston: Allyn & Bacon.

Comer, J. P. (1988). Educating poor minority children. *Scientific American, 259* (5), 42–48.

Cox, J., Daniel, N. and Boston, B. (1985). *Educating able learners: Programs and Promising Practices.* Austin, TX: University of Texas Press.

Davis, G. A., & Rimm, S. B. (1998). *Education of the gifted and talented.* Boston: Allyn & Bacon.

Hilliard, P. (1976). *Identifying gifted minority children through the use of non-verbal tests.* Unpublished doctoral dissertation. Yeshiva University, New York.

Feldhusen, H. J. (1993). *Individualized teaching of gifted children in the regular classroom.* West Lafayette, IN: STAR Teaching Materials.

Feldhusen, J. F. (1991). Full-time classes for gifted youth. *Gifted Child Today, 14* (5), 10–13.

Hoover, S. M., Sayler, M. F., & Feldhusen, J. F. (1993). Cluster grouping of gifted students at the elementary level. *Proper Review, 16* (1), 13–15.

Illinois State Board of Education. (1993). *Gifted education resource guide.* Springfield, IL.

Jacob K. Javitz. Gifted and Talented Students Education Act, 20 U.S.C. § 3061–3068 (1988).

Johnsen, S. K., & Ryser, G. R. (1996). An overview of effective practices with gifted students in general-education settings. *Journal for the Education of the Gifted, 19* (4), 379–404.

Kaplan, S. (1986). Alternatives for the design of gifted program inservice and staff development. *Gifted Child Quarterly, (30)* 3, 138–139.

Kitano, M. K., & Kirby D. F. (1986). *Gifted education: A comprehensive view.* Boston: Little, Brown.

Kitano, M. K. (1991). A multicultural educational perspective on serving the culturally diverse gifted. *Journal for the Education of the Gifted, 15,* 4–19.

Kitano, M. (1989). Critique of "Identification of Gifted Asian-American Students." In J. Maker & S. Schiever (Eds.), *Critical issues in gifted education* (Vol. II): Defensible programs for cultural and ethnic minorities (pp. 163–168). Austin, TX: Pro-Ed.

Maker, C. J. (1982). *Curriculum development for the gifted.* Austin, TX: Pro-Ed.

Maker, C. J., & Nielson, A. B. (1995). *Teaching models in the education of the gifted* (2nd ed.). Austin, TX: Pro-Ed.

Marland, S., Jr. (1972). *Education of the gifted and talented.* Report to the Congress of the United States by the U.S. Commissioner of Education. Washington, DC: U.S. Government Printing Office

Moon, S. M. (1996). Using the Purdue three-stage model to facilitate local program evaluations. *Gifted Child Quarterly, 40* (3), 121–127.

Nidiffer, L. G., & Moon, S. M. (1994). Middle school seminars. *Gifted Child Today, March/April,* 24–27.

North Carolina State Department of Public Instruction. (1988). *Excellence for the future: Program options for the academically gifted.* (ERIC Document Reproduction Service No. ED 300 966).

Office of Educational Research and Improvement. (1993). *National Excellence: A Case for Developing America's Talent.* Washington, DC: United States Department of Education.

Passow, A. H., & Rudnitski, R. A. (1993). *State policies regarding education of the gifted as reflected in legislation and regulation.* The National Research Center on the Gifted and Talented. (ERIC Document Reproduction Service No. ED 379 849).

Renzulli, J. S. (1975). *A Guidebook for Evaluating Programs for the Gifted and Talented: Working Draft.* (ERIC Document Reproduction Service No. ED 119 426), Washington, DC:

Renzulli, J. S. (1996). Schools for talent development: A practical plan for total school improvement. *The School Administrator, January,* 20–22.

Renzulli, J. S., & Reis, S. M. (1994). Research related to the schoolwide enrichment triad model. *Gifted Child Quarterly, 38* (1), 7–20.

Richert, S. (1985). Identification of gifted children in the United States: The need for pluralistic assessment. *Roeper Review, 8* (2), 68–72.

Sapon-Shevin, M. (1995). Why gifted students belong in inclusive schools. *Educational Leadership, 52* (4), 64–68, 70.

Silverman, L. K. (1993). *Counseling the gifted and talented.* Denver: Love Publishing.

VanTassel-Baska, J. (1998). *Excellence in educating gifted and talented learners.* Denver: Love Publishing.

VanTassel-Baska, J., Patton, J., & Prillaman, D. (1989). Disadvantaged gifted learners: At risk for educational attention. *Focus on Exceptional Children, 22* (3), 1–15.

Wood, B., & Feldhusen, J. F. (1996). Creating special interest programs for gifted youth. *Gifted Child Today, July/August,* 22–28.

Woods, S. B., & Achey, V. H. (1990). Successful identification of gifted racial/ethnic group students without changing classification requirements. *Roeper Review, 13,* 21–26.

7 Addressing the Curriculum, Instruction, and Assessment Needs of the Gifted Bilingual/ Bicultural Student

A. JIM GRANADA

The student that is acquiring a second language, assimilating into a second culture, and dealing with the asynchronous development of being gifted is not only elusive to identify, but a very complex student, indeed. We must understand the many facets of this student before we even think about the appropriate curriculum to design, the best instructional approaches and strategies to use, and the best instruments to select to assess his or her progress and performance.

The first issue to address is that of language. The teacher needs to determine the degree to which the bilingual/bicultural gifted student can use the primary language, in addition to the proficiency level at which he or she is operating. The teacher also must determine the extent to which the active and passive vocabularies have developed in the second language, and the rate at which they were acquired. The teacher should also become aware of regional differences in a language such as Spanish—from significant differences (which might exist between native speakers from two different Spanish-speaking countries) to more subtle differences, such as the terminology used for common objects or actions. A student may be proficient in a language but may not be using the formal language, as would be taught in school.

An aspect of language that may reflect giftedness in linguistic abilities is the level of code switching that a student demonstrates. Switching between two languages may reflect a more complex process than initially meets the eye, or ear, if you will. To various degrees, code switching indicates the ability to manipulate language, and students who combine two languages when speaking, using the right phonetic and grammatical structures within the merging of the two languages, may be displaying a much greater skill than students who insert words when they can't bring into active vocabulary a term they are trying to use.

Collecting these data may provide the baseline indicators for linguistic emphasis in gifted services if the data indicate a high level of proficiency in one or both languages, advanced-level active or passive vocabularies, or an accelerated rate of acquisition of the new language.

The second issue is that of culture. Caution should be taken at this point regarding overgeneralization of the Hispanic cultural umbrella. The student may or may not practice the customs and traditions of his or her cultural heritage. The degree to which a student relates to a culture of another country is dependent on the student's level of acculturation and the family's level of acculturation, which may be different. To understand the cultural perspectives of the bicultural/bilingual gifted student, we must become familiar with the various cultural settings in which the student currently functions and learn what we can about the contexts of which he or she may have also been a part.

Four distinct cultural contexts should be examined if culture is to become an integral piece of the completed gifted programming puzzle: the academic setting, the family setting, the neighborhood in which the student resides, and the community in which the student lives, particularly if that community is not the same as the one in which the school is located. The first cultural setting that should be analyzed is that of the school, with an examination of how the student is operating in the culture of the classroom and the school as a whole. If the student has quickly assimilated into the operations of both, and is at ease in both settings, the student may be demonstrating advanced levels of socialization and adaptation. The teacher should also seek out information regarding any other academic settings in which the student may currently take part, such as a religious setting, as well as previous school experience. If all indicators are positive in the various educational settings, the teacher may not need to focus as much on transitioning the student into the current learning environment and can instead focus attention on other programmatic aspects.

The second cultural setting of which the teacher should gain awareness is that of the family. The culture of the family may be reflective of a culture outside that of the mainstream, and may or may not reflect the traditions and beliefs of another country. Some family information that could be helpful as the gifted education program is designed may relate to familial structure (nuclear or extended, gender roles, expectations of family members), the dynamics in the home (leadership, responsibilities, who provides support and assistance with school-related tasks), and the things that family members consider indicators of giftedness. It is also helpful to know with whom the student primarily interacts at home, because interaction with older siblings, for example, may have a significant impact on the student's language acquisition, cultural assimilation, and academic attitude. Knowledge of the role the family plays in the life of the bicultural/bilingual gifted child can help guide the selection of the advanced-level educational tasks to be assigned to the student.

The neighborhood may provide the student the context in which he or she is most comfortable, depending on how many other similar students share the same residential area. This author has been in various cities and towns in which the neighborhood gives one the impression that they have stepped outside of mainstream America. This is not exclusive to large metropolitan areas but depends on the relative number of individuals that share enough commonalities to draw them to the same areas of the community to reside. The neighborhood may influence the bicultural/bilingual gifted student, because it may provide the most relative role models for the student, which, in turn, may have an impact on the student's academic and career aspirations. The youth of the neighborhood also may influence the attitude of the student regarding school and being gifted, because the student may value peer relationships over what others might consider more important factors in the student's life.

The community as a whole may have an impact on the bicultural/bilingual gifted student in a variety of ways, and it may be particularly important if the student reflects on what occurs in the community. Politics, particularly if those who hold office are a source of community conflict, may leave a gifted student with a confused sense of justice. The things on which the community places value may also create conflict for the bicultural/bilingual gifted student, particularly if that student's giftedness is not in alignment with what is valued. Examples of this conflict include the student gifted in the performing arts in a community that holds athletics in high esteem, or the bilingually gifted student who resides in a community that places more value on one language than on another. Some communities may consider academic achievement important, but if the livelihood of the community depends on those with skills other than academic, a student may be more encouraged to develop work-related skills than areas of giftedness.

The impact of popular culture also should be noted, because a student may more quickly embrace what is directly reflected by peers (dress, entertainment, ways of communication, extracurricular interests). Individual student interests may springboard from popular culture, and because interests are one means of customizing gifted curriculum and instruction, knowledge of current trends within popular culture has merit.

Language and culture add considerable complexity to the gifted bilingual/bicultural student, and this complexity may prevent the student from being identified as gifted. So much focus may be placed on language acquisition and acculturation that a student's giftedness may remain masked, perhaps until he or she reaches a level of English proficiency and acculturation that allows those that nominate for gifted programs to measure the gifts. Giftedness may take many forms, and teachers should be searching for the linguistically gifted among students that speak more than one language or who live in two distinct, major cultures. Knowledge of the areas of giftedness is critical for the design of learning experiences that will allow talents to blossom.

This chapter is devoted to the components involved in providing the gifted student who speaks more than one language and who adapts to more than one culture the best learning environment possible to achieve high levels of ability. This chapter also examines the areas of curriculum, instruction, and assessment and makes recommendations for each of two distinct delivery models: the pull-out program and the cluster-grouping model. The chapter begins with an overview of the interrelatedness of each component and then details each component.

Curriculum, Instruction, and Assessment

Curriculum, instruction, and assessment are components of education that, when integrally connected, provide sound learning experiences for all students. The same applies to the gifted bilingual/bicultural student, with additional variables to be considered.

Curriculum for these complex students should be developed within a structured framework and should reflect both a philosophy based on theory and practice in gifted education, bilingual education, and multicultural education, and the program design within which gifted services will be delivered. The curriculum should also be grounded in the standards that have been developed for content areas. Modification of curriculum content also may be necessary if the content does not extensively address higher levels of thinking.

Instruction of the gifted bilingual/bicultural student should include the best practices in the areas of gifted, bilingual, and multicultural education. Differentiation of instruction, although an appropriate means of meeting the needs of high-ability students, may take place in isolation or may not be occurring in a systematic fashion. Operating from within a curriculum framework and matching authentic assessment targets and multiple teaching approaches, combined with effective teaching strategies, will provide the gifted bilingual/bicultural student with learning experiences that address the unique combination of attributes he or she brings to the gifted program.

Assessment of the gifted student who is acquiring a second language and adapting to multiple cultural settings should be designed to measure targeted outcomes without placing undue emphasis on language limitations or cultural differences. Assessment measures should not only indicate levels of mastery, but also be used to document rates of gain. Well-planned assessment practices utilizing well-structured instruments are much better indicators of gifted productivity for these students than a haphazard approach of measuring student performance.

Yong (1994) summarized the importance of conscientious decision making regarding curriculum, instruction, and assessment for diverse student populations:

> Self-concepts and internal locus of control of ethnically diverse students can be enhanced through numerous approaches, such as setting realistic goals and objectives, using instructional material and resources that have a multicultural perspective, encouraging parental participation in their children's learning, providing consistent and positive feedback on students' performance, stressing independent learning, and helping students to become aware of their own attributions. (p. 194)

General Considerations

Curriculum for the Gifted Bilingual/Bicultural Student

Teachers face many challenges at the beginning of each academic year as they prepare for the new groups of students they will teach, guide, and support for the next nine months. Some of these challenges arise from what seems to be an ongoing cycle of curriculum changes and the teaching expectations related to those changes. One year, new textbooks are adopted. The next may see new state guidelines. The following year may bring a new math or science program. And, periodically, teachers are presented with what has been labeled "gifted curriculum."

The intent here is not to undermine the importance of having a curriculum for the gifted program. Differentiation practices, when used sporadically and stemming independently from lesson to lesson, may lack the structure that curriculum models, or frameworks, can provide. Too often, however, this gifted curriculum is a loosely connected series of ideas and lessons that has been churned out during the summer by a dedicated, but underprepared, group of teachers of the gifted.

Curriculum should be designed only by those that have expertise in curriculum writing. Although it is important to gather teachers together to provide input into the design and content of the curriculum they will be asked to teach, it is highly likely that only a few have been trained to design curriculum or to align curriculum with standards and state-mandated curricular guides. Leadership in the development of curriculum for gifted students, which reflects a population of bilingual/bicultural students, should go to those in the district who already have either coursework or training in curriculum principles and development, with a secondary level of leadership assigned to those willing to obtain professional development in the writing of curriculum. This leadership team can then become the curriculum design team; in a diverse district this team should include not only teachers of the gifted, but also bilingual teachers.

Good curriculum comes from a merging of theory, frameworks or models, and a thorough understanding of teaching practices. Lloyd (1998) examines four theories of learning that designers of gifted curriculum may consider when developing the first piece, a philosophical foundation, of a gifted curriculum framework. Schema theory is based on the premise that the brain collects information in the form of long-term memory, which is organized into schemata, analogous to a complex computer filing system. Learning takes place when the schemata are accessed, adding new information to "files" that already exist or replacing information as these "files" are updated.

Cognitive flexibility is a theory that addresses the type of learning that requires accessibility to multiple schemata in order to understand concepts of greater complexity. Learning occurs as data from these schemata are manipulated by the brain to create new connections and concepts.

Reader response theory focuses on the direct and extended learning that takes place through the intake of information that is read. At one level, learning is literal, such as remembering content presented in textbooks. The continuum extends to a level at which valuing and personal reactions are encouraged.

The fourth theory described by Lloyd is sociocultural theory. This interpretation of learning focuses on movement from independent operations to those requiring assistance, with a strong emphasis on social interactions.

These four theories of learning can provide the philosophical backbone of a curriculum for the gifted, and they reflect important considerations for the bilingual/bicultural learner. Aspects of each should be considered when developing gifted curriculum for this special group of learners, with particular emphasis on schemata development and social interactions.

Curriculum Standards   Content standards are a second foundational piece in the design of curriculum for gifted students. These standards have resulted from extended periods of development and review by specialized educators from many arenas of learning. Standards reflect current trends and thinking within a specific discipline and should be incorporated into curriculum created at the local level. Rather than ask teachers to juggle multiple documents and try to determine how one relates to another, gifted curriculum should integrate content standards and provide a vehicle to help teachers make critical connections between theory and practice, as well as between the disciplines.

Scope and Sequence   One of the first design components of a gifted curriculum is a conceptual scope and sequence. The initial mapping of what is to be learned as students move vertically (from grade level to grade level) and horizontally (from the beginning to the end of a school year) provides the designers of gifted curriculum the first look at how curriculum for the gifted is different from that for the mainstream. Content and skills are outlined in scope and sequence, and the mapping provides a spiral curriculum design, a design that encourages vertical teaming and that provides a link across both the scope of the curriculum and the sequence that is to follow. The scope and sequence also provide guidance in dealing with the varied entry points along the continuum, which typically occur when gifted students are identified at different points in the K–12 system. The scope and sequence also provide the starting point for discussions related to the needs of diverse students who will enter the program, including gifted learners who are bilingual and bicultural.

Multicultural Curriculum Considerations   The gifted curriculum that is to be used with ethnically diverse learners should not only reflect appropriate and varied cultural resource materials, but also integrate multicultural content at a more complex level. Banks and Banks (1993) describe four levels of multicultural content integration. The first two levels, contributions and additive, are relatively self-descriptive. These levels of integration, involving heroes, holidays, and traditions in the former, and concepts, themes, and perspectives in the latter, do not significantly change the structure of the curriculum and certainly do not reflect the complex levels of thinking expected of gifted students. Emphasis should be placed instead on the transformational and social action levels. The transformational level creates structural changes in curriculum to allow students to view concepts, issues, and themes from diverse perspectives, while the social action level infuses into the curriculum real-life experiences involving decision making and action on social issues. These two levels reflect many traditional curriculum practices in gifted education, including application of problem-solving processes and the inclusion of real problems for real audiences. The combination of multicultural education and gifted education is relatively new in the field of gifted education, and more research is needed in this area.

Linguistic Considerations in Curriculum Design   Curriculum for the gifted learner who is also bilingual is unique in many ways, and scope and sequence provide the initial structure within which to consider needs of this type for the gifted student.

Kitano and Espinosa (1995) approached the gifted bilingual learner from the bilingual education perspective and pointed out that four basic types of programs exist for the student acquiring English as a second language: the immersion program, the early-exit bilingual program, the late-exit bilingual program, and the two-way bilingual program. Each design creates a different learning scenario, but in all cases some fundamental curricular considerations apply.

Curriculum for the gifted English-language learner should be conceptual in content emphasis and should allow the development of a learning environment in which a student can freely use either language to help define the concepts and generalizations they are learning. Even in the English immersion program, students need to be able to communicate more complex thinking in whatever manner they can, using one or both languages. If this emphasis is not built into the curriculum, false "ceilings," based on language usage limitations, may be placed inadvertently on these students.

Curriculum for these learners also should heavily emphasize language usage, even for the gifted bilingual student whose giftedness may be more nonverbal. This language emphasis allows students to not only learn language, but also use and manipulate it in a variety of ways. The gifted curriculum should support language acquisition in general, without having the learning of English as its focus. Rather, the curriculum for the gifted bilingual student should emphasize the high levels of thinking and performance that are expected of any gifted student.

Kitano and Espinosa (1995) also surveyed the literature in search of effective bilingual education practices that would have a positive impact on gifted English-language learners. These researchers concluded that a firm foundation in the primary language should be established prior to transitioning to a second language, encouraging the continued development and refinement of conceptual knowledge and skills in the first language. When transition to English instruction does occur, content should be challenging, with instruction supporting transition into mainstream classes. The classroom and school should focus on student empowerment, structured to reflect a valuing of diverse languages and cultures.

Curriculum Frameworks and Models   Numerous perspectives on curriculum design exist, and they reflect the diversity of thinking in the field. The gifted bilingual/bicultural child would benefit from a curriculum that is concept-based, fostering giftedness through conceptual thinking, as well as providing learning experiences that could allow more extensive use of language. Erickson (1998) proposes a systems design for curriculum that is concept-based:

> A systems design for curriculum is coherent, balanced, and systematically develops sophistication in knowledge, understanding, and the ability to perform. A systems design addresses four critical components: (a) the student outcomes (what students should know, understand, and be able to do based on the identified knowledge, skills, and abilities they will need as "educated" and successful citizens in the 21st century); (b) the critical content, key concepts, and essential understandings that form the knowledge base of different areas of study; (c) the major process and skill abilities that ensure quality performance; and (d) quality assessments for measuring standards-driven performance. (pp. 45–46)

Erickson also points out, through example, the difference between curriculum based on topics and one based on ideas:

> The difference between a topic-centered and an idea-centered curriculum/instruction model is the difference between memorizing facts related to the American Revolution and developing and sharing ideas related to the concepts of freedom and independence as a result of studying the American Revolution. (p. 50)

Once those who are designing curriculum have determined the fundamental premise upon which the gifted curriculum will be based—one that is supportive of the bilingual/bicultural child that is gifted—a curriculum framework should be established. One such framework, based on how students arrive at understanding, is illustrated in the work of Wiggans and McTighe (1998). The authors propose a purposeful curriculum design that is based on six facets of understanding: explanation, interpretation, application, perspective, empathy, and self-knowledge. Each of these facets reflects a way of understanding that fosters complex thinking, which should be an emphasis of a curriculum for the gifted. The facets also emphasize ways of understanding that are supportive of the process of language acquisition within a culturally diverse environment.

The first facet, explanation, emphasizes sophisticated explanations that provide accounts of events, actions, and ideas that are knowledgeable and justified. The use of higher levels of thinking within this facet is apparent. The implied focus on more sophisticated levels of communication would foster language experiences for the English-language learner that are broader and more challenging than some more highly structured approaches.

Interpretation, the second facet, focuses on the use of interpretations, narratives, and translations that lead to understanding. Language usage and the interpretive nature of second-language learning are inherent in this facet, as are the higher level operations required to achieve meaning through interpretation.

The third facet of the design is application, which is somewhat more complex than the meaning we typically think of—the application of skills acquired. This facet focuses on the ability of a student to use knowledge effectively in new situations and within diverse contexts. Bilingual/bicultural gifted students would have many opportunities to apply the knowledge they are rapidly acquiring in new situations and diverse contexts, which they would be experiencing on a daily basis.

The bicultural gifted student would function naturally within the fourth facet of the design, perspective. This facet emphasizes critical and insightful points of view. Learning opportunities based on this facet could effectively tap diverse cultural points of view and, in turn, emphasize the value of diversity.

Students who feel as different from the mainstream population as the gifted bilingual/bicultural student might feel, require settings in which these differences are understood. Empathy—the ability to understand another person's feelings or view of the world—would provide the instructional foundation upon which a supportive learning environment could be established.

The final facet, self-knowledge, promotes understanding through self-awareness, including the ability to know how one's thinking and actions inform as well as prejudice. This seems to be a universal goal in education and certainly supports the individual needs of the gifted bilingual/bicultural student.

The facets that make up the design are not taught in a sequential manner, providing the flexibility to design a curriculum scope and sequence that integrates them and can emphasize any single one where most appropriate. The design can also better focus the thinking of teachers as they create units of study based on the six facets.

Defensible Designs and Practices   Literature focusing on curriculum for gifted bilingual/bicultural students is limited; the emphasis of those examining this specific population tends to be on identification methods. Udall (1989) approaches curriculum as it relates to the broader population of Hispanic gifted students, but her recommendations readily apply to the gifted bilingual/bicultural student.

An important point made by Udall is that "curriculum for gifted Hispanic students cannot be discussed in isolation from the issues of definition and identification" (p. 41). This statement illustrates the importance of connecting curriculum to the type of student that is selected for gifted education services. Whatever criteria are used for selection of the gifted bilingual/bicultural student, criteria representative of the school or district definition of *giftedness* should be the basis for curriculum focus. If nonverbal or creativity measures are used to identify students, then the curriculum must have a nonverbal or creative component or strand in order to ensure success of students with nonverbal or creative strengths in the gifted program.

Udall also emphasizes two key requirements for successfully serving gifted Hispanic students. The first is to follow established guidelines in the development of a qualitatively differentiated curriculum. The second key requires a design that supports individualization. This design should extend from a logical framework and should be determined by the program delivery model and the profiles of the gifted students that will be served.

Finally, Udall considers the following as important curriculum principles upon which a successful curriculum is built: (1) an accelerated/advanced content that is interdisciplinary and at a high level of abstractness, (2) an emphasis on real problems, (3) the development of research skills and allowance for independent study, and (4) the generation of new information or products that allow development of personal growth.

Two Program Delivery Options and Recommended Curricular Considerations
The curriculum used in a gifted program for students who are bilingual and bicultural not only should be designed with the unique needs of these students in mind, but also should fit the delivery model in which gifted education services are being provided. The suggestions that follow are based on this author's work in the field with practitioners serving bilingual and bicultural students, including the potentially gifted, as well as effective curriculum practices observed.

The Pull-out Program Model   Pull-out gifted program models, in which students are pulled from the regular education classroom for designated periods of time, provide unique curriculum opportunities in spite of the time parameters within which services can be delivered. It is within this delivery model that a separate curriculum for gifted students is most viable. Although the pull-out curriculum design should connect, to a degree, with the required regular education curriculum, the teacher providing gifted instruction may have much more flexibility in customizing a curriculum that addresses the unique population that he or she serves as a learning facilitator, including the gifted bilingual/bicultural student.

Fogarty (1991) provides a series of detailed descriptions of various curriculum structures in general education that also match the attributes of a pull-out delivery model. These structures include shared planning/teaching, integration, and immersion designs.

Shared planning and teaching takes place in two disciplines, in which overlapping concepts or ideas emerge as organizing elements. In a gifted education context, the teacher that works with gifted students instructs these students independently, yet in harmony, with the regular education teacher or teachers. This model could provide an effective collaboration between the teacher of gifted and the bilingual/ESL teachers with whom students are shared, particularly when schedules limit joint planning or teaching time.

The integrated structure is an interdisciplinary approach, matching subjects for overlaps in topics and concepts. This structure includes team teaching, which, in this case, would involve the pull-out teacher and the regular education teacher. Thematic units, a popular curriculum focus in gifted education, are a component of this structure. The pull-out teacher of gifted bilingual/bicultural students would be able to readily integrate into the curriculum diverse cultural perspectives with delivery of content in two languages.

The immersed curriculum structure is appropriate when the disciplines become part of the gifted learner's lens of expertise; the gifted learner, by design, is provided an environment in which he or she filters all content through this lens and becomes immersed in his or her own experience. In a pull-out setting, an individualized educational plan could be designed for select students based on this structure, and be customized to the unique needs of the bilingual/bicultural students.

Finally, the networked curriculum structure permits the gifted learner to filter learning through the expert's eye, leading to extensive networking with experts in various fields. Independent studies combined with levels of mentoring fit within this structure and can provide bicultural students the opportunity to interact with experts that share their heritage.

The Cluster Program Model   Gifted bilingual/bicultural students who are provided gifted education services through a cluster program model stay in regular education classrooms and receive gifted instruction from regular education teachers. When this program is designed appropriately, the regular education teachers are trained to provide continuous support for gifted students in all academic areas through curriculum differentiation and authentic assessment. To meet the unique needs of bilingual/bicultural students who are gifted, the cluster program teacher should also be fully trained in both bilingual and multicultural education practices. However, teachers with extensive preparation in all three areas are difficult to find.

The cluster program teacher faces many challenges that the pull-out teacher does not, including addressing the educational needs of students with a wider range of abilities. This teacher also bears responsibility for mastery of grade-level objectives for all students. These expectations may result in gifted education taking the form of curriculum extensions—enrichment activities that take place only after a student has completed required assignments. Teachers who may be more skilled in curriculum and instruction for gifted students may cluster skills and objectives, or they may compact the curriculum to allow more individual opportunities for gifted students. Curriculum extensions, clustering skills/objectives, and compacting offer a better method for enhancing the attributes of gifted bilingual/bicultural students, but they may not address the additional attributes these individuals bring to the classroom.

Fogarty (1991) addresses additional curriculum models that may, when placed in a gifted education context, not only provide frameworks for improved gifted educational instruction, but also better support the added language and multicultural needs of the bilingual/bicultural students who are gifted. These structures include connected, nested, sequenced, threaded, and networked designs.

The connected model structures a single content-area curriculum so that the content is connected from topic to topic and concept to concept. The opportunity is also in place to connect one year's work to the next's. Ideas within this model are explicitly related. For gifted students, this model allows better acceleration opportunities and the application of generalizations and themes. Bilingual students are provided a structure in which to allow the continuous development of language that is connected within each content area. As with all of the curriculum models, the connected model allows the integration of multicultural themes, resources, and learning experiences.

Advanced-level learners could benefit from the nested model. In this model, multiple skills are targeted within each content area—a social skill, a thinking skill, and a skill specific to the content being taught. The skill-development areas in this model could focus on giftedness, dual language acquisition, and biculturalism. This model, however, might have limited use with regular education learners who are sequential in their learning and who require instructional support and modification.

Gifted learners, capable of making leaps in their learning, could benefit from a sequenced curriculum. This model, particularly useful in the departmentalized structure of secondary level education, requires that topics or units be arranged and sequenced to coincide with one another. Subjects remain separate, but ideas are taught in concert. The gifted student could arrive at concepts independently by connecting content from subject to subject; the bilingual student would be allowed to explore language to a greater breadth and depth within the sequenced presentation of topics and concepts.

The threaded curriculum focuses on thinking and social skills, multiple intelligences, and technology, which are threaded throughout each content area. Teachers and students operating within this model would need to be highly organized and flexible in their approaches to teaching and learning, respectively. This model has the potential for development of a highly dynamic curriculum, which would be beneficial to the student who is cognitively, academically, and linguistically gifted.

There will be times that the regular education teacher will need to seek experts in various fields to serve in mentoring roles for gifted students who exhaust the available resources in an area of study or interest. The networked curriculum provides a structure for an extensive mentoring experience. Cluster model teachers who have a highly gifted student among those identified would be encouraged to explore this model. Technology and community contacts can provide the network, and specific efforts can be made to create a design that allows learning that is multicultural and bilingual in nature.

Simply having a good curriculum in place for gifted bilingual/bicultural learners is not enough to provide a learning environment that is commensurate with the abilities and special needs of these students. A sound curricular framework must be accompanied by appropriate instruction and authentic assessment. The instructional aspects of learning are explored next.

Instruction for the Bilingual/Bicultural/Gifted Student

Good instruction benefits all students, regardless of any special needs the students may have. Good instruction reflects high levels of differentiation within various instructional approaches. Good instruction is well designed and is not simply a series of loosely connected activities written in a lesson plan book. This section covers instructional practices that provide the learning environment best suited for gifted students who are bilingual and bicultural.

The Teacher of Bilingual/Bicultural/Gifted Students   There are some fundamental considerations of the instructional agent that should underlie the assignment of bilingual/bicultural gifted students to a classroom. Perhaps the most obvious is that their teacher should be bilingual. However, being bilingual alone, particularly if the teacher's proficiency in both languages is not extreme, does not suffice. The teacher of bilingual/bicultural gifted students should have extensive preparation in bilingual education and at least fundamental knowledge of sound principles in multicultural education. One cannot expect advance levels of instruction bilingually, or a sophisticated level of integration of multiculturalism, if the primary deliverer of both is not adequately equipped with skills and knowledge in both areas.

The instructor also should be highly flexible. This flexibility is pertinent when the teacher is asked to move from a comfort zone of instruction into the delivery of approaches and strategies that may not fit his or her own teaching or learning styles. This required flexibility also relates to the ongoing need for modification of instruction, particularly when students come to the educational setting with such diverse needs.

Skills in curriculum writing are useful to the teacher of gifted bilingual/bicultural students. Commercial curriculum for these unique students is limited, at best, as are school districts with comprehensive gifted/bilingual/bicultural curricula in place. A teacher working with these students will need to be able to modify available curricula if no specialized curriculum has been designed.

A Child-Centered Focus   Grant and Piechowski (1999), in an article addressing the need for child-centered gifted education, wrote the following:

> Being child-centered means respecting children's autonomy, providing experiences that enable children to follow their passions and be self-actualizing, and seeking to understand things from the child's point of view. The strongest argument for child-centeredness is that it regards children as ends, not means. It provides conditions for children to flourish, become themselves, and it does not impose a way of being on them. (p. 8)

This philosophical approach is especially appropriate for students who are as complex as those who are gifted, bilingual, and bicultural. In addition, the authors stated that "an understanding of the child's perspective and inner life aides us in assisting children in finding their own way in life" (p. 8). In instructional design for bilingual/bicultural gifted students, this understanding can make the difference between selecting resources and designing learning experiences that are tangential to a child's language and culture and those that directly relate to the day-to-day life experiences of the child.

Grant and Piechowski also pointed out that, often, the emphasis in working with giftedness is on accomplishments that are recognizable and valued, and on production, likening the expectations for the gifted to the expectations a farmer has for livestock—increased production. This becomes an elusive outcome for the gifted student whose giftedness is in the acquisition of languages and/or adaptability to multiple cultures. Teachers need to keep in mind how giftedness works when dealing with this special segment of the gifted population. Productivity takes many forms and can be greatly influenced by what is valued in a culture and community. Finding out how each bilingual gifted child thinks, feels, and experiences all aspects of life can help teachers better understand their students' unique giftedness and better plan to meet their academic and other needs.

Another aspect of a child-centered approach to teaching relates to how the learner approaches what is being taught. Howard Gardner (1993) suggests that teachers design learning experiences using multiple entry points. These entry points map onto the multiple intelligences described in his theory. The entry points encourage students to approach content from varied perspectives. Gardner's proposed entry points include the narrational, the foundational/existential, the esthetic, the logical-quantitative, and the experiential. Each entry point focuses on a different way of thinking, ranging from the asking of questions and connecting of ideas in the foundational/existential entry point to the creation of images and mood interpretation in the esthetic entry point.

Instruction and Language Development   Designers of instruction for students who are bilingual, bicultural, and gifted should emphasize language development in all areas of instruction. These designers, ranging from theorists to classroom practitioners, should base the level of second-language development emphasis on the specific needs of the students they are teaching, and should not make the assumption that every student in the classroom is a second-language learner.

Kitano and Espinosa (1995) examined the unique combination of language diversity and giftedness. They found that many instructional strategies recommended for English-language learners appear to have face validity for these students who are also gifted, especially those strategies that emphasize higher level thinking. These include incorporating gifted education strategies (in general, not dependent on level of language acquisition), focusing on student strengths (including primary language ability), providing a content-rich curriculum that provides in-depth study, promoting students' active engagement in learning, developing oral and written language development in all aspects of instruction, and promoting students' self-esteem through valuing of their languages, cultures, and experiences.

Kaplan (1999) also wrote about the unique needs of language-diverse gifted students and pointed out one of the shortcomings of educating gifted English-language learners:

> While this could be considered to be a semantic rather than a philosophical or pedagogical argument, the coupling of gifted and English language learner without the insertion of the word AND has inhibited rather than facilitated the type of teaching and learning available to these students. In teaching the gifted, the emphasis should be on giftedness, not on the student's status as an emergent English language learner. (pp. 1, 20)

Kaplan emphasized the need to use strategies appropriate for gifted learners without diminishing them due to language differences. Among the strategies Kaplan considered as necessary for evolving scholars are the use of inquiry and questioning techniques, developing the language of the discipline being studied (including use of figurative and technical language), and the reinforcement of the ability to perceive from multiple perspectives.

Recommended Practices   A few researchers in gifted education have studied effective practices used with gifted bilingual/bicultural learners. Udall (1989) recommends seven teaching strategies, synthesized from the literature on curriculum needs of gifted minority students:

1. The use of concrete materials to teach abstract concepts
2. Instructional examples relevant to culture and experience
3. Community involvement
4. Integration of leadership components in the gifted curriculum
5. The use of mentors
6. Tapping creative and problem-solving strengths
7. Concentration on affective needs

Kaplan (1999) adds this additional perspective:

> There are many examples of how teachers can fill in the gaps to facilitate the participation of gifted and emergent English language learners. All of these fill-in-the-gaps activities must be identified as inherent features of an exemplary differentiated gifted curriculum and not just as good teaching practices. Too often, English language learners who are gifted are either excluded from the differentiated gifted curriculum because of limited experience, or the experience is given to the students in a limited manner. (p. 20)

Kaplan suggests these strategies for use with gifted English-language learners:

1. Sequencing information, or presenting information and skills in a developmental order
2. Clustering, which enables students to determine the connections among ideas and skills, such as superordinate and subordinate
3. Paralleling, a technique encouraging student use of prior concepts or skills in the acquisition of new concepts and new skill mastery
4. Teaching backwards, a strategy based on the idea that we do not always have to teach sequentially, and that the learning progression need not always be from simple to complex. Students may be stimulated to learn by the unknown and the abstract

TABLE 7.1   Appropriate Practices in Gifted Education

Gifted Education Practice	Questions to Consider when Applying Strategy to Gifted Bilingual/Bicultural Learner
Program arrangements influencing academic and affective outcomes and learning characteristics	Do we understand the cultural aspects of the learning environment, and the impact of language and culture on learning styles?
	Can we effectively target the affective needs of the bilingual/bicultural gifted student, given the added complexities of culture and language differences?
	Should we be even more cautious regarding the selection and use of texts as the sole source of curriculum and instruction, given the broad target for which these materials have been designed?
Ability grouping	Must we only group bilingual students with other bilingual students (limited to the "ability" to use language) or pair them with students who have a command of content in English?
	If ability grouping or flexible grouping is not common practice, and if gifted students are not frequent recipients of differentiated instruction, does that imply that bilingual gifted students would first and foremost receive instruction to improve language acquisition rather than to develop talent?
	Does the tendency to not group by ability have an impact on the opportunities for individual pacing and acceleration?

Finally, Shore and Delcourt (1996) address practices they consider uniquely appropriate to gifted education. Two practices, supported by research as particularly effective, are outlined in Table 7.1.

The research on instructional practices appropriate for gifted students who are bilingual and bicultural is limited but strongly indicates that strategies typically used with gifted students are equally beneficial to bicultural English-language learners. With this in mind, teachers must have as their goal a learning environment that allows gifted bilingual/bicultural students to extend and refine their first and second languages, that celebrates the students' cultures, and that establishes an atmosphere conducive to risk taking. The latter ensures that the gifted thinker will feel secure in conveying complex ideas and concepts in either language.

Teachers must also create a playful environment, one in which the second-language learner can approach language acquisition as they would a new toy, enjoying each new word or phrase learned, exploring the many ways it can be used. This is particularly important for the linguistically gifted student. With this in mind, we will now look at some specific strategies used in gifted education and their implications for use with bilingual/bicultural students as well as within two programming models.

Two Program Delivery Options and Recommended Instructional Considerations
Gifted education instructional strategies can be utilized in both the pull-out program and
the cluster group model. Modifications of the strategies should be considered when
working with students who are bilingual and bicultural. Table 7.2 lists some of the more
commonly used strategies, implications of the strategies within the two program delivery
models, and recommended considerations when used with bilingual/bicultural students.

**TABLE 7.2   Pull-out Program and Cluster Group Model:
Strategies, Applications, and Implications**

Differentiation Strategy	Application within a Pull-out Program	Application within a Cluster Model	Implications for the Bilingual/Bicultural Student
Flexible skills grouping	Allows cross-age grouping and interest grouping, as well as grouping based on skills and knowledge	Broadens the grouping practices used in classrooms beyond cooperative groups and often-avoided ability groups	Students may be grouped based on conceptual understanding, individual or cultural interests, and, when appropriate, language abilities
Tiered assignments	If groups are large, or if multiple age ranges are taught simultaneously, can be an effective strategy	Allows the teacher to differentiate within a single lesson or unit of study	Takes into consideration language differences; appropriate resources based on language or cultural aspects can be incorporated into the tiers
Learning centers/stations	Can provide individualization of instruction and can be adapted for use with multiple grade levels	Allows differentiation for all levels in the classroom, with specific tasks designed for high-ability students	Tasks can be designed to match language abilities and can integrate multicultural activities and resources
Interest groups	Somewhat limited due to numbers of students seen in one setting, but can provide a means to broaden students' interests	Can better personalize instruction, providing additional means of motivation for students that are a challenge to motivate	Cultural interests can be addressed; groups can provide bilingual instruction

Individual educational plans (IEPs) used in special education may be appropriate for use with some students in either of the program delivery models. These educational plans can be instrumental in designing learning experiences for students when large or small group experiences are not appropriate, such as when a student is highly gifted in areas beyond the levels of his or her intellectual peers in either program. An IEP would also be appropriate if the student is dealing with multiple variables that are having an

Differentiation Strategy	Application within a Pull-out Program	Application within a Cluster Model	Implications for the Bilingual/Bicultural Student
Independent study	For small groups, could provide the structure for regular curriculum extension; may provide a means for extending contact time if planned jointly with regular education teacher	Specifically applicable at the secondary level when course selections do not match with level of ability or interest areas; useful strategy for the highly motivated, self-disciplined students	Can allow students the option to study an area of cultural significance in either or both languages
Compacting	Effective strategy when the pull-out teacher assumes some responsibility for mastery of grade-level skills; can be utilized on an individualized basis	Effectively used in conjunction with regular preassessment and independent projects; allows the variability of student academic strengths from unit to unit	Can provide a greater emphasis and more time on language development if student compacts in areas of giftedness
Mentoring	Teacher can arrange for mentoring for a greater number of students, building into the schedule support and facilitation time	Very useful when a single student or small group has expanded skills and knowledge far beyond the classroom experiences needed by the majority of students	Provides an opportunity to pair students with mentors of similar cultural backgrounds and who are bilingual, emphasizing the value of being bilingual and bicultural
Questioning techniques	Methods such as Socratic questioning can be incorporated into all instruction, with discussion as a component; higher level complex questions can be used with consistency	Various strategies can be integrated into small group and whole class discussions, resulting in improved questioning for all students	As teachers utilize more questioning in teaching, students are allowed to better develop and use the languages they are acquiring and refining

impact on his or her education, which could be the case with the gifted bilingual/bicultural learner. Though somewhat cumbersome, IEPs should not be immediately ruled out when designing instruction for these unique students.

Appropriately developed instruction based on a solid curricular framework will still lack effectiveness if not paired with authentic assessment. The final section of this chapter deals with assessment practices that best fit the learning experiences of gifted students.

Assessment for the Bilingual/Bicultural Gifted Student

Differentiation of instruction within a well-designed curricular framework provides the opportunity for gifted bilingual/bicultural students to perform at levels indicative of their areas of talent. However, without appropriate assessment techniques, advanced-level products and performance will be inconsistently and inadequately measured. Assessment tools and procedures that are sound and that match targeted outcomes need to be developed and used. Authentic assessment takes place when assessors are skilled in the design and use of multiple types of assessment, are basing instructional decisions on data provided by assessment, and follow principles of sound assessment.

Stiggans (1997) proposes seven guiding principles of assessment that should be the foundation upon which assessment practices are based:

1. Assessments require clear thinking and effective communication.
2. Classroom assessment is key.
3. Students are assessment users.
4. Clear and appropriate targets are essential.
5. High-quality assessment is a must.
6. Understand personal implications.
7. Assessment can be used as a tool for teaching and learning.

These principles provide a learning environment that is positive for all types of learners. When the principles guide the development and use of assessment instruments, the unique profiles of individual students are carefully considered. The complexity of the gifted bilingual/bicultural student requires this focus if this type of learner is to be successful in a gifted program.

Preassessment   When a student's performance in an educational setting is complicated by a number of variables, it is critical that the teacher has baselines upon which to measure gains and rate of skill and knowledge acquisition. This can be accomplished only through the use of preassessment. For the gifted bilingual/bicultural learner, the use of well-designed preassessments allows the teacher to identify areas of the curriculum that merit the use of compacting without limiting these opportunities due to diversity of language. Preassessments also can produce data that reflect the rate of language acquisition and the level of language usage and development in both languages used by the bilingual gifted learner. Without the use of preassessments, the teacher may unwittingly base instructional decisions on English-language abilities only, preventing the development of areas of talent.

Selected-Response, Essay, and Performance Measures   Typical assessment practices, in which objectives are taught and then measured by some type of selected-response measure, may not be the best way in which to measure the growth of the bilingual student who is also gifted, unless the measure is administered in the primary language of the student and the concepts being measured were taught in this same language. Unless the assessment practices are designed accordingly, selected-response instruments are limited, in that they may be measuring as much the acquisition of language as they are the intended mastery of objectives. They are also only a snapshot of learning, and unless compared over time for relative gains, are narrowly focused.

Essay measures, which are likely used at upper elementary and secondary levels, share many characteristics of the more analytical selected-response assessments, but essay measures are more complex in design. The bilingual and bicultural gifted student should have the opportunity to develop, at a pace and level commensurate with abilities, skills in responding to essay questions. These questions should be of high-quality design and systematically created based on techniques recommended by experts in assessment. Additional time should be given to the bilingual/bicultural gifted student to respond to an essay question. This measure may require that a student use multiple means to convey the abstract thinking that may be taking place, but that is limited by the level of language proficiency. The student may have a strong desire to respond in English, and this desire should be fostered, but not at the sake of limiting the potential response. The student may need to discuss his or her ideas in their primary language in order to acquire and use a similar level of language sophistication in English.

Illustrations also may be a means to bridge the gap between conceptualizing thinking in the primary language through discussion and committing the ideas in writing in English. The gifted bilingual/bicultural learner potentially has the ability to conceptualize what has been taught and, given the right vehicle, can be very expressive linguistically. Essay measures used with this student may require transcribing or translation. Additionally, the essay assessment experience should be nonthreatening so that, if the student chooses to respond in English, he or she will not be penalized for doing so.

Performance assessment tools may measure a broader range of gifted bilingual/bicultural student capabilities than will selected-response assessments. Checklists, in particular, may be very useful not only as performance measures, but also as structured teaching tools. A checklist provides more concrete criteria for assessment, because it is analytical in nature, as opposed to popularly used rubrics that, due to the more abstract structure of criteria on a continuum, may be more difficult for the English-language learner to conceptualize. The checklist can be delineated into essential components of the task assigned, with these components detailed to the degree necessary to communicate the requirements effectively. This more detailed structure may then lend itself more readily to translation, and the student will have the option to move between the two language formats. In addition, a checklist may be easier for parents or guardians to understand, particularly if these individuals are supporting the educational efforts of the school by extending learning at home and providing assistance to the child in the completion of homework. However, once a student reaches a developmental age at which point rubrics are better understood in either language, they should be used whenever they best match the task that has been assigned for evaluation.

Use of portfolios may be the best method when assessing advanced products and performance of gifted bilingual/bicultural students, because portfolios may not only illustrate mastery of objectives, but also reflect the kinds of growth that occur over time. Portfolios are comprehensive by design and can incorporate a variety of assessment tools. Portfolios also provide a strong communication base for sharing student performance with parents, and they provide opportunities for gifted bilingual/bicultural learners to improve skills in self-assessment.

Exemplary and professional levels of performance can be realistic targets of gifted bilingual/bicultural students if their performances are defined and assessed with the special needs of these students in mind. This may require individual conferencing with the student to analyze, through bilingual discussion, the details of the targeted performance and the criteria to be applied in assessment. Attention also should be given to determining the level of language usage, in either language, that is required to be successful at these high levels.

The teacher who combines authentic assessments with differentiated instruction provides a learning environment in which all learners, including those that are gifted, bilingual, and bicultural, can maximize their potential. Selected-response, essay, performance assessments, and portfolios are all effective means of determining at what level a gifted bilingual/bicultural student is achieving, regardless of program delivery model.

Summary

The gifted student who is bilingual and living within two cultures is like a moving target. Students of this complexity are hard to identify and, if identified, provide numerous challenges in meeting their unique combination of needs. By providing these students with a flexible, creative, and supportive learning environment, not only will we be able to find more of them, we will be better able to provide learning experiences that will tap their talents and maximize their performances. This can be accomplished only in a program that is operating within a solid curricular framework, in which qualitatively differentiated instruction is taking place and in which authentic assessments are being used. Only then are we doing justice to this underrepresented population.

REFERENCES

Banks, J. M., & Banks, C. M. (1993). *Multicultural education: Issues and perspectives* (2nd ed.). Boston: Allyn & Bacon.

Erickson, H. L. (1998). *Concept-based curriculum and instruction: Teaching beyond the facts.* Thousand Oaks, CA: Corwin Press.

Fogarty, R. (1991). *The mindful school: How to integrate the curricula.* Palatine, IL: Skylight Publishing.

Gardner, H. (1993). *Multiple intelligences: The theory into practice.* New York: Basic Books.

Grant, B. A., & Piechowski, M. M. (1999). Theories and the good: Toward child-centered gifted education. *Gifted Child Quarterly, 43* (1), 4–12.

Kaplan, S. (1999). Teaching up to the needs of the gifted English language learner. *Tempo, 19* (2), 1, 20–21, 25.

Kitano, M. K., & Espinosa, R. (1995). Language diversity and giftedness: Working with gifted English language learners. *Journal for the Education of the Gifted, 18* (3), 234–254.

Lloyd, C. V. (1998). Engaging students at the top (without leaving the rest behind). *Journal of Adolescent and Adult Literacy, 42* (3), 184–191.

Shore, B. M., & Delcourt, M. A. (1996). Effective curricular and program practices in gifted education and the interface with general education. *Journal for the Education of the Gifted, 20* (2), 138–156.

Stiggans, R. J. (1997). *Student-centered assessment* (2nd ed.). Upper Saddle River, NJ: Prentice-Hall.

Udall, A. J. (1989). Curriculum for gifted Hispanic students. In C. J. Maker & S. W. Schiever (Eds.), *Critical issues in gifted education: Defensible programs for cultural and ethnic minorities* (pp. 41–56). Austin, TX: Pro-Ed.

Wiggans, G., & McTighe, J. (1998). *Understanding by design.* Alexandria, VA: Association for Supervision and Curriculum Development.

Yong, F. L. (1994). Self-concepts, locus of control, and Machiavellianism of ethnically diverse middle school students who are gifted. *Roeper Review, 16* (3), 192–194.

8

The Intersection of Language, High Potential, and Culture in Gifted English as a Second Language Students

JO ANN ROBISHEAUX

As a teacher of English as a Second Language (ESL) in an elementary school, I quickly noticed the differences in my students' ability to learn English. While some students labored to remember new vocabulary and grammatical forms, others enthusiastically dove into the new language. Once these students had mastered enough English to communicate their thoughts and feelings, I perceived a qualitative difference in their thinking processes. These more capable students processed information quickly, sought creative solutions to problems, devoured new material and asked for more, and were not easily dissuaded when English challenged them. I was already familiar with Wong Fillmore's (1983) work on characteristics of successful language learners, but these students exceeded those characteristics in terms of their thinking abilities.

I then looked into the identification of giftedness in students and quickly realized that some of my ESOL students fit many of those qualifications. One definition of *giftedness* that particularly fit my students with high potential was Cohen's description of gifted students as "possessing an abundance of certain abilities that are most highly valued within a particular society or culture" (1988). Likewise, Gardner's (1983) description of multiple intelligences highlighted these students' abilities beyond the domain of linguistic and/or mathematical intelligences. Many of the students demonstrated strengths in Gardner's other identified intelligences (spatial, bodily-kinesthetic, musical, interpersonal, and intrapersonal). Furthermore, the families of these students often remarked on their children's proclivities in these areas. It quickly became apparent that I was witnessing the same phenomenon that Bernal (1978) had identified in his research on the characteristics of Spanish-speaking gifted students. He identified gifted Mexican American students as those that

1. Rapidly acquire English language skills once exposed to the language and given an opportunity to use it expressively
2. Exhibit leadership ability, be it open or unobtrusive, with heavy emphasis on interpersonal skills
3. Have older playmates and easily engage adults in lively conversations
4. Enjoy effective risk-taking behavior, often accompanied by a sense of drama
5. Are able to keep busy and entertained, especially by imaginative games and ingenious applications, such as getting the most out of a few simple toys and objects
6. Accept responsibilities at home normally reserved for older children, such as the supervision of younger siblings or helping others do their homework
7. Are recognized by others as a youngster who has the ability to make it in the Anglo-dominated society

However, convincing the educators who screened students for entry into classes for the gifted proved to be quite a battle. I heard comments such as, "They can't be both bilingual and gifted" and "Once they exit the ESOL program, we'll screen them for gifted classes." As incredulous as I was about these responses, I was faced with the problem of having gifted students in my ESOL classes who were not likely to be formally identified as gifted for many years. When I turned to the academic literature for suggestions, I discovered that I was not the only educator faced with this frustration. Frasier (1995) identified barriers that language-minority students must overcome when they enter school. On reviewing her list, it became obvious that the educators themselves had established all of these barriers. Among these obstructions were

- A school environment that differed greatly from any of the students' previous experiences
- A lack of communication between the school and parents
- An assumption that language-minority students had a deficit that must be overcome
- Testing instruments that were not free of language and cultural bias
- A lack of referrals to gifted and talented programs because of teachers' assumptions about language-minority students' limitations

On investigating the strategies used for teaching gifted students, I discovered the appropriateness of those strategies to use when teaching a second language. I decided to teach all of my ESOL students (those I suspected of being gifted, as well as the others) as if they were all gifted. It was not until much later that I learned of Levin's Model for Accelerated Schools, which was also designed to advance the learning rate of students by transforming instruction into a gifted and talented approach (Levin & Chasin, 1994).

By challenging the ESOL students to use all of their linguistic and nonlinguistic talents, the learning of English as a second language became more naturalistic and fun for the students. The activities I adapted for my classroom engendered authentic communication situations, and the students acquired English in many of the same situations in which they had acquired their native languages.

In this chapter, I discuss the evolution of second-language education, the best practices in teaching gifted children, the specific problems that language and ethnic minority students encounter when tested for entry into gifted programs, and how these variables intersect for ESOL students with high potential.

The Evolution of Second-Language Education

In the past several decades, the pedagogy of helping students become proficient in a second language has reflected a continuum from sequenced drills to natural usage of a second language. Language-learning methodologies such as the reading method and the grammar-translation method focused on explanations of grammar rules and vocabulary and, as such, sacrificed authentic communication in the second language. Likewise, the goal of audiolingualism was to produce language learners who could form grammatically proper sentences after participating in numerous patterned response drills and controlled conversation. However, this idea of language as a system of skills that should be taught through drill and by the formation of stimulus–response associations was eventually challenged by cognitivists such as Noam Chomsky, who reminded educators that language is not fabricated by humans, but develops as a result of our genetic structures (Chomsky, 1980). Support for this idea came from Brown (1973) and Slobin (1971), who found that children from different language backgrounds all use similar linguistic structures in their language development, that they make the same kinds of errors, and that linguistic structures are learned in the same order. The implication of this theory and research was that second languages, just as first languages, should be allowed to grow and develop in appropriate environments.

In a move away from memorization and drill, language teachers began to develop approaches that supported a second-language student's comprehension and communication abilities. This belief gave rise to language-teaching methodologies such as Gattegno's Silent Way (1972), Curran's Community Language Learning (1972), Lozanov's Suggestopedia (1978), Asher's Total Physical Response (1972), and Krashen's and Terrell's Natural Approach (1983). A brief description of these methodologies follows.

The Silent Way

The goals of the Silent Way are to use language for self-expression, to develop independence from the teacher, and to develop inner criteria for correctness. Teachers see students' errors as clues to where the target language is unclear, and they adjust instruction accordingly. Students are urged to take responsibility for their learning, and additional learning is thought to take place during sleep. The teacher is silent much of the time but very active in setting up situations and listening to students. The teacher speaks only to give clues but not to model speech (Doggett, 1994).

Community Language Learning

The goals of Community Language Learning (CLL) are to learn language communicatively, to take responsibility for learning, to approach the task nondefensively, and to never separate the intellect from the emotions. The teacher acts as a counselor, supporting students with understanding of their struggle to master a different language. At first, students are seen as dependent clients of the counselor, but they become increasingly independent as instruction proceeds. Because students design the course, they determine the aspects of language to be studied. Grammar, pronunciation, and vocabulary are dealt with based on the students' expressed needs (Doggett, 1994).

Suggestopedia

The goals of Suggestopedia are to learn the second language by overcoming psychological barriers and tapping mental powers, which lead to learning at an accelerated pace. Students choose an identity to use in the second language, and they use texts of dialogues accompanied by translations and notes in their native language. Each dialogue is presented during two musical "concerts"—once with the teacher matching his or her voice to the rhythm and pitch of the music while students follow along, and then a second time, with the teacher reading normally and students listening while in a meditative state. The students gain facility with the new language through activities such as dramatizations, games, songs, and conversations (Doggett, 1994).

Total Physical Response

The goal of Total Physical Response (TPR) is to provide an enjoyable learning experience while having a minimum amount of the stress that typically accompanies learning a second language. At first, the teacher gives commands and the students follow them. (Teachers recombine their instructions in novel and often humorous ways.) Once students are ready to speak, they take on the role of director. Grammatical structures and vocabulary are emphasized, although they are embedded in the imperative form (Doggett, 1994).

The Natural Approach

The goal of the Natural Approach is authentic communication in the second language. Students move through four basic stages: comprehension, early speech production, speech emergence, intermediate fluency, and fluency. The length of time spent in any one stage varies greatly, depending on the individual, the amount of comprehensible input received, and the low-anxiety environment created by the teacher (Richard-Amato, 1988).

In what was viewed as a radical departure from the rigorous practice of drilling language forms until they became unconsciously functional, the communicative and comprehensive approaches to second-language learning specified that the successful learning of a second language must follow the same patterns as native language acquisition. This belief system can best be summarized by looking at the four principles upon which Krashen and Terrell (1983) developed the Natural Approach as a method.

The first principle states that *comprehension precedes production.* Just as young children acquire their first language through many experiences of listening and trial utterances (Brown, 1980), second-language learners must also comprehend the messages they are receiving before they can attempt to speak. In classroom practice, this translates as understanding that second-language learners must proceed through a "silent period" (Asher, 1972), during which they are basically listening to the new language and constructing meaning for themselves.

The second principle reminds us that production *must be allowed to emerge in stages.* If we again think of the young child acquiring his or her first language, we remember the babbling infant, the one- and two-word utterances of toddlers, and finally, the construction of sentences by three- and four-year-olds. Although second-language learners are generally able to progress through stages of language production at a much faster rate, the stages of second-language production are identifiable and predictable. In the second-language classroom, the teacher can note the students' progress through the stages of preproduction, early production, speech emergence, intermediate fluency, and fluency. The behaviors that identify second-language students as they progress through these stages are described as follows:

Stages of Language Acquisition[1]
Characteristics of the preproduction *student*
1. Does not talk at all or says only isolated words, phrases, or routine expressions
2. Cannot understand initially what is said or written in English
3. Begins to associate sound and meaning, building a receptive vocabulary
4. Develops listening and comprehension strategies
5. Begins to understand the main idea of an utterance by focusing on the key words
6. Does not get actively involved, preferring to "hold back" and watch for awhile
7. Sometimes appears quiet or expressionless
8. Does not follow directions
9. Gets distracted, frustrated, and lost easily
10. Relies on contextual cues for understanding

Characteristics of the early production *second-language student*
1. Begins to say a few simple words or short phrases in response to comprehensible input
2. Understands some of what is said or written in English
3. Continues to focus on key words in an utterance
4. Starts to get involved, but still holds back and acts shy
5. Continues to use contextual cues to understand utterances
6. Sometimes appears quiet or expressionless

---

[1]Adapted from the Riverside Unified School District, Riverside, CA, and *The Rainbow Collection,* Alvarez-Martina, C., Marino, E., Raley, T., & Terrell, S. Miami, FL: Santillana Publishers, 1984.

7. Follows a few directions
8. Continues to be distracted and frustrated, but not as often
9. Gets lost less often
10. Responds only minimally in the native language
11. Has minimal academic achievement in English

Characteristics of the speech emergent *second-language student*
1. Begins to speak in longer phrases, often producing whole sentences
2. Does not speak fluently; has noticeable gaps and errors in vocabulary, grammar, and pronunciation
3. Possesses vocabulary and facts necessary to get the message across, but expressive abilities are still limited
4. Can understand most of what is said in general conversation in English
5. Begins to refine listening strategies and comprehending more than key words in utterances
6. May still have difficulty understanding abstract concepts or academically demanding tasks in the new language
7. Continues to develop his or her vocabulary, still maintaining a larger comprehension vocabulary than production vocabulary
8. Can follow more complex directions
9. Gets lost less frequently
10. Responds in English more and more frequently
11. Participates more in class discussions

Characteristics of the second-language student with intermediate fluency
1. Demonstrates native or near-native speaking ability
2. Understands most of what is said in English
3. Has mastered basic vocabulary in English, but needs expansion and refinement in subtle, descriptive vocabulary and terms used in subject-area classes
4. Continues to have difficulty understanding and expressing abstract concepts or completing academically demanding tasks in English
5. Produces fewer errors in speech

Characteristics of the fluent *second-language student*
1. Demonstrates native speaking ability
2. Understands everything that is said in English
3. Has mastered basic and descriptive vocabulary in English and is able to use academic language with facility
4. Is able to understand and express abstract concepts and complete academically demanding tasks in English
5. Produces few errors in speech

The third principle asserts that *the course syllabus must be based on communicative goals.* Very few second-language learners enroll in a class with the goal of memorizing scripted dialogues and drilling new vocabulary words. Like children acquiring their native language, second-language learners want and need to communicate. Here, it is wise to remember that there are four language arts: listening, speaking, reading, and writing. Too many of the traditional grammatical approaches focus solely on reading and writing and, as such, sacrifice the equally important forms of communication—listening and speaking. This principle also reminds us that grammatical forms are eventually internalized by first- and second-language learners after multiple experiences with the language. As an example of this principle, one need only think of the following conversation between a two-year-old, who was acquiring English as her native language, and her mother:

> **CHILD:**   Mommy, you goed to store?
>
> **MOTHER:**   No, I went to the store.
>
> **CHILD:**   Yes, Mommy. You goed to the store. You buyed juice?

The goal of the two-year-old was to communicate. Her mother's attempt to teach correct grammatical form through modeling was wasted on the child because the child's goal was quite different from the mother's. This is also true for second-language learners and their teachers. Although the teacher may wish to impose correct grammatical forms on the students, the students' goal of communication must be met first.

The fourth principle, *activities must be planned so that they will lower the affective filter,* relates to second-language learners' emotional state. Krashen (1987) coined the term *affective filter* to represent the emotional barriers, such as anxiety and lack of self-confidence, that some second-language learners may raise. If the teacher is aware of this possibility and consciously creates an environment in which experimentation with language is encouraged, in which errors are corrected gently (or ignored), and in which students feel supported and safe, the language learner is more likely to create an affective filter that is permeable by the teacher's input. On the other hand, a classroom in which grammatical form is more important than successful communication may cause the learner to create an impermeable affective filter, which will block out all or most of the teacher's input.

Translating these four principles into classroom practice gives rise to activities such as songs, games, role-playing, storytelling, art, exploration, cooking, self-selected reading, and other forms of natural interaction. The main focus is on creating activities that foster an atmosphere that encourages second-language learners to explore, experiment, acquire, and learn their second language. As discussed in the next section, these activities mirror those recommended for students with high potential.

Best Practices in Teaching Gifted Students

In many ways, reaching a consensus about the best curriculum for gifted students is as difficult as determining the best approach for teaching language-minority students. Educators in the field of gifted education debate the advantages of academically rigorous programs in which the curriculum is accelerated with those who advocate an enrichment approach that allows gifted children to explore and delve into their own interests. Likewise, some experts in the field of second-language learning advocate drill and practice, while others understand second-language acquisition to be a natural extension of human learning and thus provide numerous, rich language-learning experiences that strive to replicate the conditions under which a first language was acquired. In this section, I review the recommendations of educators in the field of education for gifted children and then highlight those methodologies that meld with the methodologies for second-language learning.

One ongoing argument among educators is the debate between those who believe that knowledge can be transmitted from the teacher to the student and those who believe that all knowledge must be constructed by the student. Constructivists such as von Glasersfeld and Cobb (1983) and Wittrock (1977) argue that knowledge cannot be absorbed by students, but rather that they must construct the knowledge for themselves through experience. Again, we see the parallel to second-language educators. Some believe that through drill, the second-language learner will absorb the information and eventually become proficient in the second language. Others believe that a second language must be naturally constructed by the learner through numerous authentic experiences with the second language.

In Goodlad's (1984) extensive study of schools, he found that most teachers use some form of didactic instruction as their primary, if not exclusive, method of instruction. This reflects a strong belief that knowledge can be transmitted from teacher to student. This belief system is reflected in classrooms for gifted children as well as in classrooms for ESOL students. In classrooms for gifted students, this belief manifests in methodologies that only promote lecture and curriculum acceleration. In ESOL classrooms, this belief is reflected in activities such as drilling phonics, distributing vocabulary worksheets, and overusing basal readers.

By contrast, if we look at Renzulli's (1977) ideas about education for gifted students, we see that the goals of student-centered, constructivist learning experiences are:

1. To assist youngsters in becoming actual investigators of real problems or topics by using appropriate methods of inquiry
2. To provide students with opportunities for taking an active part in formulating problems to be investigated and the methods by which the problems will be attacked
3. To allow students to use information as *raw data* rather than reporting about conclusions reached by other persons
4. To provide opportunities for students' inquiry activity to be directed toward some tangible product
5. To provide students with an opportunity to apply thinking and feeling processes to real situations rather than to artificially structured exercises

These goals of the Renzulli Enrichment Triad model set the perfect stage for educators of ESOL students who support the natural acquisition of a second language.

Consider the following goals for second-language learning, which are based on Renzulli's five goals:

1. To assist ESOL students in becoming actual users of their second language by investigating real problems or topics
2. To provide students with opportunities for taking an active part in formulating the learning activities to be conducted in their second language
3. To allow students to become the actual writers, researchers, scientists, historians, and so on, rather than relying on the decoding and comprehension of academic works written by others
4. To provide opportunities for students' language-learning activity to be directed toward some tangible product, such as short stories, poetry, plays, and so forth
5. To provide students with an opportunity to apply second-language learning processes to real situations rather than to mechanical exercises

Wheatley (1988) synthesized the recommendations for teaching gifted students and formulated general guidelines for developing strategies to teach gifted learners. I have included those guidelines that most closely suit teaching a second language for ESOL students.

1. Make extensive use of generative instructional strategies such as discovery, discussion, small-group problem solving, and other nondidactic methods.
2. Provide a learning environment with a variety of options that enable students with different learning styles to choose activities and materials that fit their own learning styles.
3. Deemphasize competition and encourage cooperative learning.
4. Use little or no drill and practice.
5. Make differentiated assignments to meet the needs of students of different levels.
6. Encourage students to set their own goals and make decisions about what to study. Provide vehicles such as planning forms and lists of options to enable students to develop their own learning plans.

Of particular interest to those who work with gifted minority students is Gardner's conception of Multiple Intelligences (1983). In his theory, Gardner describes the seven intelligences:

1. Linguistic intelligence, which includes verbal comprehension, syntax, semantics, and written and oral expression
2. Logical-mathematical intelligence, which includes inductive and deductive reasoning and computing
3. Spatial intelligence, the capacity to represent and manipulate three-dimensional configurations
4. Musical intelligence, which includes such abilities as pitch discrimination; sensitivity to rhythm, texture, and timbre; the ability to hear and perform themes in music; and music composition

5. Bodily-kinesthetic intelligence, the ability to use all or part of one's body to perform a task or create a product
6. Interpersonal intelligence, which is the ability to understand the actions and motivations of others and to act sensibly and productively based on that knowledge
7. Intrapersonal intelligence, which refers to a person's understanding of self; one's own cognitive strengths and weaknesses, thinking styles, feelings, and emotions

These ideas for teaching gifted students were synthesized in Levin's Model for Accelerated Schools (Levin & Chasin, 1994). Originally designed to meet the needs of at-risk students, Accelerated Schools seek out the strengths of their students and use those strengths as a basis for providing enrichment and acceleration. Like language-minority students, the strengths of at-risk students are often overlooked. These include not only the various areas of intelligence identified by Gardner's Multiple Intelligences Model (1983), but also areas of interest, curiosity, motivation, and knowledge that come from the culture, experiences, and personalities of the students (Levin & Chasin, 1994).

At the core of the Accelerated Schools Model is the goal of improving student achievement by providing "powerful learning" opportunities. For a lesson to meet the requirements of powerful learning, the activities must be authentic, interactive, learner-centered, inclusive, and continuous. If students can relate what they are experiencing in the classroom to real issues and situations, then the material is considered *authentic*. *Interactive* lessons must allow students to collaborate with others in the learning process and to work together toward a common purpose. Student exploration and continual discovery are essential for powerful learning lessons and, as such, are considered to be *learner-centered*. Lessons must also focus on giving all students equal access to learning opportunities to be considered *inclusive*. Finally, lessons are considered to be *continuous* if they strengthen connections between different learning contexts so that students perceive knowledge in a more holistic manner (Levin & Chasin, 1994).

As such, the Accelerated Schools Model synthesizes the constructivist-based teaching strategies that have been shown to be successful with gifted learners. An interaction among the components of a powerful learning lesson would also lead to a natural acquisition of a second language. Again, it is clear that the methodologies developed for gifted students are applicable for the teaching of English to ESOL students.

Problems Faced by English-Language Learners with High Potential

The final variable to be considered in this chapter is that of the students' cultures. Because ESOL students typically come from cultural backgrounds that could be described as "minorities," a few words about the effect of students' cultures are appropriate. In this section, I discuss (1) the problem of minority students being identified as gifted, (2) the problem of ESOL students being identified as gifted, (3) recommendations for alternative methods of identification, and (4) teaching ideas for ESOL students with high potential.

It has long been recognized that students from minority cultures have not been represented in the population of students classified as gifted. African American, Hispanic, and Native American children appear in gifted programs at only about one-half or less their prevalence in the larger society, whereas Asian Americans appear at twice their percentage in the U.S. population (Gallagher & Gallagher, 1994). Zappia (1989) and Machado (1987) looked at the percentage of minority students in the United States and compared that number with the percentage of students participating in gifted programs. They likewise found that, nationwide, Caucasians and Asian Americans are overrepresented, while the percentage of African Americans and Hispanics is only half what would be expected in programs for gifted students. Cohen (1988) summarized these findings as follows:

Minority Group	*General Enrollment (%)*	*Enrollment in Gifted Programs (%)*
Caucasians	71.2	81.4
African Americans	16.2	8.4
Hispanics	9.1	4.7
Asians	2.5	5.0

In addition to testing, the concept of giftedness as it relates to teachers' expectations can help explain why more Asian American students have been identified as gifted than any other group. Although these children comprise only 2.5 percent of the nationwide school-age population, they constitute 5 percent of the identified gifted students. The traditional Asian American values of educational attainment and obedience to authority support achievement in U.S. schools despite the fact that Asian American cultures differ in many ways from the dominant American culture.

Different learning styles, which are influenced by the home culture, may also contribute to the underrepresentation of minority-language students with high potential. Cohen (1988) notes that Native Americans are often caught between the schools' value of independence and the community's value of interdependence: "In school, students generally sit in rows and face the teacher, whereas in Native American culture, everyone would be seated in a circle and decisions would be made collectively."

Previous explanations for this skewed representation have been the discredited idea that intelligence is based on genetics and the bias that is inherent in tests used to measure intelligence. IQ tests are constructed in such a way that they have built-in limitations and assumptions that can discriminate against students who do not closely identify with the dominant culture. The widely used Stanford-Binet IQ test, for example, was standardized by using children of White English-speaking parents. Additional problems have been documented concerning the higher scores received on nonverbal intelligence tests by Mexican American children (Mercer & Smith, 1972), the effect of examiner variables found by Bordie (1970), and the diminishing of children's creativity due to imposed time limits (Torrance, 1969). Nevertheless, many states and local school boards still rely on a narrow definition of *giftedness* in which students must meet strict IQ scores to qualify for inclusion in curricula for gifted students.

These problems also exist for ESOL students who fail to qualify for gifted classes, not only because educators identify them as belonging to minority cultures, but also because of their perceived lack of English fluency. Students who are learning English as their second language are rarely referred for placement in gifted programs. Even the terminology sometimes used to describe these students, such as "limited English proficient" (LEP), implies the existence of an educational problem rather than the potential for academic excellence. School personnel frequently view language differences as deficits that disable students rather than as strengths that empower them. For example, the use of code switching (mixing languages) is seen as a positive stage of interlanguage by ESOL professionals. However, non-ESOL professionals often see this same phenomenon as dependence on the first language.

Students learning English as a second language are a subgroup of a culturally diverse population. Not only is their primary language different from the majority of students, but they also have different home cultures, family dynamics, historical and experiential backgrounds, motivational patterns, values, and learning styles. There is a body of evidence (Baca and Almanza, 1991; Barkan & Bernal, 1991) that indicates traditional standardized tests do not adequately measure the ability levels of ESOL students. Therefore, identification of these individuals should focus on informal and dynamic assessment procedures that provide a holistic measure of a student's performance across varied and meaningful contexts.

Therefore, identification and assessment of language-minority students with high potential is complex because it involves students who are both gifted and from a language or cultural background different from that of middle class, native-English-speaking children. Many researchers and practitioners recommend multiple assessment measures to give students several opportunities to demonstrate their skills and performance potential (Cohen, 1988). DeLeon and Argus-Calvo (1997) suggest that a multidimensional approach to identification be developed that includes nomination by parent, teacher, or self. In a program that focused on artistic ability and the teaching of art to support student persistence and achievement, they also elicited assessment ideas from a community artist. Then, the identification committee's recommendations were cross-referenced with the community artist's recommendations. This use of community resources was novel in its approach and helped educators see beyond any perceptions of limitations based on the students' languages or cultures, because the community artists were judging the students' products without actually knowing the students.

Other researchers have concurred that the best way to include language-minority students in programs for the gifted and talented is to provide alternatives to existing assessment practices. Working with a population of rural Mexican Americans in the southwestern United States, Reyes (1996) discovered that students using multidimensional and holistic procedures showed cognitive and performance profiles similar to those identified using traditional methods. McIntosh (1995) also espouses identification in the primary grades, enrichment programs, parental involvement, and specialized teacher training. Garcia (1994) recommends that assessment strategies move away from strict quantitative measures and also include qualitative data that feature student production, informant data, language and cognitive-style data, and data organization systems.

FIGURE 8.1   Sample Checklist for Identifying Language-Minority Students with High Potential.

_____ Learns English quickly

_____ Takes risks in trying to communicate in English

_____ Practices English skills by him- or herself

_____ Initiates conversations with native English speakers

_____ Does not frustrate easily

_____ Is curious about new words or phrases and practices them

_____ Questions word meanings; for example, "How can a bat be an animal and also something you use to hit a ball?"

_____ Looks for similarities between words in their native language and English

_____ Is able to modify his or her language for less capable English speakers

_____ Uses English to demonstrate leadership skills; for example, uses English to resolve disagreements and to facilitate cooperative learning groups

_____ Prefers to work independently or with students whose level of English proficiency is higher than his or hers

_____ Is able to express abstract verbal concepts with a limited English vocabulary

_____ Is curious about American culture

_____ Is able to use English in a creative way; for example, can make puns, poems, jokes, or original stories in English

_____ Becomes easily bored with routine tasks or drill work

_____ Has a great deal of curiosity

_____ Is persistent; sticks to a task

_____ Has good physical coordination

_____ Is independent and self-sufficient

_____ Has a long attention span

_____ Becomes absorbed with self-selected problems, topics, and issues

_____ Retains, easily recalls, and uses new information

_____ Demonstrates social maturity, especially in the home or community

The use of a portfolio or a case study procedure would help to include culturally different students in programs for gifted individuals. The use of case studies to identify giftedness has been documented by Renzulli and Smith (1977) and is recommended because it relies on multiple sources of information about a student's performance. Elements of the portfolio or case study for ESOL students could include the following:

- A checklist of behaviors identifying students with potential (Figure 8.1)
- Home data, such as parent interviews and questionnaires

- Formal assessment models that measure the growth from assisted to unassisted performance by using a pretest and posttest procedure
- Alternate assessment models, such as performance-based assessment, portfolios, and so forth
- An informal language assessment that measures the quantity and quality of functional communication competencies at home, in school, or in the community
- Peer as well as self-ratings
- Pertinent samples of student work
- Student products
- A dialogue journal between the teacher and the student that emphasizes communication and meaning over spelling, mechanics, and grammar (Robisheaux and Banbury, 1994)

Suggested Activities

Even if the classroom teacher is frustrated with the system's inability to identify culturally and linguistically different students as gifted, the teacher can instruct the students as if they had been identified as gifted. This can be done by implementing methodologies recommended for gifted students to teach the content necessary for ESOL students. However, convincing educators to adopt these types of methodologies requires nothing less than reversing those belief systems and practices that hold that limited English proficiency equals limited cognition. Despite findings by Collier (1995), Goodman (1990), and Solis (1999) that show that learning basic skills is not an absolute prerequisite for engaging in creative lessons that challenge students, many educators continue to try to "remediate" language-minority students' skills rather than capitalize on their strengths.

Blanning (1980) suggests that programs for gifted language-minority students should allow their students to do the following:

1. Pursue topics in depth at a pace commensurate with their abilities and intensity of interest
2. Explore interests without imposing predetermined curricular expectations
3. Initiate activities within a framework of guidance and resources
4. Ask questions about the area being studied
5. Experience emotional involvement with a project
6. Learn the skills, methodology, and discipline necessary for intellectual pursuits and/or creative endeavors
7. Make interpretations, connections and extrapolations in order to develop ideas, images, and intuitive insights
8. Experience the use of intellectual abilities and senses necessary in all creative endeavors

Using the ESOL curriculum as a starting point and following the suggestions of Armstrong (1994), a unit about clothing was organized around Gardner's theory of Multiple Intelligences (Figure 8.2).

FIGURE 8.2   Ideas for Teaching ESOL Students about Clothing.

Linguistic Intelligence

Children's Literature

Many books feature articles of clothing in the text and/or illustrations. Following is a list of recommended books:

The Emperor's New Clothes	Hans Christian Andersen
Mama, Do You Love Me?	Barbara M. Josse
Just Plain Fancy	Patricia Polacco
People	Peter Spier
Phoebe's Revolt	Natalie Babbitt
Hats, Hats, Hats	Ann Morris
Grandma's Shoes	Libby Hathorn

Similes and Analogies

Even students with limited English fluency can use their creativity to complete simply worded similes about clothing.

A hat is like a _____.

A coat is like a _____.

Shoes are to feet as _____ are to plants.

A hat is to a head as _____ is to a house.

Jewelry is to clothing as _____ is to _____.

Journals

Daily practice in writing has been shown to be a valuable exercise for students learning a second language. The following are suggested journal topics:

The important thing about clothing is _____.

I wanted my parents to buy _____ for me, but they said it was too expensive.

I get dressed up in my best clothes for _____.

Publishing

Create a catalog of clothing. Categorize the clothing into separate sections (e.g., sportswear, evening wear, pajamas, work clothes).

Logical-Mathematical Intelligence

Calculations and Quantifications

Use a newspaper advertisement or sale circular to calculate the price of clothing during a sale (25% off, 40% off, etc.).

Classifications and Categorizations

Students can classify different styles of clothing by drawing conclusions about the effects of climate on the way people dress. Create timelines that depict the types of clothing that have changed the most and the least over the past one hundred years.

Concept Maps

These graphic organizers help ESOL students understand the relationships among concepts.

Venn Diagrams

This is another type of graphic organizer, which helps to show the relationships among groups.

Visual-Spatial Intelligence

Picture Metaphors

A picture metaphor expresses an idea in a visual image. This helps ESOL students to link a new idea to a familiar visualization. Example:

> If the clothes we wear were animals, which ones would they be?
>
> How is a clothing store like a grocery store?

Idea Sketching

In this "Pictionary"-type game, one student sketches an article of clothing and the other students guess what it is. Other types of idea sketching are to ask students to design clothing for the future or to photograph or videotape samples of clothing.

Bodily-Kinesthetic Intelligence

Body Answers

Ask students to respond by using their bodies (e.g., blinking one eye, holding up fingers, scratching their heads, etc.).

The Classroom Theater

These activities include role-playing, pantomime, puppet shows, skits, and so forth.

Hands-on Thinking

These activities allow students to learn by manipulating objects or by making things with their hands. Example: Sculptures or collages of different types of uniforms.

Musical Intelligence

Rhythms, Songs, Raps, and Chants

This exercise gives students the opportunity to create their own lyrics about clothing and set them to well-known tunes or to compose an original song about clothing.

Supermemory Music

Based on the same idea behind Suggestopedia, this activity suggests having students enter a relaxed, meditative state, with the help of music, as a way of learning new vocabulary and/or concepts.

(continued)

FIGURE 8.2   Ideas for Teaching ESOL Students about Clothing. *(continued)*

Mood Music

Present music that represents various moods and then ask the students to select the type of clothing that they identify with that music.

Musical Accompaniment

If a student chooses to create a video or slide show on clothing, as described in the section on Visual-Spatial Intelligence, finding or creating a musical accompaniment for the presentation would enhance musical intelligence.

Interpersonal Intelligence

Peer Sharing and Cooperative Groups

There are several models of cooperative learning groups that lend themselves well to interpersonal intelligence. In cooperative learning, students work together in small groups on tasks that require cooperation and interdependence among all individuals in each groups.

People Sculptures

Students work together to create a living sculpture of a sewing machine. Students move to show how the different parts of the machine work.

Board Games

Create a board game that focuses on situations that require specific types of clothing. Cards can be made from pictures found in catalogs or magazines. In what situations would each type of clothing be appropriate? For example, would it be appropriate to wear a swimsuit to church?

Simulations

Similar to role plays, simulations require students to work together to investigate a situation. For example, "It's 1919 and you and your friends are going to a party. Will you wear a short skirt or a long skirt?"

Interviews

Interviews help ESOL students improve their listening and speaking skills, because they must go out and communicate with the interviewee. For example, interview someone who wears a uniform. What are the positive and negative aspects of wearing a uniform?

Surveys

Like interviewing, conducting a survey gives ESOL students a reason for interacting with English-speaking peers. For example, students could collect information on T-shirts and caps that feature logos or that support specific causes.

Intrapersonal Intelligence

This type of intelligence can be supported by giving students one-minute reflection periods, independent projects, and personal-learning logs. Examples of suggested topics are the following:

> I never knew that clothing was . . .
> I would like to wear . . .
> Arguments I have with my parents about clothing

Recommendations

Effective instruction of ESOL students emphasizes the functions of language, not merely the form of and focus on meaningful, interactive activities that motivate students to use English. This is a fundamental change from artificially created dialogues that require memorization, performance, and drill. In fact, the most significant shift in Teaching English to Speakers of Other Languages (TESOL) theory and practice is the current belief that language learners are not merely passive recipients in the learning process, but active learners who create rules from available language input and who are learning language through content (Morley, 1987).

The strategies of teaching gifted students are closely aligned with this philosophy of teaching English as a second language. Learning activities that establish a learning environment that promotes creativity, integration, and synthesis encourage cooperation and idea exchange. In turn, cooperation and idea exchange necessitate the natural usage of language in a grammatically unstructured setting. A summary of these ideas is presented as follows:

Effective instruction of ESOL students
- Focuses on the functions of language, not merely the form
- Focuses on meaningful interactive activities that motivate students to use English
- Believes that language learners are active learners who create rules from available language input and who learn language through content in order to communicate, regulate, interact, and imagine

Strategies for teaching gifted students
- Incorporate learning activities that establish a learning environment that promotes creativity, integration, and synthesis
- Encourage cooperation and idea exchange
- Assist students in constructing knowledge through experience

By adopting the strategies normally used with gifted students, ESOL students with high potential can discover new and richer avenues for creative language expression. The two separate teaching fields can be blended. Therefore, the following recommendations are made for the identification and instruction of ESOL students with high potential:

1. Identification of ESOL students must incorporate a portfolio approach, which includes verbal and nonverbal intelligence tests, samples of students' work, teacher recommendations, parent interviews, peer recommendations, and a checklist of behaviors identifying students with potential. Furthermore, the elements of the portfolio must be viewed with a balanced approach so that the results of IQ tests are not given more weight than other factors.

2. The underrepresentation of ESOL students in programs for gifted students must be brought to the attention of state departments of education and measures taken to remedy that imbalance. As such, advocates for ESOL students with high potential would come from the classroom teachers, parents, and leaders of state and national organizations that support education for ESOL and gifted students.

3. Teachers of ESOL students must be made aware of behaviors that potentially indicate giftedness in the students. Because a lack of fluency in English may limit the students' abilities to communicate their knowledge to the teacher, teachers must be aware of other indicators.

Instruction of all ESOL students must shift to a constructivist view that more closely parallels the ideas of second-language acquisition as a natural process. Furthermore, instruction of ESOL students with high potential must utilize those strategies that are recommended for gifted students, because those strategies also engender worthwhile experiences with the second-language. Finally, action research, which supports the efficacy of using teaching strategies usually applied only to gifted students in order to promote the acquisition of English, must be undertaken.

Summary

The five goals of this chapter are the following:

1. To review the evolution of second-language education
2. To review the philosophies that influence the education of gifted students
3. To highlight some of the problems faced by gifted language-minority students
4. To make recommendations for changes that would positively affect gifted language-minority students
5. To present sample activities that illustrate how the methodologies used to educate gifted children can be adapted for use with second-language learners

Over the past fifty years, second-language education has moved along a continuum that began with an emphasis on skill-based lessons and memorization and evolved into a recognition that first-language acquisition could be used as a model for second-language acquisition. With the distinction made between language acquisition and language learning, educators began to realize that a second language could be naturally acquired before skill lessons and grammar were learned. This realizaton led to second-language teaching strategies that allowed students to participate in activities that mirrored first-language acquisition. Drill and memorization were replaced by activities that encouraged learners to explore, experiment, acquire, and learn their second language.

Likewise, the debate over best practices for the education of gifted students has moved toward a more constructivist-based philosophy embodied by the Accelerated Schools Model, which requires lessons to be authentic, interactive, learner-centered, inclusive, and continuous. If these components are viewed from the perspective of a second-language lesson, it is clear that the methodologies developed for gifted students are applicable for teaching second-language learners.

Despite these changes in second-language and gifted education, many gifted language-minority students are still not being identified and served. Teacher expectations, culturally influenced learning styles, test biases, and uninformed school personnel often serve as hurdles that most gifted language-minority students never clear. Therefore, alternative methods of identification must be implemented.

Many researchers and practitioners recommend multiple assessment measures that give students several opportunities to demonstrate their skills and performance potential. These assessment measures could include a checklist of behaviors, parent interviews and questionnaires, portfolios, informal language assessments, peer as well as self-ratings, and student performance–based products.

REFERENCES

Armstrong, T. (1994). *Multiple intelligences in the classroom.* Alexandria, VA: Association for Supervision and Curriculum Development.

Asher, J. (1972). Children's first language as a model for second language learning. *Modern Language Journal, 56,* 133–139.

Baca, L. M., & Almanza, E. (1991). *Language minority students with disabilities.* Reston, VA: The Council for Exceptional Children.

Barkan, J. H., & Bernal, E. M. (1991). Gifted education for bilingual and limited English proficient students. *Gifted Child Quarterly, 35,* 144–147.

Bernal, E. M. (1978). The identification of gifted Chicano children. In A. Y. Baldwin, G. H. Lear, & L. J. Lucito (Eds.), *Educational planning for the gifted: Overcoming cultural, geographical, and socioeconomic barriers.* Reston, VA: The Council for Exceptional Children.

Blanning, J. M. (1980). *A multi-dimensional inservice handbook for professional personnel in gifted and talented.* Hartford, CT: Connecticut State Department of Education, Connecticut Clearinghouse for the Gifted and Talented.

Bordie, J. (1970). Language tests and linguistically different learners: The sad state of the art. *Elementary English, 47,* 814–828.

Brown, H. D. (1980). *Principles of language learning and teaching.* Englewood Cliffs, NJ: Prentice-Hall.

Brown, R. (1973). *A first language: The early stages.* Cambridge, MA: Harvard University Press.

Chomsky, N. (1980). *Rules and representations.* New York: Columbia University Press.

Cohen, L. M. (1988). Meeting the needs of gifted and talented minority language students. *New Focus, 8,* 21–30.

Collier, V. P. (1995). *Acquiring language for school: Directions in language education.* Washington, DC: National Clearinghouse for Bilingual Education.

Curran, C. (1972). *Counseling-learning: A whole-person model for education.* New York: Grune and Stratton.

DeLeon, J., & Argus-Calvo, B. (1997). *A model program for identifying culturally and linguistically diverse rural gifted and talented students.* (ERIC Document Reproduction Service No. ED 388 024.)

Doggett, G. (1994). *Eight approaches to language teaching.* Washington, DC: The Center for Applied Linguistics.

Frasier, M. (1995). *A review of assessment issues in gifted education and their implications for identifying gifted minority students.* (ERIC Document Reproduction Services No. ED 388 024.)

Gallagher, J., & Gallagher, S. (1994). *Teaching the gifted child.* Boston: Allyn & Bacon.

Garcia, J. H. (1994). Nonstandardized instruments for the assessment of Mexican-American children in gifted and talented programs. In S. B. Garcia (Ed.), *Addressing cultural and linguistic diversity in special education: Issues and trends.* Reston, VA: The Council for Exceptional Children.

Gardner, H. (1983). *Frames of mind: The theories of multiple intelligences.* New York: Basic Books.

Gattegno, C. (1972). *Teaching foreign languages in schools: The silent way.* New York: Education Solutions.

Goodlad, J. (1984). *A place called school.* New York: McGraw-Hill.

Goodman, Y. (1990). *How children construct literacy.* Newark, NJ: International Reading.

Krashen, S. D. (1987). *Principles and practice in second language acquisition.* Englewood Cliffs, NJ: Prentice-Hall International.

Krashen, S. D., & Terrell, T. D. (1983). *The natural approach: Language acquisition in the classroom.* Englewood Cliffs, NJ: Alemany Press.

Levin, H. M., & Chasin, G. (1994). *Creating new educational communities, schools, and classrooms where all children can be smart.* Chicago: University of Chicago Press.

Lozanov, G. (1978). *Suggestology and outline of suggestopedy.* New York: Gordon and Breach.

Machado, M. (1987). Gifted Hispanics underidentified in classrooms. *Hispanic Link Weekly Report,* February, 1.

McIntosh, S. (1995). Serving the underserved: Giftedness among ethnic minority and disadvantaged. *School Administrator, 52* (4), 25–29.

Mercer, J., & Smith, J. (1972). *Subtest estimates of the WISC full scale IQs for children.* Rockville, MD: National Center for Health Statistics.

Morley, J. (1987). Current directions in teaching English to speakers of other languages: A state-of-the-art synopsis. *TESOL Newsletter, 4,* 16–20.

Renzulli, J. S. (1977). *The enrichment triad model: A guide for developing defensible programs for the gifted and talented.* Wethersfield, CT: Creative Learning Press.

Renzulli, J., & Smith, L. (1977). Two approaches to identification of gifted students. *Exceptional Children, 43,* 512–518.

Reyes, E. I. (1996). Developing local multidimensional screening procedures for identifying giftedness among Mexican-American border populations. *Roeper Review, 18* (3), 208–211.

Richard-Amato, P. (1988). *Making it happen.* New York: Longman.

Robisheaux, J. A., & Banbury, M. M. (1994). Students who don't fit the mold: Identifying and educating gifted ESL students. *Gifted Child Today Magazine, 17* (5), 28–31.

Slobin, D. (1971). *Psycholinguistics.* Glenview, IL: Scott Foresman.

Solis, A. (1999). Extending advanced skills instruction into the education of disadvantaged students. *Intercultural Development Research Association Newsletter, August,* 9–10.

Torrance, E. P. (1969). Creative positives of disadvantaged children and youth. *The Gifted Child Quarterly, 13* (2), 71–81.

von Glasersfeld, E., & Cobb, P. (1983). Knowledge as environmental fit. *Man-Environment Systems, 13* (5), 216–224.

Wheatley, G. H. (1988). Matching instructional strategies to gifted learners. In J. VanTassel-Baska (Ed.), *Comprehensive curriculum for gifted learners* (pp. 383–395), Boston: Allyn & Bacon.

Wittrock, M. C. (1977). Learning as a generative process. In M. C. Wittrock (Ed.), *Learning and instruction* (pp. 621–631). Berkeley, CA: McCutchan Publishing.

Wong Fillmore, L. (1983). The language learner as an individual: Implications of research on individual differences for the ESL teacher. In M. A. Clarke & J. Handscombe (Eds.), *On TESOL '82: Pacific perspectives on language learning and teaching* (pp. 157–173). Washington, DC: TESOL.

Zappia, I. (1989). Identification of gifted Hispanic students: A multidimensional view. In C. J. Maker & S. W. Schiever (Eds.), *Defensible programs for gifted students from underserved populations: Cultural and ethnic minorities* (pp. 10–26). Austin, TX: Pro-Ed.

9

The Schoolwide Enrichment Model

Promoting Diversity and Excellence in Gifted Education

VALENTINA I. KLOOSTERMAN

If I accept you as you are, I will make you worse;
however, if I treat you as though you are
what you are capable of becoming,
I help you become that.

—Johann Wolfgang von Goethe

Neither cultural differences nor language ability in English should be used as a parameter for excusing the exclusion of students in programs for the gifted and talented. Diversity is translated in different ways of living, values, thoughts, languages, ways of expression, and experiences. Commonalities and differences are integral parts of humankind. Education, especially gifted education, has the major responsibility of attending to the needs of all children by recognizing, valuing, and developing their gifts and talents in a meaningful cultural and linguistic environment. The insufficient information regarding the specific cognitive, socioemotional, and cultural characteristics of high-ability diverse students challenges paradigms in gifted as well as bilingual education. Paradigms and research in gifted education suggest a reality in which opportunities for those children outside of what is deemed "the mainstream group" are denied. New concepts and paradigms on the identification and development of talents and cognitive and social skills in culturally and linguistically diverse (CLD) students will gradually result in a change in definitions, conceptions, and interpretations. In the United States, these compelling reasons demand that a new generation of researchers and practitioners focus their attention on this unrecognized student population and develop new assessment, programming, and evaluation procedures.

This chapter provides a description of how implementing the Schoolwide Enrichment Model (SEM) can benefit the development of talents in CLD students. Created in the early 1970s by Joseph S. Renzulli of the University of Connecticut, this educational model was intended primarily for gifted and talented students. This model has been evolving over the past few decades and has been successfully implemented as an enrichment plan for total school improvement. The SEM is one of the most prosperous models for developing the talent potentials of young people by systematically assessing their strengths; providing enrichment opportunities, resources, and services to develop these strengths; and using a flexible approach to curricular differentiation and the use of school time (Renzulli, 1994).

The SEM promotes diversity and excellence in education by holding high standards for all learners, regardless of age, ethnicity, gender, education, or socioeconomic conditions. The implementation of this model, particularly for CLD students, could counter the underestimation of potential talents and high abilities of this student population. Although conceptions of cultural and linguistic diversity often comprise a wide range of subcultures and linguistic groups, this chapter specifically focuses on bilingual/bicultural children.

This chapter presents four interrelated areas that provide a theoretical and practical rationale for the implementation of the SEM as an educational plan to promote high abilities in diverse students. In the first section, bilingualism and talent development are described as beneficial factors for children's cognitive and social growth. The critical underrepresentation of CLD students in programs for the gifted is also discussed. In the second section, the SEM is described in relation to serving diverse populations. The possibilities of an educational project combining the SEM and a two-way bilingual program are analyzed in the third section. The fourth section focuses on the significance of research and modifications in practices used to address the needs of gifted bilingual learners. A summary of the benefits of using the SEM for this student population is also presented.

Strengthening Opportunities for Bilingualism and Talent Development

Bilingualism is a very complex phenomenon. It involves cognitive, affective, cultural, environmental, and situational factors. Interactions among these factors cause differences in bilingual students. The range of proficiency skills in the two languages can vary widely, from fluent bilingualism to limited communicative skills in either of the two languages. The optimal level is known as the "balanced bilingual." At this level, the bilingual student shows age-appropriate abilities in both languages. Several studies have suggested that bilingual children may be more flexible in their thinking, mainly because of the constant switching and the comparison and contrast of both languages.

Development and nurturance of both languages are essential contributors to the growth of talent development in all domains. Linguistic proficiency and usage of the languages evolve and so, too, the possibility of realizing talent potential. As an example, researchers have given evidence of the benefits of fostering reading skills in children's first and second languages (Cummins, 1992; Mortensen, 1984). As Krashen (1996) explains, "It is extremely efficient to develop literacy in the child's first language; the transfer to English is rapid, even when the alphabets used are very different" (p. 1). Books, resources, and other material in the students' first language in school classrooms and libraries "help validate the primary language and culture, can contribute to continued first language development, and can help literate students get subject matter knowledge" (Krashen, 1996, p. 17).

Many studies have addressed the crucial role of family with respect to bilingual development. The family is the first emotional and cognitive context in which a child can develop his or her potential bilingualism. During the first years of human development, language growth and meaning are tied to cognitive development and socioemotional interaction. Bilingual families may encourage or withdraw from bilingualism in the new generations for different reasons. One of the reasons is the lack of information and assistance available to bilingual parents regarding the advantages of raising their young children bilingually (Arnberg, 1984; Dolson, 1985).

Bilingual students are being served in the U.S. public school system through a continuum of programs. In general, bilingual programs are transitional in nature, and the bilingual student is moved as quickly as possible into the monolingual English instruction without much consideration of his or her native language. In this regard, Baker (1993) points out that there is a clear difference between "a classroom where formal instruction is to foster bilingualism and a classroom where bilingual children are present, but bilingualism is not fostered in the curriculum" (p. 151).

Teachers' negative attitudes and low expectations toward diverse learners have been described by some researchers as detrimental to the academic performance and socioemotional development of this population (Cegelka, 1988; Cummins, 1989; Kofsky, 1992; National Center for Research on Cultural Diversity and Second Language Learning, 1994a). Also, teachers' lack of awareness and knowledge of the family culture and educational needs of CLD students clearly demonstrate the provision of unequal educational opportunities.

An interesting finding emerged regarding the teachers' appreciation and knowledge of their students' bilingualism in a study that explored and described personal characteristics of twelve high-ability Hispanic students in an urban area (Kloosterman, 1999). Some, but not all, of the teachers in this study demonstrated difficulty in differentiating between students for whom English was their second language and bilingual children who were fluent in two languages. Because most of the teachers were not aware of the CLD students' language development other than English, they appeared to believe that, if the student was not in the English as a Second Language (ESL) program, he or she was not bilingual.

Teachers should be given the opportunity to improve their knowledge and skills by working with CLD students through inservice programs and training. Consequently, educators will benefit from professional development opportunities that empower them to overcome prejudices, attitudinal barriers, and provide a high-quality curriculum and instruction. Terms such as *gifted limited English proficient, culturally and linguistically diverse gifted, gifted English as a Second language,* and *gifted bilingual* all address particular characteristics of children who demonstrate talent potential or outstanding talents while simultaneously developing two languages.

Considering the problems stated so far, six major needs regarding the development of talents in bilingual students can be addressed. These include a need to (1) develop appropriate identification tools and procedures for bilingual students, (2) develop professional training of staff for the identification and development of exceptional abilities in bilingual students, (3) create programs and evaluate services that enrich the regular bilingual curriculum, (4) provide training and assistance services to parents and community members, and (5) develop bilingual, culturally sensitive techniques and resources that help to unfold bilingual students' cognitive strengths, abilities, learning styles, interests, and languages.

Expression of Diversity in Programs for the Gifted

Each culture values and recognizes different sets of talents, and for this reason, educators not only need to be aware of the culture of each student but, more specifically, need to ask what talents or outstanding abilities are recognized by that particular cultural group. Moreover, educators themselves need to conduct some type of research on how these valuable talents are exhibited and developed. Demographic information has revealed that in the United States, CLD students are underrepresented in gifted and talented programs (Castellano, 1995; Frasier, Garcia, & Passow, 1995) and overrepresented in special education programs (Voltz, 1995). In addition, CLD teachers are underrepresented at all educational levels (American Association of Colleges for Teacher Education, 1994).

A research study conducted on high-ability Hispanic bilingual students (Kloosterman, 1999) indicated that the "attitudes" of school faculty and staff toward CLD students were one of the most significant factors that needed to change in order to recognize and stimulate the talents and academic and socioemotional skills of the participants. Certainly, changing attitudes is difficult. In this study, teachers, specialists, and administrators representing the mainstream society lived by certain rules, values, and traditions that maintained the status quo of this particular institution. Acceptance of differences, but moreover, respect and integration, remain challenges in U.S. public schools.

Due to diverse student populations in the United States, teachers need to understand and encourage students' cultural and ethnic identities in their classrooms (Banks, 1993; Dean, Salend, & Taylor, 1993; Diamond & Moore, 1995; Garcia & Malkin, 1993; Weil, 1993). The 1990 census data indicate that nearly thirty-two million people in the United States speak languages other than English in their homes. Today, ten million children, or one-fifth of school-age children, live in homes in which languages other than English are spoken, with Spanish being the most widely spoken language. Many of these students are immigrants of various ages who usually come to school with varying degrees of cultural and academic preparation. In addition, although an overwhelming number of recent studies describe bilingualism as an asset, CLD students in the United States continue to perform below the academic standards and score comparatively lower than the mainstream student population (De La Rosa & Maw, 1990; Dolson, 1985; Orfield, 1986). Also, CLD students from certain groups have higher dropout rates (U.S. Department of Commerce, 1986).

Furthermore, Passow and Frasier (1996) point out the difficulty that CLD students have expressing their potential talents or high academic skills in educational settings that have "fewer challenging curricula, fewer instructional resources, and environments that provide limited educational opportunities" (p. 201). The absence of knowledge about or the misunderstanding of the cultural, linguistic, and cognitive skills of these students results in limited educational policies, school programs, or educational services that address their unique needs, interests, and strengths.

It is important that "teachers have an awareness of their own culture and a general understanding of how culture mediates school learning" (Voltz, 1995, p. 2). Weil (1993) criticizes the way schools approach multiculturalism by simply "transmitting information about others that students are told to appreciate and forced to memorize for test taking purposes" (p. 215). Weil adds that teachers' practices and materials, such as textbooks, are embedded with an Eurocentric point of view in which "the significant us [majority] and the insignificant others [minorities]" (p. 215) are permanently promoted through the curriculum. In this regard, Banks (1993) addresses the fact that

> . . . school knowledge is more consistent with the cultural experiences of most White middle-class students [and teachers] than for most other groups of students, these students have generally found the school a more comfortable place than have low income students and most students of color. (p. 8)

The United States Department of Education report (1993), *National Excellence: A Case for Developing America's Talent*, states that "special efforts are required to overcome the barriers to achievement that many economically disadvantaged and minority students face" (p. 28). Various sections in this report also address the need to identify and nurture talents in youngsters of different socioeconomic and cultural backgrounds. In this regard, although several efforts have been made in the past decade to overcome these limitations, school districts and individuals still find themselves lacking systematic research support or guidance in designing, implementing, and evaluating their efforts.

Today, very few educational programs have been specifically designed to identify and develop talents in CLD students. These programs promote primary and secondary language development as well as cultural expression through the different academic areas. Programs that provide enrichment opportunities in both languages are highly recommended in order to promote talent development in all bilingual students, especially high-ability bilingual students. Enrichment programs in general emphasize students' strengths and allow teachers to facilitate more challenging and differentiating learning experiences.

Learning environments that encourage bilingualism and value cultural differences also support students' expressions of strengths and interests. Within these enriched environments, students have the opportunity not only to develop higher levels of bilingual proficiency, but also to advance their knowledge in a particular interest area. An extensive and enriched multicultural curriculum better serves the cultural and socioemotional needs of all students, and certainly those of CLD students. Bilingual education and multicultural education are strongly related to each another. A common goal joins them: the creation of an educational environment in which culture and language differences are valued and developed. Hence, it is essential that gifted education join in an effort to achieve this goal. Assessment, programming, and evaluation with a multicultural perspective should improve the actual inequity experienced by CLD students in gifted education.

Professional development should be used to promote an understanding among teachers, specialists, and administrators regarding awareness and knowledge of the learning and cognitive style preferences of CLD students. Also, school personnel must become familiar with the cultural and linguistic characteristics and needs of this population. Information and inservice training sessions on topics related to the education of CLD students, such as bilingualism, ESL practices, gifted education, and multiculturalism, are essential for the entire staff, especially classroom teachers.

Classroom teachers should have access to information regarding the assessment, programming, and evaluation of gifted and talented programs that are appropriate for CLD students (in the event that the school or district has a gifted program in place). Also, teachers should be aware of the goals and objectives of the gifted program. The same situation should exist relative to the goals for ESL programs or bilingual programs in the school.

An interdisciplinary approach should be implemented in schools in which CLD students are present, and programs such as the ESL or bilingual program and the gifted program should be integrated into the total educational experience of these students. Teachers and professionals in different areas can be informed and trained by colleagues in basic aspects of these fields. This perspective would not only benefit CLD students, but also teachers' pedagogical practices.

The Schoolwide Enrichment Model for Culturally and Linguistically Diverse Students

The Schoolwide Enrichment Model (SEM), developed by Joseph Renzulli and contributed to by Sally M. Reis, both from the University of Connecticut, was originally created for gifted and talented students. For the past twenty years, research and practice on this model have demonstrated its success in developing interests, talents, and high order thinking skills not only in high-ability students, but also in all students and at all educational levels, from kindergarten to college. As a research-based practical plan, the SEM has been field tested with a variety of student populations and effectively implemented for total school improvement (Renzulli & Reis, 1994).

There is no undoubted certainty of measuring giftedness, and no dichotomy between "gifted" and "not gifted" exists in the SEM. The educational principles and practices of this model are based on a developmental approach. The SEM does not rely on labeling students or on narrow definitions of *giftedness*, such as the ones measured by IQ tests or other psychometric procedures. Rather, the SEM focuses on the manifestations of gifted behaviors or performances that very often appear unexpectedly while providing enrichment and high-quality learning opportunities.

Reis and Renzulli (1985) provide an operational definition of *giftedness* as an interaction among three basic clusters of human traits: above-average general and/or specific abilities, high levels of task commitment, and high levels of creativity. Gifted and talented children are those possessing or capable of developing this composite set of traits and applying them to any potentially valuable area of human performance. Children who manifest or are capable of developing an interaction among the three clusters require a wide variety of educational opportunities and services that are not ordinarily provided through regular instructional programs (Reis & Renzulli, 1985).

The three basic clusters are essential contributors to, and their interaction results in, the manifestation of gifted behaviors or performances. A graphic representation of this definition is presented in Figure 9.1.

Two indisputable factors that determine the identification of underserved CLD students in programs for the gifted and talented are the definition of *giftedness* being used and the type of assessment process selected. The primary reason cited for their underrepresentation is the absence of adequate assessment procedures and programming

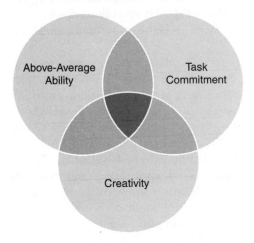

FIGURE 9.1   Definition of Giftedness.

efforts (Cohen, 1988; Frasier, Garcia, & Passow, 1995; Kitano & Espinosa, 1995; Mills & Tissot, 1995; Smith, LeRose, & Clasen, 1991).

There exists a detrimental impact as a result of using IQ tests and/or other traditional methods as the sole measure for identifying giftedness among CLD children. In spite of the research that supports eliminating biased tests and modifying traditional methods, many school districts still place a heavy emphasis on standardized test cut-off scores for student placement in gifted programs (Frasier, Garcia, & Passow, 1995). Traditionally, assessment tools and procedures commonly used in gifted programs rely on measures and techniques that are primarily dependent on English oral and written language (Hartley, 1987).

Assessment should include not only the selection of appropriate techniques and screening procedures, but also an in-depth knowledge of the student being assessed by sensitive and well-trained school personnel. The assessment procedure, as well as the educational program, should be carefully considered in the design and development of any gifted program. The cognitive, linguistic, and socioemotional characteristics of CLD students should be measured by standards reflecting the students' ethnic and cultural backgrounds, and validated by an ethnolinguistic approach. The design, implementation, and evaluation of new assessment procedures are critical for the identification and development of learning styles and high academic abilities in CLD students.

Flexible criteria using multiple sources to assess talents in CLD students are needed in order to identify and nurture students' outstanding abilities (Kitano & Espinosa, 1995; Kloosterman, 1997). Observations, autobiographies, behavioral checklists, nominations, parent interviews, student interviews, student portfolios and reports, anecdotal logs, interest surveys, case studies, student journals, and exploratory enrichment activities are some of the multiple possibilities that can be used to assess potential interests and abilities in CLD students. This type of assessment should always take into account the cultural and linguistic background of the child and should be conducted in the student's native language (if the talented child is also bilingual). Indeed, all children benefit when multidimensional assessment procedures are used to explore their interests, abilities, and learning styles.

The SEM proposes a continuum assessment, whereby the selection of students for the gifted program is not fixed. Rather, it is a process in which multiple methods of assessment, including students' work products, give substantial information about a particular student. This type of alternative assessment minimizes the effects of biases continuously addressed in the literature on traditional academic achievement tests and psychometric tests for CLD students. The SEM considers self-description of interests, high abilities, and learning styles of students as extremely valuable. The model focuses its assessment primarily on performance-based types of measures rather than on standardized measures. For example, valuable information could be gathered from the usage of simple surveys. A teacher survey helps educators obtain basic data of students' bilingualism and high abilities. Surveys for bilingual parents, written in English and a second language (e.g., Spanish), provide teachers with meaningful information on children and their home environments (Figure 9.2).

FIGURE 9.2   Sample Survey for Bilingual Parents.

Parent/Guardian Survey
Encuesta a Padres o Tutores

Date/Fecha: _____

Student Name/Nombre del Alumno: _____   **Age/Edad** _____

Parent or Tutor Name/Nombre del Padre o Tutor: _____

Please mark or write your answer in the spaces below. Por favor marque y escriba sus respuestas en los espacios dados. (Sus respuestas pueden ser en español.)

(1) What language do you usually speak at home?   _____   _____
      ¿En qué idioma usualmente hablan en el hogar?   English   Spanish
                                                          Inglés   Español

(2) What language does your child usually speak at home? _____   _____
      ¿En qué idioma usualmente habla su hijo/a en el hogar? English   Spanish
                                                          Inglés   Español

(3) Name three things your child likes to do at home.
      Mencione tres cosas que a su hijo/a le gusta hacer en
      el hogar.

_____   _____   _____
       (1)   (2)   (3)

(4) Name three abilities of your child.
      Mencione tres habilidades de su hijo/a.

_____   _____   _____
       (1)   (2)   (3)

Thank You/Muchas Gracias

Source: From V. I. Kloosterman, copyright © 1997.

The Schoolwide Enrichment Model:
Components and School Structure

The SEM is a coherent, systematic, and flexible plan in which assessment, programming, and evaluation processes are interrelated. Although its principles, definitions, and goals remain constant, this model allows for changes and adaptations, depending on school structures, specific characteristics of the school (human and material resources), student populations, families, and community involvement. The SEM has been well accepted and implemented in many schools and districts throughout the United States and overseas, because it

- Emphasizes the development of multiple potentials of young people. It provides broad and rich experiences for all students by implementing a variety of services and resources.
- Focuses on students' strengths, interests, and learning styles. Therefore, it allows teachers to develop a more challenging curriculum by individualizing the personal needs (affective, cognitive, linguistic, and cultural), interests, and abilities of each student.
- Embraces both excellence and equity in education by creating a school environment in which personal and cultural characteristics are valued and nurtured.
- Is a practical plan that promotes the development of relevant collaborative partnerships among enrichment specialists, students, teachers, administrators, parents, and community members. A graphic representation of the SEM is presented in Figure 9.3.

School Structures

The Regular Curriculum   The implementation of the SEM as a total school plan directly infuses the regular curriculum. As Renzulli (1995) explains, the major goal of the SEM is to promote high levels of challenging and satisfying learning across the full range of abilities, interests, and learning styles by incorporating enrichment learning and teaching practices into existing school structures and school improvement activities. For all students, but certainly for CLD students, the principles underlying this model raise expectations by empowering the learning and performances of this underserved population. As Renzulli (1995) states,

> This approach reflects a democratic ideal that accommodates the full range of individual differences in the entire student population, and it opens the door to programming models that develop the talent potentials of many at-risk students who traditionally have been excluded from anything but the most basic types of curricular experiences. (p. 3)

Enrichment Clusters   Essentially, clusters are enrichment alternatives for stimulating interests and developing talents in students as well as school personnel. Renzulli (1994) defines *enrichment clusters* as nongraded groups of students who come together

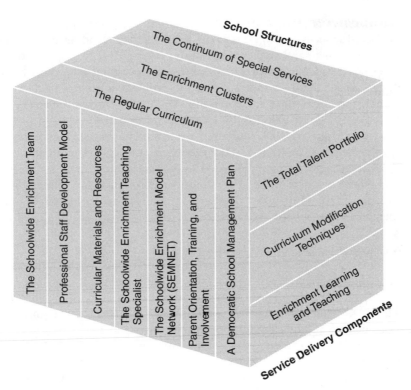

**FIGURE 9.3   The Schoolwide Enrichment
Model: Components and School Structures.**

Source: From Renzulli & Reis. (1985). Copyright © 1995 by Creative Learning Press, Inc.

during specified blocks of time during the school day to pursue common interests (p. 64). A wide variety of topics and disciplines not usually covered by the regular curriculum, at least not in an in-depth manner, could be developed in multiple enrichment clusters.

Family and community members are welcomed to participate as facilitators of enrichment clusters that are related to their areas of interest or expertise. This type of enrichment strategy gives students the possibility to (1) explore interest areas, (2) express style preferences and talent potentials, (3) acquire knowledge in a specific topic and develop individual or small group projects, and (4) interact with students of different ages and grade levels, meet with different adults, and learn about their many skills and experiences.

Because the entire school is involved in organizing and implementing the enrichment clusters, an excellent opportunity arises to allow for integration and diversity. In a school where diversity is well expressed in its student population, it should be important to invite parents and community members representing the diverse cultural and linguistic groups to propose and create clusters. This invitation will promote acceptance, diversity, and caring while learning in a meaningful way.

The Continuum of Special Services   Learners who perform at the highest levels require special services or programs to challenge their outstanding achievements. A rich variety of enrichment and acceleration options are available to respond to the needs of students whose academic performances surpass the possibilities of the school. Summer programs, special schools, complex real-world problem-solving projects, competitions, internships, apprenticeships, and counseling and mentoring assistance are some of the many educational alternatives for this student population.

Mentorships are valuable and often-strategic services used by schoolwide enrichment programs. Reis and Renzulli (1985) created a mentor system to implement at the secondary level. This system facilitates the search for mentors as well as their activities. Candidates could be found in the school or the community. The key issue regarding working with mentors is that there is willingness to help a student or a small group in a specific area. Furthermore, a passion for learning is usually infused in students' experiences.

A successful example of a mentor program is the *UConn Mentor Connection*, an enrichment summer program, coordinated and developed at the University of Connecticut. This program allows diverse learners to expand their knowledge on a certain interest topic or area by giving them opportunities to show their talents in creative projects and investigations. The *UConn Mentor Connection* targets highly talented secondary students who, for a three-week period, participate in real-world research projects and consult directly with university mentors who share a common interest field or subject area.

This type of mentor program is especially beneficial for CLD students when (1) there is someone to assist them on interesting projects and (2) the mentor shares the students' cultural and linguistic backgrounds or is knowledgeable about them. Whenever possible, it is highly recommended to have bilingual mentors for high-ability, bilingual students. Bilingual mentors are excellent resources to enrich students' knowledge and bilingualism. However, it is important to keep in mind that mainstream students also benefit greatly when they are able to interact with CLD mentors.

Service Delivery Components

Enrichment Learning and Teaching   The SEM stresses the process and products of learning and teaching experiences. In this model, the enrichment process is based on the idea that learning is more successful if there are enjoyment and meaning in the process and content, and better if students get involved in real-world problems. An enrichment plan called the Enrichment Triad Model (Renzulli, 1977) gives shape to this process (Figure 9.4). High-level enrichment and acceleration activities are developed, and students' responses are documented to continue with new, exiting, and higher level experiences for individuals, small groups, classrooms, or entire schools. The Enrichment Triad Model is a dynamic model, configured by three interrelated types of enrichment experiences (types I, II, and III). Type III activities are the most advanced types of enrichment (see Figure 9.4). They are also the types of enrichment self-selected by students.

The Enrichment Triad Model allows for activities in which CLD students could develop their two languages, and it organizes bilingual materials and resources. It is

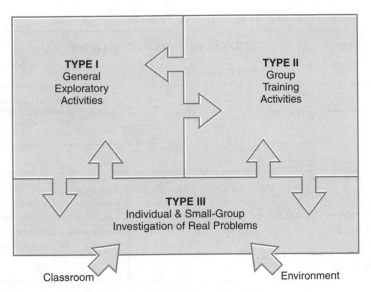

FIGURE 9.4   The Enrichment Triad Model.

highly recommended that school personnel be bilingual when working with bilingual/ bicultural students. Culturally and linguistically diverse parents and community members are powerful resources for helping teachers organize and implement a wide variety of Type I, II, and III enrichment activities.

The regular classroom and/or the resource room are suitable places for implementation of the different types of enrichment activities. It is recommended that the enrichment learning and teaching activities be developed at school, at home, and in the community. Some independent projects need to be planned outside the school setting. For example, Type III enrichment gives students the possibility to develop individual and group projects by selecting an interest topic or area of study. Students may be able to accomplish enrichment projects by using bilingual material at a higher proficiency level. On the one hand, students expand their knowledge on a particular interest area, and on the other hand, they develop the ability of using their two languages.

Curriculum Modification Techniques   The primary procedure used as a curriculum modification technique is called *curriculum compacting*. This is an enrichment procedure that modifies the regular curriculum by eliminating repetition of material already mastered, increasing the level of learning experiences, and providing advanced enrichment and acceleration activities (Reis & Renzulli, 1992; Renzulli & Reis, 1997; Renzulli & Smith, 1978). The SEM uses two other curriculum modification procedures: (1) the analysis of textbooks to eliminate repetitious drill and practice and (2) the exchange of these textbooks for in-depth selective-learning material to use in enrichment experiences. Figure 9.5 provides a graphical representation of two compactors, one in English and its translation in Spanish.

FIGURE 9.5 Sample Compactors: English and Spanish Versions.

INDIVIDUAL EDUCATIONAL PROGRAMMING GUIDE

The Compactor

Prepared by: Joseph S. Renzulli
and Linda M. Smith

NAME _____ AGE _____ TEACHER(S) _____

Individual Conference Dates and Persons Participating in Planning of IEP

SCHOOL _____ GRADE _____ PARENT(S) _____   ____ ____ ____

Curriculum Areas to Be Considered for Compacting Provide a brief description of basic material to be covered during this marking period and the assessment information or evidence that suggests the need for compacting.	**Procedures for Compacting Basic Material** Describe activities that will be used to guarantee proficiency in basic curricular areas.	**Acceleration and/or Enrichment Activities** Describe activities that will be used to provide advanced level learning experiences in each area of the regular curriculum.

GUIA DE PROGRAMACION EDUCATIVO INDIVIDUAL

El Compactador

Preparado por: Joseph S. Renzulli y
Linda M. Smith

NOMBRE _____ EDAD _____ MAESTRO(S) _____

Fechas de Entrevistas Individuales y Nombres de los Participantes en al Planificació de la GPEI

ESCUELA _____ GRADO _____ PADRE(S) _____   ____ ____ ____

Areas del Curriculum Consideradas Para Compactar Describa breve-mente el material básico a ser cubierto durante este periodo y información o evidencia que sugiera la necesidad de compactar.	**Procedimiento Para Compactar el Material Basico** Describa las actividades que las realizarán para garantizar el dominio de las áreas curriculares básicas.	**Actividades de Aceleracion y/o de Enriquecimento** Describa las actividades que se realizarán para proporcionar experiencias de aprendizaje de nivel avanzado en áreas del curriculum regular.

Basically, the compactor is an instrument that helps educators organize information on students' previously mastered material and select more challenging activities to replace the initial ones. The use of this instrument in languages other than English (see Figure 9.5) could assist bilingual educators in documenting CLD students' highest academic performances, programming enrichment or acceleration activities, and selecting bilingual material that reflects their strengths and ethnolinguistic characteristics.

The Total Talent Portfolio   There are many different types of portfolios, depending on the rationale, information, audience, and setting in which they are used. As with any instrument, a portfolio also may vary in shape and size. Usually, issues such as age appropriateness, capacities, and previous knowledge of managing a portfolio influence the accessibility of this instrument. Teachers need to evaluate these issues before using the portfolio in the classroom. Teachers willing to develop their own portfolios could share and plan their ideas with other colleagues and even with students at the upper grades. The design of the portfolio (the way information and students' work and products are gathered and recorded) could be a creative project to develop with the whole class. Students' work has unlimited potential for presentation. Portfolios help to record and keep track of their accomplishments as well as their learning progress in different subject areas and interest topics. A representation describing the major dimensions of the Total Talent Portfolio (TTP) is depicted in Figure 9.6.

The Bilingual Talent Portfolio   The Bilingual Talent Portfolio (BTP) is based on the TTP developed by Renzulli (1994). The key issues to be discovered are students' interests and talent potential by assessing the students in different domains and in formal and informal ways. Based on Renzulli's TTP, the BTP is an instrument to be used with bilingual/bicultural students for collecting and recording information about their needs, interests, abilities, learning-, thinking-, and expression-style preferences in two languages. The emphasis is on collecting information of CLD students' strengths in both languages and cultures (Kloosterman, in progress).

When describing the TTP, Renzulli (1994) explains that this instrument consists of both status information and action information. Status information is anything we know or can record about a learner's characteristics prior to the instructional process. Action information consists of annotated recordings of events that take place within the instructional process (p. 102), the new things we learn about our students.

The focus of both the TTP and the BTP is on students' strengths: (1) abilities or highest competencies of a student in a particular area or areas of human domain, (2) interests, and (3) learning-style preferences or ways in which students adapt and organize the assets in various learning situations. A form entitled "Action Information Message," depicted as a lightbulb, is used to record and communicate teacher's observations. In the upper primary grade levels and secondary level, this form is also completed by students. The form could take different shapes and sizes. In the event that a school has bilingual students, an alternative could be to create this form in the students' first languages. The students should then be allowed to complete the form in his or her language of preference. As Renzulli and Reis (1985) explain, action information is always something that grows out of the interests of students. By completing the Action Information Message, teachers have relevant information on students' true interests,

FIGURE 9.6   The Total Talent Portfolio.

DIMENSIONS OF THE TOTAL TALENT PORTFOLIO

Abilities	Interests	Style Preferences			
Maximum Performance Indicators	*Interest Areas*	*Instructional Styles Preferences*	*Learning Environment Preferences*	*Thinking Style Preferences*	*Expression Style Preferences*
Tests • Standardized • Teacher-Made Course Grades Teacher Ratings **Product Evaluation** • Written • Oral • Visual • Musical • Constructed (Note differences between assigned and self-selected products) Level of Participation in Learning Activities Degree of Interaction with Others Ref: General Tests and Measurements Literature	Fine Arts Crafts Literary Historical Mathematical/ Logical Physical Sciences Life Sciences Political/Judicial Athletic/ Recreation Marketing/ Business Drama/Dance Musical Performance Musical Composition Managerial/ Business Photography Film/Video Computers Other (Specify) Ref: Renzulli, 1977b	Recitation & Drill Peer Tutoring Lecture Lecture/ Discussion Discussion Guided Independent Study* Learning/ Interest Center Simulation, Role Playing, Dramatization, Guided Fantasy Learning Games Replicative Reports or Projects* Investigative Reports or Projects* Unguided Independent Study* Internship* Apprenticeship* *With or without a mentor Ref: Renzulli & Smith, 1978	**Inter/Intra Personal** • Self-Oriented • Peer-Oriented • Adult-Oriented • Combined **Physical** • Sound • Heat • Light • Design • Mobility • Time of Day • Food Intake • Seating Ref: Amabile, 1983; Dunn, Dunn, & Price, 1975; Gardner, 1983	Analytic (School Smart) Synthetic/ Creative (Creative, Inventive) Practical/ Contextual (Street Smart) Legislative Executive Judicial Ref: Sternberg, 1984, 1988, in press	Written Oral Manipulative Discussion Display Dramatization Artistic Graphic Commercial Service Ref: Renzulli & Reis, 1985

Source: From Renzulli (1994). *Creative Learning,* with permission.

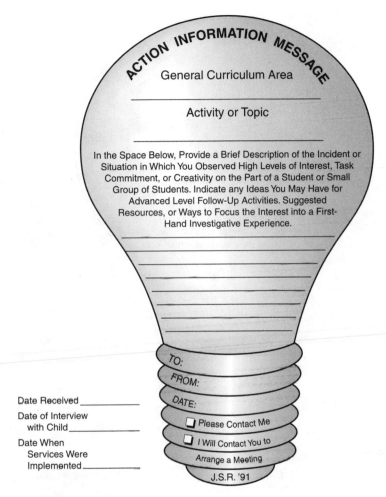

FIGURE 9.7　Lightbulb.

From Renzulli & Reis (1985).

which could be expressed through working on advanced-level projects or activities. Figure 9.7 presents a lightbulb, and the same lightbulb translated into Spanish is presented as Figure 9.8.

　　As in the TTP, the BTP should travel with a student from grade to grade, and should serve as the basis for briefing subsequent-year teachers about an individual's strengths and accomplishments (Purcell & Renzulli, 1998; Renzulli, 1994). Also, information collected during each academic year should be analyzed together by the regular teacher, the bilingual teacher or enrichment specialist, and the student. The primary purposes of the BTP are to assist educators in recording what they already know about a CLD student and to collect and assess information on the student's interests, talents,

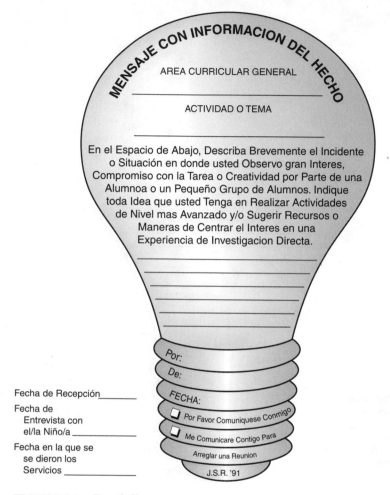

FIGURE 9.8 Bombilla.

From Renzulli & Reis (1985).

learning styles, and cultural expressions in English and another language. The BTP is also helpful for keeping notes on the student's academic performance and progress. Included in the BTP could be samples of a student's independent projects, such as type III products.

Real possibilities have to be evaluated for scheduling the BTP as part of the regular curriculum. As long as the regular curriculum is covered, the BTP is an excellent alternative for the development of students' academic and social skills across languages. In essence, the BTP is an assessment instrument that, if used well, could demonstrate CLD students' outstanding talents or potential talents more effectively than could any standardized measure. As a culturally and linguistically sensitive assessment measure, the BTP provides relevant information about students' bilingual development. In addition, the lack of information and the presence of misconceptions about learning- and cognitive-style preferences among CLD students are addressed in many studies (DeLeon, 1983). By implementing the BTP for diverse learners, research-based information on learning-, thinking-, and expression-style preferences could be collected and analyzed to contribute to the limited data on this aspect. In practice, educators may be able to program enrichment activities that promote the development of diverse styles by being knowledgeable of students' preferences.

Organizational Components

The organizational components proposed by the SEM (see Figure 9.3) are essential contributors to the development of the different services and activities for bright students. In general, these components address the many significant activities that are possible to develop via collaboration among the school, students' homes, and the community. It is of significant importance that students', families', and communities' cultural and linguistic characteristics be collected and used as valuable information to consider at the time of implementing the model.

As an example, the development of the Schoolwide Enrichment Model Network (SEMNET) allows for what Renzulli (1994) explains as the possibility of teachers and administrators to share a wide variety of SEM know-how, such as instructional materials, program-development tips and tactics, and professional development resources (p. 278). Teachers could search for appropriate CLD material on the SEMNET and subsequently use it in the classroom. Enrichment bilingual resources are highly recommended for any regular classroom in which CLD students are present. The SEMNET simplifies the search for high-quality, innovative material, a time-consuming activity for teachers.

The role of the enrichment specialist is essential, because she or he provides advanced-level enrichment activities to students, coordinates and supervises enrichment projects, and provides training to staff members. This specialist also informs and invites parents and the community to enrichment activities and programs and evaluates the progress of the enrichment plan in place. Partnerships among the school, the families, and the community play essential roles in both discovering students' talents and providing a caring and meaningful education. Family and community members can offer useful information regarding the students' cultural backgrounds, experiences, and abilities, which in turn can be used to improve the identification procedures and educational services. Family and community members also support the development of talents outside the school context by creating a rich and challenging environment.

Educators should inform CLD parents about the academic progress of their children. Also, the school staff needs to create different channels of communication suitable for specific CLD families. For example, a more direct and personal approach is recommended with Hispanic families. Culturally and linguistically diverse families should be welcomed to the school by having teachers appreciate and consider their values, traditions, and thoughts. In addition, CLD parents need to be encouraged and informed about gifted education identification and program services as well as activities that will enable them to assist their high-ability children at home.

The success of CLD parents' involvement in the school is associated with the use of the home language (a language other than English). A positive parent participation has been suggested when adults can apply their first language to assist their children with schoolwork and activities that are designed in their home language and when their children learn the home language in school over a longer grade span (Ramirez, Pasta, Yuen, Ramey, & Billings, 1991).

The following important aspects must be kept in mind when working with CLD parents:

1. Offer parent educational services and assistance in identifying and fostering the expression of talents and the maintenance of the first language at home.
2. Provide professional development opportunities for staff, as well as training and assistance for parents in English and their first language.
3. Establish family–community–school partnerships.
4. Develop and implement a challenging curriculum for bilingual students.

Promoting the Expression of Talents in a Schoolwide, Two-Way Bilingual Enrichment Program

Research evidence exists that the implementation of two-way bilingual education programs benefits all students by enhancing their bilingualism and academic performances (Thomas & Collier, 1995). Although these types of enrichment programs have been described as very effective in promoting oral bilingualism and biliteracy (Cummins, 1992; Krashen, 1991), as well as positive cognitive and socioemotional development (Genesee, 1987), there are very few programs in place. The Center for Applied Linguistics (1997) reported the total number of schools in the United States using the Two-Way Immersion Model as follows: 167 (Spanish/English), four (Korean/English), three (Cantonese/English), two (Navajo/English), two (French/English), one (Arabic/English), one (Japanese/English), one (Russian/English), and one (Portuguese/English).

The two-way curriculum is content-based and focuses on the development of strong academic achievement in both languages. However, although the goals of this type of bilingual program remain constant, the modes of instruction and the model of language development vary from program to program. Various reports indicate that the two-way approach is effective not only in the teaching of two languages to both language groups, but also in the development of academic excellence.

A Schoolwide Two-Way Bilingual Enrichment Program could identify and provide responsive educational experiences to talented bilingual students. The educational framework for this program is based on Renzulli's SEM. Because this model focuses on both outcome and the process of learning, this results in high-end learning experiences for all students, but especially for bright underserved students.

Independent research and practice in the two-way bilingual program design and the SEM suggest that the integration of these two exemplary programs has great potential in successfully meeting the needs of high-ability, bilingual/bicultural students (Kloosterman, 1997). Diverse learners will be more motivated to learn a second language if the enrichment learning and teaching process is configured in a positive and challenging atmosphere in which students' cultural backgrounds as well as personal characteristics are protected and valued.

The program should be able to provide students with opportunities to be fully engaged in challenging academic work while they work toward full mastery of English and another language. The program can also have an impact on national efforts to improve the education of CLD populations by identifying these students and providing them with high-quality learning and curricular experiences. This model program will identify talented bilingual students, develop and implement an enriched bilingual curriculum that advocates the expression and development of talents and languages, and train educators and parents to identify and develop talent potential and support academic excellence in this student population.

Because this Schoolwide Two-Way Bilingual Enrichment Program is designed whereby both nonnative-English-speaking and native-English-speaking students work together toward bilingualism, all students could benefit from the program. The additive bilingual environment proposed by this particular program provides both sets of students with ample opportunities to develop the two languages while, at the same time, allowing them to progress academically in both languages and gain an appreciation of another culture (National Center for Research on Cultural Diversity and Second Language Learning, 1994b).

Efforts need to be made to ensure that the modified educational procedures and techniques proposed for an educational project such as the Schoolwide Two-Way Bilingual Enrichment Program are valid and reliable to use with CLD students. Practice needs to be parallel with ongoing research that could evaluate the effects and reach relevant conclusions about this model for high-ability bilingual/bicultural learners.

A Promising Future for Gifted Culturally and Linguistically Diverse Students

To date, it is unquestionable that the United States is a diverse and pluralistic society. Its citizens differ in many ways, including culture, ethnicity, language(s), and religious preferences. These differences have influenced the expression of values, norms, and customs of the different immigrant groups since the foundation of the United States. People from different cultural and linguistic backgrounds who share the same historical background and geography give identity to a nation. A diverse society exhibits beliefs, thoughts, feelings, and values from different cultural perspectives, and the development of these aspects could be part of or absent from the formal educational system. However, every child should have the right to see his or her culture expressed and developed at school, as it is at home or in the community.

Although not explicitly addressed, in what Renzulli (1994) calls "The Act of Learning" (dynamic interaction between the teacher, the learner, and the material to be learned), three other important dimensions infuse the learning and teaching process. These dimensions could be described as (1) situational factors (socioeconomic, historical and demographic), (2) interpersonal and intrapersonal factors, and (3) cultural and linguistic diversity factors.

Renzulli (1995) clearly explains that the SEM is not meant to replace the existing school structures, but to influence and improve them. Thus, for example, if a bilingual program or ESL services are provided in a school in which an enrichment program is also in place, strategies and services provided by the SEM could enrich and promote high-quality education for diverse learners.

The adequate implementation of the SEM as an educational plan with alternative procedures and modification of enrichment techniques is a promising path for the development of interests, talents, and learning styles of CLD students. The SEM benefits all students, but certainly those who are underserved in programs for the gifted, because of the following:

1. The SEM adheres to a behavioral definition of *giftedness*. This conception of giftedness allows different ways of expression of talents and high academic performances rather than the narrowing concept of high IQ or intelligence. Also, a wide range of ability levels is considered without excluding students from services by only one score measure; the SEM does not rely on traditional standardized tests to determine whether a student is gifted or talented. Not all of the assessment procedures developed by the SEM depend on language. This is meaningful for bilingual students. The SEM proposes a continuum assessment procedure, whereby students' products and academic achievements are key components in the evaluation of strengths. Assessment strategies may include tasks in the students' first languages.

2. The SEM is flexible enough to develop talents by allowing the expression of diverse cultural and linguistic characteristics of the student population.

3. The SEM advocates for differentiated curriculum and instruction by attending to the unique needs of each learner.

4. The SEM provides high-quality education by improving the regular curriculum and promoting excellence in the school system. This model gives CLD students the opportunity to improve their academic performances and skills, and subsequently better prepares them for a challenging future.

5. The SEM actively involves the participation of the students and their teachers or facilitators in the enrichment learning and teaching process. Enrichment and acceleration opportunities for exploring, researching, and manipulating objects in different domains give students new knowledge and cognitive skills.

6. The SEM encourages and gives meaning to teacher training and schoolwork by promoting a sense of ownership and decision-making opportunity, while providing educational strategies and techniques to respond to students' interests, talents, learning- and expression-style preferences, and ethnolinguistic backgrounds.

As Renzulli (1994) discusses, one of the major goals of the SEM is "to create a learning community that honors ethnic, gender, and cultural diversity, mutual respect and caring attitudes toward one another, respect for democratic principles, and preservation of the Earth's resources" (p. 53). Nobody can say this is an easy task. A change of attitudes cannot be imposed, but individuals can be inspired to pursue these fundamental principles in school, at home, and throughout the whole community. The quality of education for all students in general, and high-ability diverse students in particular, will improve, and equitable educational opportunities will be provided, only when educators become aware, informed, and trained in the acceptance and expression of diverse cultural, ethnic, and linguistic backgrounds in their classrooms.

Summary

This chapter presented the Schoolwide Enrichment Model as an educational plan that can be utilized to simultaneously pursue excellence and equity as goals for talent development in all students. Students from diverse cultural and linguistic backgrounds could be particularly afforded opportunities to be identified and served in programs for the gifted and talented via the SEM. However, no changes are possible unless educators, parents, students, and the entire community understand the many ways that talent can be meaningfully expressed in a diverse sociocultural, educational environment. If this understanding is put into practice, the ultimate expression of diversity, in which every child learns from each other's cultural and linguistic background, will be actualized. This goal is not only for those who are underrepresented, but also for those in the mainstream.

Diversity is reflected in the SEM by allowing multiple and flexible alternatives of implementation, adapting the different components to the specific needs and characteristics of each community. There are no rules written in stone; on the contrary, after a thorough analysis of the characteristics of its student population as well as human resources and materials, each community will determine the appropriate ways through which to serve its students.

REFERENCES

American Association of Colleges for Teacher Education. (1994). *Teacher education pipeline III: Schools, colleges, and departments of education enrollments by race, ethnicity, and gender.* Washington, DC: Author.

Arnberg, L. (1984). Mother tongue playgroups for preschool bilingual children. *Journal of Multilingual and Multicultural Development, 5* (1), 65–84.

Baker, C. (1993). *Foundations of bilingual education and bilingualism.* London: Multilingual Matters.

Banks, J. A. (1993). The canon debate, knowledge construction, and multicultural education. *Educational Researcher, 22* (5), 4–14.

Castellano, J. (1995). Revisiting gifted education opportunities for linguistically and culturally diverse students. *National Association for Bilingual Education News, 18* (6), 27–28.

Cegelka, P. T. (1988). Multicultural considerations. In E. W. Lynch & R. B. Lewis (Eds.), *Exceptional children and adults. An introduction to special education* (pp. 545–587). Glenview, IL: Scott Foresman.

Center for Applied Linguistics. (January 1, 1997). *Directory of two-way immersion programs in the US.* Available at: <www.cal.org>.

Cohen, L. M. (1988). *Meeting the needs of gifted and talented minority language students: Issues and prac-*

tices. (ERIC Document Reproduction Service No. ED 309 592.)

Cummins, J. (1989). A theoretical framework for bilingual special education. *Exceptional Children, 56* (2), 111–119.

Cummins, J. (1992). Bilingual education and English immersion: The Ramirez report in theoretical perspective. *Bilingual Research Journal, NABE, 16* (1–2), 91–104.

Dean, A. V., Salend, S. J., & Taylor, L. (1993). Multicultural education: A challenge for special educators. *Teaching Exceptional Children, 26* (1), 40–43.

De La Rosa, D., & Maw, C. (1990). *Hispanic education: A statistical portrait.* Washington, DC: National Council of La Raza.

De Leon, J. (1983). Cognitive style differences and the underrepresentation of Mexican Americans in the programs for the gifted. *Journal for the Education of the Gifted, 6* (3), 167–177.

Diamond, B. J., & Moore, M. M. (1995). *Multicultural literacy: Mirroring the reality of the classroom.* White Plains, NY: Longman.

Dolson, D. (1985). The effects of Spanish home language use on the scholastic performance of Hispanic pupils. *Journal of Multilingual and Multicultural Development, 6* (2), 135–155.

Frasier, M., Garcia, J., & Passow, A. H. (1995). *A review of assessment issues in gifted education and their implications for identifying gifted minority students.* (RM Series No. 95203.) Storrs, CT: The University of Connecticut, The National Research Center on the Gifted and Talented.

Garcia, S. B., & Malkin, D. H. (1993). Toward defining programs and services for culturally and linguistically diverse learners in special education. *Teaching Exceptional Children, 26* (1), 52–58.

Genesee, F. (1987). *Learning through two languages: Studies of immersion and bilingual education.* Cambridge, MA: Newbury House.

Hartley, E. A. (1987). *How can we meet all their needs? Incorporating education for the gifted and talented into the multicultural classroom.* (ERIC Document Reproduction Service No. ED 336 968.)

Kitano, M. K., & Espinosa, R. (1995). Language diversity and giftedness: Working with gifted English language learners. *Journal for the Education of the Gifted, 3* (18), 234–254.

Kloosterman, V. I. (in progress). *The bilingual talent portfolio: An instrument for assisting educators on the assessment, development and educational progress of high ability, bilingual students.*

Kloosterman, V. I. (1997). *Talent identification and development in high ability, Hispanic, bilingual students in an urban elementary school.* Unpublished

doctoral dissertation, University of Connecticut, Storrs.

Kloosterman, V. I. (1999). *Socio-cultural contexts for talent development: A qualitative study on high ability, Hispanic, bilingual students (RM99142).* Storrs, CT: University of Connecticut, The National Research Center on the Gifted and Talented.

Kofsky, G. E. (1992). *Increasing the number of minority elementary students found eligible for placement in a gifted program by enhancing the quality of screening instruments and inservice training provided to school staff.* Unpublished doctoral dissertation, Nova University, Fort Lauderdale, FL.

Krashen, S. D. (1991). *Bilingual education: A focus on current research.* Washington, DC: National Clearinghouse for Bilingual Education.

Krashen, S. D. (1996). A gradual exit, variable threshold model for limited English proficient children. *National Association for Bilingual Education News, 19* (7), 1, 15–18.

Mills, C. J., & Tissot, S. L. (1995). Identifying academic potential in students from under-represented populations: Is using the Raven's Progressive Matrices a good idea? *Gifted Child Quarterly, 39* (4), 209–217.

Mortensen, E. (1984). Reading achievement of native Spanish-speaking elementary students in bilingual vs. monolingual programs. *The Bilingual Review/La Revista Billingüe, 11* (3), 31–36.

National Center for Research on Cultural Diversity and Second Language Learning. (1994a, February). *Funds of knowledge: Learning from language minority households.* (ERIC Digest, EDO-FL-94-08). Washington, DC: Center for Applied Linguistics.

National Center for Research on Cultural Diversity and Second Language Learning. (1994b, December). *Two-way bilingual education programs in practice: A national and local perspective.* (ERIC Digest, EDO-FL-95-03). Washington, DC: Center for Applied Linguistics.

Orfield, G. (1986). Hispanic education: Challenges, research, and policies. *American Journal of Education, 95,* 1–25.

Passow, A. H., & Frasier, M. (1996). Toward improving identification of talent potential among minority and disadvantaged students. *Roeper Review, 18* (3), 198–202.

Purcell, J. H., & Renzulli, J. S. (1998). *Total talent portfolio: A systematic plan to identify and nurture gifts and talents.* Mansfield Center, CT: Creative Learning Press.

Ramirez, J., Pasta, D., Yuen, S., Ramey, D., & Billings, D. (1991). *Final report: Longitudinal study of structured English immersion strategy, early-exit and late-exit bilingual education programs for language-*

minority children (Vol. II). (No. 300–87–0156). San Mateo, CA: Aguirre International.

Reis, S. M., & Renzulli, J. S. (1985). *The secondary triad model: A practical plan for implementing gifted programs at the junior and senior high school levels.* Mansfield, CT: Creative Learning Press.

Reis, S. M., & Renzulli, J. S. (1992). Using curriculum compacting to challenge the above-average. *Educational Leadership, 50* (2), 51–57.

Renzulli, J. S. (1977). *The enrichment triad model: A guide for developing defensible programs for the gifted.* Mansfield, CT: Creative Learning Press.

Renzulli, J. S. (1994). *Schools for talent development: A practical plan for total school improvement.* Mansfield, CT: Creative Learning Press.

Renzulli, J. S. (1995). *Building a bridge between gifted education and total school improvement.* (BDM No. 9502.) Storrs, CT: The University of Connecticut, The National Research Center on the Gifted and Talented.

Renzulli, J. S., & Reis, S. M. (1985). *The schoolwide enrichment model. A comprehensive plan for educational excellence.* Mansfield, CT: Creative Learning Press.

Renzulli, J. S., & Reis, S. M. (1994). Research related to the schoolwide enrichment model. *Gifted Child Quarterly, 38,* 2–14.

Renzulli, J. S., & Reis, S. M. (1997). *The schoolwide enrichment model. A how-to guide for educational excellence.* Mansfield, CT: Creative Learning Press.

Renzulli, J. S., & Smith, L. H. (1978). *Compactor.* Mansfield, CT: Creative Learning Press.

Smith, J., LeRose, B., & Clasen, R. E. (1991). Underrepresentation of minority students in gifted programs: Yes! It matters! *Gifted Child Quarterly, 35* (2), 81–83.

Thomas, W. P., & Collier, V. P. (1995). Language-minority student achievement and program effectiveness studies support native language development. *National Association for Bilingual Education News, 18* (8), 5, 12.

U.S. Department of Commerce. (1986). *School enrollment: Social and economic characteristics of students.* Washington, DC: Bureau of Census, Current Population Reports.

U.S. Department of Education. (1993). *National excellence: A case for developing America's talent.* (Office of Educational Research and Improvement.) Washington, DC: U.S. Government Printing Office.

Voltz, D. L. (1995). Learning and cultural diversities in general and special education classes: Frameworks for success. In B. A. Ford (Ed.), *Multiple voices for ethnically diverse exceptional learners* (pp. 1–11). Reston, VA: The Council for Exceptional Children.

Weil, D. (1993). Towards a critical multicultural literacy: Advancing an education for liberation. *Roeper Review, 15* (4), 211–217.

10 Portraits of Success

Programs That Work

NILDA AGUIRRE AND
NORMA E. HERNÁNDEZ

There is nothing more unequal than equal treatment of unequal people.
—Thomas Jefferson

Historically, language and culturally diverse (LCD) students have been excluded from gifted programs due to their inability to function both linguistically and culturally in the language of the dominant culture. Traditional IQ tests have not adequately assessed the knowledge and achievement that students from diverse backgrounds possess. In any given school, the majority of the gifted program consists of students from the middle to upper classes of the mainstream society. Too often there is an obvious lack of minority representation in the gifted and talented programs. Amodeo (1982) defines the gifted and talented as the top 5 percent of any cultural group. Yet, there is ample evidence that children from LCD groups are still not being identified to satisfy the 5 percent mark of their culture group.

The administration of these instruments has also posed a problem in obtaining valid test results. The effect of examiner variables, such as bilingualism, ethnic group membership, and style of test administration, can induce inaccurate test results (Bordie, 1970; Palomares & Johnson, 1966; Sattler, 1970; Thomas, Hertzig, & Fernandez, 1971; Torrance, 1977). Research still indicates that the instruments used for identifying English-language learners (ELLs) are not reflective of the potential that these students possess (Cohen, 1990; Fraiser, 1990; Frasier, Garcia, & Passow, 1995; Passow et. al., 1996; Plucker et. al., 1996; Reyes et. al., 1996). Many of these instruments are the contributing factors that have hindered the process. This has greatly affected access to categorical programs and increased the underrepresentation of this special population in gifted education programs.

Research has always conferred that children exposed to early nurturing and stimulating environments have a greater chance of developing high levels of intelligence

(Clark, 1986; VanTassel-Baska, 1989). Children who come from an environment in which social and emotional development is obstructed have a difficult time in the pursuit of developing their potential *self-actualization* (Maslow, 1971). Giftedness results partially from an early interaction with a stimulating environment. Family patterns or persons who provide this environment can be found in any cultural, language, and socioeconomic circumstance. However, because these factors differ from the traditional pattern of the dominant culture, traditional identification procedures will most likely be ineffective for discovering gifted ability (Fraiser et al., 1995; Sternberg, 1981, 1982, 1988).

Multiple criteria assessment has become the focus when identifying students who are LCD. Torrance (1982) believes that testing culturally diverse children should include mood setting or activities that will awaken the creative process. Renzulli (1977) suggests that non-language-dependent identification strategies be developed. Also, the process needs to be a continuous one among the culturally diverse. Frasier et. al. (1995) believe that nominations should come from other sources in addition to the teacher (i.e., community leaders, peers, and self).

The purpose of this chapter is to present alternative educational programs for gifted and talented ELL *that have worked*. In each section, you will find that the authors have outlined their programs in the hopes of providing practitioners with components that are essential for planning and implementing successful programs. Key elements involve the philosophy of each program and the program goals and objectives.

In this chapter, we emphasize what writers and researchers alike have known for sometime: The teacher is the single most important element in the instructional process. The teacher's cultural sensitivity, the ability to respect and understand students from diverse ethnic backgrounds, the desire to provide these students with successful experiences, and the quality of the instruction and preparation promote and foster a learning environment that is true to the students' self-actualization. Perhaps we can also add another element: teacher attitudes toward the target population. Students who are challenged and teachers who have high expectations form a winning combination. However, when teachers perceive the target population based on cultural and ethnic stereotypes and lower the expectation, the students will fail to succeed. These practices may perpetuate lowered teacher expectations that are communicated to the students, which may become self-fulfilling prophesies. As educators, we need to embrace programs that are of high caliber, programs that through adversity and resistance have proved that language minority, culturally diverse, and economically disadvantaged students can be gifted, talented, and successful.

Identification procedures for the programs included in this chapter provide a multidimensional definition of *giftedness* and a multiple criteria approach to selecting potentially gifted students. Careful attention needs to be paid to teachers' referrals. In many cases, teachers are regarded as the sole source for recommending potential candidates for assessment. Teachers are usually the ones who are most familiar with the students' achievements, abilities, aptitudes, and strengths, and, foremost, teachers can provide daily observation and anecdotal records of behaviors during formal and informal situations. The underlying current in all of the programs is the belief that both cognitive (verbal and nonverbal) and behavioral traits are an intricate part of the process. Giftedness should be inclusive and offer flexibility in identifying bilingual and bicultural students. Local norms for the school district and target population should play important roles in the development of criteria for determining giftedness.

Taking this into consideration, the instructional approach needs to be based on sound educational practices that combine English as a Second Language (ESL) methodologies, gifted strategies, and techniques such as Bloom's Taxonomy (Bloom & Krathwohl, 1977), creative problem solving (Parnes, 1965; Sternberg, 1985; Treffinger & Firestein, 1989), critical thinking skills, questioning techniques (divergent, convergent, evaluative, open-ended) (Runco & Vega, 1990), use of multiple intelligences (Gardner, 1983), and aspects of creativity (fluency, elaboration, originality, and flexibility) (Guilford, 1975; Torrance, 1979).

The assessment portion of these programs also suggests the following alternative approaches: portfolios, performance-based, product evaluation, rubrics, and assessments reflecting evaluation made by self, peers, audience, parents, and teachers.

All in all, successful programs make one fundamental claim: Early intervention combined with unique and innovative instruction yields excellence in the education of the potentially gifted and talented ELL. The work reported herein was supported under Grant no. T003G30006-87-96, Title VII Academic Excellence Program of the Office of Bilingual Education and Minority Language Affairs (OBEMLA), U.S. Department of Education. However, the contents of this chapter do not necessarily represent the positions or policies of OBEMLA or the U.S. Department of Education.

Project GOTCHA:
An Academic Excellence Program

Historical Perspective

Title of Project/Program   Project GOTCHA (Galaxies of Thinking and Creative Heights of Achievements) is a former Title VII Academic Excellence Program of the OBEMLA, U.S. Department of Education. GOTCHA was developed and implemented in the Broward County Public Schools, Fort Lauderdale, Florida, during the funding cycles from 1987 to 1996. Currently, dissemination activities have been assumed by the coordinator and trainers of the GOTCHA Program under International Educational Consultants, Inc.

Model Sites   The following are model sites of the GOTCHA programs in Florida: Palmetto Elementary School in Palm Beach County (1996–present), and Pompano Beach Middle School (1992–1996), Dwight D. Eisenhower and Nova Blanche Foreman Elementary Schools (1987–1992), and Nova Middle Schools (1987–1992) which are in the Broward County Public School System, Fort Lauderdale.

Adoption Site   Project GOTCHA was funded by the Academic Excellence Program for the purpose of dissemination. The schools that demonstrated a need asked to adopt the program. The teachers, administrators, and parents were trained by the coordinator/trainer of Project GOTCHA. The adoption sites received a three-day intensive training, complete with assessment instruments, GOTCHA curriculum resource guides, GOTCHA production activity cards, training manuals and parent training manuals.

Funding/Seed Money   The GOTCHA program evolved from the Bilingual Exceptional Student Education Demonstration Project, funded by the OBEMLA from 1980 to 1985.

Funding/Implementation Cycle   Project GOTCHA was awarded dissemination funds under the Academic Excellence Program, which was authorized by Congress in the Education Amendments of 1984. It is a dynamic system for sharing and disseminating successful bilingual and ESL projects among public and private educational agencies. Administered by OBEMLA, the Academic Excellence Program was funded to distribute information about exemplary projects across the United States.

Project GOTCHA was one of the original nine programs to be awarded in 1987. Thereafter, the program was awarded funds for dissemination for three cycles (1987–1990, 1990–1993, and 1993–1996). When funds were no longer available, the coordinator and trainers assumed the dissemination activities.

Program Overview   Project GOTCHA identifies and serves gifted, creative, and talented ELLs in grades 1 through 8. This nationwide program is designed to reach local education agency personnel who wish to develop similar programs and individual teachers who wish to incorporate these methods in classroom activities. There are two major characteristics that differentiate the GOTCHA Program from other ESL gifted programs. First, there is the emphasis on the unique creative abilities of each child. Second is the early intervention of ELLs. The program consists of four components: student identification, staff development, instructional approach/materials, and parent training.

Program Goals   The goals of the program are to achieve the following:

- Develop a coordinating plan with national, state, and local educational agencies to disseminate information about the GOTCHA project.
- Develop, validate, and disseminate information on instructional materials, guides, and training modules used in the project.
- Train potential users in the adoption of the program.

History of Program   Project GOTCHA evolved from the Bilingual Exceptional Student Education Demonstration Project funded by OBEMLA in Broward County, Florida, from 1980 to 1985. After seven years of successfully meeting its objectives and providing data to document its success, project GOTCHA was awarded for its best promising practices and claims of effectiveness. Project GOTCHA became one of the Academic Excellence Programs in 1987. For the following nine years (1987–1996) Project GOTCHA disseminated its program practices and trained teachers who met eligibility criteria.

Program Features   Project GOTCHA assists educational agencies with the design and structuring of gifted and talented programs by providing a model that has met rigorous Academic Excellence standards. Its unique features include the following:

- Transportability of the program components
- Successful implementation in diverse cultural and ethnic settings
- Cost effectiveness
- Maximization of student strengths
- Performance-based, content-based language acceleration curriculum
- ESL methodology integrated with gifted strategies
- A specialized parent education program
- A multifaceted and multidimensional identification criteria
- Staff development that emphasizes gifted and ESL training
- Evaluation reports that evidence claims of effectiveness
- Easy correlation with Goals 2000, National ESOL standards, state standards, and benchmarks

Instruction and Curriculum   Perhaps one of the most interesting aspects of the curriculum is the flexibility that has been built into every unit. The lessons are designed to include the following: (1) multiple levels of achievement, (2) a variety of learning styles, (3) language proficiency levels, (4) degree of cognitive challenge, (5) creative strands, (6) product process, (7) alternative assessment, (8) critical thinking (Bloom's Taxonomy), and (9) self-evaluation.

Delivery is a priority for the success of the program. Teachers are trained in delivery as well as the content of the curriculum. The focus is to empower teachers to extend the existing curriculum by training them to apply the techniques used in the GOTCHA curriculum. Teachers are trained to view the curriculum as a springboard from which they can expand, create, and elaborate.

Project Components

As mentioned, the program consists of four components: student identification, staff development, instructional approach and instructional materials, and parent training.

Identification Component   The identification of students is one of the main components of the program. It is unique in its reliability for selecting students who possess creative and talented characteristics within a unique population. Linguistically, these children are most likely to demonstrate their superior abilities in their home languages. Consideration, therefore, is given to their experiential backgrounds, home, community, and school values; and other cultural factors. There are three stages in the identification process:

1. *Nomination:* Teachers nominate children for the program based on supportive information (such as informal observations and samples of students' work) and orientation sessions. A parent/community form is also sent home for parents to nominate their child.

2. *Identification:* During this stage, more information is collected about the nominated students. This information is based on the scores obtained from the Renzulli Behavioral Checklist, the Aguirre/Hernandez Gifted LEP Characteristic Checklist (1999), the Torrance Test of Creative Thinking (Figural), and/or the Universal Nonverbal Intelligence Test (UNIT), as well as additional projects and work samples. If available, achievement test scores and /or report card grades are considered.

3. *Placement:* The GOTCHA team (ESL teacher, principal, resource bilingual teacher, other) evaluate the Matrix Form, which contains a profile of the student's performance. Students that meet the eligibility criteria are then placed in the GOTCHA Program. Students need to qualify on five of the seven criteria on the matrix. The program consists of two models: inclusion or pull-out. The curriculum responds to the fact that many of these students may come from poverty-level families, have academic limitations in their backgrounds, be unfamiliar with the mainstream culture, and lack proficiency in the English language. Therefore, the curriculum is aimed at enriching these students' educational backgrounds as well as providing them with the skills to function and/or compete with English-speaking peers. The instruments used for the identification of students include the following:

- *The Torrance Test of Creative Thinking:* This instrument is nonlanguage dependent. Nominated students are given the test, which is scored using the established norm-referenced criteria. The raw scores are converted to t scores and recorded on the matrix. Scores above the 50th percentile are considered acceptable for placement in the program if additional validating criteria are found. A few students scoring under the 50th percentile have been accepted into the program per the recommendation of their teachers.
- *The Universal Non-Verbal Intelligence Test (UNIT):* The UNIT is a multidimensional measure of intelligence that assesses a broad range of complex memory and reasoning abilities. Normative data were collected from a comprehensive national sample of 2,100 children and adolescents from the ages of five years through 17 years 11 months. Data were collected in 108 sites across thirty-eight states. When individuals from reliability, validity, and fairness studies were included with the standardization sample, a total of 3,865 children and adolescents were examined. The following nine variables were used to select participants for the standardization sample: age, gender, race, Hispanic origin, region, community setting, classroom placement, special education services, and parental educational attainment. *Reliabilities were high* (0.83 to 0.98), meeting or exceeding the technical standards often cited by experts in the field for both standardization and clinical samples. The UNIT appears to be a moderately good predictor of academic achievement. In addition, discriminant validity evidence is reported, demonstrating that UNIT differentiates among individuals with mental retardation, learning disabilities, speech-language impairments, and those that are *gifted.*
- *The Renzulli Behavioral Checklist (Adapted):* This instrument places the student in different situations in which their behavior could demonstrate creative skills. The scoring consists of four categories: from 0 = not observed to 4 = always observed. Students scoring in categories 3 or 4 remain in consideration for the program.

- *The Aguirre-Hernandez Gifted LEP Checklist:* The characteristics of the Aguirre-Hernandez Gifted LEP checklist are provided in Table 10.1.
- *Project Evaluation and Teacher Recommendations:* Teachers are asked to assess the projects and work samples developed by the students. This assessment is based on the four aspects of creativity: flexibility, originality, fluency, and elaboration.

Curriculum Model   The lessons and activities found in the elementary and secondary curriculum guides have incorporated Gardner's Multiple Intelligences Theory. The social studies and science portions of the curriculum provide opportunity for developing problem-solving and critical-thinking skills. The learning environment focuses on developing cooperative learning skills. Creativity is fostered through the use Torrance's Creative Thinking Skills of fluency, flexibility, originality, and elaboration. There is an emphasis on ensuring that metacognitive skills are taught in order to instill the desire to become lifelong learners. See Tables 10.2 and 10.3 for curriculum model components associated with Project GOTCHA.

The schedule for program implementation is at the discretion of the adopting district. The recommended model calls for grouping identified students by language proficiency levels and instructing them for a minimum of two hours a week. An alternative model is inclusion, in which students are identified and the classroom teacher modifies curriculum and contracts extension assignments.

TABLE 10.1   Characteristics of the Culturally and Linguistically Diverse Gifted and Talented Child

- Eagerly shares his or her native culture
- Shows a strong desire to teach peers words from his or her native language
- Has a strong sense of pride in his or her cultural heritage and ethnic background
- Eagerly translates for peers and adults
- Balances appropriate behaviors expected of the native culture and the new culture
- Possesses advanced knowledge of idioms and native dialects with the ability to translate and explain meanings in English
- Understands jokes and puns related to cultural differences
- Reads in the native language two grades above his or her grade level
- Functions at language proficiency levels above that of his or her non-gifted LEP peers
- Is able to code switch
- Possesses cross-cultural flexibility
- Has a sense of global community and an awareness of other cultures and languages
- Learns a second or third language at an accelerated pace (formal or informal)
- Excels in math achievement tests
- Possesses strengths in the creative areas of fluency, elaboration, originality, and/or flexibility
- Demonstrates leadership abilities in nontraditional settings: playground, home, church, clubs, etc.

Source: Characteristics based on study of students participating in Project GOTCHA, Galaxies of Thinking and Creative Heights of Achievements, Title VII, Academic Excellence Program (1987–1996).

TABLE 10.2   Instructional Component Chart: Curricula for Gifted, Talented, and/or Creative Language Minority, Culturally Diverse, and LEP Students

Subcomponents	Activities	Assessment (Authentic)
Listening	Drama/art/poetry/music	Product/demonstration
Speaking	Brainstorming	Portfolios
Reading	Projects/presentations	Observation
Writing	Role-playing	Group presentations
Critical thinking	Related classroom activities	Alternative assessments
Multiple intelligences	Transformation activities	Self-evaluation
Bloom's Taxonomy	Student-centered tasks	Peer-evaluation
Accelerated language	Manipulatives (creative)	Video documentation
Technology	Multimedia projects	Power-point presentations

Components: Language, social studies, science, math, special thematic units, and performance-based curricula.

Instructional Materials

GOTCHA ESL/Gifted/Creative and Talented Elementary Resource Guide   This resource guide is used in grades 1 through 5. The topics covered in the units include Performing Arts, Visual Arts, Media Production, Communications, Transportation, Archaeology, Toys and Games, Future World, Plants, Volcanoes, Seasons, Weather, Astronomy, Earth and Space Beyond, Animals, Human Body, Creative Writing, Alphabet, Vocabulary, Special Days, Foods, Manners, I Am Special, Knowing Myself, Book Reports, and other gifted resources.

GOTCHA ESL/Gifted/Creative and Talented Secondary Resource Guide   This curriculum guide is used in grades 6 through 8. Topics covered in the units are Origin and History

TABLE 10.3   Curricular Componant for Addressing Diversity

Subcomponents	Activities	Assessment
Prejudice	Mentors/guest speakers	Demonstration
Bias reduction	Field trips	Portfolio
Social action	Related classroom activities	Group activities
Tolerance	Community-related activities	Observation
Cultural awareness	Action plans	Newsletter
	Penpals	

Components: Multicultural communication, cross cultural understanding, and self-esteem.

of English, Letter Writing, Composition, Speech, Poetry, Mythology, Folklore, Tall Tales, Fairy Tales, Newspaper, Journalism, and Media Production.

Parent Training Manual   Parent involvement is a critical part of any educational program. This manual provides parents with the following: description of the program objectives, goals, identification process, instructional approach, rights and responsibilities, suggestions and recommendations for improving their child's education, and activities to motivate creativity at home.

Teacher Training Manual   This manual contains the complete process for an effective and successful implementation of the program. This manual includes the following: background information, overview goals, objectives, identification criteria, instruments used, placement criteria, instructional approaches, delivery techniques, implementation guidelines, assessment, forms, research articles, and program evaluation forms. Teachers implementing Project GOTCHA receive specialized training in "Power Teaching." Power Teaching is the compilation of strategies and techniques that have been validated as exemplary practices to produce effective academic gains.

Independent Learning Center Activity Kits   Activity cards adaptable for all levels of language proficiency are provided. The purpose of this kit is to facilitate the design of a learning center and provide opportunity for independent or small-group activity.

Student Outcome

Claims of effectiveness were made in 1987 when Project GOTCHA was awarded funds for dissemination activities under the Title VII Academic Excellence Program. The evaluation of student achievement was used as baseline data in the original proposal submitted to the U.S. Department of Education. Students in the GOTCHA Program were scoring above average in the areas of language arts, reading, and math. English language proficiency was attained at twice the rate of LEP students not participating in the GOTCHA Program.

The data collected thereafter was to evaluate the dissemination process of the project. Specific forms were developed as a result of Title VII guidelines and resulted in obtaining the following information from each adoption site and model site: (1) evaluation of the program by teachers, students, parents, and administrators; (2) evaluation of the curriculum materials; (3) evaluation of the awareness and training sessions; and (4) information of identified students through the Individual Profile Form. These data were compiled and analyzed by an external evaluator and then reported to the Project Director of the Academic Excellence Program. Consistently during the three funding cycles, Project GOTCHA excelled in its dissemination practices. This is exemplified by the number of adoption sites that implemented the program (Table 10.4).

Project Impact

Project GOTCHA had the following impact on the districts that adopted and implemented the program: (1) increased representation of ELLs in gifted and talented pro-

TABLE 10.4   Project GOTCHA: 1993–1996 Summative Evaluation Data

Number of Sites Implementing Project GOTCHA	Attendance Record for Project GOTCHA Classes	Language Classification	Standardized Scores	Referrals to Districts' Gifted and Talented Programs
N = Students	*Percentage of students present throughout the 3 years*	*No. of students scoring 2 levels or higher per year on a language proficiency screening instrument*	*No. of students scoring above the 34% NP after 1 year in the program*	*No. of students referred for gifted evaluation*
Three Model Sites, Elementary n = 18 students	90	12	15	3
Two Model Sites, Secondary n = 25 students	80	16	18	6
Twenty Adoption Sites, Elementary n = 618 students	87	502	586	111
Six Adoption Sites, Secondary n = 131 students	85	97	95	21

Source: Data compiled by Nilda M. Aguirre and Norma E. Hernandez, Consultants for Project GOTCHA under International Educational Consultants, Inc. (1996–1999).

grams, (2) increased rate of language proficiency levels, (3) increased student achievement scores, (4) teachers trained to recognize characteristics of special populations of students to meet their needs, and (5) a shift in paradigm: "Students do not need to be proficient in English to be identified as gifted."

The major systemic reform is twofold: (1) the instruction of the target student population using a specialized curriculum enriched with gifted strategies and integrated with ESL methods and (2) increasing awareness and representation of ELLs in gifted and talented programs. The training of teachers is also a major reform, because it incorporates the most promising practices, review of current research, cultural awareness, gifted strategies, ESL methodologies, alternative assessments, program evaluation, and multiple criteria evaluation. Parental participation is highly regarded by all involved, therefore, parents take an active part in learning about their gifted child. The most significant accomplishment of Project GOTCHA has been assisting educators in the identification, implementation, and awareness of gifted and talented ELLs.

Summary

Project GOTCHA has changed the attitudes held by many about the LCD minority student being identified as gifted and talented. Teachers felt that their nominations were considered and that students were being identified in other areas of giftedness, not just in the academic areas. The rationale for adopting a program like GOTCHA goes beyond meeting the needs of ELLs. Project GOTCHA has been at the forefront of gifted ESOL education. It promoted the concept of identifying LEP students, using multiple criteria. It promoted instructing LEP students, using critical thinking skills and gifted strategies. It promoted teaching LEP students with a specialized curriculum containing integrated and interdisciplinary units. It promoted performance-based outcomes and portfolio assessment, and it promoted student-centered and cooperative learning environments. Project GOTCHA has lead the way for many gifted and talented ESOL programs for the past twenty years. Visit Project GOTCHA'S website at <www.kreative-kids.com>.

The Milwaukee Public Schools Bilingual Gifted/Talented Program

Location, Model Sites, and Funding

Location
Allen-Field Elementary School
730 W. Lapham Boulevard
Milwaukee, WI 53204
Phone: (414) 645–8580
Fax: (414) 645–1638

Model Sites
Golda Meir Gifted/Talented Elementary School
1555 Martin Luther King Jr. Drive
Milwaukee, WI 53212
Phone: (414) 271–6840

Samuel Morse Gifted/Talented Middle School
4601 N. 84th Street
Milwaukee, WI 53225
Phone: (414) 616–5800

The funding implementation cycle is July 1 to June 30. Funding/seed money for the program was provided by the Milwaukee Board of School Directors.

Program Overview

The Milwaukee Public School System is a pioneer in gifted and talented education. As a result of its early efforts, the Bilingual Gifted/Talented Program was developed. The

Bilingual Gifted/Talented Program for grades 3 through 5, located at Allen-Field Elementary School, is a districtwide program and was established in September of 1980. This intensive effort is to fully educate bilingual students with unique and challenging needs beyond the programs and services normally available within the regular bilingual classroom program.

Program Philosophy

The philosophy of the Bilingual Gifted/Talented Program is to afford each student the quality of instructional materials and resources necessary for each student to develop to his or her maximum potential.

Program Goals

In keeping within the program's philosophy, the Bilingual Gifted/Talented Program seeks to create a stimulating environment in which the potential of every student is challenged through a variety of intensive learning experiences. Program goals include the following:

- Develop an awareness of each pupil's abilities and talents.
- Foster respect for the abilities and talents of others.
- Provide experiences in critical/creative thinking and problem solving.
- Nurture the leadership potential in each student.
- Develop independence, self-direction and discipline in learning.
- Access and stimulate reading/writing in English/Spanish.
- Use cultural facilities to develop and expand students' artistic skills and talents.
- Stimulate parental involvement in school activities, events, and learning situations.

History (Program Biography)

In 1980, the Milwaukee Board of School Directors accepted and adopted a proposal from parents, teachers, and administrators recognizing the need to establish and provide a bilingual specialty program. Thus, the Bilingual Gifted/Talented Program was implemented in order to educate bright, capable, and industrious children who benefit from a fast-paced, stimulating environment. These bilingual children require an ability-challenging educational program to achieve their potential. This particular population of students also represents the next step toward attendance at the Morse Gifted/Talented Middle School. Bilingual Gifted/Talented students may demonstrate performance or potential in one or more of the five areas identified by the U.S. Department of Education:

1. General intellectual ability
2. Specific academic aptitude
3. Creative and productive thinking
4. Leadership ability
5. Ability in visual performing arts

Program Features (Personnel)

The Division of Bilingual Multicultural Education in the Milwaukee Public Schools System includes the following:

- One program director
- One curriculum/department specialist
- One teacher supervisor
- One administrator and assistant principal
- One bilingual coordinator (Gifted and Talented fifth-grade teacher)
- One bilingual Gifted and Talented teacher
- Two educational assistants

Instruction (Curriculum Focus)

The art of teaching gifted and talented students resides in teachers challenging children's enthusiasm for learning while gradually increasing responsibility and ownership for their success. Districtwide grade-level expectations and objectives for reading/writing in English/Spanish, math, science, and oral communication have been written for grades 3 through 5. These objectives are appropriate for guiding the growth of bilingual gifted and talented children. However, the staff has accelerated and enriched the curriculum in these basic subject offerings as well as in other areas of the curriculum, such as creative and visual arts programs.

The curriculum provides students with opportunities to extend their abilities to think, analyze, evaluate, and learn rather than only to acquire facts. Higher level questioning, analysis, problem solving, and divergent and critical thinking are among the techniques used to stimulate learning. Constant assessment of student educational progress and needs is made by using teacher-made tests, along with other criterion-referenced and standardized tests.

Ongoing assessment of student progress occurs daily, and the need for additional instruction is provided. Curriculum extensions are flexible and vary according to the time of year, current events, curriculum impact, and availability and talent of personnel. The summative evaluation of program objectives provides information that is used to make the necessary adjustments in the Effective School's Plan, which is developed annually.

Program Components

The components of the Milwaukee Public School Bilingual Gifted/Talented Program, which unlocks student ability, include the following:

- Well-defined criteria for identification
- Use of different learning styles
- Development of language skills in English/Spanish
- Building on strengths

- Higher level questioning
- Independent learning and group activities
- Multisensory approach
- Career education
- Critical and creative problem solving
- Curriculum extensions
- Research and study skills
- Stimulating learning environment
- Development of leadership and organization
- Multidiscipline approach
- An appropriate reporting system to students, parents, teachers
- Open-ended activities
- Community involvement
- Laboratory experiences in computers, distance learning, and science labs
- Provision of giftedness in all areas

An additional part of this program's component focuses on parents, volunteers, and community resource persons, who are often called on to enrich and enhance program activities by sharing information on their careers and life experiences.

Student Selection/Recruitment and Identification

Criteria for identification include the following:

1. Above-average ability (grades and quality of work)
2. Task commitment (motivation and responsibility)
3. Creativity
4. Leadership qualities

Classroom teachers, parents, and peers from the fourteen bilingual elementary schools in Milwaukee identify and recommend potential students to grades 3 through 5 during the annual school selection period. The procedure consists of submitting a student information form, a copy of the current-grade report card, a gifted/talented indicator, and a student writing sample. A random selection of students is then made from among those children who have been identified to participate.

Population

There are two classrooms, housing approximately sixty students. The current enrollment consists of a split classroom for grades 3 and 4, and a fifth-grade classroom. Both classes have thirty bilingual gifted/talented students. A waiting list of at least eight to ten students remains active throughout the year. Limited space is a major factor, which constricts the increase of the student population in the program. Most children are transported to the school daily by bus.

Learning Environment/Instructional Strategies

The program is organized into two self-contained classrooms of thirty students possessing a wide range of abilities. It is an action-oriented program in which instruction and learning occurs mainly through large- and small-group work and individualization. Students also are grouped for special projects according to interests and special assignments.

Assessment/Pupil Progress

Periodic assessment of pupil progress and program effectiveness is made by the teachers, parents, and students. These evaluations lead to improved curricular offerings so that each pupil's potential is maximized. A bilingual report card, using letter grades, indicates a student's achievement effort, and progress is reported to parents on four occasions throughout the school year. Handwritten teacher comments in English and Spanish add to the student's and parents' understanding of the student's progress. Conference days also are well attended. Effective student, parent, and teacher communication is recognized as a most essential ingredient in a stimulating educational program.

Program Impact

Student achievement and attendance is well recognized and rewarded. Throughout the year, students are recognized through the Honor Roll. They also participate in writing and art contests, ballet, theater, cultural exhibits, a college for kids program, and intramural sports. A personal goal of all students is to be accepted to the Morse Middle School for the Gifted/Talented. Considering that this is a direct placement, the students try to excel and do their best to maintain their grades. Many of them continue on to college and universities with great success. This generates a great impact in the Allen-Field Elementary School, the district, and the Hispanic community.

Summary

The Milwaukee Public Schools Bilingual Gifted/Talented Program, located at Allen-Field Elementary School, is a positive, exciting, and unique experience. The program recognizes, develops, and nurtures students' creative and academic abilities by meeting their individual needs in a multicultural society, while acknowledging and respecting various learning and teaching styles.

Project EXCEL: San Diego City Schools

Names of Projects

Project EXCEL (Title VII) is a K–2, self-contained, gifted bilingual (English/Spanish) program with dually certified (bilingual and gifted) teachers. Project First Step (Javits) is a program for all linguistically diverse groups in grades Pre-K–2.

Location, Model Sites, and Funding

These projects are located in the San Diego City Schools, San Diego, California. The model sites comprise ten schools with the highest percentage of English language learners and diverse students. The projects are funded by Title VII (1989–1994) and the Javits Act (1992–1995).

Project Focus and Goal

The focus is on early intervention in preschool through second grade. The goal of the projects is to identify a talent pool of potentially gifted learners at an early age and provide a differentiated curriculum.

History of the Program

San Diego City School's Gifted and Talented Program is a long-standing program in the district (30 years). The Gifted and Talented Education (GATE) Program serves 20,000 students, of which 1,700 are highly gifted. Students are identified in grades 2, 5, and 7. There are self-contained GATE cluster classrooms and (25) seminar centers for the highly gifted. Currently, there are 1,300 teachers of the gifted and about 250 bilingual teachers of the gifted.

Program Features

There is one GATE program administrator, two curriculum resource teachers, and five psychologists. The GATE program is in 131 of 164 total schools. All of the secondary schools have a GATE program. In the San Diego, California, city school district, teachers of the gifted are required to have GATE District Certification. We offer the competency-based certification on a yearly basis. The parent involvement components include a District Advisory Committee of parents that represent all areas of the city.

Instruction (Curriculum)

Instruction in the GATE Program is driven by the *GATE Curriculum Framework*. This handbook includes current theories and practices in June Maker's book, *Models for the Education of the Gifted* (e.g., Abraham Tannenbaum's Enrichment Matrix).

Project Components

The design for both projects was based on the structure of the GATE Program. The three major components are student readiness, teacher training, and parent involvement.

Project EXCEL: Bilingual Gifted and Talented

Project EXCEL is an elementary school bilingual program for gifted English-language learners (ELLs). About one in every three Hispanic children who enroll in the San Diego City Schools is an ELL. Prior to Project EXCEL, the ELL children had to wait to become fluent in English before they could be considered for testing in the district's all-English GATE program. Indeed, Hispanic children historically have been under-represented in San Diego's referral process for the GATE program by a factor of 4 (Saccuzzo & Johnson, 1995); that is, one-fourth as many Hispanic students are referred to the GATE program as one would expect, based on their representation in the San Diego schools.

In the early 1980s, the student population in the GATE program was 20 percent minority and 80 percent White, while the district was 48 percent minority and 52 percent White. So the San Diego City Schools, under the guidance of a new superintendent and in response to suggestions from the Mexican American Advisory Committee, made a concerted effort to identify more minority students for its GATE program and to identify them during the early elementary years. District funds were allocated to the GATE program so that it might service all the schools in the district. An additional psychologist and resource teachers were hired. The GATE program's identification process was also changed to accommodate multiple criteria.

In 1986, the Developing Gifted Potential (DGP) Project was established at the ten elementary school sites with the highest percentage of minority students. English language learners posed a special problem, however, because they could not be tested in English. Project EXCEL, building on the philosophical and methodological bases of the DGP Project, but with an early intervention focus, set about in six elementary schools with high enrollments in bilingual programs to provide a developmentally and linguistically appropriate elementary educational experience to bright ELL students and to facilitate their successful transition into the GATE program at a later time. Project EXCEL was funded by Title VII and operated officially for five years, from 1989 to 1994.

An evaluation committee was formed early in the project's implementation year to work with the district's evaluation staff. It consisted of internal and external evaluation consultants, GATE administrators, school psychologists assigned to GATE screening, and some participating schools' principals.

Project EXCEL was well founded both in the research on early intervention in gifted education and in the research on primary language instruction in bilingual education. The design of the project consisted of three integrated components: student readiness, teacher development, and parent involvement. In the identification process, the project utilized a talent pool of children nominated as potentially gifted by teachers at every grade level. In addition to introducing certain IQ tests, such as Ravens Progressive Matrices, Project EXCEL used a portfolio, the California Learning Record, to supplement the psychometric test used for identification. The *La Prueba* test was used to measure the academic achievement of LEP students in Spanish reading during the 1989–1990 and 1990–1991 periods, but this test was replaced by the *Aprenda* series in 1992.

EXCEL was not the first attempt to provide a developmentally and linguistically appropriate education for primary-grade ELLs, but it was among the longest running projects, and appears to be the only one to date to demonstrate an impact on the ethnic composition of the host district's gifted program (Perez & Bernal, 1996).

Teacher Selection and Development Component

The Project recruited from the selected schools credentialed bilingual teachers with no previous experience in GATE. Project teachers volunteered or were selected by principals to participate in Project EXCEL. The goal of this component was to develop a cadre of certified bilingual teachers of the gifted by providing them with a comprehensive professional development program, opportunity to express their own professional creativity in a new curricular departure, and a chance to serve an important segment of the population of ELLs. The desired outcome was that these teachers develop positive attitudes toward giftedness to help define and implement a curriculum for gifted students that are differentiated by bilingualism.

The foundation for this component was an extension of the San Diego City School's GATE teacher certification process, with a focus on the culturally and linguistically diverse gifted learner. This competency-based certification process included five categories and eighteen competencies. Project teachers received both district credit (professional development units) and, by special arrangement with San Diego State University, three semester hours of college credits for these professional development experiences.

Parental Involvement Component

Parental training began in earnest right from the start of the project. The project manager offered five workshops to parental groups throughout the project's first year at various school sites. The parental involvement component emphasized information and training during the project's second to fifth years. Topics of discussion at the parents' workshop included the following:

- An orientation to the district's Gifted and Talented Education Program (GATE)
- An orientation to Project EXCEL and the concept of early intervention
- Characteristics of giftedness
- Early childhood development and intellectual abilities
- Multiple intelligences
- The project's instructional strategies
- Developing creativity at home through math, science and language arts activities

In the second to fifth years of the project, there was an average of three workshops per project site. This component developed into a two-tier program to meet the needs of parents who were new to the project, while parents of longer standing received training that built on the topics mentioned before. Each site provided two morning training sessions for parents. In addition, the district provided two regional sessions at night.

Summary

Overall, the number of GATE-eligible Hispanics at the six project schools increased by a factor of 9 over the project's five-year history. This was due in no small part to a change from very traditional instruments, such as the Henman-Nelson, WISC-R, or

Standford-Binet (LM), to tests that measure more fluid intelligence without relying on English proficiency alone, such as Ravens Progressive Matrices. These changes also reflect the influence of Project EXCEL on the district's GATE program. Today, there is an effective programmatic option in place in the six Project EXCEL schools to educate bright ELLs that did not exist in 1989. Project EXCEL, which covers grades K–5, ultimately led to project First Step, an early-childhood program for very able ELL students, which added four other schools offering gifted education programming. The San Diego School's GATE Program has made progress in the way it selects its historically underrepresented students for gifted education programming.

REFERENCES

Aguirre, N. M., & Hernandez, N. E. (1999). *Characteristics of the culturally and linguistically diverse gifted and talented child.* Baton Rouge, LA: Project GOTCHA; Title VII; Academic Excellence Program; International Education Consultants, Inc.

Amodeo, L. (1982) *Parental involvement in the identification of gifted Mexican children.* Paper presented at the Council for Exceptional Children National Conference for the Exceptional Bilingual Child, Phoenix, AZ.

Bloom. B. S., & Krathwohl, D. R. (1977). *A taxonomy of educational objectives: Handbook I: Cognitive domain.* New York: Longman.

Bordie, J. (1970). Language tests and linguistically different learners: The sad state of the art. *Elementary English, 47,* 814–828.

Clark, B. (1986). *Optimizing learning: The integrative education model in the classroom.* Columbus, OH: Merrill.

Cohen, L. (1990). ERIC EC Digest no. E480; ERIC Document No. 321485.

Frasier, M. (1990). Identifying the typical and atypical gifted: A paradigm for the 21st century. In *Education of the gifted in the 21st century: Applying new ideas and innovative approaches to gifted education* (pp. 41–46). Santa Barbara, CA: The Townes Foundation.

Frasier, M. M. et al., (1995). *A review of assessment issues in gifted education and their implications for identifying gifted minority students.* (ERIC Document Reproduction Service No. ED388024.)

Gardner, H. (1983). *Frames of mind: The theory of multiple intelligences.* New York: Basic Books.

Guilford, J. P. (1975). Varieties of creative giftedness: Their measurement and development. *Gifted Child Quarterly, 19,* 107–121.

Maslow, A. (1971). *The farther reaches of human nature.* New York: Viking.

Palomares, U., & Johnson, L. (1966). Evaluation of Mexican American pupils for EMR classes. *California Education, 3* (8), 27–32.

Parnes, S. J. (1965). *The moral judgement of the child* (M. Gabin, Trans.). New York: Free Press. (Original work published 1932)

Passow, A. et al., (1996). Toward improving identification of talent potential among minority and disadvantaged students. *Roeper Review, 18* (3) 198–202.

Perez, R. I., & Bernal, E. M. (1996, March). Project EXCEL: Gifted bilingual. Paper presented at the meeting of the Southwestern School Boards Association, San Diego, CA.

Plucker, J. A. et al., (1996). Wherefore art thou, multiple intelligences? Alternative assessments for identifying talent in ethnically diverse and low income students. *Gifted Child Quarterly, 40* (2), 81–92.

Renzulli, J. (1977). The enrichment trend model. A plan for developing defensible programs for the gifted and talented. *Gifted Child Today, 12* (4), 35–39.

Reyes, E. I. et al., (1996). Developing local multidimensional screening procedures for identifying giftedness among Mexican American border population. *Roeper Review, 18* (3), 208–211.

Runco, M. A., & Vega, L. (1990). Evaluating the creativity of children's ideas. *Journal of Social Behavior and Personality, 5,* 439–452.

Saccuzzo, D. P., & Johnson, N. E. (1995). Traditional psychometric tests and appropriate representation: An intervention and program evaluation study. *Psychological Assessment,* (2), 183–194.

Sattler, J. (1970). Racial "experimental effects" in experimentation, testing, interviewing, and psychotherapy. *Psychological Bulletin, 73* (2), 137–160.

Sternberg, R. J. (1981). A componential theory of intellectual giftedness. *Gifted Child Quarterly, 25,* 86–93.

Sternberg, R. J. (1982). Lies we live by: Misapplication of tests in identifying the gifted. *Gifted Child Quarterly, 26,* 157–161.

Sternberg, R. J. (1988). *A triarchic theory of intellectual giftedness.* In R. J. Sternberg & J. E. Davidson (Eds.), *Conceptions of Giftedness,* (pp. 223–243). New York: Cambridge University Press.

Thomas, A., Hertzig, I., & Fernandez, P. (1971). Examiner effect in I.Q. testing of Puerto Rican working-class children. *Measurement and Evaluation in Guidance, 4* (3), 172–175.

Torrance, E. P. (1977). *Discovery and nurturance of giftedness in the culturally different.* Reston, VA: Council for Exceptional Children.

Torrance, E. P. (1979). Unique needs of the creative child and adult. In A. H. Passow (Ed.), *The gifted and talented: Their education and development. 78th NSSE Yearbook* (pp. 352–371). Chicago: National Society for the Study of Education.

Torrance, E. P. (1982). Identifying and capitalizing on the strengths of culturally different children. In C. R. Reynolds & J. B. Gutkin (Eds.), *The Handbook of school psychology.* (pp. 481–500). New York: Wiley.

Treffinger, D. J., & Firestein, R. L. (1989). Update: Guidelines for effective facilitation of creative problem solving. *Gifted Child Today, 12* (4) 35–39.

VanTassel-Baska, J. (1989). The role of the family in the success of disadvantaged gifted learners. *Journal for the Education of the Gifted, 13* (1), 22–36.

11 Programming for Identification

Young, Gifted English-Language Learners

ROSA ISELA PÉREZ

The fastest-growing population of diverse gifted students consists of students acquiring English, or English-language learners (ELLs). The number of ELL students in the United States is projected to be 15 million, or 25 percent, of the K–12 enrollment by the year 2026 (Garcia, 1994). Over the next 30 years, the proportion of gifted students who are acquiring English will grow from one in twenty to one in four (Kitano & Espinosa, 1995). School leaders need to educate themselves about the knowledge base in effective practices for serving gifted children whose first language is other than English. These children can be appropriately identified and serviced by gifted programs if school districts adopt the value of equity or equality of opportunity for all learners (Perez, 1993).

This chapter seeks to encourage implementation of enriched developmental programming to increase identification and services to young gifted ELL students. San Diego City Schools' (SDCS) Project EXCEL is discussed as one model that is effective in addressing the needs of young, gifted ELLs. A literature review and historical perspective on SDCS's Gifted and Talented program provide the context and purpose of Project EXCEL. The program elements of Project EXCEL are described, and the evaluation methods and findings of the project are discussed. The chapter concludes with the summative considerations and recommendations from Project EXCEL and, more importantly, implications for gifted programs nationally.

Literature Review

The challenge of serving gifted students from culturally and/or linguistically diverse backgrounds is well documented in the literature of gifted education. Passow (1980) notes that strategies developed by concerned educators for dealing with barriers to appropriate accommodation of diverse gifted learners generally include (1) new criteria for defining *giftedness*, which depend on other measures in addition to IQ; (2) a bilingual approach to language; (3) renewed teacher training that embraces cultural diversity; (4) an emphasis on teaching skills that enhance creativity and expressiveness; and (5) accountability from gifted programs regarding minority group participation that is enforced by the school board.

During the past two decades, two programs were successful in identifying and nurturing young, culturally diverse, gifted students and implementing program strategies as outlined by Passow. These programs are Bring Out Head Start Talents (Project BOHST) and the Program of Assessment, Diagnosis and Instruction (PADI). The approach for both programs was grounded in the belief that potential giftedness can be found among a very diverse group of students, including those with deficits in basic skills, those with limited English proficiency, those that are economically disadvantaged, and non-White students whose experiences may distance them from the mainstream. The primary focus was to identify and foster potential to enable "hidden" gifted students to emerge and refine their skills sufficiently to move into programs for the gifted.

Both Project BOHST and PADI implemented similar components: (1) general enrichment programming, both in the classroom and at home, to enhance the critical thinking skills and creativity of all children; (2) identification processes for determining the gifted and/or talented child in the program, using both parent and teacher input; and (3) specific programming to involve parents of gifted and talented children.

According to the evaluation findings of Project BOHST, the program had a positive impact not only on children in the intervention group identified as gifted, but also on children not so identified and on the project teachers: Both identified bright/gifted/talented children and nonidentified children made gains on the Kaufman IQ test over their comparison group counterparts. Moreover, the biggest gains on the Kaufman test were made by children who were not identified, indicating that exposing children to higher order thinking skills may have a beneficial impact on all children. In addition, the attitudes of the teachers in the intervention group was changed: The way they described their students became significantly more positive (Karnes & Johnson, 1986).

Gregory (1988) suggests that one of the real strengths of PADI is in the assessment approach, which the project called "identification through teaching." The approach permitted staff members to refine their judgments about how individual students met the cognitive demands of the program, based on their observations over time. PADI also encouraged a teacher-coaching network to break down potential isolation in individual classrooms. Companionship, according to Gregory, became an important key; a coaching partner, struggling to achieve the same instructional goals with the same kind of students, provided collegial support that was not otherwise available. After five years of the project's being operational, more than forty teachers have been trained to instruct over 1,000 children, and it has fostered the screening of approximately 8,000 students. San Diego's Project EXCEL drew from the experiences of BOHST and PADI, but in the context of districtwide reform.

Project History and Description

About one of every three Hispanic children who enroll in the San Diego City Schools (SDCS) is an ELL. Prior to Project EXCEL, a Title VII–sponsored bilingual project, ELL students had to wait to become fluent in English before they were considered for testing in the district's all-English gifted and talented education (GATE) program. Indeed, Hispanic children historically have been underrepresented in San Diego's referral process for the GATE program by a factor of 4 (Saccuzzo & Johnson, 1995); that is, one-fourth as many Hispanic students are referred to the GATE program as would be expected, based on their representation in the SDCS.

In the early 1980s, the student population in the GATE program was 20 percent minority and 80 percent White, while the district was 48 percent minority and 52 percent White. The SDCS, under the guidance of a new superintendent and in response to community concern from the Mexican American Advisory Committee, made a concerted effort to identify more minority students for its GATE program. District funds were allocated to the GATE program so that it might serve all the schools in the district, and additional psychologists and a bilingual Hispanic resource teacher were hired. The GATE program's identification process was also modified to accommodate multiple criteria.

In 1986, the Developing Gifted Potential (DGP) Project was established at the ten elementary school sites with the highest percentage of minority students. ELL students posed a special problem, however, because they could not be tested in English. Project EXCEL, building on the philosophical and methodological bases of DGP (Ciriza, 1987), but with an early-intervention focus, set about to provide a developmentally and linguistically appropriate educational experience for gifted ELL students in six elementary schools, and to facilitate their successful transition into the GATE program. Project EXCEL operated officially for five years, from 1989 to 1994.

Project EXCEL was well founded both in the research on early intervention in gifted education and in the research on primary language instruction in bilingual education. The design of the project consisted of three integrated components: student readiness, teacher development, and parent involvement. In the identification process, the project utilized a talent pool of children nominated as potentially gifted by the teachers at every grade level. In addition to introducing certain IQ tests, such as Ravens Progressive Matrices, Project EXCEL used a portfolio, the California Learning Record, to supplement the psychometric tests used for identification, with an authentic assessment of selected students. The La Prueba test was used to measure the academic achievement of all students in Spanish during the 1989–1990 and 1990–1991 periods. This test was replaced by the Aprenda series in 1992.

The aim of this project was to identify and develop the potential of Hispanic ELL primary-age students by providing a developmentally enriched curriculum in bilingual K–5 classes prior to formal identification for entry into the program for the gifted. Kitano and Espinosa (1995) note that enriched curricula to foster potential is a promising practice and that, once validated, may replace traditional identification models for identifying diverse gifted students.

Project bilingual teachers were offered inservice training and peer coaching in strategies for enhancing, observing, and recording potential. Instructional methods included strategies for promoting the inductive thinking, creativity, and problem-solving skills typically used in classrooms for gifted learners. Barkan and Bernal (1991) argue that there is no inherent need to delay the education of limited English proficient (LEP) gifted children if bilingually competent teachers of the gifted are available.

The parent involvement component included parent workshops designed to be sensitive to the cultural and linguistic needs of Spanish-speaking Hispanic families. Few would dispute the importance of parent involvement as a contributing factor in the academic success of most children. With respect to gifted children, some implications from research pertain to how parent interaction affects the development of gifted children and how parent training might be affected.

Tannenbaum (1992) reports that some adults attribute their success to childhood home environments that were nurturing and challenging, while others excelled despite having troubled, nonsupportive childhoods. These two situations indicate that no generalization can be drawn, but the special relationship between child and parent is most influential. Determining what works best for individuals is most challenging, and providing parent training to develop gifted potential is paramount.

The following sections describe in greater detail the participants and project elements of Project EXCEL: student readiness, teacher development, and parental involvement.

EXCEL Participants

Project EXCEL utilized a study design with two experimental formats and one control-group format (referred to hereafter as the "project talent pool students," "project non-talent pool students," and the "control students"). Hispanic ELLs randomly assigned to self-contained K–5 bilingual project classrooms comprised the two project groups. The project talent pool students were selected by project teachers as students that demonstrated gifted potential, whereas the non-talent pool students were not. The control students consisted of Hispanic ELLs who were randomly assigned to self-contained K–5 bilingual classrooms at the project schools but were not enrolled in project classrooms.

The district bilingual regulations require that schools identify students who are ELLs and provide them with "appropriate instruction." When a student enters the district as a new enrollee, the parents/guardians are asked to complete the Home Language Survey, which indicates the language(s) spoken in the home. If a language other than English is indicated for students in grades K–6, the IDEA Proficiency Test (IPT) is administered in English to assess the students' listening and speaking abilities.

Those students who score below the "fluent" level are classified as ELLs and are placed in the district's second-language program. The IPT is subsequently administered to these students in their primary languages (in the case of Project EXCEL students, the Spanish version) to determine the level of proficiency in their first languages. Both project talent pool and non-talent pool students and the control group of students in this study scored below the "fluent" level on the IPT as new enrollees and were placed in bilingual classrooms.

Of the 1,167 project students involved during the 1993–1994 academic year, the teachers selected 443 of these (38%) for the project's talent pool of students that demonstrated gifted potential. The two campuses that had at least one project teacher at each grade level identified the largest number of students for the talent pool. Overall, 51.9 percent of the talent pool students were girls—a virtually perfect gender representation.

School sites were selected on the basis of their high representation of Hispanic ELL students from low-income families, as determined by the free and reduced-price lunch data at each site. The six project schools rank in the top thirty of 160 schools in SDCS with 90 percent of children in poverty.

Student Readiness

In Project EXCEL, the purpose of the student readiness component was to provide enriched programmatic opportunities for the identification of students with gifted potential. All project students participated in a differentiated curriculum for gifted learners, with a focus on process and content modifications conducted in two languages, Spanish and English. The project classrooms offered a bilingual program that included a one-hour session in English as a Second Language (ESL) and all other content areas in the children's first language, Spanish. The instructional strategies of Hilda Taba's Model for Cognitive Development (e.g., concept development, resolution of conflict), Parnes' Creative Problem-Solving Model, and Kaplan's Model for Thematic Interdisciplinary Instruction were implemented in project classrooms. The students' program was further differentiated by providing out-of-school augmentation (e.g., community classroom consultants and field trips) so that students used the cultural, linguistic, and social resources of their communities in their learning.

Teacher Professional Development

The project recruited credentialed K–5 bilingual teachers from the selected schools with no previous experience in GATE. Project teachers volunteered or were selected by the principals to participate in Project EXCEL. The goal of this component was to develop a cadre of certified bilingual teachers of the gifted by providing them a comprehensive professional development program, an opportunity to express their own professional creativity in a new curricular departure, and a chance to serve an important segment of the population of ELLs. The desired outcome was that these teachers develop positive attitudes toward giftedness in order to help define and implement a differentiated curriculum for young, gifted ELL students.

The foundation for this teacher component was an extension of the SDCS GATE teacher-certification program, with a focus on the culturally/linguistically diverse gifted learners. This competency-based certification process includes five categories and eighteen competencies (Table 11.1). Project teachers received both district credit and, by special arrangement with San Diego State University, three units of college credit.

The first year, EXCEL teachers participated in three full-day conferences and ten additional days of training throughout 1989–1990 to complete the GATE district certification program. The curriculum text for this component was the district's *GATE Curriculum Framework*, which contains work from some of the leaders in the field of gifted education at the time. Project teachers were introduced to qualitatively differentiated programs as those that modify or adjust the content, process, products, and learning

TABLE 11.1 SDCS GATE Certification Competencies

I. Characteristics and Behaviors of Gifted and Talented Students
   a. Gain knowledge and understanding of varied expressions of cognitive, social, and emotional characteristics and behaviors of gifted students.
   b. Understand special needs within the gifted population.
   c. Understand the impact of culture, ethnicity, socioeconomics, language, and other factors on the development, expression, and recognition of giftedness.

II. Identification and Certification of the Gifted and Talented
   d. Gain knowledge of district's GATE identification approaches and procedures.
   e. Become familiar with the relevance of cultural, ethnic, and socioeconomic factors to the assessment and achievement of individual students.

III. Differentiated Curriculum and Instruction for Gifted and Talented Learners
   f. Gain an understanding of curricular differentiation for the gifted.
   g. Be able to build from the core program a differentiated curriculum.
   h. Be able to plan and design a classroom program based on student assessment data.
   i. Develop an awareness of a variety of learning styles and strategies appropriate to gifted students.
   j. Acquire knowledge of a variety of classroom management techniques.
   k. Be able to identify current issues and trends as they affect the education of the gifted and utilize research findings in program implementation.

IV. Parenting the Gifted
   l. Be exposed to a variety of resources to share with parents on parenting skills and understanding the gifted child at home.
   m. Gain knowledge of the variety of processes which involve parents in ongoing decision-making affecting the planning, implementation, and evaluation of site and district GATE programs.

V. Professional Development
   n. Enhance understanding of self as learner and the impact of self-knowledge on gifted student' learning.
   o. Acquire the ability to convey and defend to a wide variety of persons the appropriateness of their program for the gifted.
   p. Increase his/her awareness of professional and nonprofessional organizations that promote gifted education.
   q. Be provided with information of opportunities for continued professional development with respect to gifted education.

environment in ways that build on and extend the special characteristics of gifted learners. Emphasis was placed on broadening the concept of giftedness and tying students' needs to instruction.

The project's training of teachers began with process modifications to develop high-level thought and strategies that allow open-ended responses, discovery, and freedom of choice. The Hilda Taba Model for Cognitive Development (e.g., concept development, resolution of conflict) and Parnes' Creative Problem-Solving Model were introduced in the first year by the EXCEL teachers in both Spanish and English in all content areas, as indicated by classroom observations. In addition to the formal training, the project provided monthly individualized peer-coaching sessions in the project teachers' own classrooms. Peer coaching was used to support teachers in learning, implementing, and adjusting the strategies to fit their classroom instruction. Teachers were observed throughout the schoolyear in order to document the phases of implementation, especially the trial and experimentation period. In teacher training research, this process is considered "mutual adaptation."

The second year's inservice training of the project's teachers continued with the intent of building and expanding their GATE competencies. The training at this point sought to refine the teachers' ability to observe gifted behaviors, become more effective in selecting project students for the talent pool, and, of course, continue to implement the project instructional strategies. During the second year, project teachers received training in thematic, interdisciplinary instruction and developed thematic bilingual gifted units. The teachers attended two full conference days and ten partial days. In addition, several separate training workshops were set up to accommodate the teachers that were new to the project in the 1990–1991 schoolyear.

The number of teachers in Project EXCEL grew from nineteen to twenty-three during its second year, of which ten were new, and from twenty-three to twenty-eight during the third year. Ten of the second-year teachers were new, recruited from the bilingual program in the upper grades as project EXCEL expanded from K–2 to include K–5 in most sites.

Additional training was provided to these teachers, as well as opportunities to be informally mentored in their own schools by teachers with previous experience in the project. By the end of the third year, all twenty-eight bilingual teachers had earned district GATE certification.

Teachers' regularly scheduled training sessions during the third year consisted of three full conference days. Over 90 percent of the teachers attended all sessions, and the teachers rated all of the training sessions at the highest level. The training continued to emphasize a differentiated curriculum, with inductive thinking strategies, creative problem solving, and peer coaching. The nature of giftedness and how to identify potentially gifted children for the talent pool remained as an ongoing focus in the training. The project manager continued to give classroom demonstrations and provide peer-coaching sessions at each project site.

In the project's fourth year, the number of teachers grew from twenty-eight to thirty-one, but the project lost seven veteran teachers and added ten new teachers. Thirty of the thirty-one teachers added GATE certification to their bilingual credentials, and nine of them also received graduate-level credit for these studies. At this point, teacher training included the use of a portfolio assessment instrument, the California Learning Record (CLR), for the identification of students for the project talent pool.

The CLR is an extended portfolio, essentially, but is based largely on language and literacy development and expanded to include learning in the classroom and elsewhere, so that parents can participate in the documentation of children's performances as well. Properly and fully implemented, a completed CLR is basically a case study and serves to supplement whatever standardized test data may be gathered on a youngster. In a few instances, the CLR was the deciding factor in admitting a child into the GATE program for the district. The CLR requires a cooperative effort over a period of time and provides excellent documentation of what goes on in and out of school that impacts the child's academic and personal development. Several teachers noted that using the CLR further sensitized them to observe gifted behaviors. The CLR is perhaps most appropriately used on gifted children who are at greatest risk of being excluded in the selection process for gifted programs.

By the project's fifth year, inservice training included how to better involve parents. The project manager designed a training-of-trainers workshop so that the more experienced EXCEL teachers jointly planned and conducted the parents' workshops at the individual project sites, and involved the newer teachers as well.

Sustained training over time was the hallmark of EXCEL's teacher professional development component. In subsequent years, a cadre of EXCEL teachers have demonstrated leadership and become GATE Bilingual Mentor Teachers for the district and active participants in the Association of San Diego Educators for the Gifted (ASDEG) and the California Association for the Gifted (CAG). These teachers have also presented workshops on bilingual gifted instruction at the Annual National Association for Bilingual Education (NABE) conference.

Parent Involvement

Parental training began in earnest right from the start of the project. The goal of this component was to provide opportunities for parents to actively participate in the project and become knowledgeable in identifying and nurturing gifted potential at home. The project staff offered five workshops in Spanish to parent groups throughout the first year at each project school. The parental involvement component emphasized information on gifted education and on home activities that foster higher level thinking and creativity.

Project staff modeled the instructional strategies to enable parents to experience the processes of high order thinking and demonstrated how parents might apply these strategies at home with their children. Parents were encouraged to volunteer in their child's classroom and to attend field trips so that they would experience the importance of utilizing community resources that have relevance to the growth and development of their child. Topics of discussion at these parent workshops included the following:

- An orientation to the district's Gifted and Talented Education Program (GATE)
- An orientation to Project EXCEL and the concept of early intervention
- Characteristics of giftedness
- Early childhood development and intellectual abilities
- Multiple intelligences
- The project's instructional strategies (of Taba and Parnes)
- Fostering higher level thinking and creativity at home through math, science, and language arts activities

As in the teacher development component, sustained training over a period of time was critical. In years 2 to 5 of the project, staff continued to offer workshops. In the fifth year, project teachers took over the role as trainers and implemented this component. Eventually, a two-tier program was developed to meet the needs of parents who were new to the project, while parents of longer standing received training that built on previous topics.

The acquisition of a sound knowledge base and an understanding of the special challenges of parenting a potentially gifted child supported the parent advocacy goals. A site principal commented that parents knocked on her door to inquire, if not demand, that their children continue to be placed in a project classroom.

Project Evaluation

Evaluation Questions

Evaluation questions addressed over the five-year funding period of Project EXCEL were the following:

- Did students in the project talent pool demonstrate greater achievement over time in Spanish reading and math, as compared with the control students?
- Did the identification of gifted Hispanic ELLs increase at the project schools?
- How did the project influence teachers' professional development over time?
- How did the project influence parents over time?

Evaluation Design

As mentioned earlier, the study design utilized two experimental groups and one control group (the project talent pool students, project non-talent pool students, and the control students) to report various measures of student progress, most specifically, Aprenda scores and GATE identification results. Hispanic students who were ELLs and enrolled in project classrooms comprised the experimental groups. The one control group was comprised of Hispanic ELLs who attended project schools but were not enrolled in project classrooms.

Achievement Instruments   To measure achievement in Spanish reading and math, project students were administered the Aprenda, a standardized achievement test in Spanish, for all district students in grades K–8 who demonstrated LEP. The academic achievement of project students was assessed, in part, by comparing the Aprenda reading scores of project students with those of the control students. The students' progress in reading during the project's fourth year was measured by comparing their 1993 Aprenda scores with baseline data from 1992, when Aprenda replaced La Prueba (the former Spanish standardized achievement test used by the district).

Gifted Identification Procedure   During each year of the project, GATE staff psychologists administered a nonverbal/spatial test instrument, Ravens Progressive Matrices, to students in the project and in nonproject classrooms who were recommended for testing to determine qualification for participation in the gifted program.

Ravens Progressive Matrices is a nonreading test of cognitive processing. It was designed to cover the widest possible range of mental ability and to be equally useful with persons of all ages. This test consists of sixty matrices divided into five sets (A, B, C, D, and E), each made up of twelve problems.

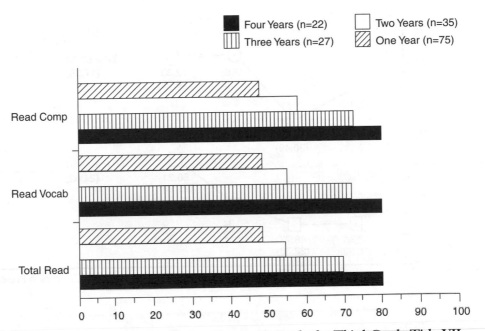

FIGURE 11.1   1993 Aprenda Mean Percentile Ranks for Third-Grade Title VII Students (Combined) by Number of Years of Project Participation.

Teacher and Parent Surveys   Survey data from teachers were collected to assess their opinions about various aspects of the project, including the teacher training program, the implementation of newly acquired instructional strategies, and student performance. Similarly, data from a parent survey provided information regarding parent attitudes and opinions about the project and its implementation, student performance, and their participation in the project workshops.

Student Achievement   Aprenda results of a longitudinal nature (from Spring 1992 to Spring 1993) indicate that project talent pool and project non-talent pool students at all grade levels, except grade 3 increased in Spanish reading. Furthermore, both groups of project students at grade 2 showed the greatest gains, followed by students in grades 5 and 4. A separate analysis compared 1993 Aprenda results (Figure 11.1) for all project students who were in the project for one, two, and four years, and these data indicate that performance was highly correlated with number of years of participation in the project. This is one of the significant indicators of effectiveness of the project, because its long-term effects can be assessed longitudinally in order to discount some of the confounding effects of cross-sectional data posed by the high rates of mobility in the project schools.

Figures 11.2 and 11.3 display the Aprenda (Spanish) reading vocabulary and reading comprehension data, respectively, for project students for 1992 and 1993. The points along the baseline represent the number of years that the children were in the project, so that the long-term impact of the project can be noted on the same cohorts of students.

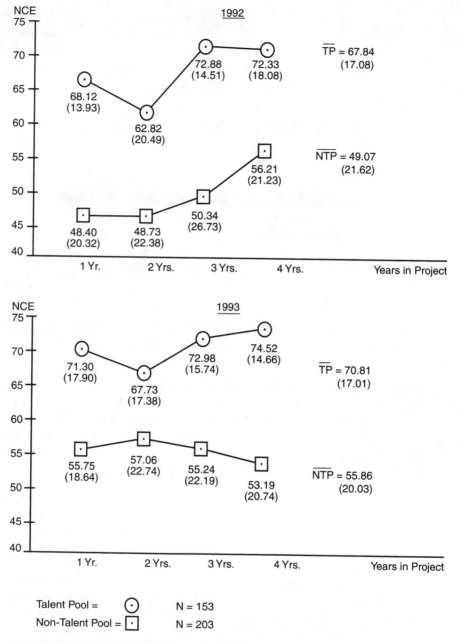

Talent Pool = ⊙ N = 153
Non-Talent Pool = ▢ N = 203

FIGURE 11.2   Longitudinal Analysis of 1992 and 1993 Aprenda Reading Vocabulary Data (NCEs) for Project EXCEL Students by Number of Years in the Project.

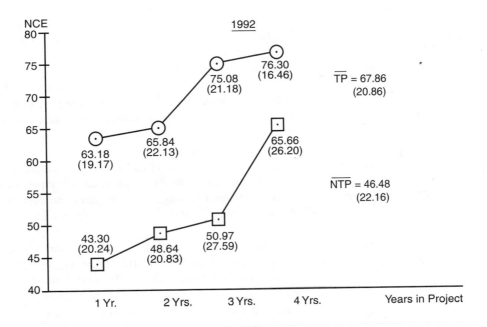

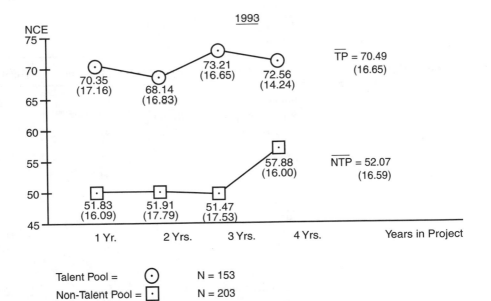

FIGURE 11.3   Longitudinal Analysis of 1992 and 1993 Aprenda Reading Comprehension Data (NCEs) for Project EXCEL Students by Number of Years in the Project.

In Figure 11.2, no significant differences between students are noted for cohorts within the project talent pool and within the project non-talent pool across the years, although differences in reading vocabulary clearly exist between the project talent pool students and the project non-talent pool students.

Figure 11.3, however, presents an ambiguous picture for reading comprehension. The 1992 data show that the fourth-year project talent pool and the project non-talent pool students scored considerably higher than did the first-year students, which is what one might expect, but the trend disappears one year later (1993), when first-year students in both groups raised their scores.

Special longitudinal analyses of children who had been in the project for at least three years were also conducted to gauge the effects of extended participation in Project EXCEL, but the numbers were small. Table 11.2 displays the results on the Aprenda (Spanish) reading comprehension and vocabulary subtests for students in grades 1 through 5.

Analyses of variance with Scheffé post-hoc comparisons show that reliable differences occur between the average scores of talent pool and control students. Effect size (Cohen, 1988) was also computed for each statistically significant difference to check on its educational significance in terms of standard deviation units. For the 1992 reading comprehension data, $f = 13.36$ with 2 and 25 d.f., $p = .001$, and effect size = 2.0, a highly significant finding, given that Cohen's criterion for a large effect is 0.8. The 1993 data

TABLE 11.2   1994 Mean Aprenda Scores* Reading Project and Comparison Group Students

Grade in 1993–1994	Student Group	n	Comprehension	Vocabulary
1	Talent pool	42	66	60
	Non-talent pool	50	42	36
	Control	42	42	43
2	Talent pool	32	70	71
	Non-talent pool	36	43	44
	Control	37	48	53
3	Talent pool	6	58	78
	Non-talent pool	13	43	64
	Control	31	50	60
4	Talent pool	32	63	77
	Non-talent pool	38	53	60
	Control	79	50	54
5	Talent pool	24	60	52
	Non-talent pool	22	56	46
	Control	111	55	56

* Expressed in normal curve equivalents.

TABLE 11.3   Aprenda Math Concepts for Students in Project EXCEL for Three Consecutive Years

	1992	1993	1994
Talent pool (n = 9)	65.6	81.1	84.6
Non-talent pool (n = 3)	47.4	58.4	60.4
Control (n = 13)	40.0	57.7	47.2

show $f = 6.64$, $p = .005$, and effect size = 1.2. The 1994 data show that $f = 10.20$, $p < 0.001$, and effect size = 1.4. Data from the reading vocabulary subtest show a similar pattern and comparable effect sizes for mean differences between project talent pool and control students across the years.

Aprenda mathematics subtests follow a similar but not identical pattern, whereby the project talent pool students consistently show superior performance over the control group. In math concepts, for example (Table 11.3), scores for twenty-five students who were in the project for three consecutive years are expressed as normal curve equivalents (NCEs). Analyses of variance were conducted with Scheffé comparisons. For the 1992 data ($n = 25$, $f = 6.64$ with 2 and 22 d.f., $p < 0.01$, effect size = 1.2), the project talent pool students outperformed the control students. The 1993 data ($f = 5.28$, $p < 0.02$, effect size = 1.2) and 1994 data ($f = 11.82$, $p < 0.001$, effect size = 1.6) show the same outcome. Furthermore, by 1994, the project talent pool students, on average, were performing more like gifted students: The mean NCE of 84.6 is equivalent to the 95th percentile. This same pattern is repeated for the Aprenda math applications and math computation subtests. The small sample is due to attrition through mobility and undoubtedly affected the reliability of observed mean differences between the project talent pool and project non-talent pool students and between the project non-talent pool students and the control students.

Although the number of children in the three-year longitudinal panel (See Table 11.4) is low, the district's Assessment, Research, and Reporting Team has discovered that for all but one of the project sites, the "stability rate" for the students in the six project schools is below the district's average. High mobility causes significant attrition and, therefore, reduces our ability to estimate the long-term impacts of the project. Nevertheless, the Aprenda reading and mathematics data are suggestive of Project EXCEL's positive long-term results.

TABLE 11.4   Aprenda Reading Comprehension for Students in Project EXCEL for Three Consecutive Years

	1992	1993	1994
Talent Pool (n = 10)	73.2	68.2	80.0
Non-talent pool (n = 5)	53.7	53.8	63.3
Control (n = 13)	32.5	41.8	48.8

TABLE 11.5   Number of Gifted Hispanic ELLs Identified by Year and School

	1988–1989 (Baseline)	1989–1990	1990–1991	1991–1992	1992–1993	1993–1994	Totals
School A	4	12	16	9	10	13	60
School B	3	8	8	11	10	15	52
School C	0	6	12	6	7	14	45
School D	0	0	3	6	9	5	23
School E	0	3	4	4	8	11	30
School F	0	5	3	5	5	5	23
Totals per year	7	34	46	41	49	63	233

Gifted Identification

Table 11.5 presents the results of GATE identification, by school, for the five years of Project EXCEL. The number of gifted-identified Hispanic ELLs increased by a factor of 9 over the project's five year history.

By the end of the first year, thirty-four project talent pool students were GATE-identified. In comparison, none of the ELL students in the comparison group were identified as gifted. In year two, forty-six additional project students were identified as gifted, and forty-one of the project talent pool were GATE-identified during the third year.

As part of the GATE program's ongoing evaluation efforts, a random sample of the GATE students are rated by their teachers each year. A follow-up study of thirty-seven former project talent pool students who were certified GATE, along with a random sample of 1991 GATE children districtwide found no significant differences in their teachers' ratings of these youngsters' learning skills or subject-area performance.

In the fourth year, 1992–1993, an additional forty-nine project talent pool students were identified gifted, compared with only four students in the control group during this same year. Altogether, 233 students from Project EXCEL were identified for the GATE program, compared with only seven Hispanic ELL students in the baseline year of 1988–1989.

Project Teachers   A survey of the nineteen teachers was conducted in the first year of the project. These returns suggested that the typical level of use of instructional strategies by the participating teachers was "once a week," and inservice training was rated by the teachers as "very useful." Three classroom observations per teacher were made by an external consultant. The consultant's findings indicated that teachers continued to implement the strategies throughout the first year.

Project teachers again responded to a survey in the second year, and the project training again received high marks. During the second year, teachers went beyond concept development to further implement the other two instructional strategies (resolution of conflict and Parne's Creative Problem-Solving Model). The independent evaluator, who visited each class in the project at least three times throughout the year, observed a greater use of the resolution of conflict strategy both in English and Spanish literature, and also documented the teachers' use of the advanced steps in Parnes' Creative Problem-Solving Model. Perhaps most important, almost all subject areas were influenced by these instructional strategies. The teachers' self-reported use of the concept development and resolution of conflict strategies increased during the second year from once a week to about twice a week.

Classroom observations in the second and third years of the project indicated an increased implementation of a differentiated curriculum, including a greater use of thematic interdisciplinary instruction. The teachers noted that peer coaching among the project teachers occurred about once per month. In the fourth and fifth years of the project, the surveys indicated that the more experienced project teachers utilized the various instructional strategies to a greater extent than did those new to EXCEL.

Project Parents   Attendance at the parent workshops was generally low, and only about one-fifth of the parents who participated in the training returned the evaluation questionnaire handed out or mailed to them: from 43 respondents to 59 over the five years of the project. Those who did respond, however, indicated a great awareness of the phenomenon of giftedness in children, considerable knowledge about the instructional strategies used by the program, special parenting skills for nurturing giftedness at home, and a somewhat greater understanding of whom to contact and how to help their children than they did in year 1. Nevertheless, the results were disappointing, because such an unrepresentative number of parents returned the questionnaire. The returns, however, are comparable to other surveys conducted by the district. The parents who responded knew about EXCEL and liked it, had discussed the project with their children's classroom teachers, and had grown in their understanding of giftedness and of their role as parents in supporting the development of this trait.

Summary

Project EXCEL illustrates that to serve diverse gifted learners demands an effort to reform an entire gifted program. Project EXCEL was part of a major change in the SDCS Gifted and Talented program demanded by the community. Identification procedures were modified districtwide, and EXCEL students were identified in a manner similar to the identification method used for GATE students. Overall, the number of GATE-identified Hispanic ELLs at the six project schools increased by a factor of 9 over the project's five-year history. This was due in no small part to a change from very traditional instruments, such as the Henman-Nelson, DCAT, and WISC-R or Stanford-Binet (LM), to tests that measured more fluid intelligence without relying on English proficiency alone, such as Ravens Progressive Matrices. These changes also reflect the influence of Project EXCEL on the district's GATE program. Today, there is an effective programmatic option in place in the six Project EXCEL schools to educate gifted ELL children that did not exist in 1989. Project EXCEL brought attention to the promising practices of programming for identification and academic success.

The long-term effects of Project EXCEL have extended to teachers and parents. Bilingual teachers of the gifted not only have access to the GATE program, but now have an additional leadership role as trainers in the long-standing GATE teacher certification program. Also, parents of gifted ELL students have acquired the knowledge base to demand appropriate programs for their gifted children.

School districts eager to serve the culturally and linguistically diverse gifted learners must make a long-term commitment. It requires a collaborative effort among categorical programs to ensure that the educational principles of each program, bilingual and gifted, are honored. Finally, as noted by Passow (1980), school boards must hold gifted programs accountable for the participation of minority students, as found in the San Diego City Schools.

REFERENCES

Barkan, J. H., & Bernal, E. M. (1991). Gifted education for bilingual and limited English proficient students. *Gifted Child Quarterly, 35* (3), 144–147.

Ciriza, F. (1987, July). *Title VII Preschool Project evaluation report.* San Diego: San Diego City Schools' Planning, Research, and Evaluation Division.

Cohen, J. (1988). *Statistical power analysis for the behavior sciences* (2nd ed.). Hillsdale, NJ: Lawrence Erlbaum Associates.

Garcia, E. (1994). *Understanding and meeting the challenges of student cultural diversity.* Boston: Houghton Mifflin.

Gregory, D. A. (1988). *Finding and nurturing potential giftedness among Black and Hispanic students.* (ERIC Document Reproduction Service No. ED298707).

Karnes, M. B., & Johnson, L. J. (1986). Identification and assessment of gifted/talented handicapped and nonhandicapped children in early childhood. *Journal of Children in Contemporary Society, 18* (3–4), 35–54.

Kitano, M. K., & Espinosa, R. (1995). Language diversity and giftedness: Working with gifted English language learners. *Journal for the Education of the Gifted, 18* (3), 234–254.

Passow, A. H. (1980, January). *Nurturing the potential of the gifted disadvantaged.* Paper presented at the Biennial National Conference on Disadvantaged Gifted/Talented, New Orleans, LA.

Perez, R. I. (1993). Early intervention practices for diverse students. *Gifted Child Today, 16* (5), 40–41.

Perez, R. I., & Bernal, E. M. (1996, March). *Project EXCEL: Gifted bilingual.* Paper presented at the meeting of the Southwestern School Boards Association, San Diego, CA.

Ramirez, D. (1991, March). Study finds native language instruction is a plus. *NABE News, 14* (5), 20–22.

Richert, E. S. (1985). Identification of gifted children in the United States: The need for pluralistic assessment. *Roeper Review, 8* (2), 68–72.

Ross, P. O. (1991). Advocacy for gifted programs in the new educational climate. *Gifted Child Quarterly, 35* (4), 173–176.

Saccuzzo, D. P., & Johnson, N. E. (1995). Identifying traditionally underrepresented children for gifted programs. *The National Research Center on the Gifted and Talented Newsletter,* 1:4–5.

Shaklee, B. D. (1992). Identification of young gifted students. *Journal for the Education of the Gifted, 15* (2), 134–143.

Tannenbaum, A. (1992). Early signs of giftedness: Research and commentary. *Journal of the Education of the Gifted, 15*(2), 104–133.

12 Recruiting Teachers for Bilingual Gifted and Talented Programs

ERNESTO M. BERNAL

It has long been established that students from nondominant ethnic groups are generally underrepresented in educational programs for the gifted and talented (GT) (O'Connell-Ross, 1993), and that language-minority students are especially underidentified (Bermudez & Rakow, 1993). The matter of general underrepresentation has received considerable attention over the past thirty years or so, and some progress in ethnic equity has been noted (Bernal, 1997b), especially in California and Texas, states that give some latitude to school districts in specifying the tests and steps used to nominate and identify children for GT programs.

One reason why the number of language-minority students in GT programs remains so low is that most districts rely too heavily on testing in English to select or identify GT students, because school personnel frequently cannot provide for assessment, much less for accelerated instruction, in these students' first languages. The author's experience of visiting dozens of GT programs suggests that, in addition, few GT teachers know English as a Second Language (ESL) methods. (A similar situation exists in special education [Wald, 1996].) The result of this deficit in GT programs is that bright students who enter school and are less than proficient in English are selected for the GT program later than their native-English-speaking peers, even under the best of circumstances. This in turn affects the program's demographics (Bernal, 1998) and requires the bilingual GT students to "catch up," a demoralizing prospect for many students and their parents, which is made even worse if the GT program is not prepared to deal sensitively with these culturally different learners.

At present, however, the outlook for public school districts is not so bleak, especially for those that have in place strong GT and bilingual programs and a cadre of well-prepared bilingual teachers. A few viable examples of bilingual GT programs exist (see, e.g., Barkan & Bernal, 1991; Gallagher, 1991; Perez & Bernal, 1996), and others are starting up. Early in 1997, a joint meeting in Washington, DC, of the U.S. Department of Education's Office of Bilingual Education and Minority Languages Affairs (Title

VII–OBEMLA) and the Javits Program (GT) of the Office of Educational Research and Improvement (OERI) augured well for a new departure in federal funding opportunities for bilingual GT program development and evaluation. In 1997, for example, the Javits Program funded the Region One Education Service Center in south Texas for three years to produce a bilingual GT curriculum.

There have always been a few elementary school GT programs that offered a course in a modern language for enrichment, whereby language was studied as a separate subject, but that is not what is contemplated in this book or in this chapter. Instead, what is proposed is nothing less than a GT program that offers *content* instruction in *two* languages to English-language learners (ELLs), using appropriate methodologies.

The essential element in implementing such a curriculum, of course, is in the recruitment of highly proficient bilingual teachers who can also become good teachers of the gifted. This chapter deals exclusively with the recruitment of experienced teachers for bilingual GT programs. It does not address preservice models because there are none that are designed to certify teachers in both fields simultaneously and economically, that is, without having to "add" a complete certification program through postgraduate or graduate courses.

Approaches to the Recruitment of Bilingual Teachers for the Gifted and Talented Classroom

Despite general shortages in the number of qualified bilingual teachers (Bernal & Amabrisca, 1996; Boe, 1990; Wald, 1996), experience over the years indicates that bilingual teachers can be positively recruited to serve bright ELLs in GT programs (Bernal, 1989, 1990, 1995; Perez & Bernal, 1996). Recent experiences in the Chicago Public Schools and in the El Paso, Texas, independent school district (ISD) suggests that bilingual teachers who have been specifically prepared to teach in two-way bilingual programs can transfer their skills into a GT setting. These teachers know how to teach English-proficient learners and ELLs each other's languages. What these teachers need to learn are the ways to accelerate and enrich the classroom setting in ways that differentiate a good gifted program from an albeit innovative but "regular" program. The anecdotal observations of this author suggest that this transition is not so difficult for effective, bilingually fluent teachers who already are on the frontiers of educational development.

The General Appeal to Service and Professional Growth

Designating certain bilingual teachers for recruitment, in the experience of the San Diego City Schools (Bernal, 1995; Perez & Bernal, 1996), seems to be very effective. Selecting bilingually fluent teachers with a penchant for creativity and for promoting higher order thinking skills, teachers who also possess a willingness to take the lead from their students in order to capitalize on the "teachable moment," is in itself an important form of recognition. This, coupled with the opportunity to add a GT credential to their professional qualifications, can be a very persuasive inducement to dedicated educators.

San Diego's recruitment effort was built around six schools with the greatest percentage of Spanish-speaking ELL students. Baseline studies (Perez & Bernal, 1996) indicated that relatively few children in these schools were selected for the GT program, regardless of their proficiency in English. A Title VII (OBEMLA) grant was initially obtained, pursuant to a proposal submitted in consultation with the schools. Information was shared with the bilingual teachers, who indicated their interest and were subsequently trained to meet the district's requirements for local GT credentialing. (Details of their training are presented later in this chapter.) In addition, many of these teachers took university coursework in the area of the gifted.

In El Paso, the appeal to service seemed to be further strengthened by the obvious collaboration between the district's bilingual and GT program directors, the associate superintendent in charge of the geographic area, the articulated support of a respected school principal, and the fact that the proposal for an ethnically and linguistically integrated, bilingual GT program had been endorsed enthusiastically by the parents whose children would participate. In both San Diego and El Paso, the teachers were also trained and visited regularly by university professors and consultants who had an interest in the bilingual GT project or had a stake in the participating schools' success.

Another source of bilingual teachers that should not be overlooked is the GT program itself. Many GT programs, in the author's experience, have used native speakers of modern languages as well as highly proficient second-language speakers of these languages to enrich the GT students' curriculum by offering foreign language studies. Given the chance, some of these teachers may want to engage in teaching academic content through these media as well. These teachers, of course, could benefit from an internship in a bilingual program as well as the inservice or formal coursework necessary to secure a bilingual credential.

Financial Incentives and Scholarships for Training and Certification/Endorsement

Diaz-Rico and Smith (1994) describe a recruiting technique for bilingual teachers that includes financial support for teacher credentialing. This technique has been employed successfully to secure bilingual teachers for GT programs in California, Arizona, and Texas, in the author's experience, and the formal coursework or workshops to prepare these teachers for their enhanced roles has been paid by using local funds, the state's allocations to the districts for GT programs, and special federal grants awarded to the schools or to universities. Region One's Javits Project in Texas, for example, has sponsored five to ten teachers per year to attend graduate education courses in gifted education to obtain a GT teaching credential.

Some districts have also used local monies to pay bonuses to bilingual teachers, but in these instances, the teachers have been assigned either to compensatory or to non-GT, two-way bilingual classrooms. It remains to be seen whether such bonuses would be made available to bilingual teachers assigned to work with gifted children in a bilingual mode.

Release Time, Travel to Professional Meetings, and Other Perquisites

Release time; money to support travel to professional meetings that support the work of the bilingual GT program, where the teachers can meet other teachers to share ideas and practices; a larger budget for teaching materials and hardware/software in two languages; an extra computer for each of the classrooms; a special fund for field trips; and the like have variously been used (Diaz-Rico & Smith, 1994). Done collaboratively with other teachers at the sites where the bilingual GT program will operate, benefits can accrue to students and teachers who are not formally a part of the program. To avoid internal problems at a school site where the bilingual GT program is being implemented, each and every perquisite should help the bilingual GT teachers bring the new program on line, as it were, and support active experimentation and professional sharing as well. Innovative programs are, perforce, resource-hungry (Fullan & Miles, 1992). The other teachers at the site can be convinced of the desirability of these expenditures and opportunities if they (and their students) can also benefit from the new desktop printer and software, can access the new fiber-optic line that runs by their classrooms to the GT classroom, can receive training in giftedness and the process of nominating students for the program as a way of meeting their obligation to earn some continuing professional educational credit, and can learn about using GT instructional methods (Beecher, 1995) in their regular classrooms.

Effective Recruitment Is Contextually Bound to the Conditions of Good Retention

Good leadership working through a cross-role group of professionals (Fullan & Miles, 1992), in short, can reduce professional envy and give the bilingual GT teachers the opportunities to receive the necessary training, work and bond together, plan the bilingual units and the applications of the strategies, and secure the public recognition and administrative support to protect them through the "vulnerable" period and consolidate their commitment to the program. Ultimately, it may reasonably be expected that these outstanding teachers will play an integral role in recruiting minority students *and* teachers into gifted education (Ford, Grantham, & Harris, 1997).

The basic process of recruitment, then, if not simple, is disarmingly straightforward, in the professional sense. It consists of identifying exceptionally creative and proficient bilingual teachers from either GT education or bilingual education; inviting them to participate in shaping the new bilingual GT venture; pointing out the particular contributions one is expecting them, as individuals, to make to the overall plan; showing them the actual commitment of the school district's bilingual and GT programs to support the new program with resources; training them as necessary in GT or in bilingual methodologies; and then allowing them to network with each other, with the GT and bilingual coordinators, and with their school principals in order to evolve the bilingual GT curriculum over several years.

In the author's experience in consulting and evaluating bilingual GT efforts in five projects involving seven school districts, high levels of commitment from the district result in (1) the selection of a highly competent and stable cadre of teachers and (2) the design and implementation of a sound and efficacious curriculum. Lesser levels of commitment, provided that good training is forthcoming, will still yield high-quality teachers, but their levels of frustration subsequent to deployment in their new roles without good support will burn them out, cause them to experience high turnover rates, and not yield a sensible, integrated curriculum from them.

The Preparation of Bilingual Teachers for a Gifted Bilingual Program

The short inservice courses offered by districts or agencies of the state to prepare teachers to teach gifted children typically address such topics as the nature of giftedness, its assessment, basic instructional strategies (such as improved questioning techniques and brainstorming), the cultivation of higher order thinking skills (including creativity), and the special needs of GT students. In Texas, state guidelines to achieve the "acceptable" level of compliance for the professional development of GT teachers are general: the nature and needs of GT students, assessing student needs, and curriculum and instruction for gifted students (Texas Education Agency, 1996), although extended participation by teachers, counselors, administrators, and even local school board members is required to achieve the "recognized" and "exemplary" levels of review. Some schools also provide some release time for the inservice teachers to visit each other's classes or observe an experienced GT teacher work with GT students. University-based credentialing programs take the time to explore these topics in greater depth; introduce special topics, such as the teacher's role in counseling the gifted; study instructional models for the gifted; and frequently provide supervised practice.

Very few district, state, or university programs, however, make explicit provision for dispelling the stereotypes of minority students (Tonemah, 1992), much less for incorporating multicultural or bilingual education into GT classrooms. Neither do they prepare the teachers of the gifted to help the parents of these children to better support their children. The skills of working with parents can be learned on the job, of course, out of a sense of urgency to help certain children. The multicultural educational concerns, however, will probably not be so readily addressed (Banks, 1994) unless strong leadership and direction is provided at the program level and at the school site to make these accommodations without sacrificing the GT program's standards or rigor (Bernal & Amabrisca, 1996), or unless a particularly sensitive and willing group of teachers decides to take on the task (Ford, Grantham, & Harris, 1997) of preparing all of today's GT students to function together effectively and peacefully in twenty-first century America.

Within the gifted education literature, empirically based articles about staff development are extremely few in number (Johnsen, 1998, p. 29). The experience of two districts is recounted here from the point of view of one who observed many of the staff development activities take place. Keep in mind that in both districts, the teachers selected had high levels of fluency and literacy in the non-English language of choice, which was Spanish in these instances.

San Diego City Schools' Project EXCEL (Bernal, Perez, & Rode, 1997) began the inservice preparation of their bilingual GT teachers by using a local certification process that incorporated certain major topics and objectives, which are adumbrated as follows:

Characteristics and behaviors of GT students
- To gain an understanding of the varied expressions of cognitive, social, and emotional characteristics and behaviors of gifted students and the concomitant needs arising from the students' atypical development
- To understand special needs within the gifted population
- To understand the impact of culture, ethnicity, socioeconomic status, home language, and other factors on the development, expression, and recognition of giftedness

Identification and assessment of the GT
- To become familiar with the district's GATE identification philosophies and procedures
- To understand how cultural, ethnic, and socioeconomic factors can affect the assessment and achievement of individual students

Differentiated curriculum and instruction for GT learners
- To understand curricular differentiation for the gifted
- To be able to build, from the core program, a differentiated curriculum
- To be able to plan a classroom program based on student assessment data
- To become aware of the variety of learning styles exhibited by GT students and teaching strategies appropriate to meet their instructional needs
- To acquire knowledge of several classroom management techniques
- To develop an awareness of the variety of program models appropriate for gifted education
- To become knowledgeable about current issues that affect the education of the gifted, to identify trends in the field, and to be able to utilize current research in GT education to improve program implementation

Parenting the gifted
- To acquire a variety of resources to share with parents on parenting skills and understanding the gifted child at home
- To learn how to involve parents in the planning, implementation, and evaluation of classroom and site GT programs

Professional development
- To enhance the teacher's understanding of self as learner and the impact of self-knowledge on gifted students' learning
- To acquire the knowledge and ability to defend the appropriateness of GT education
- To learn about professional and lay organizations that promote gifted education
- To be provided with information about opportunities for continued professional development in GT education

All training sessions involved the teachers in discussion and "make and take" activities, and follow-up at each campus occurred through the project coordinator and other observers (Perez & Bernal, 1996), so that levels of implementation were reported in the annual evaluation summaries (Bernal, Perez, & Rode, 1997).

The teacher training program for the El Paso program was linked from the beginning to a particular school and to the needs and desires of the teachers who were invited to participate by the GT and bilingual program coordinators and the school principal (Bernal, 1999). Mesita School was considered the ideal site, because the parents were well organized and wanted dual language instruction for their GT children. Grades 1 to 3 were selected to start the project, because the GT parents were clamoring to see a well-organized GT program at these levels. The three teachers were already dually certified in bilingual and gifted education; indeed, one of them was teaching in the gifted program at the selected school. All three accepted the challenge and became part of the planning group, which thereafter met frequently with consultants, university professors from the area, and district administrators in what this author observed to be an atmosphere of joint decision making and a commitment to excellence.

The preparation of the El Paso teachers continued into the summer before the project started and consisted of a course in two-way bilingual immersion methodology (Montes, 1998), the district's planned inservice in bilingual and GT, opportunities to review and purchase many new educational materials, and joint planning for acceleration and continuity of curriculum across the years. By February of the project's first year, a teacher for the fourth grade was selected. This teacher had completed student teaching in the program's third grade during the fall term. This process, which involved all of the stakeholders in the project, not only yielded a teacher who was a "known quantity" for the program, but also provided her with mentoring in a supportive, site-based environment, which, generally, is so important to the success and retention of bilingual teachers (Gonzales & Sosa, 1993).

Models of Teacher Preparation for a Bilingual Gifted and Talented Program

Reflecting on the experiences of the San Diego and the El Paso public schools in recruiting and preparing teachers, as well as on the subsequent success of these individual programs, led this author to propose some models that combine teacher recruitment, teacher preparation, and program design. These models are subject to change in the light of new data and documented experience. No one program to date incorporates all of the features in either model. Figure 12.1 is the basic model of recruiting bilingual teachers for the purpose of establishing a bilingual GT program that operates in parallel with the English-monolingual GT program, at least until the ELL GT students have become proficient in academic-level English. Ideally, the bilingual teachers who volunteer for such training will have the opportunity to serve some type of internship in a GT classroom to develop their intuition about how GT classrooms and children function, and the special roles that GT teachers must assume. The option at the top of the chart is for the bilingual GT program to continue, at the parents' behest, for a time *after* the children have achieved English-proficient status, so that they may take advantage of a *developmental* bilingual program (also known as the maintenance or late-exit model) to instill advanced cognitive/academic skills in both languages. The late-exit model is contrasted

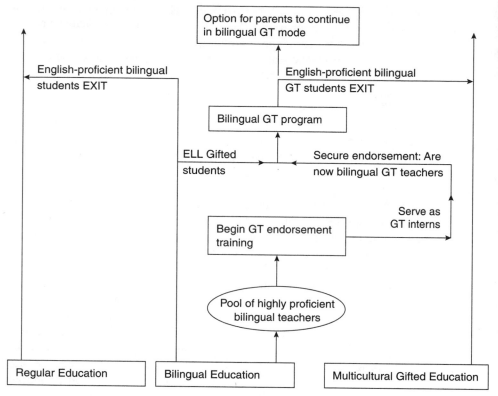

FIGURE 12.1   Basic Bilingual GT Program Model for Teacher Training and Student Assignment.

with the more popular transitional (or early-exit) model, which removes ELLs from a bilingual or ESL program as soon as they are deemed to be basically English proficient. The developmental model allows the now *bilingually* proficient GT students to continue to receive core content instruction in both languages as the way to qualitatively differentiate and enrich their curriculum. Whether the developmental option is exercised, however, does not diminish the need for the English-monolingual program to become multicultural in nature; otherwise, it will place the additionally selected children from nondominant ethnic groups at risk of deracination (Bernal, 1997a) by the simple act of placing them in a prestigious academic environment that neither reflects their cultures nor is responsive to their interpersonal expectations. (See Gopaul-McNicol & Thomas-Presswood [1998] for a thorough discussion of student elements that impact educational and emotional needs, including bilingualism, and current best practices in assessment and instruction of culturally or linguistically different children.)

As Bernal (1997a) pointed out, however, this option—or the entire model adumbrated in Figure 12.1, for that matter—could be regarded as a type of "reverse segregation" in some quarters. Other options are available, however, that teach the English-proficient children the modern language of choice and then integrate the students in developmental bilingual programs. Bilingual GT programs actually come in several models (Bernal, 1998)—from a transitional bilingual GT program that exits the ELL children into the all-English GT program once they achieve a sufficiently high level of proficiency in their second language (L_2) to a two-way (or dual immersion) bilingual program designed to produce fully proficient and literate bilingual GT students over many years of bilingual instruction, regardless of which language was their L_1 and irrespective of their ethnicities. (See Crawford [1997] for a discussion of various bilingual models used in regular educational programs.) This very important and current option extends the invitation to participate in the bilingual GT program to GT students who are English proficient and whose parents believe that bilingualism is the key to a multicultural and international future or that it represents levels of enrichment reminiscent of a classical past (Bernal, 1997a).

Figure 12.2 modifies Figure 12.1 by proffering both bilingually endorsed and GT-endorsed teachers an opportunity to "cross over" to become prepared to teach in a bilingual GT program, in this instance, a two-way immersion program, because it

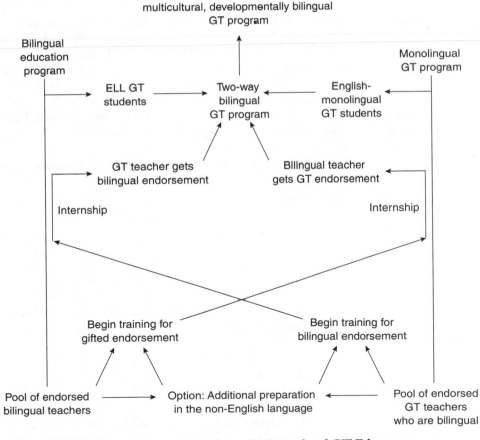

FIGURE 12.2   Recruitment and Training of Bilingual and GT Educators for a Bilingual GT Program.

incorporates both English-monolingual and ELL GT students from the beginning in a very demanding bilingual GT program. Indeed, the demand characteristics of the two-way program are such that there should be an option for the teachers to receive additional preparation in the modern language of choice, so that they will feel more comfortable teaching the core areas in that language. Unlike simple transitional bilingual programs—essentially regular programs in two languages—the bilingual immersion model places an emphasis on the development of bilingual language to very high levels of fluency and literacy; therefore, the teachers in this program must be very smart and very bilingual. One alternative to giving teachers the opportunity to enhance their non-English-language skills is to select only those teachers from the bilingual or GT programs who have been educated formally in the other language to a great extent, so that they can teach the core areas in both languages. The other alternative is to select pairs of teachers to alternate in the same classroom—one teacher who is a native speaker of English, with the other having native-like proficiency in the modern language of choice, each teaching half the curriculum in all subjects, with no repetition or translation (Bernal, 1998).

Note that both the English-proficient students and the students who are proficient in the other modern language can learn cooperatively in the model represented in Figure 12.2, much in the manner envisioned by Slavin's (1990b) Student Team Learning (STL) Model, which he advocates for use with gifted students to accelerate their learning within the regular classroom (Slavin, 1990a). In the case of the linguistically integrated bilingual program, however, the problems posed by widely divergent levels of ability, in which the GT students find themselves doing too much of their assigned groups' work (Robinson, 1998) or being used as peer tutors (Ray, 1997), would be averted. This cooperative educational model should be especially useful during the first few years that the students are integrated, when they, perforce, must rely on each other's mastery of their native tongues in order to complete their bilingual assignments. Consultation with the group of selected teachers can guide the decision to include STL in the GT bilingual teachers' preparation.

Because an internship is envisioned here for both the GT and the bilingual teachers, so that each group can learn the work and methods required in each program, the teachers can work cooperatively as well, showing each other the inner workings of their classrooms, sharing their knowledge and insights, and selecting or designing educational materials in both languages. Peer coaching, of course, is a natural outgrowth of this cross-contact. It is a technique that should be emphasized, because the designated bilingual and GT teachers are in a unique position to help each other achieve success within a reasonable period of time by preparing instructional plans, critiquing lessons, and actively experimenting with the two-way bilingual approach in the GT setting.

Such training is absolutely essential for any group of teachers who need to be creative enough to make their own way collaboratively on the still largely uncharted seas of bilingual GT education. In the meantime, project directors, project evaluators, and the classroom teachers themselves will have to document in great detail the materials, methods, and activities selected and actually used for instruction, and evaluate the results as well, so that those who follow will have a validated base of experience upon which to build.

Teacher Retention in the Bilingual Gifted and Talented Program

The San Diego program's experience with teacher turnover occurred mainly in the period between the second and third year of the program. Not many of the Project EXCEL teachers left, but reflection on the experience suggests that a number of factors were involved, including demographic and bureaucratic influences. The Post and Bid provisions for new openings elsewhere in the district attracted some of the teachers who, having been recruited to EXCEL as new teachers to the district, were, by the end of their second year, eligible to bid on jobs in more favorable school environments, where less poverty and less crowding and better facilities were available. The Southeast region of the district has traditionally been plagued by high teacher turnover, and Project EXCEL was not immune. The schools in this region are large and overcrowded, and many new teachers feel overwhelmed by the situations they encounter. However, most teachers stayed in the program because of their commitment to these same schools, especially to the children in these settings.

The moral seems clear: Select teachers who are more experienced and committed to working in these school settings. Care must be taken, of course, not to accept any teachers whose marginal skills have forced them to take refuge in these types of sites, but local recruitment of known teachers seems to be a definite plus. It also seems likely that inner-city schools that adopt an innovative GT program will have a somewhat higher turnover rate than will programs in the affluent suburbs. Project evaluators on larger projects should consider making turnover comparisons within these sites part of their evaluation reports.

Summary

Ford et al. (1997) remind us that teachers from nondominant ethnic groups not only "work effectively with minority students," but "also have a positive influence on the development of White students" (p. 216). Given the relative scarcity of teachers from nondominant ethnic groups and the relatively high potential of GT students to provide the leadership, the material innovations, and the cultural substrate necessary for social change, perhaps more teachers of color should dedicate their efforts entirely to the education and moral formation of the gifted.

Multicultural education can promote multicultural understanding among the gifted. Bilingual GT education has the potential to achieve parity for culturally and linguistically different learners in the GT program. In ethnically and linguistically integrated settings, bilingual/multicultural GT education can also promote the academic skills and lifetime achievements of all GT children preparing to live as adults in the new millennium. As with any curricular innovation, bilingual GT education depends on the quality of the teachers recruited and the quality of the support given them. Recruitment of such teachers, if done on a highly personalized basis, is not difficult, experience shows, but retention of good teachers whose services are in demand requires, initially, good training and, later, an exceptional—even gifted—administrator and a program that calls on the teachers' initiative and creativity to keep it dynamic.

REFERENCES

Banks, J. A. (1994). Multicultural education: Historical development, dimensions, and practice. In L. D. Darling-Hammond (Ed.), *Review of research in education* (pp. 3–49). Washington, DC: American Educational Research Association.

Barkan, J. H., & Bernal, E. M. (1991). Gifted education for bilingual and limited English proficient students. *Gifted Child Quarterly, 35* (3), 144–147.

Beecher, M. (1995). *Developing the gifts and talents of all students in the regular classroom: An innovative curricular design based on the Enrichment Triad Model.* Mansfield Center, CT: Creative Learning Press.

Bermudez, A. B., & Rakow, S. J. (1993). Examining identification and instruction practices for gifted and talented limited English proficient students. In L. Malave (Ed.), *Proceedings of the National Association for Bilingual Education Conferences, 1990 and 1991* (pp. 99–114). Washington, DC: NABE. (ERIC Document Reproduction Service No. ED 360 871.)

Bernal, E. M. (1989, October). *Year two (1988–89) evaluation report, Title VII bilingual gifted project, Tucson U.S.D.* Unpublished report.

Bernal, E. M. (1990, April–May). *The gifted migrant student.* Paper presented at the National Migrant Education Conference, San Antonio, TX.

Bernal, E. M. (1995, May). *An evaluative overview of Project EXCEL.* Unpublished report. San Diego, CA: San Diego City Schools.

Bernal, E. M. (1997a, February). *Gifted English-language learners: Opportunities for enriching the gifted and talented program.* Invited address to the West Texas Association for the Gifted and Talented, El Paso, TX.

Bernal, E. M. (1997b, Spring/Summer). Some thoughts on the changing complexion of GT education: The demographic shift could revitalize the field. *Baylor Educator, 22* (1), 10–17.

Bernal, E. M. (1998). Could gifted English-language learners save gifted and talented programs in an age of reform and inclusion? Texas Association for the Gifted and Talented. *Tempo, 18* (1), 11–14.

Bernal, E. M. (1999, December). *Second year evaluation report on Mundos Unidos-Connecting Worlds.* Evaluation report to El Paso ISD.

Bernal, E. M., & Amabrisca, E. (1996, November). *A survey of bilingual/ESOL program directors and a survey of bilingual/ESOL teacher-preparation programs in Arizona to determine the priority needs of educational personnel.* Paper presented at the Sixth Bilingual Education Institute, Phoenix, AZ.

Bernal, E. M., Perez, R. I., & Rode, R. (1997). *Project EXCEL: An elementary school bilingual program for gifted English-language learners.* Unpublished manuscript.

Boe, E. E. (1990, September). Demand, supply, and shortage of bilingual and ESL teachers: Models, data, and policy issues. In U.S. Department of Education, Office of Bilingual Education and Minority Languages Affairs, *Proceedings of the 1st research symposium on limited English proficient students' issues, September 10–12, 1990* (pp. 23–83). (ERIC Document Reproduction Service No. ED 341 262.)

Crawford, J. (1997). *Best evidence: Research foundations of the Bilingual Education Act.* Washington, DC: National Clearinghouse for Bilingual Education.

Diaz-Rico, L. T., & Smith, J. (1994). Recruiting and retaining bilingual teachers: A cooperative school-community-university model. *Journal of Educational Issues of Language Minority Students, 14,* 255–268.

Ford, D. Y., Grantham, T. C., & Harris, J. J., III. (1997). The recruitment and retention of minority teachers in gifted education. *Roeper Review, 19* (4), 213–220.

Fullan, M., & Miles, M. (1992). Getting reform right: What works and what doesn't. *Phi Delta Kappan, 73,* 744–752.

Gallagher, R. M. (1991, November/December). Programs for gifted students in Chicago Public Schools: Yesterday, today, and tomorrow. *G/C/T, 14* (6), 4–8.

Gopaul-McNicol, S., & Thomas-Presswood, T. (1998). *Working with linguistically and culturally different children: Innovative clinical and educational approaches.* Boston: Allyn & Bacon.

Gonzalez, F., & Sosa, A. S. (1993, March). How do we keep teachers in our classrooms? The TNT response. *IDRA Newsletter, 20* (3), 1, 6–9.

Johnsen, S. (1998). Staff development for gifted education. Texas Association for the Gifted and Talented. *Tempo, 18* (2), 29–31.

Montes, E. (1998). Sharing the wealth. Texas Association for the Gifted and Talented. *Tempo, 18* (2), 12–25.

O'Connell-Ross, P. (1993). *National excellence: A case for developing America's talent.* Washington, DC: U.S. Department of Education, Office of Educational Research and Improvement.

Perez, R. I., & Bernal, E. M. (1996, March). *Project EXCEL: Gifted bilingual.* Paper presented at the meeting of the Southwestern School Boards Association, San Diego, CA.

Ray, J. (1997). The gifted student in the regular classroom: A survey. Texas Association for the Gifted and Talented *Tempo, 17* (4), 18–20.

Robinson, A. (1998). Cooperative learning, curriculum access, and the challenge of acceleration. Texas Association for the Gifted and Talented *Tempo, 18* (1), 1, 6–7.

Slavin, R. E. (1990a). Point-counterpoint: Ability grouping, cooperative learning and the gifted. *Journal for the Education of the Gifted, 14* (1), 3–8.

Slavin, R. E. (1990b). Research in cooperative learning: Concerns and controversy. *Educational Leadership, 42,* 52–54.

Texas Education Agency (1996, November). *Texas state plan for the education of gifted/talented students.* Austin, TX: TEA, Division of Advanced Academic Services.

Tonemah, S. A. (1992, November). *The American Indian teacher training program: The next to the last piece of the puzzle.* Paper presented at the meeting of the National Indian Education Association, Albuquerque, NM.

Wald, J. L. (1996). *Culturally and linguistically diverse professionals in special education: A demographic analysis.* Reston, VA: National Clearinghouse for Professions in Special Education.

13 A Parent–Family Involvement Model to Serve Gifted Hispanic English-Language Learners in Urban Public School Settings

ROSINA M. GALLAGHER

The benefits of parent involvement in children's education are indisputably documented in the literature. Children whose parents volunteer or participate in school programs have better attendance. They complete homework more consistently. They achieve higher grades and test scores. They show higher graduation rates and greater enrollment rates in postsecondary education. After two decades of research in the field, Henderson and Berla (1995) conclude the following:

> The most accurate predictor of student achievement in school is not income or social status, but the extent to which a family is able to: 1) create a home environment that encourages learning; 2) communicate high but reasonable expectations for their achievement and future careers; and 3) become involved in their children's education at home, school and in the community.

Parent and family involvement also improves school quality. Parents who volunteer at school give teachers higher ratings. Teacher morale increases. Children who may be failing improve dramatically. Schools enjoy better reputations in the community. To be effective in the overall effort to effect school improvement, however, researchers point out that parent involvement must be well planned, inclusive, and comprehensive.

To promote meaningful parent and family participation, the National Parent Teachers Association published the *National Standards for Parent/Family Involvement Programs* in 1997. The standards address six components of effective programs:

1. Communication between home and school is regular, two-way, and meaningful.
2. Parenting skills are promoted and supported.
3. Parents play an integral role in assisting student learning.
4. Parents are welcome in the school, and their support and assistance are sought.
5. Parents are full partners in decisions that affect children and families.
6. Community resources are used to strengthen schools, families, and student learning.

Because these standards are closely related, "quality indicators" clarify specific elements. For example, communication can be promoted through newsletters, assignment notebooks, and parent–teacher conferences. Parenting skills may be supported by holding parent meetings on topics such as building social skills, offering English-language workshops or computer training, and linking parents to community resources. School administrators may help parents promote student learning by establishing a homework hotline and providing written guidelines to develop study skills, plan long-term projects, or set educational goals.

Parents feel important when a committee is established to welcome new members to the school and when there is an organized volunteer program with activities such as running special interest centers in classrooms or planning special events. Schools may also offer leadership training for parents to become child advocates at the local, district, or state level. Finally, parents may be instrumental in helping to establish and maintain partnerships with local business and community groups. The National PTA proposes revision of these standards periodically to ensure they are dynamic and responsive to demographic trends and related school reform initiatives.

The focus of this chapter is to describe a model for parent involvement that has been developed over the past ten years as part of a gifted center for bilingual students in a large, urban public school district. To place the parent component in context, it is helpful to describe the administrative structure and magnet center model that is one of ten paradigms used to serve a diverse population of high-ability learners. The model parallels the one started in the late 1960s to meet the needs of gifted children in an urban public school district, which currently serves over 431,000 students.

The Administrative Structure

A central office and six satellite offices administer the gifted programs across the city. Each regional office generally manages a variety of elementary and high school program models in thirty-five to forty school sites, serving 3,500 to 4,000 identified gifted students per region. The office that services the bilingual gifted centers in each region includes a team of bilingual professionals, which includes, but is not limited to, a resource teacher, a school psychologist, and a social worker who provides such support services as tutoring, mentoring, and counseling. The offices collaborate in systemwide activities such as the identification and placement of students and planning and coordinating staff development, parent involvement, and program evaluation.

The Magnet Center Model

The magnet centers for gifted Hispanic students who are in the process of developing proficiency in English offer a comprehensive, differentiated curriculum from grades 1 through 8. The primary grades are self-contained, while the upper grades are departmentalized. Bilingual teachers provide instruction in Spanish and English, affording students the opportunity to develop both languages as they are challenged in core subjects and specific areas of interest at levels commensurate with their academic potential and linguistic abilities. The goals of the program include nurturing responsibility, initiative, creativity, problem solving, and leadership skills among age peers of similar interests and abilities.

The core curriculum includes special features, such as literature-based language arts in English and Spanish, laboratory science, computer education and research, social studies, fine arts, band or folkloric dance, athletics, and health and career awareness. Students have the opportunity to earn high school credit in at least one academic area, and they are expected to complete twenty hours of community service prior to graduation.

Identification and Selection Criteria

Candidates for the Spanish–English bilingual gifted centers are recruited from public and private schools across the city. To be eligible, students first must have participated in a bilingual program or be classified as beginning English-language learners. Second, teachers nominate students by using a checklist of observed behavior and providing evidence of high academic potential as indicated by standardized achievement tests and academic portfolios. Eligible candidates are then invited to take an aptitude test. A selection committee recommends placement based on the data collected and the center locations closest to the students' homes. Transportation is provided at designated stops for students living more than 1.5 miles from the school.

Establishing the Parent Component

The parent component was initiated as part of the summer orientation for students entering the first grade in the magnet gifted centers established throughout the city. Because children for these centers are transported from some distances to a different neighborhood, such a program has been helpful in facilitating early adjustment to a new environment. Children form friendships and become acquainted with the teachers and the school prior to beginning the regular schoolyear. The parents are also invited to seminars in which program goals and expectations are discussed in addition to broader issues in gifted education. Special activities and field experiences are also planned to help parents work with their children on a long-term project.

Planning the Summer Orientation

The summer orientation has been adapted to the bilingual gifted centers with modest available resources. To meet the needs of gifted Hispanic English-language learners and their families, the orientation includes three components: (1) a project-oriented instructional program for incoming students, (2) structured activities for accompanying siblings, and (3) seminars and English conversation practice for parents. (Each of these components are discussed subsequently in greater detail).

The staff includes one teacher for incoming first- and second-grade students; a second teacher for students entering grades 3 through 6; one teaching assistant for siblings who accompany the new center students; and the bilingual school psychologist and social worker to conduct the parent workshops.

In addition to the professional staff, two to four incoming eighth-grade students are invited to complete their community service by assisting the classroom teachers in planning and organizing student projects. These volunteers are invaluable to the program, and they in turn gain factual knowledge and practical experience working with children under supervision. They maintain a log of their activities with personal observations, problems encountered, and how these problems were resolved. The students eventually discuss their experiences with the supervising teacher and submit their journals as a record of their community service.

Other budgetary expenses to consider are provisions for a snack and/or lunch for the children, instructional materials and supplies, light refreshments for the parent workshop, and public transportation tokens for the students and parents who need assistance. The parents usually organize and contribute a "pot-luck" luncheon after the culminating activity. At this event, the staff also awards formal certificates of participation to the parents.

Generally in late spring, the parents of eligible candidates are invited to enroll the children in the center and register for the summer orientation. To encourage parent participation, brothers and sisters of the new center students also are invited. This activity requires the preparation of a flyer in Spanish and English announcing the site, times, and the tentative program. Because many Hispanic parents may not be familiar with the educational system, a number of personal telephone contacts also are necessary to ensure that parents have the opportunity to ask questions or resolve issues that may prevent their participation. From experience, working parents frequently find a family member or relative to participate with the children in their place. Others rearrange vacation schedules. Mothers constitute the majority of participants, but fathers make an effort to attend some of the sessions. Approximately twenty to twenty-five parents attend each summer.

Purpose and Goals

The purpose of the summer orientation is to enable the teachers, students and their parents to become acquainted with one another in the school setting. They meet daily from 9 A.M. to 12 P.M. for two weeks in the school that houses the gifted center. The goals are the following:

> Goal 1: To provide incoming students with activities that will help them develop socialization and communication skills and build greater confidence in becoming independent learners

> Goal 2: To help teachers become familiar with student reasoning and linguistic abilities, skills, and interests, and begin planning curriculum differentiation activities

> Goal 3: To include siblings in appropriate learning activities according to their abilities and interests. This component is essential to enable most parents to participate

> Goal 4: To help parents become familiar with program goals and expectations, practice English communication skills, review school and community resources, and consider ways of becoming involved in school activities and governance

Two important points should be noted. First, the fact that the sibling program is not a baby-sitting service. The teacher aide, if not trained in early-childhood pedagogy, is usually oriented to designing appropriate activities for young children. Careful planning ensures that meaningful learning activities are included for all age groups. In addition, the staff convenes regularly at the end of each day for fifteen to twenty minutes to review the group's progress. Frequently, the staff may modify activities, request supplementary materials, and brainstorm various alternatives to difficult situations.

Instructional Component

The instructional program for each classroom is generally developed around a theme and a project-oriented activity that calls for guidance from parents. Teachers plan high-interest, hands-on activities and a field experience. One summer, the primary-age group studied simple machines. A simple machine was defined as "any device that makes work easier." The children studied concepts such as force, energy, and friction and how to measure them. They investigated simple machines and attended a special exhibit at the local museum. Finally, each child made his or her own machine with parental guidance, and all projects were demonstrated in operation at the final assembly. The project and learning objectives are described in Figure 13.1.

Another summer, the popular Olympic games became the theme for all three classrooms. Students working individually, in pairs, and in small groups engaged in different projects involving the games. They used computers, the Internet, and other resources the teachers had made available. One group presented a timeline on butcher paper tracing the Olympics from its Greek origins to the first modern games held in Athens in 1896, through the interruptions during the World Wars and the political difficulties in 1976, to the current summer and winter events. Other students looked at

FIGURE 13.1   **Project and Learning Objectives.**

Machines Made Fun!
by Analicia Ramos,
First-Grade Teacher

Project Description
This project allows students to use problem-solving skills and creativity, with guidance from family members, to construct a working model of a simple machine from recycled materials and materials purchased from a hobby shop. To make the best model possible, the students learn about machines, perform simple experiments, and practice making machines in the classroom. They also visit local industry or special museum exhibits. These hands-on projects and experiments teach the children to identify simple machine parts, such as gears, levers, inclined planes, wedges, screws, wheels and axles, and ball bearings. Students become mechanical engineers and receive patents for their models.

Learning Objectives
Students will be able to do the following:

- Identify simple machines and describe how they help people work
- Describe force as a push or pull
- Define vocabulary: machine, simple machine, work, friction, and force
- List/categorize simple machines that make work easier at home and in school
- Discuss science-related careers/avocations, focusing on mechanical engineers
- Describe the uses of a patent

nutrition issues and what constitutes a healthy diet to maximize athletic performance. One young swimmer reported how several Olympians train to win a gold medal. For instance, Pablo Morales, a gold medalist from the United States, believed, athletes should concentrate on improving incrementally rather than in leaps and bounds.

Two boys investigated Olympians who had established new records. They organized and displayed their findings on a poster table, showing the athletes' names, genders, ages, countries of residence, events, records, and the years the records were established. A trio examined why warm-up and cool-down exercises are important and demonstrated a routine. Younger children discussed and illustrated their favorite sports with personal captions and integrated their work on a colorful group mural on butcher paper.

Finally, a larger team planned and organized the closing ceremony, in which the entire group presented its work. This activity required planning a budget for materials needed, including refreshments; keeping track of expenses; designing a logo, the program, and decorations; and organizing the parade of all performers who dressed in the school gym uniforms. The children came to the same conclusion as Baron Pierre de Coubertin, past president of the International Olympic Committee, that athletic competitions between countries help to improve world relations. The important notion about competition, the children emphasized, is not winning but taking part in order to improve, as the Olympic motto in Latin states: *Citius, Altius, Fortius,* which means "swifter, higher, stronger."

Parent Workshop Schedule

As the teachers implement the instructional component, the coordinating staff concentrates on the parent program. They also meet daily for two weeks from 9 A.M. to 12 P.M. When mothers bring infants and toddlers that are still unwilling to separate, arrangements are made to have an activity center in the corner of the classroom. A playpen, rug, puzzles, and developmental toys are available, and parents may bring a child's favorite toy and snack. Experience shows that young children generally adapt to a parallel situation, in which mothers are allowed to participate with minimal disturbance by the children. An eighth-grade volunteer may be asked to help toddlers engage in parallel play and begin to share toys. Once they are comfortable in the new environment, young children may readily join the sibling group in an adjacent classroom.

The parent activity schedule is organized as follows, but modifications are made as necessary. For instance, when appropriate, time is allowed for parents to visit the classrooms to observe their children at work.

9:00	Topic presentation by staff member
9:45	Topic discussion through Cooperative Learning groups
10:30	Break and light refreshments
10:45	Discussion in English through Counseling–Learning/Community Language Learning (C-L/CLL) structured by staff facilitators
11:45	Reflections in the large group
12:00	Adjournment

Seminar Topics

The first session is divided into three periods of approximately forty, twenty-five, and fifteen minutes. The facilitator (bilingual school psychologist, social worker, or support staff member) introduces one of the following topics in Spanish, accompanied by brief articles or hand-outs in English or Spanish. These topics have been found to support parenting skills and stimulate discussion on how to begin planning long- and short-term educational goals for children. A list of topics follows.

- Education in the Twenty-first Century: The Challenge for Hispanics
- Attitude and Acculturation
- Giftedness and Creativity
- Developing Language and Communication Skills
- Building Self-esteem
- Developing Problem-solving and Critical-thinking Skills
- The Art and Science of Discipline

During the second, twenty-five-minute session, parents share their understanding of the concepts, adding their personal experiences in cooperative learning groups. They refer to specific passages of the printed material, helping one another if texts are in English. The facilitator rotates among the groups, providing guidance as needed. Finally, reporters from each group summarize their discussions before the entire group to conclude the session. As can be seen, the staff strongly believes in serving as facilitators rather than as experts. Each parent's point of view is respected, and all have an opportunity to assume a specific role within the groups.

To address specific concerns parents may have about the school, program, or neighborhood, school administrative staff and an experienced parent representatives are invited to welcome the new members toward the end of the orientation. New parents generally inquire about school policies with regard to the uniform, homework, transportation, discipline, athletic and fine arts activities, and parent involvement.

Counseling–Learning Theory and the Community Language Learning Model

Parents in the bilingual gifted centers usually welcome the opportunity to practice English communication skills. To meet this need, the staff has adapted the Community Language Learning (CLL) approach to second-language acquisition. This model is an integral part of Counseling-Learning (C-L) theory in education and is thus recognized as C-L/CLL. An introductory explanation of this instructional approach is helpful before presenting its current application.

Counseling-Learning theory evolved from basic principles in psychology. This theory proposes that learning is a unique, personal process that requires self-investment, risk taking, and communication. Learning occurs best in a "matrix of personal relationships." Rardin, Tranel, Tirone, and Green (1988) explain:

> The matrix of personal relationships involved in the classroom is seen as the actual medium of learning . . . the relationship of the teacher with herself, the relationship between the teacher and the student, and the relationship of the student with himself and that which is being learned, as well as with the other students in the class. It is the quality of the interaction of these personal relationships which dictates the kind of learning that takes place and it is for this reason that one can say, "learning is persons." (p. 1)

The CLL model thus creates a safe and secure environment in which individuals acquiring a second language move at their own pace through five developmental stages (Curran, 1976). The learners are initially totally dependent on the language counselor (teacher) to interact, using the target language in small groups. In the second stage, the learners begin to use the words and phrases they have retained. In the third, or "adolescent," stage, the learners grow in confidence and ability to communicate independently, assured that the language counselor will correct errors and provide appropriate expressions. In the fourth stage, individuals communicate freely in the target language, although they may need assistance with subtle expressions and grammatical structures. Few learners reach the fifth stage of nearly native proficiency, unless they have had the opportunity to interact daily, using the second language in a natural setting.

Establishing the Community Language Learning Groups

At the initial meeting, parents are asked to help the staff organize the English conversation workshop by completing a rating scale to indicate their language proficiency levels in English and Spanish. Instructions are provided in both languages. Parents are reassured that they can be beginners in either language.

After having worked with Hispanic parents in the public school system for many years, this author has found that in a group of twenty-five parents, two or three rate themselves 16 or above in English, a perfect score being 20. A few total scores range from 8 to 12. The majority range from 0 to 8. Parents who rate their English language skills at 16 or above are invited to assist in the groups as language counselors, and they are trained briefly after demonstrations of activities that constitute the typical C-L/CLL cycle (described subsequently). Often, high-ability speakers of English may have been born in the United States and thus rate themselves weak in Spanish-language skills. There are also a few that have limited formal schooling and identify weaknesses in both languages, and a few who rate themselves high in Spanish due to having attended a university.

Regardless of English proficiency levels, parents begin communicating in English from the first day. The class is divided into groups of five or six members to form CLL Conversation Circles. An English–Spanish bilingual language counselor (LC) is assigned to each group. The CLL staff trainer demonstrates the process to the class as follows.

A Description of the Typical Counseling–Learning/ Community Language Learning Cycle

The typical cycle includes the following activities, which may be carried out in a simple or more complex fashion, depending on the group, the time available, and specific circumstances. A detailed description of each process follows this list.

- Conversation Circles
- Playback of Recorded Conversation
- The Human Computer
  - Practicing Pronunciation
  - Creating New Sentences
- Recycling Activities to Reinforce Learning
- Reverse Role-Playing at Advanced Stages
- Reflection: Group Process, Journals, and Portfolios

Conversation Circles

Conversations may or may not be recorded using a tape recorder with a remote-control microphone. If an electronic tape recorder is used, it is placed on a stool or small table in the center of the group, with the remote-control mike accessible to all. Alternately, the LC, as facilitator, asks for an advanced learner with a language proficiency of stage II to IV, to volunteer as English recorder (ER). The ER sits outside the circle and listens attentively, because the ER may not disrupt the conversation. The ER prints the date and each group member's name at the top of a lined sheet of paper. The object is to print and number the statements spoken by each member in English. If the ER is not sure of a word or phrase, the native language may be substituted. The ER is reassured that not every statement needs to be included and that corrections will be made when the conversation is terminated. The sequence follows as illustrated here:

1. Seated in a circle, learners engage in free conversation. Speaker 1 (S1) raises his hand or takes the microphone and poses a statement in the first language (Spanish, in this case) to the group.

2. The LC, standing outside the circle, moves just behind S1, leans to his shoulder and translates the statement in English, phrase by phrase, in a clear, soft voice that is audible to S1 and the rest of the group.

3. S1 repeats the statement in English, phrase by phrase, to the group. If a tape recorder is used, S1 switches the microphone on/off switch to record *only* his repetition of phrases in English. This process takes practice, but, when carried out smoothly, learners are elated to hear themselves speak in fluent, correct English.

4. Speaker 2 (S2) raises her hand or requests the microphone to respond to the initial statement and continue the conversation.

5. The LC moves quickly toward S2, stands just behind her, leans in and translates the second statement as described previously.

6. S2 repeats the statement in English to the group. The microphone is used as noted previously if the conversation is being recorded.

7. Each person in the circle takes a turn as spontaneously as possible.

8. A conversation is sustained for approximately five to seven minutes initially.

Playback of Recorded Conversation

1. If a tape recorder is used, *only* the learner statements are recorded in the target language. Thus, the group finally listens to a tape of their conversation in English only.

2. Seated in a circle, the learners recall and translate what they said in the first language, to ensure all understand the content.

3. An LC is available to assist when necessary. At first, the LC prints each sentence clearly in English only on a sheet of paper for each speaker. Each person's sheet may include three to five statements apiece. Not all statements need to be included. Variety and clarity should be the guide. Errors are corrected.

Materials needed for this activity are graph, self-adhesive, newsprint easel paper and multiple color markers. Fold each sheet vertically into eight segments to guide size of letters and number of sentences per sheet. Label each sheet with the date and group name or number to facilitate record keeping.

1. Learners now number and copy their sentences in English only, on the newsprint, using clear, large print that can be read from a distance.

2. The LC asks group members to print each sentence in a different color. Alternating colors helps to distinguish sentences from a distance.

3. The LC may model the activity; learners follow and help one another.

The Human Computer

The purpose of the Human Computer (HC) is to allow learners to practice pronunciation and/or create new sentences from their conversation transcriptions. The groups may convene individually or as a class. Transcriptions are posted on a wall. The LC adopts the role of a computer by giving the following instructions:

> I am a language computer that is programmed to give information only in English; however, I understand both English and Spanish, so if you would like to practice a particular sound, word, phrase or sentence with the computer, you can give the data either in English or Spanish. If you want an entire sentence pronounced, simply give the number of the sentence you wish to hear. The HC makes no judgmental observations. It is up to you to listen carefully to the differences, if there are any, between what you say and what the computer gives back. HC is programmed to repeat your input request up to three times. Raise your hand to activate or stop the computer. You have complete control over the computer. (Rardin, et al., p. 133)

1. Seated in a semicircle and facing the transcriptions on the wall, the first speaker (L1) raises his hand to activate HC, calls out the number of the statement, and pronounces the word, phrase, or the entire sentence to the best of his ability.

2. The HC stands behind L1 and repeats input in native English pronunciation. L1 has up to three opportunities to echo the pronunciation as closely as possible.

3. The rest of the group overhears and repeats silently to themselves.

4. L2, L3, and so on, take turns in a similar fashion.

At a more advanced level, learners can write sentences on the chalkboard or on transparencies for the overhead projector. The HC can be used for transformation drills, giving the following instructions:

> I am your English computer. I am programmed to change affirmative statements into negative ones. You may feed any of the written sentences as they appear, or you may change them into negative statements. Either way will activate the computer, but the HC will only give back the negative statement. It will not tell you whether you are right or wrong, so you need to listen carefully for any differences. HC is programmed to allow three attempts at a time. (Rardin, et al., p. 133)

The group proceeds as indicated previously.

Recycling Activities to Reinforce Learning

A variety of games, puzzles, or graphic organizers can be designed to give learners control over their own learning in an enjoyable and absorbing way. At more advanced stages, songs and literature pieces can be "re-programmed" to reinforce vocabulary, grammar, themes, and so on. These activities help learners shift their perception of themselves as passive receptors of "content" to active and creative designers and processors of information.

A popular game for beginners is "Concentration." Learners are asked to play in pairs or groups of three or four. They are seated around tables or in student desks in such a way that they can see the transcriptions on the wall. The LC asks them to decide among themselves on ten words, phrases, or sentences they wish to remember. Each group receives ten to twelve pairs of blank playing cards in two different colors. Each person chooses a word or phrase and prints the English on a blue card and the Spanish on a white card. The cards are then spread on the table face down.

The first player turns up a blue card, "I would like . . . " and then turns a white card to find its match in Spanish. If it is not a match, he places it back on the table with the Spanish facing down. The second player turns up another white card to "Me gustaría . . . . " If it is the proper translation, she collects both cards and turns another blue card, " . . . to learn to drive a car." She then turns up another white card to find its match. If it is not a match, she puts the white card face down, and another person takes a turn. The game is over when all the cards have been properly matched and collected.

At an advanced level, players can create new sentences from several conversations that appear transcribed on newsprint posted about the classroom. In a group of four, each player chooses to print, on separate 3×5-inch cards, two English nouns, verbs, adjectives, and adverbs and three articles, pronouns, and prepositions. Each player then take turns placing a card on the table to make up as many different sentences as possible. Depending on learner readiness, simple sentences may be combined or turned into questions or negative statements.

Reversed Role-Playing at Advanced Stages

At the advanced stages of development, a language learner may adopt the LC or teacher role to explain or clarify rules for pronunciation or grammar. The LC graciously gives up superiority and control, and assumes a learner role. The benefits of yielding or the idea, "I shall decrease so that you may increase," empowers young adult learners in stages III and IV.

Reflection: Group Process, Journals, and Portfolios

Reflection aids learning, whether it is about content or experience. The playback of conversations, transcriptions, listening attentively to pronunciation, and recycling new language concepts through games and puzzles constitute rethinking about "content," in this case, the English language. Reflecting on a learning experience, however, can help students gain a better understanding of the reactions, feelings, and strategies that facilitate learning. Insights gained through journal entries, group process, or maintaining a portfolio of growing language abilities can extend understanding and appreciation of self and others as well as content.

In the present application, the class as a whole spends fifteen minutes twice a week commenting on their learning experiences. Sample individual comments are discussed in the Evaluation section.

Evaluation

Formal evaluation has helped to improve the summer orientation program over the years. The parent questionnaire in English and Spanish asks for a rating of the various activities under the instructional component for new students and their siblings and the parent workshops, as well as open-ended questions to elicit descriptions of overall strengths and suggestions for improvement. The questionnaire is given to the parents at the end of each summer session.

The results for 1999 are similar to those from previous years. The overall rating for the entering student component was 4.19 of a possible 5.0, with a standard deviation (SD) of 0.60. Particular benefits, as perceived by this group of parents, were the children's ability to work with one another (4.65, SD 0.61) and the interest and motivation they showed for classroom activities (4.52, SD 0.68). The lowest, but still high, ratings were in demonstrated independence (4.00, SD 0.90) and ability to express ideas and feelings (4.13, SD 0.85). Both of these areas are specifically addressed each summer.

The overall rating of the parent component is generally ranked higher (4.48, SD 0.96) than the student component (4.19, SD 0.60), probably due to the parents' intense involvement described previously. One mother commented at a final group reflection, "I feel like I'm at a university." Others stated, "I'm learning about my children, about myself and also some English!"; "I'm impressed to hear how knowledgeable and sensible my new friends are . . . even my Spanish is improving!"; "I was only going to come one day, but I took some vacation time from work because I was learning a lot and I also felt it was important to represent the fathers."

Parents found the topics meaningful (4.71, SD 0.53) and the readings challenging (4.81, SD 0.40). New parents also welcomed practical information from school staff (4.65, SD 0.55). Suggestions on how to promote language development (4.61, SD 0.67) and creativity (4.61, SD 0.56) were ranked the highest by this group.

Data on the practice of English communication skills is also consistent from year to year. While actual gain in competency to understand (3.68, SD 1.05), speak (3.39, SD 0.99), and write (3.29, SD 1.04) English is clearly above average, confidence is usually higher in all three areas. This finding is in keeping with C-L/CLL philosophy; namely, that learners who gain increased confidence are likely to work harder and smarter at developing strategies to increase competency levels across the board.

Finally, the significance of the sibling component is that a high percentage of Hispanic mothers generally would be unable to participate in the summer orientation if they could not bring their other children along. Sibling participation aids future recruitment efforts, as many of the children eventually qualify to enter the magnet centers.

Individual Case Studies

The following case studies are vivid examples of the impact that parent involvement may have on individual families.

Parents of Gifted Children Are Risk Takers

The mother of a sixth-grade student, Jaime, initially became involved as plans for the summer orientation were underway. Early one spring, the author became aware of scholarships available to minority students who would be able to attend an enrichment program at a private suburban school during the first three weeks in August. Jaime and three classmates in one of the magnet centers were encouraged to apply for a scholarship. However, a daily forty-five-minute ride from the opposite part of the city was a problem. Jaime's mother, Maria O., hesitatingly reported she was learning to drive an automobile. After exploring a number of resources, Maria. was the only alternative. With support and coaching, she practiced her driving diligently, passed the driver's license written test in Spanish, and secured her driver's license in time to drive her son and other students to the summer private school program.

Convincing Maria's husband to allow her to carpool the group was another story. After several conferences, securing written parent permissions, and trial runs using ordinary streets versus the expressway, Maria was able to carpool the group, which thoroughly enjoyed their first experience "away from home." Later that year, Maria proudly reported, "I now drive the kids everywhere; I even helped my husband drive to Disneyland for our vacation!"

As Jaime's parents became more involved in school governance, Mr. O. agreed to fill an unexpected vacancy for a primary teacher in the center. Although Mr. O. had a successful year of teaching, he returned to his job as machine operator for a freight train company. He apologetically admitted, "It is a considerable difference in annual income, and I now need to pay for my eldest son's tuition at a private university."

From Parent to Advocate

A second case study is that of Marisol, a young woman who had studied communications at the Universidad Autónoma de México. After immigrating with her husband from Chiapas to the United States, she began raising daughter Yolanda, or Yoli, who enrolled in one of the magnet gifted centers as a first grader. "I remember being a language counselor in the summer orientation, even though my English was awful!" commented Marisol, "but I improved several years later when Tony was accepted into the program."

During a recent interview, Marisol admits, in Spanish, "Ese verano me empujaron a regresar a la universidad," or "That summer I decided to go back to the university." "I also participated in the evening, ten-week workshop that you and Dr. Beltrán conducted on the needs of gifted children," Marisol recalls quietly. "My husband is a bus driver for the city transit authority but would have liked to teach math. He encouraged me to become a teacher when the children started school," she concludes.

Now a certified primary bilingual teacher, Marisol continues to be vigilant about her children's education. Tony is a fourth grader who, interested in anthropology, has become knowledgeable about dinosaurs and enjoys frequenting museums. Yoli is in sixth grade, and, as part of the annual Academic Talent Search, has recently taken the Scholastic Aptitude Test to gain a realistic picture of her academic potential and to continue formulating appropriate educational goals. Marisol is also active in the local school council and has recently volunteered to help with advocacy efforts in support of higher standards for teacher training.

Yoli has participated in several summer university programs and, as a result, has become interested in studying turtles and constructing automobile models that can be propelled in nontraditional ways. When asked what high school Yoli is considering, Marisol indicates that her husband is willing to move to any part of the city where their daughter can attend "the best" secondary school.

Summary

Parents and families are an essential link in improving U.S. education. If families are to help educators instill a love of learning in children and youth, schools need to design a comprehensive plan to involve the parents in the educational process. This chapter offered a specific model to bring parents and primary caregivers to school and keep them engaged for a brief period of time. However, the impact of the summer orientation program can extend throughout the schoolyear.

To initiate the process of designing a comprehensive program for parent and family involvement, the National PTA recommends that schools undertake seven essential steps. First, create an action team consisting of parents, educators, administrators, and appropriate community representatives to clarify and set goals to which all are committed. Second, examine current practices. Third, based on evaluation findings, outline a plan for improvement, establishing priorities in each of the standard areas discussed at the beginning of this chapter. Fourth, write a policy containing the vision, common mission, and foundation for future plans. Fifth, secure financial resources and support from all stakeholders, those who will implement the plan, those who will be affected, and those outside the system who have influence over the outcome. Sixth, provide professional development for school and program staff, including ample opportunity for them to work together and evaluate their progress. Finally, make a commitment to continuous evaluation and improvement to ensure long-term success.

REFERENCES

Curran, C. A. (1976). *Counseling-Learning in second languages.* Apple River, IL: Apple River Press.

Henderson, A. T., & Berla, N. (1995). *A new generation of evidence: The family is critical to student achievement.* Washington, DC: The Center for Law and Education.

Rardin, J. P., Tranel, D. D., Tirone, P., & Green, B. (1988). *Education in a new dimension: The Counseling-Learning approach to Community Language Learning.* Fort Lee, NJ: C-L/CLL Publications.

14 Educational Policy and Gifted/Talented, Linguistically Diverse Students

BEVERLY J. IRBY AND RAFAEL LARA-ALECIO

This chapter addresses (1) federal and state policy issues related to students who are gifted and talented and linguistically diverse; (2) implications of the lack of policy for gifted and talented, linguistically diverse populations; and (3) policy recommendations for generating better services for those students identified as gifted and talented and linguistically diverse. Herein, we primarily explore macro-level educational policy for gifted and talented, linguistically diverse students and do not address such micro-level policy issues as idiosyncracies or similarities between or among gifted classrooms or bilingual classrooms across schools or in like kinds of schools, which would generate unique implications specific to those campuses or districts.

Federal Policy Issues

Educational policy related to students who are both gifted and talented and linguistically diverse is lacking at the federal level. Although there are federal mandates through Public Law (P.L.) 94-142 and the Individuals with Disabilities Education Act (IDEA) for free and appropriate public education for students with other types of exceptionalities, there have been no specific federally mandated policies that require action by states to enforce educational programming at the local level for gifted and talented students in general or, more specifically, for gifted and talented, linguistically diverse students.

The decades of the 1970s and 1980s brought attention to gifted and talented education through the development of what McDonnell (1994) refers to as capacity-building policies, not mandated policies. Capacity-building policies provide for additional funding to enhance local or state efforts in their provision of gifted and talented education. Although the capacity-building policies, P.L. 95-561 and P.L. 100-297, gave special contingencies to children who were designated as gifted and aided significantly in supporting their education, again, neither of these laws were mandates, nor did these laws, themselves, lead to major systemic educational reform. August, Hakuta, and Pompa (1994) related systemic reform to limited English proficient (LEP) students as follows:

> Systemic reform holds promise for improving instruction and learning for all students, including LEP students. But such an outcome is not a foregone conclusion. Thus far the reform movement has generally sidestepped the particular conditions, needs, and strengths of LEP children. Difficult issues remain to be addressed in many areas including curriculum, instruction, and leadership. (p. 5)

We add policy to their list of remaining reformation needs.

Public Law 100-297 continues today in its capacity-building mode, providing support through competitive grant funds to programs for gifted and talented students that emphasize economically disadvantaged students, LEP students, and students with disabilities who are gifted and talented (*Federal Register*, 1998).

Because no federally mandated policy exists for programming for students designated as gifted and talented, educational policy at the state level is muddled, at best, in relation to students who are gifted and talented and who are also codified as minority to some degree. In fact, minority students, particularly those from low socioeconomic status (SES) backgrounds, from other cultures out of the mainstream, middle-class, Anglo culture, or from the LEP ranks, are not represented fairly in programs for the gifted and talented (Lara-Alecio & Irby, 1997).

Ortíz and Gonzalez (1989) testified in a report from the U.S. Department of Education's Office of Civil Rights, and revealed that "minority groups such as Hispanics, Blacks, and Native Americans are underrepresented by as much as 70% in gifted programs" (p. 152). Moreover, Brown (1997) indicated that between 1980 and 1992, these same populations were constantly underrepresented in thirty-four of the fifty states. Those who live in rural areas continue to be overlooked and underidentified (Spicker, Southern, & Irby, 1987), and those who are LEP are further exploited (Irby, 1993). Because there are gifted students in all realms of society, it is important to develop mandated policies for programming designed for all groups (Passow & Rudnitski, 1993).

State Policy Issues

Because mandated policies solely aimed at the gifted and talented do not exist, nor have they ever existed at the federal level, it falls to the states to mandate policies that are in the best interest of their own gifted and talented students. According to Passow and Rudnitski (1993), there is no common model that shapes policies related to gifted and talented education among the fifty states. However, every one of the fifty states has some type of policy that acknowledges the need to appropriately educate *all* students or acknowledges the existence of students who are gifted and talented and their need for appropriate educational programs (Irby & Lara-Alecio, 1999).

Even though all states had a policy that acknowledged gifted and talented students early in the 1990s, as of 1994, twenty states (40%) still did not have state-level mandates for the education of gifted and talented students[1] (Coleman, Gallagher, & Foster, 1994).

---

[1]These twenty states did not have mandated gifted and talented education, but did urge local district to serve this population.

TABLE 14.1   States without Mandated G/T Policies in 1994. Updated from 1999.

Colorado	Michigan	North Dakota
Connecticut**	Minnesota	New Hampshire
Delaware	Mississippi*	New Jersey
Indiana	Missouri	New York
Maine	Montana*	Vermont**
Maryland	Nebraska	Washington
Massachusetts**	Nevada	Wyoming*

*States with mandated policies after 1992 or 1994.

** Some alterations in policy mentioned, but no mandated policy is in effect. If no asterisk is provided, there is no change in gifted education services.

Mississippi passed a mandated policy for gifted education services in 1992.

Wyoming altered its policy in 1998 to include a mandate for gifted/talented education.

Montana mandates gifted education; however, there is no funding attached.

Vermont, in 1992, did not mention gifted and talented students in state policy (Coleman & Gallagher, 1992); however, by 1999, as a part of the Educational Support Team Law, Vermont provided support so that all children can succeed in their classroom, and the phrasing includes gifted and talented.

Massachusetts, in 1992, did not mention gifted and talented students in state policy (Coleman & Gallagher, 1992); however, by 1999, gifted and talented are mentioned as part of education of all students.

Connecticut does not have a mandate for services, but requires districts to identify the gifted students.

Source: Data from Coleman & Gallagher, 1992; Coleman, Gallagher, & Foster, 1994; and Irby and Lara-Alecio, 1999.

By 1999, the number changed by 10 percent. Table 14.1 indicates the states that did not have mandated policies regarding legislation during the first few years of the 1990s (Coleman & Gallagher, 1992; Coleman, Gallagher, & Foster 1994). In a phone follow-up survey interview of those twenty state contacts for gifted or special education, two mandates had been passed for the states listed in Table 14.1 (Irby & Lara-Alecio, 1999).

Based on the phone follow-up survey interviews (Irby & Lara-Alecio, 1999), there are currently eighteen states (36%) that do not have mandated policies for gifted education. The six states that made changes after 1992 or 1994 were Massachusetts (changed from no mention to mentioned supportively, but not mandated), Mississippi (changed in 1992 to mandated gifted education for intellectually gifted grades 2 to 6, voluntary in other areas of giftedness and at various grade levels), Wyoming (changed in 1998 to mandated gifted education), Montana (changed law to mandate gifted education after 1994), Connecticut (requires districts to identify gifted students), and Vermont (mentions gifted students in law related to services for *all* students).

Gifted Education Policies and Special Populations

In the Coleman and Gallagher (1992) report, it was noted that, within state policies, references were made to special populations of gifted students. Two years later, Coleman, Gallagher, and Foster (1994) checked state documents for references to culturally diverse populations, economically disadvantaged students, and students with disabilities. Forty-one states included specific references to students from culturally diverse backgrounds in their policies; forty-two states included references to economically disadvantaged students; and forty-four states mentioned students with disabilities (Coleman, Gallagher, & Foster, 1994, p. 21). According to a study by Landrum, Katsiyannis, and DeWaard (1998), percentages of minority students served in gifted education as reported by eighteen states ranged from less than 1 percent in Alabama, Idaho, New Mexico, and North Carolina to more than 5 percent in California, Louisiana, and Pennsylvania. Types of minorities were not specified in their report of the study; however, they did indicate that "California had increased educational opportunities specifically for students with limited English proficiency" (Landrum, Katsiyannis, & DeWaard, 1998, p. 363).

A further delineation of diverse populations was addressed by Coleman, Gallagher, and Foster (1994) when they analyzed the state gifted and talented identification documents for the inclusion of students who had an English as a second language (ESL) background. Accordingly, twenty-three states included statements in their gifted education documents that directly mentioned inclusive identification of students with ESL. Coleman, Gallagher, and Foster (1994) reported that Florida and Kansas changed their policies to include students who had ESL after the original report by Coleman and Gallagher in 1992.

States with the highest linguistic diversity population (U.S. Department of Education, 1997) (i.e., Arizona, California, Hawaii, New Mexico, New York, and Texas) all, with the exception of New Mexico, mentioned students with linguistic diversity in their gifted education identification policies (Coleman, Gallagher, and Foster, 1994). As noted earlier, all states with high linguistically diverse school populations have mandated gifted education policies, with the exception of New York (Coleman, Gallagher, & Foster, 1994; Irby & Lara-Alecio, 1999).

Mandated Gifted Education Policy and Program Stability

Mandated programs currently exist in 64 percent of the states (Coleman & Gallagher, 1992; Irby & Lara-Alecio, 1999; Seaberg, 1991).[2] Passow and Rudnitski (1993) suggested that mandates are needed for program stability; however, they indicated that

---

[2]Coleman and Gallagher (1992) indicated that 66 percent of the states mandated policy related to gifted and talented, while Seaberg (1991) reported that 52 percent of the states had mandated policies. Discrepancies may lie in data collection and analysis. Our follow-up report on the Coleman and Gallagher (1992) report indicates that 64 percent of the states have mandated policies for gifted education.

even if states mandate a policy through law, the mandates may not be funded. Landrum, Katsiyannis, and DeWaard (1998) found that state funding varied widely from state to state, with support ranging from local assistance for ensuring programs to limited technical assistance. The lack of funded mandates adds to the instability of the policy itself, as could be the case, for example, with New Jersey and Montana, which mandate gifted education but do not supply state funding to local school districts (Coleman, Gallagher, & Foster, 1994; Irby & Lara-Alecio, 1999).

Lack of funded mandates is but one assumption that is problematic to policy instability. The often-considered notion that policy, itself, will invoke stability, equity, and access within programs or organizations is rudimentary at best. Howley, Howley, & Pendarvis (1986) best reflected on this by stating,

> Students who are identified as gifted are usually white students from comparatively affluent backgrounds. If the issue of equal access is not dealt with reasonably in policy and in practice, the public may perceive that the lack of access by all socioeconomic classes, all races, and all ethnic groups makes gifted programs elitist and undemocratic. (p. 4)

Access to programs through mandated policies alone does not necessarily guarantee that children with exceptional talents will receive a meaningful education (Ross, 1993). Brown (1997) furthers this argument in this way:

> The national data, as well as the data from 34 states show that Caucasian and Asian American students have been identified at a much higher rate than they are found in the total population. Native Americans, Hispanic Americans, and African Americans are consistently under-represented. It is possible, then, that those states have "*imposed* no inequality, but [their] instruments encourage it, expressly permit it" (emphasis added by the court) (*Hall v. St. Helena Parish School Board*, 1961, p. 658). (p. 159)

Indeed, policy must be designed within a context that affects all gifted and talented students and that requires that context to be translated into policy. Policy development also requires, among other components, consideration of background information related to the issue as well as ideas used to stimulate further discussion of different dimensions. Policy must be established and initiated in an appropriate emotional atmosphere and in an environment that acknowledges the policy and is agreeable to it (Hoctor & Kaplan, 1989). In considering the emotional atmosphere and an acknowledging environment, Brown (1997) suggested that the use of model language that would be advantageous for underserved populations be taken from Passow and Rudinski (1993) or Coleman, Gallagher, and Foster (1994). Despite all of the language included in their statements for guiding model legislation, none included specific references to the linguistically diverse. This may be implied in some of the language of the models, such as in the words *ethnicity* and *culturally diverse*. The point herein is that even with mandated or funded policies, the language of the policy may invoke instability and inequities if not considered carefully and written prudently.

TABLE 14.2   Representative District Data: Number of
Hispanic LEP Students in Gifted and Talented Programs

District Number[a]	Percent of Hispanic LEP Students Identified and Served in Gifted Education
1	1.65
2	0.1
3	2.0
4	0.1
5	0.25
6	0.5
7	0.1
8	0.7
9	1.0
10	0.25
11	0.1

[a]Taken by telephone interview (Irby, 1997) with district gifted coordinators and/or bilingual coordinators. To report the findings, the researcher assured the districts that the district name would not be reported in relation to the percentage of Hispanic LEP students identified and served in gifted education programs.

Gifted Education Policy and Its Contextual Nature

The context of culture and understanding in which gifted education policy is interpreted—the local school district—is critical to the inclusion of the subgroup of gifted students whose native language is not mainstream English. Those students are the linguistically diverse gifted (LEP).

The contextual, problematic nature of policy related to identification of and services to students who are potentially gifted and linguistically diverse within a local district is easily represented by the numbers of these types of students being served in gifted programs. Table 14.2 depicts data from a representative group of districts from a major urban center in Texas[3] with percentages of Hispanic students who were identified as gifted and linguistically diverse and who were served through gifted education programs.

The most notable statistic from the data in Table 14.2 is that out of the 85,000 identified LEP elementary (K–6) students in the targeted urban area districts, less than 0.5% (425) were identified and served in gifted programs (Texas Education Agency, 1995; Lara-Alecio & Irby, 1997). This numerical phenomenon is happening in a state

[3]The numbers represented in Table 14.2 are dismal examples of what is happening in one state that has had mandated gifted education for over a decade and a state that identifies 12 percent of its students as receiving services in bilingual/ESL programs (LEP students).

that has mandated gifted education, along with high numbers of students who are classified as linguistically diverse. Additionally, in Texas, much emphasis is placed on general educational services to the LEP population through bilingual and ESL programs. The question concerns what is happening in states that do not have such high numbers of students who are linguistically diverse and that do not mandate gifted education programs? Through the analysis of the data in Table 14.2, it becomes apparent, once again, that policy does not necessarily increase program stability, guarantee service, or provide access to a meaningful education.

Gifted Education Policies and Existing Needs

To improve policies that support inclusion of linguistically diverse students is paramount. The data from Table 14.2 clearly demonstrate a biased system, emanating from a lack of clear policy related to identification of and services to linguistically diverse, gifted students. It is evident from the low numbers of linguistically and culturally different students participating in gifted education programs that either the policies themselves, or lack of them, or the implementation of those that do exist do not respect minority rights. Gifted education programs, as they have been constructed from policies, even in the states that have large numbers of linguistically diverse students and that recognize their needs, still remain programs for the privileged majority. Two reasons exist for this prevailing situation. The first is that there is a popular attitude among educators, politicians, and the general public that gifted education is not necessary and that the gifted child will make it on his or her own (Christensen, 1999; Medlyn, 2000; NSW Association for Gifted and Talented Children, Inc., 2000; Winner, 1997). The second, and most politically controversial, reason is that linguistic minorities are viewed as second-class citizens, being asked to give up their language, because not to do so would be un-American (Hinton, 1999).

Therefore, there are several needs that emerge from these political situations related to the policies of various states. There is a need to challenge the Eurocentric values related to diversity. This, of course, cannot be done overnight; rather, it must be done through the passage of time and through reform movements in general education policies and language policies. A second need is that of clearly written policies mandating identification and services to students who are gifted *and* linguistically diverse. Third, a need exists for a better understanding, by those who administer and enact the policies, of who gifted and linguistically diverse students are. Following this third need and closely tied to it is a fourth need for policies that are sensitive to the demographics and cultural needs of the children that are served in public schools.

Examples of these needs can be observed in Tables 14.1 and 14.2. Yet another example of the lack of a clear, sensitive policy interpretation and application is found in enrollment data analyzed by the *Austin American Statesman* (Associated Press, 1996), which indicated that Hispanic, linguistically diverse students are four times less likely than are Anglo students to be placed in gifted education programs, and this underrepresented group is but one of the ethnically, linguistically diverse populations educated in public schools today. Again, policies must be clear, sensitive, and able to be interpreted and implemented appropriately. A policy that does not have an impact on those who are intended to derive benefit from it is a policy bereft of its own actualization and not worth the paper on which it is written.

Gifted Education Policies and Implications Related to Lack of Clarity

At least five main implications result from a lack of clear and sensitive policies that have excluded, and continue to exclude, those students who are or have the potential to be identified as gifted and linguistically diverse and served in appropriate programs: access, equity, social justice, democracy, and administrative procedures ultimately generated from policy. A synopsis of these implications is noted in Table 14.3.

First, the lack of a definitive policy that includes mandated services for the gifted, linguistically diverse student sends a negative message to the underrepresented populations who are not included in district gifted and talented educational programs. It implies that they are somehow less able than those in other populations. Opinions such as "There are just no gifted minorities" or "Minority children are in need of academic remediation, particularly those who are LEP" are common, even among the teachers (Davis & Rimm, 1989). Not only have LEP gifted students been underrepresented in gifted programs (Marquardt & Karnes, 1994), but our most precious national resource of potentially fully bilingual, gifted citizens, who can help this country compete internationally in the political and economic arenas, is neglected without a clear and mandated policy.

The few studies related to identification of gifted LEP students have not addressed the need for dual language assessment and instruction (Bermudez & Rakow, 1990; Irby & Lara-Alecio, 1996; Maker, 1993; Márquez, Bermúdez, & Rakow, 1992; Santos de Barona & Barona, 1991). In fact, research indicates that most gifted programs in the United States focus on English development at the expense of the first or native language (L1); however, research has also shown that LEP students improve their academic and English performance when their L1 is also used (Cummins, 1984; Ramírez, Yuen, Ramey, & Pasta, 1991). If linguistically diverse students' giftedness, L1, and second language (L2) abilities continue to be ignored, low achievement is bound to prevail (Ogbu, 1992; Shakelee, 1992). In fact, dropout rates among the Hispanic linguistically diverse population hover at 30 percent (NCES, 1997).

Second, without clear policies related to the inclusion of LEP students in gifted programs, isolation of these students becomes a perpetual factor. The isolation inherent among LEP children from low SES creates a minority subculture in and of itself. Their isolation begets isolation. Linguistically diverse children, like other disadvantaged or at-risk students, are affected by multiple isolating factors, not just by their language. According to Crawford (1999), these isolating factors are unequal resources and facilities, uncaring bureaucracies, insensitive treatment of parents, poorly trained staff, unchallenging curricula, and low expectations (p. 228). These factors only remove them further from the mainstream and further from appropriate services if they are potentially gifted. Hakuta (1990) suggested that this isolation is furthered by societal attitudes

TABLE 14.3   Implications Resulting from a Lack of Mandated, Clear, and Sensitive Policy

Implication 1: Linguistically diverse students are less able than are those who are in the mainstream.

Subproblems: First language and culture are devalued.

Dual language assessment is not viewed as a need.

Achievement and potential are not realized.

Implication 2: Linguistically diverse students are isolated.

Subproblems: Linguistically diverse students are affected by isolating factors.

Fewer LEP students are placed in gifted programs.

Implication 3: Meaningful educational experiences for the linguistically diverse student are diminished by the lack of dually certified (gifted and bilingual/ESL education) teachers.

Subproblems: Identification of the linguistically diverse and gifted is problematic.

Appropriate staff development for teachers is questionable.

Implication 4: Exclusionary practices are being implemented.

Subproblems: Equitable services are not uniform.

Uniform and appropriate identification procedures do not exist.

There is little match between programmatic services and the identification plan.

Implication 5: Teachers and administrators must learn how to influence policy that can be responsive to student needs.

Subproblems: School board members who make policy must be educated about the issues of service to linguistically diverse, gifted students.

Personnel who implement policy must be educated about service issues for linguistically diverse, gifted students.

toward immigrants, that somehow these immigrants are less able or are inferior to mainstream Americans, although mainstream Americans are themselves a rainbow of varied cultures.

An example of isolation is observed in Texas, where school districts that had Hispanic LEP students who were in the minority had a disproportionately low number of these same children in gifted classes (Texas Education Agency, 1991). School districts generally have had a proportionately smaller percentage of their Hispanic LEP children in gifted programs than their non-ethnic, language-minority counterparts (2% for

Hispanic LEP versus 97% for the mainstream non-LEP culture [Texas Education Agency, 1995]).

Third, the lack of clear policy in the area of certification of teachers who are both bilingual and gifted presents a problem in provision of meaningful services to the gifted students who are also linguistically diverse. According to Passow and Rudinski (1993),

> Most states acknowledge the crucial role of teachers in the identification and education of the gifted, the necessity of ensuring the selection of appropriate teachers for the gifted, and the need for providing staff development. Yet, only a third of the states have any kind of special certification or endorsement policy for teachers of the gifted. (p. 73)

In the study by Landrum, Katsiyannis, and DeWaard (1998), twenty-five of the states offered teacher certification in gifted education. The question still remains as to the discrepancy in the number of states that offer a certificate in gifted education and those states that mandate the certificate to practice in gifted education.

Further complicating this lack of policy for teacher training and certification is that the direct link to providing instruction to the gifted, linguistically diverse child is lacking. The majority of the school districts do not have teachers who can speak other dominant languages, who also know the premises and instructional academic needs of linguistically diverse children, and who are currently teaching in gifted education programs. According to Lara-Alecio & Irby (1997), district administrative personnel indicated that teacher training, better identification procedures, and programming are needed so that more linguistically diverse students may be identified and served in gifted programs with appropriate curriculum. This information indicates that some administrators acknowledge the need, but little is being done to actualize this need.

Fourth, the very act of exclusion is contradictory to the American principles of egalitarianism (Gintis, 1988). The task of providing equitable services for the gifted is made more difficult by the lack of policies demanding uniformity in objective identification procedures and in appropriate needs-based curriculum services. Uniformity does not preclude the use of a multidimensional approach to the identification of giftedness.

When reviewing evaluations of programs for the gifted, it was determined that, in many cases, there is little or no match between the programmatic services being provided and the districts' plans for identification (Irby, Henderson, & Berry, 1992). This phenomenon is likely due to a lack of clear policy.

Fifth, practitioners and school leaders must learn how to develop policies and administer them in order to change the programmatic services and/or the identification plans so that they merge at a point that is responsive to specific populations within the community. Identification policies may not be biased; that is, they may indicate that LEP students should be identified, but the policies may be unclear and can lead to biased identification procedures. In identification, if standardized tests or IQ tests are used exclusively, students' English language proficiency and cultural backgrounds may be reflected in their test results. Frasier, Hunsaker, Lee, Finley, Frank, Garcia, and Martin (1995) identified other barriers to identification of LEP students: teachers' inability to recognize indicators of potential giftedness; lack of a stimulating early home environment, more prevalent in children from economically disadvantaged backgrounds; and teachers' prejudicial attitudes.

Policies that do not address the programmatic service of relevant curriculum create problems for subgroups within the general gifted population. An effective curriculum cannot be discussed or developed in isolation of the definition of *giftedness* and identification of the particular ethnic or linguistic group. Currently, there is a large number of theoretical claims regarding who gifted children are and what type of curricular programming they need, but there are little empirical data to support these claims, particularly when referencing the linguistically diverse, gifted student (Frasier, 1991; Irby & Lara-Alecio, 1996; Zappia, 1989).

Recommendations for Policy Initiatives for Linguistically Diverse, Gifted Students

The final section of this chapter advances two concepts for policy initiatives that can better define programming for the gifted, linguistically diverse students. One concept is that of contextual, systemic policy development: observing how the policy situated within a state or district is impacted by the implementation and then by program redesign or policy revision. Another concept is the use of existing policies in bilingual/ESL education to support meaningful education for linguistically diverse, gifted students.

Concept 1: Contextual Systemic Policy Development and Implementation

Policy makers and educators simply are unable to either predict or directly experience the results that policies will produce. However, the most dangerous consequence of not providing appropriate educational experiences as a result of appropriate policy may be the undermining of the future of a large portion of our population over time, rather than the advancement of it. There must be policy development that investigates potential consequences or outcomes based on data input in the context of the state or district population that it serves. Gifted education services for linguistically diverse students need such models for policy development and implementation.

Policy development and implementation should include an examination of the impact of each of the following components on each other within a state or school system: (1) the inventory of outcomes or consequences of identification, (2) a model program design that is sensitive to the population being served, (3) type of teacher training (dual, simultaneous training), (4) ongoing staff development, (5) parental involvement and training, and (6) needs-based curriculum and instruction. Further systemic examination would initiate model program redesign, which in turn would have an impact on identification procedures and teacher training. This systemic type of policy development would examine the impact of all outcomes of gifted education services, not only for the linguistically diverse students, but also for mainstream students. Perhaps by investigating policy and its implementation from a systemic point of view, practitioners would be more aware of the outcome and impact the policy has on society as a whole. A model for this systemic policy development plan is depicted in Figure 14.1.

Concept 1 for policy development and implementation entails at least five components, as suggested by Figure 14.1. First is the idea that there is a mandated policy for

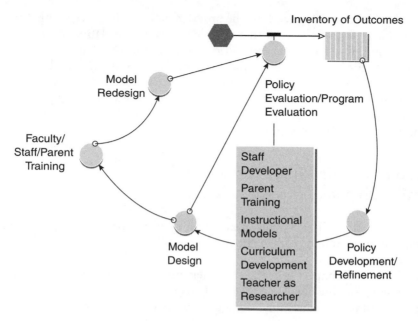

FIGURE 14.1   A Systemic Model for Contextual Policy Development and Implementation.

services to be provided to the linguistically diverse students. From that point, state and district personnel can work on implementation. Note that policy development and implementation are both cyclical and systemic; therefore, as the system is complete, the outcome may impact policy development or refinement, which in turn will impact the model used in the schools for service, and so on.

The model design suggests that there is input based on data from professionals who have received training in the particular subject of educating linguistically diverse gifted children and who have based decisions on their own investigations. It also suggests that, at the state level, model programs for the linguistically diverse, gifted students should require teachers to have dual certification. For example, teachers should have a certificate in bilingual education, should speak the language of the child, and should have a certificate in gifted education (Lara-Alecio & Irby, 2000). This may be achieved through a field-based teacher preparation program in conjunction with area universities, through distance education training programs, or through some type of an effective alternative certification plan. Specialized programs that are sensitive to students needs require a specialized teaching staff.

Model programs also should be based on input from parents who have also received training in supporting and enriching their linguistically diverse children. Parents should receive assistance in a model program for linguistically diverse students, because parents, themselves, are also linguistically diverse in the society and need assistance to enhance the lives of their children.

Model program design also includes appropriate identification techniques, instructional models for the population, and appropriate ethnolinguistic curriculum development. All of these and the aforementioned components have an impact on model design.

The developed model further determines the type of faculty, staff, and parental involvement and training, from which discussions, research, and learnings emerge. This, in turn, may lead to model program *redesign*. Both the model and any redesign should require an evaluation of the program, which should focus on outcomes and develop an inventory of outcomes. From the inventory of outcomes, the policy should be analyzed for accuracy, inclusivity, and appropriateness. From the preceding discussion, we see how each component is affected by the other, how a systemic policy can determine numbers of students served in a program, and whether the program furthers access, because of the appropriateness of accompanying training, identification, instruction, curriculum, and program evaluation.

Concept 2: Use Existing Federal Mandates to Provide Appropriate Services to Linguistically Diverse, Gifted Students

The Title VII, Elementary and Secondary Act, Part A, Bilingual Education Act (P.L. 103-382, October 30, 1994) is not mandated federal policy, in that it does not mandate services to LEP students; rather, it, like gifted education policy at the federal level, is a capacity-building policy, as stated:

> The Congress declares it to be the policy of the United States, in order to ensure equal educational opportunity for all children and youth and to promote educational excellence, to assist State and local educational agencies, institutions of higher education and community-based organizations to build their capacity to establish, implement, and sustain programs of instruction for children and youth of limited English proficiency. (p. 1; See <caselaw.findlaw.com/scripts/getcode.pl?type=search&frame=top&code=US&Ci Restriction=Title+VII+Bilingual+Education+Act>)

What is considered mandated policy for LEP students, including those who are gifted, comes under the auspices of federal court rulings. For example, there are four federal laws or rulings that guarantee equal protection: Title VI of the Civil Rights Act of 1964 (P.L. 88-352, 1964), amended by the Civil Rights Act of 1991 (P.L. 102-166, 1991); the Equal Educational Opportunities Act of 1974; *Lau v. Nichols* (1974); and *Casteñeda v. Pickard* (1981). Although these laws or rulings range over thirty-five years, the mandates are still powerful and may be used to guarantee rights to the LEP gifted student.

For example, Title VI of the Civil Rights Act of 1964 bans discrimination on the basis of "race, color, or national origin" in all federally assisted programs. The question to be reconciled is, "Are civil rights violated and discrimination practiced in services for second-language learners who are denied access to gifted education programs in school districts across the United States that receive federal funds?"

Another law, the Equal Educational Opportunities Act of 1974 states,

The Congress declares it to be the policy of the United States, in order to ensure equal educational opportunity for all children and youth and to promote educational excellence, to assist State and local educational agencies, institutions of higher education and community-based organizations to build their capacity to establish, implement, and sustain programs of instruction for children and youth of limited English proficiency. (p. 1; see 20 U.S.C. § 1702, <www4.law.cornell.edu/uscode/20/7402.text.html>)

The question then is, "Are LEP students who are also gifted denied the equal educational opportunity that their non-LEP gifted peers are afforded based on language barriers?"

Furthermore, the U.S. Supreme Court decision, *Lau v. Nichols* (414 U.S. 563, 1974), states, "There is no equality of treatment merely by providing students with the same facilities, textbooks, teachers, and curriculum; for students who do not understand English are effectively foreclosed from any meaningful education" (p. 2; <caselaw.findlaw.com/scripts/getcase.pl?navby=search&linkurl=%>&graphurl=<%GRAPHURL%>). The question herein is, "Are LEP gifted students provided with a meaningful education simply by being placed in a bilingual education setting, when mainstream gifted students have their regular educational services plus, or in lieu of them, enriching or accelerating curriculum, which is indicated as meaningful education for them?"

The Fifth Circuit Court of Appeals ruled in *Casteñeda v. Pickard* (1981) that there would be three criteria by which services to LEP students would be evaluated: (1) the school program must be based on "sound educational theory"; (2) the program must be implemented effectively, with adequate resources and personnel; and (3) the program must be evaluated and determined to be effective, not only in the teaching of language, but also in access to the full curriculum—math, science, social studies, and language arts (Crawford, 1999). The question to be answered is, "Are LEP gifted students provided with a program that has sound educational theory, adequate resources and personnel (teachers trained in gifted and bilingual education), and access to a full curriculum?"

A later state ruling in 1987, *Gómez v. Illinois State Board of Education*, ruled that "state educational agencies are responsible for ensuring that language minority students' educational needs are met, including identification and assessment of language minority students and placement of students in appropriate programs" (Ovando & Collier, 1998, p. 49). So, the final question of equity becomes, "Are LEP gifted students ensured that their educational needs are met through correct identification and assessment techniques, and then are they ensured placement in appropriate programs?"

To demand better services, parents and educators alike may use the five previously cited cases to advocate for mandated gifted education programs for students who are linguistically diverse. In doing so, parents must demand services of their school districts; and if parents, who are also within the linguistically different group, are unable to do so, it is left to those educators and advocates in the mainstream population who believe in social justice and equal educational opportunities to speak out and demand these services for linguistically diverse, gifted youth. Policy makers (school boards) must know the law that mandates services to the linguistically diverse population, and school district personnel must seek ways to implement these mandated policies to serve linguistically diverse, gifted students.

Even though mandated *gifted education* policies do not exist, mandated services for linguistically diverse students do. This includes linguistically diverse, gifted students. The debate is not in the *law*; the debate is in the *interpretation* and *politicized bias* against the linguistically diverse or immigrant population. Pond (1996) related this debate in the following manner:

> As if being LEP were not a great enough challenge in an educational context based on English proficiency and literacy, LMS [language minority students] must come to school in the center of a highly politicized debate about the programs that ostensibly serve them. Organized political movements, whose efforts would exclude entire populations from equal educational opportunities because of their minority status, represent a serious added challenge to both LMS and practitioners. (p. 123)

Summary

The challenge is to overcome the linguistic prejudice that dominates the views of the mainstream majority and has an impact on political viewpoints and platforms from which policy is created. At risk of being isolated further, linguistic minorities succumb to societal pressure and do not question the oppressive nature of these political viewpoints. A prime example is the centuries of oppressive policies foisted on the minority population of Native Americans. Native Americans have constantly fought against losing their cultural identities, but their sacrificial fight in this hegemonic society has placed the languages of the Navajo, the Sioux, the Cherokee, and others, on the endangered list. And these are the *indigenous* peoples of this country.

However unjust and sad these maxims are, they exist and form the basis for the struggle and challenge of developing and implementing effective policies. Effective policies interpreted in an inclusive delivery system are essential elements not only for educators in the fields of gifted education and bilingual/ESL education, but also for all educators, to maintain a society that is democratic and preserves its integrity (Lara-Alecio & Irby, 1996).

REFERENCES

Associated Press. (1996). Study: Too few minority students in gifted classes. *The Huntsville Item, 147* (337), 1.

August, D., Hakuta, K., & Pompa, D. (Fall, 1994). *For all students: Limited English proficient students and Goals 2000. FOCUS: Occasional papers in bilingual education.* Washington, DC: National Clearinghouse for Bilingual Education.

Bermudez, A., & Rakow, S. (1990). Examining identification and instruction practices for gifted and talented limited English proficient students. In L. M. Malavé (Ed.), *Annual Conference Journal. Proceedings of the National Association for Bilingual Education Conference,* Tucson, AZ, 1990, and Washington, D.C., 1991 (pp. 99–114).

Brown, C. N. (1997). Gifted education as a constitution issue. *Roeper Review, 19,* 3.

Casteñeda v. Pickard (1981). 648 F.2d 989 (5th Cir. 1981).

Christensen, S. M. (July 15, 1999). Testimony submitted for the recording: Hearing before the United States House of Representatives Committee on

Education and the Workforce Subcommittee on Early Childhood, Youth, and Families. Available at: <www.housecuv/ed_workforce/hearings/1060h/ecy/esea71599/christensen.htm.>.

Coleman, M. R., & Gallagher, J. J. (1992). *Report on state policies related to the identification of gifted students.* Chapel Hill, NC: Gifted Education Policy Studies Program, Frank Porter Graham Child Development Center, University of North Carolina at Chapel Hill.

Coleman, M. R., Gallagher, J., & Foster, A. (1994). *Updated report on state policies related to the identification of gifted students.* Chapel Hill, NC: Gifted Education Policy Studies Program, University of North Carolina at Chapel Hill.

Crawford, J. (1999). *Bilingual education: History, politics, theory and practice* (4th) Los Angeles, CA: Bilingual Education Services.

Cummins, J. (1984). The role of primary language development in promoting educational success for language minority students. In Evaluation, Dissemination, Assessment Center (Ed.), *Schooling and language minority students: A theoretical framework.* Los Angeles: California State University.

Davis, G. A., & Rimm, S. B. (1989). Culturally different and economically disadvantaged children: The invisible gifted. *Education of the gifted and talented* (2nd ed.) (pp. 227–302). Boston: Allyn & Bacon.

Federal Register. (March 18, 1998), 63, 52.

Frasier, M. (1991). Disadvantaged and culturally diverse gifted students. *Journal for the Education of the Gifted. 14*, (3), 234–245.

Frasier, M. M., Hunsaker, S. L., Lee, J., Finley, V. S., Frank, E., Garcia, J. H., & Martin, D. (1995, September). *Educators' perceptions of barriers to the identification of gifted children from economically disadvantaged and limited English proficient background.* Storrs, CT: The National Research Center on the Gifted and Talented.

Gintis, H. (1988). Education, personal development, and human dignity. In H. Holtz et al., (Eds.), *Education and the American dream: Conservatives, liberals & radicals debate the future of education.* Greenwood: Berging & Garrey.

Gómez v. Illinois State Board of Education. (1987). 811 F.2d 1030 (7th Cir. 1987).

Hakuta, K. (1990). *Bilingualism and bilingual education: A research perspective.* [NCBE Occasional papers in Bilingual Education, No. 1]. Washington, DC: National Clearinghouse on Bilingual Education.

Hall v. St. Helena Parish School Board. (1961). 197 F. Supp. 6–19, 658.

Hinton, L. (December, 1999), Involuntary language loss among immigrants: Asian-American linguis-

tic autobiographies. *Education Digest on Clearinghouse on Languages and Linguistics.* (Available at: <www.cal.org/ericll/digest/involuntary.html)>.

Hoctor, M., & Kaplan, S. (1989). *Developing policies for a gifted/talented program: A Handbook.* (ERIC Document Reproduction Service No. ED309607).

Howley, A., Howley, C., & Pendarvis, E. (1986). *Teaching gifted children.* Boston: Little, Brown.

Irby, B. J. (May 1993). Hispanic LEP gifted students. *Education Week.*

Irby, B. J., Henderson, D., & Berry, K. (1992). *State of gifted education in Texas.* An unpublished manuscript submitted to the Texas Association of Gifted and Talented for a Grants in Excellence project. Huntsville, TX: Sam Houston State University.

Irby, B. J., & Lara-Alecio, R. (1996). Attributes of Hispanic gifted bilingual students as perceived by bilingual educators in Texas. *SABE Journal, II,* 120–142.

Irby, B. J., & Lara-Alecio, R. (1999). *Phone follow-up survey interviews.* Unpublished report. Huntsville, TX: Sam Houston State University.

Jacob K. Javits Gifted and Talented Students Education Act. (1988). P.L. 100-297, Title IV, Part B, Sec. 1101.

Javits, J. K. (1998). *Gifted and talented students education program notice inviting applications for new awards for fiscal years 1998 and 1999.* Office of Educational Research and Improvement. United States Department of Education. Washington, DC.

Landrum, M., Katsiyannis, A., & DeWaard, J. (1998). A national survey of current legislative and policy trends in gifted education: Life after the national excellence report. *Journal for the Education of the Gifted, 21* (3), 352–371.

Lara-Alecio, R., & Irby, B. J. (1996). Bilingual education and multicultural education: An inclusively oriented educational delivery system. *The Journal of Educational Issues of Language Minority Students, 17,* 11–24.

Lara-Alecio, R., & Irby, B. J. (1997). Identification of Hispanic, bilingual gifted students. *Tempo, XVII (II),* 20–25.

Lara-Alecio, R., & Irby, B. (2000). Culturally and linguistically diverse gifted students. In C. R. Reynolds & E. Fletcher-Janzen (Eds.), *Encyclopedia of special education* (pp. 506–510). New York: John Wiley & Sons.

Lau v. Nichols (1974). 414 U.S. 563 (1974). Available at: <caselaw.findlaw.com/scripts/getcase.pl?navby= search&linkurl=%LINKURL%>graphurl=<% GRAPHURL%> p. 2.

Maker, C. J. (1993). Creative, intelligence and problem solving: A definition and design for cross-cultural research and measurement related to gift-edness. *Gifted Education International, 9*, 68–77.

Marquardt, R. G., & Karnes, F. A. (1994). Gifted education and discrimination: The role of the Office for Civil Rights. *Journal for the Education of the Gifted, 18*, 1, 87–94.

Márquez, J., Bermúdez, A., & Rakow, S. (1992). Incorporating community perceptions in the identification of gifted and talented Hispanic students. *The Journal of Educational Issues of Language Minority Students, 10*, 117–127.

McDonnell, L. M. (1994). Assessment policy as persuasion and regulation. *American Journal of Education, 102*, 394–420.

Medlyn, B. (June 7, 2000). Gifted funding "a joke" expert says. *The Arizona Republic*. Phoenix: The Arizona Republic.

NCES. (1997). *Dropout rates in the United States: 1995*. Washington, DC: National Center for Education Statistics, U.S. Department of Education, NCES97-473.

NSW Association for Gifted and Talented Children Inc. (2000). The myth about gifted children. Available at: <www.nswagtc.org.au/info/children/myth.html>.

Ogbu, J. U. (1992). Understanding cultural diversity and learning. *Educational Researcher, 21* (8), 5–14.

Ortiz, V., & Gonzalez, A. (1989). Validation of a short form of the WISC-R with accelerated and gifted Hispanic students. *Gifted Child Quarterly, 33*, 152–155.

Ovando, C. J., & Collier, V. P. (1998). *Bilingual education and ESL classrooms* (2nd ed.). Boston: McGraw-Hill.

Passow, A. H., & Rudnitski, R. A. (1993). *State policies regarding education of the gifted as reflected in legislation and regulation*. The National Research Center On the Gifted and Talented. (ERIC Document Reproduction Service No. ED 379 849).

Pond, W. K. (1996). Educational challenges unique to culturally and linguistically diverse students: A description and suggestions for pedagogical models. *The Journal of Educational Issues of Language Minority Students, 17*, 121–138.

Public Law 103-382. (1994). *Improving America's Schools Act*.

Public Law 100-297. (1988). *Jacob K. Javits Gifted and Talented Students Education Act of 1988*. 4101–4108, 20 U.S.C. 3061–3068.

Public Law 94-142. (1975). *Education for All Handicapped Children Act*. 613(a) (4), S.6. 94th Congress 1st session, June, Report No. 94-168.

Ramírez, J. D., Yuen, S. D., Ramey, D. R., & Pasta, D. J. (1991). *Final report: Longitudinal study of structured English immersion strategy, early-exit and late-exit transitional bilingual education programs for language minority children* (Vols. I and II). San Mageo, CA: Aguirre International.

Ross, P. O. (1993). *National excellence: A case for developing American's talent*. Washington, DC: U.S. Department of Education.

Santos de Barona, M., & Barona, A. (1991). The assessment of culturally and linguistically different preschoolers. *Early Childhood Research Quarterly, 6*, 363–376.

Seaberg, V. (Ed.). (1991). *The 1990 state of the states gifted and talented education report*. Agusta, ME: Council of State Directors of Programs for the Gifted.

Shakelee, B. D. (1992). Identification of young gifted students. *Journal for the Education of the Gifted, 15*, 134–144.

Spicker, H., Southern, W. T., & Irby, B. (1987). The rural gifted child. *Gifted Child Quarterly, 13* (4), 155–157.

Texas Education Agency. (1990). *The Texas state plan and guidelines for the education of the gifted and talented*. Austin, TX: Texas Education Agency.

Texas Education Agency. (1991). *Update on gifted education*. Division of Gifted/Talented Education. Austin, TX: Texas Education Agency.

Texas Education Agency. (1995). *Division of performance reporting office of policy planning & information management*. Austin, TX: Texas Education Agency.

U.S. Department of Education. (1997). *National household education*. Washington, DC: National Center for Education Statistics.

Winner, E. (1997). Exceptionally high intelligence and schooling. *American Psychologists, 52* (10), 1070–1081.

Zappia, I. A. (1989). Identification of gifted Hispanic students: A multidimensional view. In C. J. Maker & S. W. Schiever (Eds.), *Critical issues in gifted education. Vol. 2: Defensible programs for cultural & ethnic minorities* (pp. 19–26). Austin, TX: Pro-Ed.

15 Research Directions for Bilingual Gifted Education

JAIME H. GARCÍA

Both bilingual education and gifted education have had a tenuous history. The problems faced by these two areas of education have political and social factors that have influenced the development of programs and research. Because of this, research in bilingual gifted education has been sporadic. This chapter reviews some of the milestones in gifted education and bilingual education, both positive and negative, and suggests areas in which research is needed. Specific areas of recommendation include conceptions of bilingual giftedness, assessment issues in bilingual gifted education, programming and curriculum in the bilingual gifted classroom, and evaluation of bilingual gifted programs.

Unlike other areas of education, bilingual gifted education requires that researchers be cognizant of the complexities of components found in the literature in both bilingual and gifted education. Attempting to design programs for gifted bilingual students that are simply mainstream gifted models in two languages is limiting, not only because they ignore what is known about bilingualism, but also because of cultural and psychosocial characteristics of bilingual individuals. Therefore, researchers in bilingual gifted education need to work in concert with others if expertise in either bilingual education or gifted education is limited. Without this dual expertise, key features of bilingual education or gifted education can result in inaccurate or incomplete findings.

Given the complexity of bilingual gifted education, it is necessary to examine what is known and begin to formulate or refine lines of research in order to better understand the needs of bilingual gifted children and youth. At the same time, as each is examined and better understood, it is necessary to bear in mind that the fields of bilingual and gifted education are constantly in flux. It remains to the researcher to follow developments in each of these areas in order to provide educators with a better understanding of bilingual gifted education.

Research Directions

Research at the intersection of bilingual education and gifted education is critical if the field of bilingual gifted education is to develop further. Critical studies need to be conducted to not only identify those barriers that exist in the education of bilingual gifted students, but also ameliorate the problems we currently see in the identification of and programming for bilingual students. While there has been some research in the identification of bilingual gifted students, as well as demonstration projects, other areas are still in need of investigation. These areas include conceptions of giftedness in relation to bilingual students, programming options and practices, instructional practices, parental involvement and training, and evaluation of program effectiveness. This section addresses each of these areas in turn.

Conceptions of Giftedness and the Bilingual Student

While the greatest amount of research in bilingual gifted education has been in the area of identification, the problem of low identification rates may be a result of the conceptions of giftedness that are prevalent in gifted education, rather than how the assessments are conducted. These conceptions have resulted in narrow definitions, which have caused the underrepresentation of bilingual students and students of color in programs for gifted and talented students.

The earliest definitions of *giftedness* focused on defining the term as a specified performance on an intelligence test, as in Terman's (1959) longitudinal study with a cohort of persons scoring above 140 on the Stanford Binet test. These forms of conceptions were reinforced by the response to the Soviet Union's launching of Sputnik, when standardized tests were used to identify students who excelled in math and science. With the focus on standardized tests, often seen as strictly objective measures of innate ability, changes in conceptions of giftedness have been directed into examining some underlying, stable, cognitive structure such as intelligence. Questioning the validity of underlying stable structures has not occurred, and in the process, while new definitions have changed, the underlying beliefs about giftedness as related to scores on particular tests have prevented any change in the representation of bilingual students and students of color in programs for gifted and talented students.

Definitions found in the seventies, eighties, and early nineties appear more global, but the translation of those by both academicians and school personnel continues to hold to standardized test scores. This can clearly be seen by examining many of the research articles found in journals such as *Gifted Child Quarterly* and *The Journal for the Education of the Gifted*, in which one notices repeatedly that intelligence test scores are used as the classification variable for participants in a study being identified as gifted or nongifted.

More recently, developmental conceptions of giftedness have been suggested. These definitions take into account environmental and sociocultural factors that expand the conception of giftedness. By accounting for the influence of these factors on giftedness, it is assumed that potential giftedness needs to be nurtured; as such, we cannot rely on intelligence as the only marker of giftedness.

While the emergence of new conceptions of giftedness (Frasier & Passow, 1995; Martin, 1996) exist, research in the nature of giftedness is still lacking. Primary to understanding bilingual gifted individuals is the need to examine how these conceptions alter the views of educators of the gifted and talented. The central question that needs to be investigated is whether the personal epistemologies of persons influence their conceptions of giftedness. Does a person who is a logical-positivist tend to hold a view of giftedness as a static, measurable trait? Without understanding the relationship of our world view to our conception of giftedness, it becomes difficult to conduct research on other topics related to bilingual gifted persons, because the conception of giftedness held by researchers influences the way in which research is conducted.

Further, when giftedness is examined from a postmodern perspective, several implications can be drawn that may influence how the area of bilingual gifted education is constructed. As suggested by Foucault (1972), the knowledge–power paradigm rests on what a society agrees to in terms of definitions of specific concepts. Thus, if we examine giftedness in terms of how a particular population constructs the meaning of giftedness, direction can be provided for developing programs based on that construction. Examination of what giftedness is for a given language-minority group may suggest that the manner in which giftedness is viewed, and, subsequently, how children and youth are identified for programs and the curriculum that is delivered results in a reexamination of giftedness from a language-minority perspective.

For bilingual gifted education programs, it remains in the context in which giftedness is being constructed to begin to address the unique needs of bilingual gifted students. Communities construct meaning for a concept that may or may not be similar to other communities of the same ethnic group. For example, the definition of *giftedness* in the rural Lower Rio Grande Valley of Texas may be very different from that in East Los Angeles. Essential to the development of bilingual programs is a sound definition that is based on the understanding of the concept in a community. To use a standard definition from the dominant group may result in a program that receives little support from the community.

Identification of Bilingual Gifted Students

Perhaps no area in bilingual gifted education has received more attention than issues related to identification of students for gifted and talented programs. Recommendations have ranged from adjustment of scores (Mercer, 1977) to the development of specific instruments (Bernal, 1974) to the use of alternative methods of data interpretation (Baldwin, 1984; Frasier, García, & Passow, 1995). However, even with these changes, the number of bilingual gifted students remains low. García and Starks (1991) found, through a survey of school districts in Texas, that Hispanics are significantly underrepresented in gifted and talented programs. Given that those who are identified are more likely proficient in English, it can be deducted that there is a greater underrepresentation of bilingual gifted students. An examination of the recommendations may provide direction for further research in the identification of bilingual gifted students.

One of the earliest examinations of assessment of bilingual students for gifted programs was that of Mercer (1977), who suggested that the System of Multicultural Pluralistic Assessment (SOMPA) could be used to adjust the scores of students to provide an equitable assessment. Taking factors such as socioeconomic status and acculturation into account, Mercer suggested that it was possible to assess students in a manner that did not put them at a disadvantage. Such an approach can be used successfully but does not address the underlying question of the nature of assessment.

Others have suggested that the problem lies not in tests themselves, but in which tests are used. It has been suggested that by using nonverbal intelligence tests, much of the bias due to language can be eliminated (García, 1994). Some have suggested that tests in the student's first language are preferable in addressing questions of linguistic bias (Zappia, 1989). Finally, it has been suggested that culture-fair tests may be the key to identifying bilingual gifted students (Zappia, 1989). However, each of these recommendations may be problematic. With nonverbal tests, it may be possible to reduce linguistic bias, but there is still the issue of the cognitive styles that these tests may favor. For tests in the native language of the student, there is the problem related to the degree to which the student has received instruction in the native language. If there has been no instruction in the native language, the student is at a disadvantage. Thus, regardless of what instrumentation is used, there is a problem in both administration and interpretation of observed scores.

Another category of measurement includes teacher, parent, and self-report instruments. These have been widely used in gifted education but with little research on the efficacy of their use. High and Udall (1983) found that teacher referral instruments limited the number of Hispanic students referred for assessment. These instruments tend to be based on traditional conceptions of giftedness, which may not reflect the manner in which bilingual children and youth manifest behaviors associated with giftedness. This mismatch between global and culture-specific manifestations of giftedness is in need of examination if referral instruments are to continue to be used. Development of report instruments that are based on the community conception of giftedness may result in the increase of language-minority students referred for assessment. Another area in need of research is the efficacy of taking a global definition such as the one proposed by Frasier (1998) and developing items that are culture-specific.

Developing alternative forms of data representation and interpretation has been another approach to problems in the assessment of bilingual gifted students. Perrine (1989) proposed a case study approach, in which data are integrated to develop a global view of a student's abilities and need for services in a gifted and talented program. García (1994) and Frasier (1990) have suggested that plotting of test score data and integration of narrative data may allow more equitable assessment of bilingual gifted students, because a visual image of the data can allow patterns to be seen and nontest data to be used in interpretation. While these methods are promising, they are only as good as the data that are used in either developing case studies or profiling data. Concerns that have been voiced about the lack of cutoff scores center on inequity and the possibility of lawsuits. However, these concerns are questionable, because in the diagnosis of a condition, interpretation is everything. Thus, research on the underpinnings of such concerns presents another avenue that is attitudinal in nature and may speak more to the sociopolitical climate in which gifted programs, bilingual or not, exist.

Although some research has been conducted in the assessment of bilingual gifted students (High & Udall, 1983), there are still many unanswered questions. First, research is needed in developing a framework that will account for sociocultural factors that influence assessment so that selection of instrumentation can yield the information necessary to make placement decisions. Relatedly, research is needed on the match between the tests used and the definition of *giftedness* used in a given program. Finally, research is needed on the ability of methods used in assessment to identify bilingual students with potential.

Programming and Curriculum for Bilingual Gifted Students

Programming options for bilingual gifted students pose many questions and problems when consideration is given to the content of gifted and talented programs. While there needs to be a clear match between the programming options and the definition under which a program operates, it is necessary to address underlying questions about meeting the unique needs of bilingual gifted students. The inclusion of program options and components is critical to effective programs for bilingual gifted and talented students.

Understanding the role of language and culture is essential to the development of activities and programming options for language-minority, gifted students. However, as suggested by Cummins (1989), it is important to examine the format in which curriculum is implemented, the role of parents and community, and finally, how assessments are conducted in the schools. Each of these should be considered and addressed by identifying program options that address the needs of bilingual gifted students.

Culture and language should be a part of the programming if bilingual gifted students are to thrive in gifted and talented programs. How language is incorporated in the classroom helps determine the value placed on the student by personnel in the schools (Cummins, 1989). Thus, for bilingual gifted students, it is preferable to have bilingual teachers trained to work with these students so that language can be incorporated into the classroom. Likewise, culture should be a part of the programming for bilingual gifted students. As with valuing the child's language, including the child's language in the gifted and talented program is crucial in the development of positive experiences in the classroom. The incorporation of culture not only validates the child, but also provides enriched learning opportunities for other students in the gifted and talented classroom.

The curricular approach suggested by Cummins (1989) for working with minority students suggests that it should be interactive. This follows current suggestions by constructivists, but it also is an approach that can be found repeatedly in the literature on gifted education. Students should have a role in designing activities within the content being used as a vehicle for development of skills. The match between the needs of bilingual gifted students and their instructional program, whether it's the bilingual or gifted vantage point, indicates that they should thrive in the curricular environments advocated for gifted students. Research in this area may lead to a better understanding of the role of active learning among bilingual gifted students in strengthening languages, self-concept, and ethnic identity, among other phenomena.

Parents and community should have an active role in the bilingual gifted classroom. Enlisting parents to provide instruction on the unique facets of their children's cultures allows the classroom to be enriched and also allows acquisition of information that may otherwise not be found in the academic literature. There is much about the customs and practices of certain cultures that has not been documented and can be useful in instruction. Community members can also take an active role in the bilingual gifted program by providing their services as mentors and as resources for projects or in activities such as writing regional histories. These fit within what Moll (1990) terms *funds of knowledge*, that knowledge present within the community can be incorporated into the curriculum and enrich the classroom environment.

As programs are designed, it is important to conduct research on whether the program objectives are a match with the needs of bilingual gifted students. Research should also examine the effects of involving parents and community members in the bilingual gifted classroom and the effect of that involvement on student performance and satisfaction with the program. Finally, studies are needed that investigate the effect of language, culture, and community involvement on psychosocial factors such as self-concept, self-esteem, self-efficacy, and ethnic identity, as well as language development.

Also of importance are the attitudes and beliefs of those involved in bilingual gifted programs. Research on the attitudes of teachers, with regard to use of language, approaches to instruction, perceptions of persons from other ethnic groups, and the intersection of bilingual and gifted education should also be conducted. Student and parent perceptions of bilingual gifted programs can shed light on the degree to which unique needs are being met and how potential is being developed. Research in these areas can provide valuable information for the development or refinement of programs for bilingual gifted children and youth.

Evaluation of Bilingual Gifted Programs

Evaluation in gifted education is weak at best (Garcia & Starks, 1991). For bilingual gifted programs, this also tends to be the case. Most available evaluations are in the form of reports generated as part of funded research and demonstration projects. However, these evaluations tend to be short term in nature and do not examine the overall functioning of a program. As noted by Callahan, Tomlinson, Hunsaker, Bland, and Moon (1995), program evaluations should be an integral part of program development and should be considered early in the development phase. This is essential for programs in bilingual gifted education due to the limited research on such programs. As more programs develop, it would be useful to educators to have a clear understanding of what constitutes sound bilingual gifted programs. Thus, as schools develop bilingual gifted programs, it is necessary to enlist persons who can provide assistance in the evaluation of these programs.

Because educators tend to focus on one area of education, gifted or bilingual in this case, evaluation of bilingual gifted programs can probably best be achieved through the use of a team, so that input is received from persons with varied areas of expertise. Although experts on evaluation are available, the interaction of bilingual and gifted education requires that perspectives of both be used in the development of evaluation plans.

Research is needed on the manner in which evaluations for bilingual gifted classrooms are conducted. Determining what is unique about bilingual gifted programs results in asking questions not normally asked in the evaluation of bilingual or gifted programs. How can the evaluation of bilingual gifted programs enrich not only the programs themselves, but gifted education and bilingual education as well?

TABLE 15.1   Key Research Areas in Bilingual Gifted Education

Dimension	Questions
Conception	How does the conception of giftedness found in a given bilingual community compare with that generally found in gifted education?
	What do alternative conceptions of giftedness suggest with regard to all phases of program development?
Assessment	What types of instruments are appropriate, given the personal and social characteristics of bilingual gifted children and youth?
	Can existing referral instruments be adapted to provide potentially gifted bilingual students an equal opportunity for being considered for gifted programs?
Curriculum	What sociocultural factors should be considered in the development of curriculum for bilingual gifted students?
	How are student abilities, self-esteem, and ethnic identity affected by participation in a bilingual gifted program that considers what we know about working with diverse populations?
Evaluation	Do evaluation teams comprised of persons with expertise in the areas of bilingual education, gifted education, and program evaluation interpret evaluation data similarly?
	How do evaluation designs and instruments need to be modified or developed when examining the intersection of bilingual and gifted education?

Summary

This chapter outlined some of the issues related to research in bilingual gifted education from the point of view of conception, identification, curriculum, and evaluation. Table 15.1 provides a summary containing two questions that need to be addressed in each area. For each of these areas, key components are identified that can serve as a starting point for myriad studies that can enrich our understanding of bilingual gifted education. As changes occur in the sociopolitical arena in which education functions, greater possibilities for conducting valuable research in this area exist. Currently, we are seeing greater acceptance of dual language programs. As these programs grow, so, too, will the possibility for the development of more bilingual gifted programs.

However, as we see this increase, it is important to acknowledge that bilingual gifted education exists in two margins. Any research conducted needs to clearly delineate how the intersection of bilingual and gifted education is operationalized. Research also has to be clear, in that the topic is bilingual gifted education and not gifted programs that have bilingual students or bilingual programs that use methods developed in gifted education.

The intersection of bilingual and gifted education necessitates much research to meet the needs of bilingual gifted students, as well as to enrich the literature in both fields. As bilingual gifted programs are further developed, opportunities occur for research that allows us to understand the interaction of two facets of a unique group of students. How we conduct research in bilingual gifted education is limited only by the creativity of those who pose questions. Above all, it is necessary to keep an open mind when investigating a complex phenomenon. As questions are raised, it will become necessary to examine the very foundations on which we base the education of bilingual gifted students.

As we enter into the territory of research in bilingual gifted education, it is essential that consideration be given to the range of research tools available. The approaches we use must be both from the qualitative and quantitative paradigms for conducting research. While there is a tendency in gifted education to rely on quantitative methods, we must also consider qualitative methods that have been effective in investigations in bilingual education. Only by using all means available can we begin to understand the concept of giftedness from a bilingual perspective. The objective is clear; question all that has occurred to date, and pose questions in a different light.

REFERENCES

Baldwin, A. Y. (1984). *The Baldwin identification matrix for the identification of the gifted and talented: A handbook for its use.* New York: Trillium.

Bernal, E. M. (1974). Gifted Mexican American children: An ethno-scientific perspective. *California Journal of Educational Research, 25* (5), 261–273.

Callahan, C. M., Tomlinson, C. A., Hunsaker, S. L., Bland, L. C., & Moon, T. (1995). Instruments and Evaluation Desisions Used in Gifted Programs. (ERIC Document Reproduction Service No. ED427447.)

Cummins, J. (1989). *Empowering minority students: A framework for intervention.* Sacramento: California Association for Bilingual Education.

Frasier, M. M., & Passow, H. A. (1994). *Toward a new paradigm for identifying talent potential.* Storrs, CT: The National Research Center on the Gifted and Talented.

Foucault, M. (1972). *The archeology of knowledge and the discourse on language.* New York: Pantheon.

García, J. H. (1994). Non-standardized instruments for the assessment of Mexican-American children for gifted/talented programs. In S. B. García (Ed.), *Addressing cultural and linguistic diversity in special education: Issues and trends* (pp. 46–57). Reston, VA: The Council for Exceptional Children.

García, J. H., & Starks, J. (1991). *Final report of the Gifted Evaluation Models (GEM) Project.* Austin: Texas Association for the Gifted and Talented.

High, M. H., & Udall, A. J. (1983). Teacher ratings of students in relation to ethnicity of students and school ethnic balance. *Journal for the Education of the Gifted, 6* (3), 154–166

Martin, D. E. (1996). *Toward an understanding of the native Hawaiian concept and manifestation of giftedness.* Unpublished dissertation. Athens: The University of Georgia.

Mercer, J. R. (1977). Identifying the gifted Chicano child. In J. L. Martinez, Jr. (Ed.), *Chicano Psychology* (pp. 155–174). New York: Academic Press.

Moll, L. (1990). *Vygotsky and education: Instructional implications and applications of socio-historical psychology.* Cambridge: Cambridge University Press.

Perrine, J. (1989). Situational identification of gifted Hispanic students. In C. J. Maker & S. W. Schiever (Eds.), *Critical issues in gifted education: Defensible programs for cultural and ethnic minorities* (pp. 5–18). Austin, TX: Pro-Ed.

Terman, L. M. (1959). *The gifted group at midlife; Thirty-five years follow-up of the superior child genetic studies of genius.* Stanford, CA: Stanford University Press.

Zappia, I. A. (1989). Identification of gifted Hispanic students: A multidimensional view. In C. J. Maker & S. W. Schiever (Eds.), *Critical issues in gifted education: Defensible programs for cultural and ethnic minorities* (pp. 19–26). Austin, TX: Pro-Ed.

AFTERWORD

EVA I. DÍAZ

According to Callahan (1996),

> If we truly believe in the importance of serving the diverse needs of gifted children, then we cannot risk being dinosaurs in the field of education. Whatever we do, the highly able students will still be there in schools. Hence, we need to do our best to ensure that we don't jeopardize their welfare through lack of knowledge, inappropriate actions, or neglect. (p. 149)

Using Callahan's quote as inspiration, let us not be dinosaurs in the field of education and let us not jeopardize the welfare of gifted and talented students from culturally and linguistically diverse backgrounds through lack of knowledge (either unconsciously or consciously), inappropriate actions, or neglect. How?

The chapters included in this book have rendered a multipronged review and discussion of essential issues (theory and practice) regarding gifted and talented students from culturally and linguistically diverse backgrounds, including advanced cognitive development and bilingualism, creativity, identification of and programs for children with gifted potential or performance, curriculum and pedagogy, teacher preparation and recruitment, parent and family involvement, history, legislation, policy, and research. Throughout the book, these issues have been examined in light of the interdependent relationship between the educational ideals of excellence and equity. In this regard, several understandings were reinforced: (1) The education of gifted and talented students from culturally and linguistically diverse backgrounds must focus on students' cultural, linguistic, and cognitive strengths and resources rather than on their perceived deficiencies (e.g., limited English proficiency); (2) a focus on students' strengths and resources facilitates students' access to excellence and equity in education; and (3) in spite of the challenges to reconcile the educational goals of excellence and equity, we must commit ourselves to these ideals and to the pursuit of feasible means of procuring them.

The following are a few critical points made throughout this book:

1. An analysis of social, economic, political, and educational happenings in the United States from the late 1800s to the present, in relation to culturally and linguistically diverse students, sustains the need for change not only in the fields of bilingual education and gifted and talented education, but also in the field of education in general (Chapters 1 and 2). The way in which educational challenges related to this student population have generally been framed needs to be scrutinized and reshaped, and in this process, capitalize on the personal, social, and educational histories of culturally and linguistically diverse groups—histories most often marked by prejudice, discrimination, struggle for survival, and hope. By valuing and learning from these experiences, improvement, tolerance, understanding, and harmony could be fostered. Moreover, researchers, educators, administrators, practitioners, and others would contribute to counteracting the past, covert and overt educational "violence" against most culturally and linguistically diverse students, which in turn has resulted in their high rates of underachievement and failure in schools (e.g., the view of culturally and linguistically diverse people losing their culture and language in the name of social harmony or even as a prerequisite to equal opportunity; the blaming of ethnic minority and culturally and linguistically diverse students for the reduction in gifted education programs and services).

Because where there is struggle, there is hope, the fields of bilingual and gifted education are taking the initial steps to overcome past alienation through collaboration. In this way, the fields of bilingual and gifted education have intersected and are emerging with promising ways of achieving the goal of equal, high-quality educational opportunities for culturally and linguistically diverse students with gifted potential and talents.

2. There is a growing body of research knowledge pointing to the positive relationship between bilingualism and advanced cognitive development (e.g., concept formation, metalinguistic awareness, creativity, divergent and convergent thinking, problem solving, etc.). This body of research knowledge not only overturns deficit views of bilingualism, but also has significant implications for the identification and instruction of gifted and talented students from culturally and linguistically diverse backgrounds (Chapters 2 and 3). For instance, Gonzalez (Chapter 3) proposes that valid alternative assessments for identification purposes be based on findings from more sophisticated research designs that include qualitative and quantitative, methodologically robust, explanatory models of the positive effect of bilingualism on cognition. Likewise, Robisheaux and Banbury (Chapter 4) claim that there is a symbiotic relationship between bilingualism and creativity that could be nurtured in the classroom through a variety of instructional models and strategies. Thus, bilingualism is not an educational disadvantage, but an asset to students. Subsequently, students' linguistic challenges should no longer be used as an excuse for teachers' low expectations of these children.

3. Culturally and linguistically diverse students, especially those identified as having limited English proficiency, have been and continue to be excluded from gifted and talented programs and service. However, this pattern of exclusion could be dismantled by inclusionary approaches and strategies for their assessment, identification, and participation in gifted and talented programs and services (Chapter 5).

4. Traditional gifted programs and service delivery models need to be modified in order to become responsive to gifted and talented students from culturally and linguistically diverse backgrounds. Castellano (Chapter 6) argues that the multidimensional planning of inclusive gifted and talented programs and services must include the key elements of any well-developed gifted program in light of the strengths and needs of culturally and linguistically diverse students.

5. Gifted and talented programs designed to address the complexities of culturally and linguistically diverse students must include a solid curriculum framework, qualitatively differentiated instruction, and authentic assessments based on the current body of knowledge and practice in the fields of gifted education, bilingual education, and multicultural education (Chapters 7 and 8). Gallagher (Chapter 13) also demonstrates that comprehensive parent-involvement models contribute to the overall success of gifted and talented programs servicing culturally and linguistically diverse students.

6. Bilingual gifted and talented education is a real possibility (Chapters 9 through 11). The field does not need to be limited by gifted and talented education in its traditional forms, and creative, innovative ways should be sought. Kloosterman (Chapter 9) proposes a promising program model connecting the Schoolwide Enrichment Model, developed by Joseph S. Renzulli, and a two-way bilingual program model. This blending of theory and practice in the fields of gifted and talented education and bilingual education is an example of the possibility of achieving equity and excellence in bilingual gifted and talented education. Aguirre and Hernandez (Chapter 10) and Perez (Chapter 11) also describe in detail successful bilingual, gifted and talented programs implemented in the United States, which in turn are invaluable resources for school districts planning creative gifted and talented programs that serve culturally and linguistically diverse students.

7. Recruiting, training, and retaining outstanding teachers is a challenging yet critical endeavor in achieving the goals of bilingual, gifted and talented programs (Chapters 7 & 12). Bernal (Chapter 12) delineated a field-tested model for the recruitment and preparation of teachers for bilingual gifted and talented programs.

8. Although mandated bilingual or gifted education does not exist, mandated services to culturally and linguistically diverse students do exist and should be used in advocacy efforts for the provision of bilingual gifted and talented programs and services to culturally and linguistically diverse students (Chapter 1, 2, and 14). Irby and Lara-Alecio (Chapter 14) further argue that linguistic prejudice, which often dominates the views of the mainstream majority, coerce political viewpoints and platforms from which policy is created. In Chapters 1 and 2, I also demonstrate how powerful political, intellectual, business, and social leaders have increasingly voiced their opposition not only to policy development, but also to actual educational practice that seeks to meet the needs of culturally and linguistically diverse students in sensitive manners (e.g., attacks against bilingual education legislation and practice).

9. Rigorous research is urgently needed in the complex intersection of bilingual and gifted and talented education. Garcia (Chapter 15) suggests that opportunities for research in this regard would stream as bilingual gifted and talented programs and services are developed and put into practice. Moreover, methodologically adequate and valid research designs that go beyond the prevailing traditional–positivistic perspective and consider alternative research paradigms, such as constructivist, critical theory, and qualitative modes of inquiry, should be used.

The Potential of Bilingual, Gifted Education

Bilingual gifted and talented education has the potential of offering more suitable and responsive opportunities for culturally and linguistically diverse students with outstanding gifts and talents to obtain both excellence and equity in their education. However, not all forms of bilingual education or gifted education harmonize with the goal of promoting advanced bilingual, biliterate development. The logistics involved in planning programs of this nature are complex. However, those engaged in the decision making for programming must remain focused on the provision of programs and services that (1) honor students' linguistic and cultural backgrounds; (2) respect and nurture students' diverse (often not typical) ways of manifesting gifted potential, giftedness, and talents; and (3) advance stimulating and challenging learning experiences within accepting and caring environments, the rationale being that ignoring students' language backgrounds is detrimental to their identity and academic development, which in turn influences their display of gifted potential and talents. In addition, the active use of languages other than English would legitimize these languages and facilitate student academic engagement.

This additive approach to the education of gifted and talented students from culturally and linguistically diverse backgrounds will enable students to have a better economic and occupational future without the usurpation of their identities. In this way, programs and services would empower students for life. Otherwise, overlooking these factors will only contribute to the historical disabling of many of these students.

In sum, well-designed and well-implemented bilingual gifted and talented programs are about respecting students' dignity, empowerment, and bringing about benefits to the society at large, especially considering the increasingly global nature of our interactions. More importantly, it must be understood that students' diverse languages and cultures are not disabling forces, as are teachers' lowered expectations.

An Action Plan for Unlocking the Doors

Throughout this book, efforts have been made to conceptualize what the field of bilingual gifted and talented education intends to accomplish in regard to culturally and linguistically diverse students with gifted potential and talents. For this purpose, the historical and current conditions of the fields were scrutinized and examples of what have been accomplished so far and what holds much promise were presented. We hope that this book assists researchers, educators, practitioners, administrators, and others in engaging in personal and collective reflective thinking in such a way that a shared vision is established, as well as a road map created to provide direction and guidance to the field's efforts and actions. For this purpose, networking is critical. Once the field's efforts are articulated and acted on, constant renewal will be necessary to avoid being dinosaurs in the education of culturally and linguistically diverse students.

Sometime ago, I read a quote by H. J. Brown that triggered a comparison with bilingual, gifted and talented education. He wrote, "Talent without discipline is like an octopus on roller skates. There's plenty of movement, but you never know if it's going to be forward, backwards, or sideways" (Brown & Spizman, 1996, p. 41). For too long, efforts to provide for culturally and linguistically diverse students with gifted potential and talents have looked like an octopus on roller skates, that is, a lot of frantic movement with no clear target, no progress—mostly frustration and despair among educators, practitioners, and researchers. An opportunity now exists, with exciting paths ahead. Let us not be intimidated, but invigorated, by the challenges.

One Last Note

Although this book includes a diversity of topics, vital areas such as culture, language, and views of giftedness must be studied in greater depth. Likewise, topics such as counseling and essential support services need to be addressed further. Also, as mentioned in the preface, this book represents multiple perspectives among its contributors, hence the appearance of, at times, conflicting and contradictory positions. However, it is this diversity of views that stimulates the reader to make more informed choices.

REFERENCES

Brown, H. J., Jr., & Spizman, R. (1996). *A hero in every heart*. Nashville, TN: Thomas Nelson Publishers.

Callahan, C. M. (1996). A critical self-study of gifted education: Healthy practice, necessary evil, or sedition? *Journal for the Education of the Gifted, 19* (2), 148-163.

INDEX